Luminos is the Open Access monograph publishing program from UC Press. Luminos provides a framework for preserving and reinvigorating monograph publishing for the future and increases the reach and visibility of important scholarly work. Titles published in the UC Press Luminos model are published with the same high standards for selection, peer review, production, and marketing as those in our traditional program. www.luminosoa.org

The Social Question in the Twenty-First Century

The Social Question in the Twenty-First Century

A Global View

Edited by

Jan Breman, Kevan Harris, Ching Kwan Lee, and Marcel van der Linden

UNIVERSITY OF CALIFORNIA PRESS

BRESCIA UNIVERSITY
COLLEGE LIBRARY

University of California Press, one of the most distinguished university presses in the United States, enriches lives around the world by advancing scholarship in the humanities, social sciences, and natural sciences. Its activities are supported by the UC Press Foundation and by philanthropic contributions from individuals and institutions. For more information, visit www.ucpress.edu.

University of California Press
Oakland, California

© 2019 by The Regents of the University of California

This work is licensed under a Creative Commons CC BY-NC-ND license. To view a copy of the license, visit http://creativecommons.org/licenses.

Suggested citation: Breman, J., Harris, K., Lee, C.K., and van der Linden, M. (eds.) *The Social Question in the Twenty-First Century: A Global View*. Oakland: University of California Press, 2019. DOI: https://doi.org/10.1525/luminos.74

Library of Congress Cataloging-in-Publication Data

Names: Breman, Jan, editor. | Harris, Kevan, 1978- editor. | Lee, Ching Kwan, editor. | Linden, Marcel van der, 1952- editor.
Title: The social question in the twenty-first century : a global view / edited by Jan Breman, Kevan Harris, Ching Kwan Lee, and Marcel van der Linden.
Description: Oakland, California : University of California Press, [2019] | Includes bibliographical references and index. | This work is licensed under a Creative Commons CC BY-NC-ND license. To view a copy of the license, visit http://creativecommons.org/licenses. |
Identifiers: LCCN 2019001160 (print) | LCCN 2019005563 (ebook) | ISBN 9780520972483 (ebook) | ISBN 9780520302402 (pbk. : alk. paper)
Subjects: LCSH: Labor—History. | Capitalism—Social aspects. | Equality--Economic aspects.
Classification: LCC HD4855 (ebook) | LCC HD4855 .S63 2019 (print) | DDC 306.3--dc23
LC record available at https://lccn.loc.gov/2019001160

28 27 26 25 24 23 22 21 20 19
10 9 8 7 6 5 4 3 2 1

CONTENTS

List of Illustrations *vii*
List of Contributors *viii*

Preface: The Terrifying Convergence of the Three Worlds of the "Social Question" *ix*
Göran Therborn

1. The Social Question All Over Again *1*
Jan Breman, Kevan Harris, Ching Kwan Lee, and Marcel van der Linden

2. The Social Question in Western Europe: Past and Present *23*
Marcel van der Linden

3. The End of American Exceptionalism: The Social Question in the United States *40*
Fred Block

4. The Social Question as the Struggle over Precarity: The Case of China *58*
Ching Kwan Lee

5. Migrants, Mobilizations, and Selective Hegemony in Mekong Asia's Special Economic Zones *77*
Dennis Arnold

6. A Mirage of Welfare: How the Social Question in India Got Aborted 98
Jan Breman

7. The Labor Question and Dependent Capitalism: The Case of Latin America 116
Ronaldo Munck

8. Labor and Land Struggles in a Brazilian Steel Town: The Reorganization of Capital under Neo-Extractivism 134
Massimiliano Mollona

9. From Poverty to Informality? The Social Question in Africa in a Historical Perspective 152
Andreas Eckert

10. The Social Question in South Africa: From Settler Colonialism to Neoliberal-Era Democracy 170
Ben Scully

11. The Social Question in the Middle East: Past and Present 188
Kevan Harris

12. Post-Socialist Contradictions: The Social Question in Central and Eastern Europe and the Making of the Illiberal Right 208
Don Kalb

13. The Social Question in Russia: From De-Politicization to a Growing Sense of Exploitation 227
Karine Clément

14. Postscript: The Social Question in Its Global Incarnation 244
Jan Breman, Kevan Harris, Ching Kwan Lee, and Marcel van der Linden

Index 251

LIST OF ILLUSTRATIONS

FIGURES

Figure 5.1. Nominal and real minimum wage of garment and footwear sector, 2000–2015. *82*

Figure 11.1. Comparative trends in human development indicators, Middle East and North Africa, 1960–2000. *196*

MAPS

Map 5.1. Mekong Asia. *79*

Map 5.2. Thailand's SEZ development. *91*

LIST OF CONTRIBUTORS

Dennis Arnold is assistant professor in the Department of Human Geography, Planning, and International Development Studies at the University of Amsterdam.

Fred Block is research professor of sociology at the University of California–Davis.

Jan Breman is emeritus professor of comparartive sociology at the University of Amsterdam.

Karine Clément is associate professor in the Andrew Gagarin Center for Civil Society and Human Rights at the Faculty of Liberal Arts and Sciences at Saint Petersburg State University.

Andreas Eckert is professor of African and Asian studies at Humboldt University.

Kevan Harris is assistant professor of sociology at the University of California–Los Angeles.

Don Kalb is professor of social anthropology at the University of Bergen.

Ching Kwan Lee is professor of sociology at the University of California–Los Angeles.

Massimiliano Mollona is senior lecturer in the Department of Anthropology at Goldsmiths College in the University of London.

Ronaldo Munck is the head of civic engagement at DCU at Dublin City University and a visiting professor of international development at the University of Liverpool and St. Mary's University, Nova Scotia.

Ben Scully is a senior lecturer in the Department of Sociology at the University of the Witwatersrand.

Göran Therborn is professor emeritus of sociology at the University of Cambridge.

Marcel van der Linden is professor and senior researcher at the International Institute of Social History.

Preface

The Terrifying Convergence of the Three Worlds of the "Social Question"

Göran Therborn

Reading this great collection of planet-embracing, penetrating analyses by eminent area specialists, you can almost hear Minerva's owl flapping her wings in the social dusk of the world. We get a picture of how the social issues of the world hang together, with all their differences; we can see how global patterns become discernible, rolled out over time, as well as in space.

Poverty, inequality, and social injustice are ancient plagues of humankind. But they emerged as a "social question" rather late, in a context of the Enlightenment and the Industrial Revolution—the former by putting inequality and human rights on the agenda, though mainly existential inequality before the law, and the latter by producing poverty and misery by wage labor. The editors and authors of this book have put the social question into a broad socioeconomic dynamics of accumulation and dispossession and of class and labor.

The awareness and the notion of a social question derived from the emergence of wage labor—that is, of formally free and substantially unprotected labor, disembedded from family subsistence and constantly at risk from polluting working conditions, from accidents, sickness, unemployment, and from old age frailty. Wage labor emerged and developed on different scales and with different temporalities worldwide, spawning different responses to the question. Industrial wage labor originated in Western Europe, spreading unevenly across the world, most early and successfully to North America, giving rise to what we now call the Global North. Wage labor became the work of the majority of the world's population only recently, in the second decade of the twenty-first century, now estimated by the International Labour Organization (ILO) at 54 percent, up from about 40 percent in the early 1990s. In sub-Saharan Africa and in South Asia, wage labor is still only a fourth of people's work status.

From a perspective of wage labor in general and of industrial wage labor in particular, there was, as this book shows, a very different trajectory of social development in the Global South, reigning in Africa, Asia, and Latin America, with both intra- and intercontinental variations, just as the northern route comprises the three well-known mini-worlds of welfare capitalism. There are good reasons to distinguish as a third route—also treated in this book—the eastern route of twentieth-century communist socialism, opened by the Russian and the Chinese Revolutions, which provided another approach to the social question. The different areas of wage labor were always connected by the imperialism of European and (later) U.S. capitalism, and area developments were increasingly synchronized by a world time of crucial events, above all, the two World Wars and, decisively, the neoliberal offensive of the 1980s and onward.

THE GLOBAL ONSLAUGHT OF POSTINDUSTRIAL FINANCE CAPITALISM

Perhaps the most surprising finding of this rich worldwide overview is the synchronized turn, since the 1980s, of all the three trajectories of the social question into a neoliberal plunge. With some time lags, there is occurring a dramatic convergence of the three historical paths, toward one of social precarity, of more human exploitation and exclusion—although the legacies of their different employment developments and different social institutions are likely to lead to different responses in the medium term.

In the North, where it all started, there are de-industrialization of employment, beginning in 1965, accelerating from 1975, and the financialization of capitalism, from currency trading, credit deregulation, and the opening up to unhampered international capital movements. These tendencies provided the structural economic underpinnings of aggressive neoliberal ideology and politics.

In the South, weakened by the lure of debt, the neoliberal message spread through the International Monetary Fund–World Bank (IMF-WB) Washington Consensus and its imposition of "structural adjustment policies." A significant role was also played by the military-capitalist economics of Pinochetista Chile, namely, inspiring a worldwide World Bank campaign for privatization of pensions—which ultimately largely failed. In the Arab world, the military-corporatist compact was unraveled, leading up to the Arab Spring, in the end crushed by post-corporatist repression. India experienced how the previous, badly implemented social contract was broken by Hinduist neoliberalism.

In the East, there were the collapse of the Soviet Union and the post-Mao capitalist turn of China. The latter was managed by the Chinese themselves, in many ways very successfully, including a spurt of updated industrialization and a massive lift out of extreme poverty, although with initially brutal social effects—for example, on health care and rural education. The Russian turn was under Western tutelage, whose electoral-manipulation experts meddled forcefully in the 1996 Russian election to ensure the victory of the Western candidate. This was the most brutal economic aggression since the heyday of colonial plundering. Between 1990 and 1995, the income share of the bottom half of the Russian population plummeted from 30 percent to 10 percent, and by 2016, the latter had an income 20 percent below their income in 1989, under communist "stagnation."[1]

The worldwide commonality of postindustrial neoliberal ideology and ruling practices is highlighted by the current Chinese promotion of "entrepreneurship" and the practice of the gig economy, as Ching Kwan Lee shows in this book.[2] The worldwide structural changes that made the synchronized global political turn of the 1980s possible still awaits a full-scale analysis.

The chapters of this book provide a somber picture of what the neoliberal onslaught means to the world, and they give us, all of us outside the ever-narrowing circle of the privileged, reasons to fear for our future—but also reasons to fight against our prescribed fate.

The numbers and the proportion of wage workers in the world will continue to grow—as service workers, dispersed among decentralized or small workplaces, never reaching the concentrated mass of big industry workers. The industrial trajectory of the North will not be repeated. Industrial employment seems to have reached its world peak, at barely a fourth of the economically active world population. Deindustrialization has already started in Latin America, and industrial employment has stalled or begun to decline elsewhere.[3] Even in China, the number of industrial workers seems to have started to decrease in this century.[4] The northern trajectory of the social question, propelled by industrialization and industrial labor to workers' rights and to social citizenship, is now closed in the South and the East as well as in the North.

FROM THE WORKERS QUESTION TO "INCLUSION"

The social question of the nineteenth and twentieth centuries was the workers question. The latter is now gone, or discarded, all over the world. Does it have any successor? Perhaps none with any equally broad legitimacy, but in terms of a social issue talked about by a concerned establishment—which was the semantic field of the original social question—there is a plausible candidate. "Inclusion" was put onto the EU agenda of the 2000 Lisbon Strategy, and later adopted by the Organisation for Economic Co-operation and Development (OECD), inserted into the UN Development Goals, and sponsored by the World Bank and the Asian Development Bank in the form of "inclusive growth." The concept does point to something central in postindustrial twenty-first-century societies—the ongoing process of social exclusion and inequality, as evidenced in all of the following chapters.

However, the problem is that the workers question was not really tackled by enlightened ruling-class concern, but by the force of the workers themselves, their *mutualités,* their trade unions, their votes, their strikes and demonstrations, and their political parties, moved forward by the strong tailwind of expansive industrialization. How much force will the excluded and the marginalized of today be able to gather—the shrinking industrial working class, the "informal" workers on sub-industrial-standard employment, the precariat, the subsistence farmers under mounting pressure, the roving day laborers, the street vendors, the never-employed youth, all facing a strong headwind of global finance capitalism? To what extent will they be able to find allies among the middle-class salariat, also threatened by the ruthlessness of capital accumulation?

And into what kind of society can they be possibly included? Hardly into contemporary capitalism. The industrial response to the workers question was an extensive class compromise, a changed capitalism, of workers' rights and civic rights. Without strong forces of resistance and rebellion, what is awaiting us—all rhetoric of "inclusion" notwithstanding—would be galloping inequality and exclusion.

These are questions for a sequel to this great book.

NOTES

1. F. Alvaredo, L. Chancel, T. Piketty, E. Saez, and G. Zucman, *World Inequality Report 2018,* 118–19.
2. China cannot be comprehended in one formula, however. The official bicentenary promotion of Marx and the current mandated politburo reading of the *Communist Manifesto* indicate that.
3. International Labour Organization, *World Employment Social Outlook 2018,* 30–31.
4. Organisation for Economic Co-operation and Development, *Employment Outlook 2017,* 122.

1

The Social Question All Over Again

Jan Breman, Kevan Harris, Ching Kwan Lee, and Marcel van der Linden

Want, Disease, Ignorance, Squalor, and Idleness. These were, according to the British liberal reformer William Beveridge, the enemies of social progress. Together, the five "giant evils" express the so-called social question: that is, the problem of indigence and destitution on a mass scale. Originally a French notion, created more than two centuries ago (la question sociale), the social question became the leitmotiv for the many laws and policy measures in the nineteenth and twentieth centuries that resulted, in a relatively small part of the world—in capitalist welfare states and some "state-socialist" societies—in extensive protective arrangements for the disabled, the old, and the unemployed, as well as in health care, housing, and education accessible to (almost) all. Due to uneven development of capitalism on a world scale, however, working people in colonized and dominated Africa, Latin America, and Asia were excluded—indeed, necessarily—from the benefits and progress of the Global North. Between the 1970s and 2010s, global development has slowly led to the return of the social question with a vengeance, but without the assertive engagement that had made it publicly visible and politically urgent in earlier times. The decline of average profit rates in "old" capitalist countries, the collapse of state-socialist competitors to capitalism, and the concomitant rise of neoliberal ideologies have brought turmoil to the vast majority of the world's working population. The pernicious effects of mass immiseration have found poignant political expressions in, on the one hand, the surge in ultraconservative, nationalistic, and populist politics and trends (such as the election of Donald Trump, Britain's exit from the European Union, and xenophobic rejections of refugees arriving in Europe), and on the other, the mass protests and occupy movements against austerity and crony capitalism. And yet, the worldwide erasure of the "social" in favor of self-employment and self-reliance emphasized by neoliberal ideology has repressed the social question from public discussion.

This introduction offers a stylized global overview of the evolution of the social question since it was first articulated in nineteenth-century Europe. We attend to both its discursive constructions and its material and political manifestations. But first, it is important to differentiate the frame of the social question from the dominant paradigm of "poverty alleviation." The disappointing outcome of the postwar decades of developmentalism led to the declaration of the Millennium Development Goals at the end of the twentieth century, making the worldwide reduction of poverty the prime objective. Fifteen years later, equating the march to human progress with poverty alleviation and the diminution of development policy to this shallow ambit has been hailed as a remarkable success story. The country and regional case studies collected in this volume mount a major rebuttal to this assessment. The empirical findings in this book show that the persistent belief in a trickle-down spread of the benefits of economic growth to the subaltern classes is an illusion that ignores an accelerating immiseration resulting from dispossession, dislocation, and disenfranchisement.

It is not just the failure of poverty alleviation as development policy that gives us pause. There is an important conceptual difference between poverty and the social question. Poverty exists when people find it difficult to make ends meet. The deficit forces them to make painful choices, some of which are temporary in nature or restricted in magnitude and are made manageable by deferring gratification, occasionally or forever, of needs given a lower priority. Destitution, a more severe and chronic grade of misery, requires not incidental but institutionalized support to safeguard even sheer survival. Whereas the notions of poverty and destitution allude to the personal, immediate, and often irreversible deprivation afflicting people in that predicament, the social question points to the relational, institutional, and political economic forces constitutive of destitution as a historically specific phenomenon. As Marcel van der Linden elaborates in his contribution to this volume, the understanding and assessment of destitution as a social issue demanding public awareness, legal mediation, and state intervention did not come about until the great transformation in nineteenth-century Europe. It was linked, on the one hand, to the increasing commodification of social relations and the concomitant transition from an agrarian-rural to an industrial-urban economy and, on the other hand, to a social consciousness expressing solidarity spearheaded by an emancipatory working-class movement in Europe.

HISTORICAL TRAJECTORY OF THE SOCIAL QUESTION

Pre-Capitalist Responses to Indigence

Indigence did exist in the pre-capitalist era, before commodified labor relations became widespread, perhaps as far back as European antiquity, but historical research on this issue is underdeveloped.[1] In many pre-capitalist agrarian societies, huge differentials in wealth and income could exist, but often the poorest layers of society were at least minimally protected by forms of communal relief. Frequently, better-off agrarian or artisanal households were obliged to chip in to extend support to deprived neighbors in their small-scale midst. In Europe's late Middle Ages, for example, communal relief was institutionalized at the local level in the Poor Laws, which lightened the burden of improvidence. Redistributive mechanisms were usually endorsed by a religious code prescribing charity, as, for instance, provided by the collection of *zakat*, a payment in kind or cash made under Islamic law. To prevent or at least slow down an unwelcome trend toward increasing dispossession, many peasant societies utilized the custom of the commons, which implied open access to resources jointly held nearby, such as waste land or water, to members of the same rural community. A periodic redistribution of cultivated land, as, for instance, in the traditional Russian *mir* or among indigenous tribes in South America, was a more rigorous way to preempt progressive differentiation in property and power. Were such customary arrangements, which pressed for some modicum of redistribution, a feature of all peasant societies? It seems likely that a large part of humanity used to live and work in societies marked by inequality in all walks of life.

Capital accumulation, commodification of land and labor, and dispossession of peasants and artisans went hand in hand. This trend first became visible in Europe when the medieval communitarian economy that still leaned toward autarky was finally destroyed. Varieties of feudalism had eroded peasant property while silencing the voice of the victimized peasantry. In his early *Memoir on Pauperism*, published in 1835, Alexis de Tocqueville wrote, "from the moment that landed property was recognized and men had converted the vast forests into fertile cropland and rich pasture, . . . individuals arose who accumulated more land than they required to feed themselves and so perpetuated property in the hands of their progeny."[2] As a consequence of the enclosure movement, the large estates in England became even larger and were operated more commercially. Max Weber's treatise on the agrarian question is equally relevant for understanding how the social question was handled in the rural past. Elaborating on the concept of patrimonial rule practiced in the eastern German provinces, he characterized the relationship between the landlord (*Junker*), who maximized power and status instead of production, and the farm servant, who was tied to his employer's household on an annual contract in which he received discretionary benevolence for the permanent use made of his labor power. It was a form of attachment marked by exploitation as well as patronage.[3]

The Great Transformation in Europe

Taking stock of a large amount of data collected in a survey toward the end of the nineteenth century, Max Weber, who was commissioned by the Verein für

Sozialpolitik (Association of Social Policy) for this analysis, focused his attention on the inroads capitalism had made in the rural economy. A drastic change in the crop patterns, caused by a higher volume of international trade, led to a pronounced seasonality in the cultivation cycle. In reaction to increased commercialization, estate owners had started to replace their attached workforce with casual labor hired only when their presence was required in peak periods. Swarms of seasonal hands from Poland and Russia—"barbarian hordes," in Weber's vocabulary—with less physical ability but willing to work on very low wages, flooded the countryside of eastern Germany in the busy months, only to disappear again when employment fell. Landlords were no longer willing to guarantee the livelihood of agricultural laborers in the relentless drive to proletarianization. While seasonal migrants were hired when needed, the local landless could not survive on temporary, off-and-on work. They had become superfluous to demand and took off to the city to find employment in industry, construction, or other sectors of the now rapidly expanding urban economy.

A similar turn had taken place in Great Britain somewhat earlier on. A drastic revision of the Poor Laws in 1834, two years after the middle classes had gained suffrage under the 1832 Reform Act, took away the public relief that, since the medieval era, had been provided locally to unemployed labor in times of need. Forthwith, it was provided exclusively to the non-laboring poor—the elderly, widows, the handicapped, and the chronically ill. Their dole was granted only when they were fortunate enough to pass the "means test," confirming that they did not get support from relatives or other donors. Parliament, which still mainly consisted of members hailing from the landed aristocracy, debated why and how to amend the Poor Laws. The immediate ground for the amendments seemed to be the growing resistance of the non-poor to contribute to a public fund spent on labor labeled as unwilling to search around for waged work and thus take care of their own sustenance. Hidden sentiments behind expressing annoyance against what was portrayed as a "free rider" mentality were inspired by a steadfast refusal to accept maintenance of the idle poor as a burden to the commonweal in which the non-poor must share. Summing up the essence of the amendment, Karl Polányi wrote, "No relief any longer for the able-bodied unemployed, no minimum wages either, not a safeguarding of the right to live. Labor should be dealt with as that which it was, a commodity which must find its price in the market."[4] A covertly held consideration was the impelling need to drive the land-poor and landless away from their rural habitats, in which they found minimal security in times of distress, and to urban growth poles to feed the local stock of labor required for the new industrial economy.

Disqualified from Relief

The revision of the Poor Laws formed the main push for the falling from grace for many throughout Europe. This turned agrarian workers, who had always been stakeholders, into outsiders from the commonweal, once they lost their regular jobs and were hired off and on as casual hands. They were no longer eligible for public relief when unemployed. Over time, and as a consequence of the lengthening chain of dependency far beyond local reach and control, the segment cut loose from wherever it belonged in terms of work and life rapidly increased. Their rise to an abundant number with the worldwide advance of capitalism, multi-class in origin and joining the ranks of the stigmatized lot, is captured well in Karl Marx's description of what he rather disparagingly called the *Lumpenproletariat*.[5] Due to ongoing dispossession, the land-poor and landless classes in European countries had rapidly increased in size and were forced to vie for sources of livelihood other than what had been the prime sector of the economy in previous generations. The transformation went together with a major restructuring or destruction of artisanal forms of production. An accelerated footlooseness of adults, as well as minors, occurred within the countryside, but mobility from village to town or city increased even more. Sprawling urban locations required the presence of massive armies of labor for the transport and storage of a steadily growing volume of goods, not only at expanding industrial work sites but also for building up an infrastructure consisting of railway lines, stations, canals, dockyards, roads, and warehouses. The exploitation of men, women, and children ruthlessly put to work in the intensified process of economic activity—and their total lack of wherewithal to cope with the commodification to which they were subjected—led to stark poverty and pauperization. It was a consequence of capital becoming dominant in the new landscape of economic production.

The Struggle against Adversity and the Northern Class Compromise

The deterioration in livelihood caused by loss of employment as well as habitat instigated new forms of social security. As a first step, many from the ranks of the somewhat better-off and more regularly employed wage earners organized mutual-aid societies, usually beginning as small-scale, local operations, but gradually becoming interregional and even national. These forms of social security excluded, however, significant segments of the working population. Women were usually not admitted, and the poorest workers were not eligible because of their fluctuating and insufficient incomes.[6] Ongoing pauperization of the "dangerous classes" on a mass scale, their sporadic violent and rebellious behavior, and their deteriorating health combined with new forms of trade-union actions, leading to more encompassing forms of association in which claims for improvement were articulated. From the late eighteenth-century, trade unions began to organize the workforce; after 1848, their strength increased and, backed up by industrial action, they gradually succeeded in institutionalizing forms of collective bargaining. The threat of straightforward confrontations between capital and labor was avoided—or at least mitigated—when the state, through a variety of regulations, started to defuse the risk of havoc, which, in all likelihood, would have resulted from a head-on clash between them. Mediation was operationalized through extensive labor legislation that made basic rights of the workforce mandatory, such as fixing minimum wages (and a hike, in case of price rise), steadily lowering the ceiling for hours at work, and, in case of dispute, requiring obligatory arbitration.

The transformation that occurred until and beyond the middle of the twentieth century has resulted in a relative rise in working-class power in what were, of course, still capitalist societies. The social struggle that came about in industrializing and urbanizing Europe had two major components. In the first place, better conditions of employment ensued, such as higher wages; a change from piece rate to time rate; a shorter working day, week, and life; safety at work; paid leave; and a premium on schooling and skilling. All this culminated in a standard contract that conceded the right to collective action and representation.[7] In the second place, the provision of social security and protection took shape, which included health insurance, a pension fund for the aged, allowances in case of injuries and handicaps while at work, gratuities or bonuses, and, to cap it all, compensation for loss of employment.

Growth of the Welfare State and the Public Economy

What initially had been posed as a labor question, pure and simple, metamorphosed into a wider question expressing aspirations for a decent and dignified mode of existence. The deepening of public authority climaxed in the emergence of the welfare state that slowly came about in this part of the world during the first half of the twentieth century. An important element of the social progress made in Europe was the extension of suffrage, first for adult men and, belatedly, for women as well. The social question transfigured from the realm of labor to the realm of citizenship at large. The universalization of social security provisions—including medical insurance, compulsory education at young age, pension rights, unemployment and disability benefits, widows' and orphans' support, and supplemented, after World War II, by child benefits and an old-age allowance—often extended to a large segment of the population and made an important contribution to their well-being. In the righteous jargon of politicians and policy makers, this was known as care "from the cradle to the grave." Memories of the *trente glorieuses*, roughly from 1945 to 1975, evoke feelings of nostalgia. The working classes of the erstwhile Second World would have ample reason to share those sentiments.

Conditional to the realization of the ambition to raise people's standard of life was the intervention of the state machinery in building up a much larger and strengthened public economy than had existed before. The first steps toward this attempt to bring the former notion of the commons to the national level were taken in the late nineteenth and early twentieth centuries, with the establishment of municipal utility corporations for gas, water, and electricity and for garbage and sewage disposal, as well as sanitation. Cooperative housing societies, the postal and telephone services, public transport and insurance authorities were set up to cater to the commonweal and public works to upgrade the physical infrastructure. And, to top it all, public health and education became schemes of welfarism. The creation of the welfare state was inextricably linked to the emergence of public institutions, space, and agency. The flipside of a steadily expanding public domain was, of course, higher (albeit income-differentiated) taxation and increasing bureaucratization.[8]

The so-called Second World of the Soviet Union and its allies in Europe, as well as in the world at large, claimed to have put the social question at the top of the national agenda. After all, in its revolutionary origin was the promise to end the exploitation and suppression of the working classes by capitalism. In China, the urban laboring class employed in state-owned enterprises was a minority in a system that excluded the vast majority of rural producers and urban temporary workers from its iconic state paternalism. As Ching Kwan Lee documents in her contribution to this volume, even this exclusionary socialist welfare system gave way to a secular process of precarization and political exclusion for labor. The disappearance of the only alternative to capitalism lifted the pressure on Western democracies to demonstrate the superiority of their system through welfare provision.

Falling behind and the "Southern" Class Compromise

Vast tracts of the planet had remained exempt from the march of progress, resulting in what turned out to be a time-bound social compact. The Global South, made up of societies and economies subjected to (semi-)colonial rule imposed from the metropoles in the Global North, fell behind in stagnation. The split in the global working class, having its origin in the uneven path of development, with colonialism as a major cause, eventuated in a growing segregation between frontrunners in the Global North and latecomers in the Global South. After the abolition of slavery, new forms of unfree labor were introduced, on the pretext that the limited needs to which the "natives" were habituated made them work shy. It led to the recruitment, in the backward economies, of armies of indentured coolies deployed worldwide to enclaves of capitalist production, such as mines and plantations in the southern hemisphere. The work contracts in which they were entrapped could not be reneged, and protest or resistance against the harsh labor regime was brutally punished. The major part of humankind remained embedded in village-based economies, producing food mainly for their own livelihood. The low-level technology explained why these small-scale peasant communities went on to live and work from generation to generation without much change and were, in years of scarcity, supposed to help each other out in a pattern of shared poverty.

Sustained and intensified colonial rule was now portrayed as a civilizing mission with the pledge to "add value" where it was considered to be absent. In the early twentieth century, the international alliance of social-democratic parties endorsed the French proclamation of this *mise-en-valeur* thesis.[9] It meant the endorsement and propagation of a racist doctrine that justified the ongoing subordination of the "lower" segments of humanity held back in an imperialist setting. On the eve of independence from colonial rule, only a tiny fraction of the total workforce—a privileged contingent of modern factory hands and office workers mainly—had come to enjoy formalized conditions of employment. The large majority of men and women engaged in waged work were firmly stuck in labor relations that remained thoroughly informalized. The formal-informal divide that became so prominent in the late twentieth century has its origin in labor policies of the colonial period.

In the wake of decolonization of the Global South around the mid-twentieth century—though Latin America had gotten rid of formal colonialism earlier on—internal developments in the Global South led to a "southern class compromise." Rapid urbanization in the developing countries from 1950 to 1970 compelled governments in Latin America, the Middle East, and North Africa to pacify the urban popular groups consisting of both poor and middle classes with price subsidies, public services, and other forms of social wage guarantees. As Kevan Harris shows for the Middle East and North Africa, nationalization of major industries and expansion of state bureaucracy made the public economy a major provider of formal employment. This pact of developmentalist populism was orchestrated by a class coalition of state bureaucracy and industrial and export interests that paid the price of social peace with concessions to urban dwellers.[10] National sociopolitical formations shaped the particular mode of compromise. In South Africa, as Ben Scully discusses in his chapter, the settler colonial response to the social question was in the form of a whites-only welfare state, a racialized social compact that excluded the majority black population. Overall, whereas in advanced industrial societies the compromise was essentially an exchange between organized capital and organized labor, the southern class compromise was driven by the state, which incorporated and subordinated urban labor.[11] As Ronaldo Munck and Mao Mollona examine in Latin American cases, since the mid-1970s, this class compromise has begun to unravel, as southern states plunged into a sustained debt crisis and International Monetary Fund–inspired adjustment programs triggered widespread austerity protests by the urban classes.

The International Monetary Fund and the World Bank, the two transnational corporations set up by the Bretton Woods system of financial management, expanded their original mandate, which had mainly focused on the advanced economies. Increasingly, both agencies started to extend their operations to the provision of loans to developing countries with conditionality clauses meant to prevent or undo fiscal imbalances. Announced as structural adjustment programs (SAPs), policies were advocated that privatized and deregulated what had been the prerogative of state-directed welfare management exercised by the national treasury. Andreas Eckert has commented on the impact of this policy in Africa.

No transnational agency was set up to handle the social mandate. Instead, Poverty Reduction Strategy Papers (PRSPs) were announced to suggest that higher rates of economic growth in the catching-up countries were both a necessary and sufficient condition for welfare to trickle down. The fading away of the state as a broker between capital and labor was the outcome of the neoliberal strategy that first became mandatory in the Global South. After the turn of the century, it was also imposed on the Global North and became increasingly dominant the world over. In the former Soviet bloc countries, the shift that endeavored to boost the "free market" led to much reduced funding on social-sector expenditure and a major contraction of the sizable public economy. Carine Clément shows in her chapter how shock therapy in Russia in the 1990s took a heavy toll on Russian workers and their families and led to a rampant normalization and individualization of precarity. Don Kalb similarly highlights how liberalization and market reforms in post-socialist Eastern Europe undermined the strong and militant solidarities of the 1980s labor movements in the region.

THE RETURN OF THE SOCIAL QUESTION UNDER GLOBAL CAPITALISM

In drawing the final balance of the Millennium Development Goals, bringing a growing number of people above the threshold of deprivation is highlighted as the successful outcome of neoliberal policies. The World Bank's felicitous observation of gradually diminishing indigence all over the world—from 14.5 percent in 2011 to 12.8 percent in 2012 and, hopefully, to below 10 percent in 2015—stems from fixing the takeoff point at a budget considered to be adequate for the poorest countries in the world. In 1990, when the global poverty line became set for the first time, the yardstick was the ability to spend not less than one dollar a day per capita, the international poverty line based on the purchasing power parity (PPP) index. After a hike of this amount to $1.25 in 2005, it was further raised to $1.90 in 2011 in order to account for rising prices. In this statistical exercise, the growing part of the population sliding downward in the advanced economies is totally disregarded. It is an oversight compounded by the assumption that indigence is a condition that is absolute. It defies the point of view that poverty should be perceived as a lack of means defined both in relative as well as relational terms. The global downfall is not one of capitalism, as Immanuel Wallerstein has already been arguing for a number of years.[12] It should rather be understood and tackled as an increasing shortage of gainful employment and too low a price for rewarding an incessantly growing workforce in the world. One result of the globalizing economy is that the dominating trend of increasing inequity appears to indicate a growing divergence between social classes. While inequality between countries is slowly decreasing, inequality within countries is rapidly growing. For the Global North, Thomas Piketty has amply documented the enrichment of owners and managers of capital.[13]

Divergent Trajectories between the Global North and Global South

The notion that postcolonial countries, in the aftermath of the successful fight for national sovereignty, would be put on the track to progress by their erstwhile rulers pretending to be inclined to more altruistic policies than before was met with skeptical appraisals. To start with, it is an evolutionary imagery that does not acknowledge a substantial drain from the Global South during the era of colonialism in building up the lead position of the Global North. The early growth trajectory in the Atlantic basin had partly been achieved by extracting surplus from countries in the Global South caught up in a stultified, backward rural economy. These transfers—written up as a drain in the dissenting literature—contributed to the in-country process of accumulation going on in the Global North. To this critical assessment, other major diversions in the differential growth and development trajectories in the world, separated from each other in a prolonged time span, should be added. The most significant of these other distinctive features were limits to demands for labor and a drastically changed appraisal on the role of migration.

Of major importance is the much lower land-labor ratio in mid-nineteenth-century Europe as compared to the much higher pressure in the mid-twentieth century on agrarian resources elsewhere, particularly in Asia. While the push away from agriculture and the countryside amounted to a ballpark figure of 120–150 million people in Europe between 1850 and 1914, the exodus going on one century later out of the major countries of Asia easily adds up to a staggering above 700 million mostly land poor and landless peasants. Driven out by a stark lack of employment and income opportunities in and outside the primary sector of production in the countryside, a major segment of these uprooted masses of migrants try to establish a foothold in the expanding urban economy. However, while work in industry became an alternative after the loss of agrarian-rural livelihoods in erstwhile Europe, it has remained modest in size in the postcolonial societies. This means that the newcomers to the towns and cities of the Global South are dependent for employment on earnings made in construction, transport, petty trade, and services. Even in China, reputed to be today's workshop of the world, industrial jobs employ less than half of an estimated 300–350 million migrants who have left the countryside during the last quarter of a century. In India, as well as in other Asian countries, the size of the industrial workforce is still much lower, even if we include self-employed and mainly home-based manufacturers along with factory labor. Prospects of acceleration in industrial activity, providing jobs to a much larger percentage of the total workforce, are slight. While the first stage of the industrial revolution in the Global North continued was highly labor intensive, the transition to more advanced technology—first mechanization and automation, followed by computerization and robotization—has steadily given rise to a more capital-intensive mode of production and jobless forms of economic growth.

Centuries earlier, when the European countryside started to depopulate, part of the redundant labor in agriculture did not migrate to towns and cities within the same country but left for destinations overseas. This transfer mitigated the pressure on the swollen labor market at home. These earlier waves of emigrants settled down in the underpopulated zones of the planet—North and South America, southern Africa, Siberia, Australia, and New Zealand—to find better livelihoods than they had enjoyed before. The underpopulated territories on the global frontiers happened to be inhabited by tribal communities driven off or wiped out in the march toward what was claimed to be a higher level of civilization. There are no more "empty" regions in today's world.[14] People nowadays, driven by distress and trying to get out of the Global South in desperate search of work and life, are no longer classified as brave colonists who are bid welcome to settle down in their country of arrival but have become labeled economic refugees. If escape from poverty is their aim, they are even less welcome than newcomers better equipped with skills and physical as well as social capital to provide for their livelihood.

Informalization of Labor and Capital

By the turn of the new millennium, through different trajectories, the standard labor contract as part of the post-WWII class compromises in the Global North and the Global South has substantially unraveled. Informalization of labor has by leaps and bounds become a global trend. Its major features are as follows: no regulated jobs backed up by a labor contract, but hire-and-fire, according to the need of the moment; a variable length of the working day, fluctuating between too short or too long; extensive participation in the paid labor process at both underage and overage; no standardized wages with a fixed minimum, but piece-rated remuneration imposed unilaterally and individually by the employer or his agent; erratic payment, either given by way of advance or settled afterward, but in both cases, a modality meant to reduce the labor price; injurious working conditions at sites that are unclean, unhealthy, and hazardous or dangerous, leading to occupational diseases and accidents; no safeguard against dismissal, loss of labor power, and unemployment; and self-representation instead of collective bargaining and forced self-employment coupled with self-provisioning. The case studies presented in this volume bear witness to the practices of informality and informalization throughout the world. We cannot deny, of course, that huge differences in per capita income continue to exist between North and South. In the Global North there are still some vestiges left of the deal closed with labor when the economy was predominantly run along formalized lines of employment. Indigence in size, shape, and degree is much starker in the Global South than it has become once more in the Global North.

Not just labor, capital is also increasingly informalized. Labeled as a black circuit, massive financial transactions move around the globe, unregistered in governmental bookkeeping and beyond the reach of the national exchequer. Gabriel

Zucman estimates that $7.6 trillion, or 8 percent of the world's financial wealth, is held in tax havens. In Africa, the proportion is as high as 30 percent; in Russia and the Middle East, above 50 percent.[15] The black money in circulation is difficult to estimate but might be close to or even larger than the amount of cash legally changing hands. Free market enterprise happens to be backed up by a political order at the level of the nation-state willing to go along with the directives of predatory capitalism. Handicapped by the absence of forceful and effective public governance in the global realm, it seems rather farfetched to presume that financialized freebooting, which has a strong lobby in privatized banking, will eventually be brought under public control.[16]

All over the world, rich and poor have disappeared from each other's presence and even sight. They live in different circuits, and that lack of interaction means that the moral bearings of the social question got lost. Does the thoroughly informalized workforce in the global economy constitute a dangerous class? In our view, it might be more appropriate to label the down-and-out masses as an endangered species, no longer embedded within the rights of citizenship in mainstream society.[17] Take the case of the street vendor in a small Tunisian town who ended his life in self-immolation. Having failed to find a regular job, his efforts to scratch around at the bottom of the urban economy were met with police harassment, and in agony, he ended his life when his livelihood of the last resort was taken away from him. Such acts of defiance, though not rare, usually remain unseen and unheard in public space, but not in this instance. His refusal to bow down under lack of work and freedom fueled an outburst of popular anger. Demonstrations spread like wildfire and swept throughout North Africa and the Middle East in opposition to political, economic, and social tyranny.

Strains on Family and Reciprocity

In his contribution, Dennis Arnold highlights how, under the development regime the Asian Development Bank has imposed in Mekong South East Asia, "pro-poor" growth enclaves are set up that reproduce poverty rather than ameliorate it. The workforce is employed on an informal footing, and the migrants engaged, not earning enough to make a living, have to remain encapsulated in a fragile agrarian economy to do so. People steeped in progressive adversity have no other wherewithal than to fall back on makeshift solutions of long standing, such as support from family, neighbors, and others close to or far away from where they work and live. It is the low-profile way of mutual assistance, small-scale attempts to ward off setbacks by sharing expenses on life-cycle events or seasonal ups and downs among people in the same setting. But out of necessity, households have often become multi-locational, with members—both adults and children—pushed off to go wherever and for as long as waged work can be found. To bring dependents along would be an unbearable burden. As they drift away from home, the imposed mobility means that life for such labor migrants tends to become individualized, deprived from the nearby comfort of parents or offspring. Claims on reciprocity put enormous strains on family relations. It explains why destitution is often an ordeal that coincides with a break-up of the household and ends in alienation and loneliness. Ben Scully's chapter spotlights in particular the strain on the family, especially the women, as central organizers of informal welfare and survival among South Africa's poor.

Land Flight

Another coping mechanism for the surplus population is emigration, an option that has increasingly become perilous. In the receiving countries, migrant workers form a marginalized underclass depleted of minimal protection against exploitation and oppression, as has become standing practice over the last half century, for example, in the Arab Gulf region. A doctrine of naked racism has emerged in many parts of the world, made manifest in autochthonous domination versus alien subordination. Labor in the globalized economy is prevented from uniting and fighting for their common interest—decent work and dignified life—by promoting fault lines of segregation along what are considered to be primordial loyalties, such as gender, race, ethnicity, creed, caste, and nationality. It means that no common claims can be derived from the laboring status, since they clash with what are perceived as first-order sentiments.

The contingents of refugees from the Global South desperately trying to reach a safe haven in Europe, Russia, North America, or Australia tend to be equipped with an identity somewhat higher up in the class ranking, have enjoyed some degree of skilling or schooling, and, with familial support, are able to buy their way outside. They cross frontiers *sans papiers* and travel in the hope of good luck, often without knowing in advance where they will end up or wash ashore. Depots have been established either halfway or on the receiving end in which these flotsam and jetsam castaways are held in isolation, locked up because they have been found guilty of unauthorized trespassing at some point during their often ill-fated journey. In the middle of the twentieth century, the term *displaced person* (DP) was coined for the registration of people who had lost hearth and home. Half a century later, the abbreviation seems to express the fate of dumped people, arrested and detained out of sight for being a nuisance to citizens with a legal status of residence. When politicians insist that refugees have to be dealt with in or close to their country of origin, it is in euphemistic reference to detainment in permanent exile, end-stations for people considered to be surplus to demand. How to handle their presence? The simple pretense is that they are not there, have no right to existence, and building walls is not really necessary to keep them in a state of invisibility. Sheer lack of connectivity with faraway destinations, together with lack of money to pay the high price of the often illegal and tortuous passage, leaves them entrapped at home. The reserve armies of labor amassed in the Global South are stuck in a prolonged state of un- and underemployment, cut off from regular and decently paid jobs that, in their dreams, are available elsewhere. Together with the non-laboring poor, they are in rapidly growing numbers exposed to pauperism.

Earlier solutions for how to close or at least reduce the gap between prosperity and poverty were based on the logic of proportional representation and distributional justice, pertinent to an ethos of equity that aimed at structuring economic, political, and social life. The progressive disequilibrium has not prompted politicians to reconsider their policies of leaving the staggering bonanza of riches untaxed. Instead, they have opted to further reduce taxation and thus add to the sharply skewed splits of the spoils by rewarding capital with more subsidies and exemption from regulations prohibiting environmental degradation, pretending that this will stimulate employment. The strategy has allowed capital to escape again from societal control, but now in a context that is different from the one Polányi described and analyzed for the Western economies in the mid-nineteenth century.[18] In contrast to what happened then in this part of the world, re-embedding capitalism again within the perimeters of the nation-state is a moot possibility. While the drive to play along with the free operation of casino capitalism goes on as before, and a much required levy on financial transactions is not enacted, at the other end of the scale, the laboring and non-laboring poor are wont to bear the brunt of a fiscal policy that has led to a drastic underfunding of the budget spent on the social safety net. The punitive welfare reform, as designed and executed in the United States since the late twentieth century, as Fred Block details in his chapter, might become standard for dealing with the chronically unemployed in the front-running as well as the "catching-up" economies.[19]

Across the Global South, the social question on national agendas has taken the form of recently proposed or implemented social policies, such as small-cash transfers, old-age pensions, meager-workfare schemes, or basic-income grants. Poorer segments of the population that have gained newly available access to state-provided transfers, as in Brazil or South Africa, never had previous access to formal sector or employment-based welfare provisions. It remains to be seen if these low-quality and much restricted safety nets will have significant and lasting impacts in benefiting the poor. One objection, of course, is that a dole solely in the form of a state-provided cash transfer to the impoverished underclass does not even ameliorate the real situation of human immiseration. Evidence on the positive effects of the wide variety of new social policies across the Global South has to be matched with cases that demonstrate sustained or even hardening exclusion, as Jan Breman shows in his chapter on Indian social policies. Of even more significance than putting on record this diversity in graded practices of inclusion versus exclusion would be to point out that the strained public budget in the prolonged setting of neoliberalism does not allow governments to spend much on what is minimally required to keep the poor masses free from want, let alone provide them with income enabling a somewhat dignified livelihood beyond sheer reproduction. In much of the Global South, such down-and-out people seem to have wasted their value as a commodity, let alone their human quality.

COUNTERMOVEMENTS AT THE GLOBAL LEVEL?

Trade Unionism

Why and how has the social question failed to become raised and solved, when capital transcends beyond the nation-state and operates in predatory fashion at the globalized level? The main agencies charged with promoting the interests of the working classes in the world at large are a conglomerate of country-based trade unions and the International Labour Organization (ILO). Large-scale working-class movements had their origin in the nineteenth century in the North Atlantic basin. When, in the interwar years, interest in trade-unionism increased in the peripheral and semi-peripheral countries, it was the Communist Red International of Labor Unions (RILU or Profintern), which, after its founding in 1921, sought to put down roots in the Global South. The International Federation of Trade Unions (IFTU) followed a few years later, from about 1928, partly to counter the rival Communist organization, which was intent on gaining greater influence in the colonial and semi-colonial countries. The IFTU and its successor, the International Confederation of Free Trade Unions (ICFTU), were both dominated by the British TUC and the American Federation of Labor and Congress of Industrial Organizations (AFL-CIO), and had the reputation of being allies of colonialism and neocolonialism. Such suspicions were not entirely unfounded. The ICFTU tried for years to propagate a certain "model" of "proper unionism." One of the aims formulated at the time of its founding in 1949 was "to provide assistance in the establishment, maintenance and development of trade union organizations, particularly in economically and socially under-developed countries."[20] It was assumed that "proper" trade unions would remain fully independent of political parties and states; concentrate on collective bargaining and lobbying for social security legislation; and defend and promote parliamentary democracy. These principles often proved difficult to apply.[21] For a genuine collective-bargaining system to work, there are preconditions not found in many countries, including "a legal and political system permitting the existence and functioning of reasonably free labor organizations" (a condition that was fully compatible with the early ICFTU views) and the requirement that "unions be more or less stable, reasonably well organized, and fairly evenly matched with the employers in bargaining strength."[22] "Effective unions have rarely if ever been organized by 'non-committed' workers, i.e., casual workers who change jobs frequently, return periodically to their native village, and have no specific industrial skill, even of a very simple kind. In most (though by no means all) newly industrializing countries, large excess supplies of common labor are available for nonagricultural work. Not only are unskilled workers rarely capable of forming unions of their own under such conditions; if they succeed in doing so, their unions have little or no bargaining power."[23]

Given these long-lasting limitations, it should not come as a surprise that there are major regions in the world where trade unions have almost no influence. In countries with independent workers' organizations, union density (union members as percentage of the total labor force) generally has been declining. Table 1.1 reconstructs the trends in a number of countries with more than fifty million inhabitants in 2010, for the period 1960–2013.

Organized labor solidarity on a global scale is almost insignificant. Independent trade unions organize only a small percentage of their target group worldwide, and the majority of them are in the relatively wealthy North Atlantic region. By far the most important global umbrella organization is the International Trade Union Confederation (ITUC), founded in 2006 as a merger of the ICFTU and the Christian World Confederation of Labor (WCL). In 2014, the ITUC estimated that about 200 million workers worldwide belong to trade unions and that 176 million

TABLE 1.1 Union densities in selected countries with more than fifty million inhabitants in 2010.

	1960	1970	1980	1990	2000	2010	2013
Brazil	n.a.	n.a.	20.8 (1976)	26.7	28.3	26.5	16.6
China (People's Republic)	n.a.	n.a.	(58.6)	(76.6)	(62.3) (1997)	(34.7)	(42.6)
France	19.6	21.7	18.3	10.0	8.0	7.9	7.7
Germany	34.7*	32.0*	34.9*	31.2	24.6	18.6	17.7†
India	n.a.	n.a.	n.a.	n.a.	13.8 (2004)	10.2 (2009)	9.8 (2012)
Italy	24.7	37.0	49.6	38.8	34.8	36.0	36.9†
Japan	32.9	35.1	31.1	25.4	21.5	18.4	17.8
Malaysia	n.a.	n.a.	n.a.	16.5	10.7	9.1	9.4
Mexico					15.6†	14.4†	13.6†
Philippines	n.a.	n.a.	27.0	29.7	27.1	8.7	8.5
Russian Federation		100.0 (1968)	100.0 (1979)	72.0	55.6 (1999)	30.7	27.8
South Africa	n.a.	n.a.	n.a.	n.a.	39.1‡	29.7‡	n.a.
South Korea	n.a.	n.a.	n.a.	n.a.	11.4†	9.7†	n.a.
Turkey	10.8	25.9	42.1	24.0	12.4	7.0	6.5
United Kingdom	40.4	44.8	51.7	39.7	30.1	27.1	25.4†
United States of America	n.a.	23.5◊	19.5◊	15.5◊	12.9†	11.4†	10.8†

* Germany for 1960–1990: West Germany.
† OECD figures.
‡ ILOSTAT.
◊ Jelle Visser, "Union Membership Statistics in Twenty-Four Countries," *Monthly Labor Review*, January 2006, 38–49.
For lack of data, the following countries have not been included: Argentina, Bangladesh, Colombia, Democratic Republic of Congo, Egypt, Ethiopia, Indonesia, Iran, Myanmar, Nigeria, Pakistan, Tanzania, and Vietnam.

of these are organized in the ITUC.[24] The ITUC also estimates that the total number of workers is roughly 2.9 billion. Therefore, global union density currently amounts to no more than a meagre 7 percent.[25]

Apart from the "collective-bargaining bias," several other factors have contributed to unionism's demise. First, the composition of the working class is changing. Unions find it difficult to organize employees in the service or financial sector. The rapidly growing informal economy is complicating things further, since workers change jobs frequently and often have to earn their income under very precarious conditions. A second important factor is what labor economist Richard Freeman has called the "labor supply shock" that has manifested since the early 1990s. Through the entry of Chinese, Indian, Russian, and other workers into the global economy, there has been an effective doubling of the number of workers producing for international markets over the past two decades. And, third, in many countries, there has been a strong neoliberal offensive against old-style unions and their modus operandi: the dominant practice of collective bargaining has increasingly become decentralized, and individualized labor contracts have become much more widespread than before. Weakened trade unions have to face more and more competition from alternative associations that are better adapted to the new-style labor relations. In Brazil, India, Pakistan, Bangladesh, South Africa, the Philippines, or South Korea, militant workers' movements (social movement unions) have emerged. New forms of rank-and-file trade unionism outside the established channels appeared since the 1970s, with international connections at the shop-floor level "bypassing altogether the secretariats, which they see as too often beholden to the bureaucracies of their various national affiliates."[26] A well-known example is the Transnationals Information Exchange (TIE), an outfit in which a substantial number of research and activist labor groups exchange information on transnational corporations (TNCs). The ineffectiveness of old-style unions is underlined by the growing tendency on the part of international trade secretariats (now called Global Unions) to engage in the direct recruitment of members in the periphery. We may think, for example, of the activities of the Union Network International (the global union for the service sector) recruiting information technology (IT) specialists directly (without mediation of local unions) in India.

As before, the fight for labor rights has remained secluded within the frame of the nation-state, resulting in lukewarm interest for improving the lot of the laboring poor outside the Global North. The import of cheap durable and not-so-durable consumer goods—garments, shoes, crockery, toys, electronics, household gadgets, and a wide range of other products manufactured in homes or sweatshops in the Global South—contribute to creating the impression of ongoing welfare in the advanced economies. It is an illusion that can only be maintained in total denial of what the excessively low cost of production means for the workforce in the catch-up economies: ongoing exploitation and repression. Exemplary of the neglect and indifference are the lukewarm trade-union protests in the Global

North not only to the recent factory fires in Bangladesh and Pakistan but also to the police brutality meted out to these factory workers when they made a faint attempt in early 2017 to back up their demand for a higher wage by going on strike.

Architects of a Global Social Compact: ILO and The World Bank?

The "globalization process" weakens labor rights across the globe. Rights are only rights if a public (national or transnational) authority is capable of enforcing them. Unenforceable claims or claims that are privately enforced should not be considered rights in a strict sense. In the field of labor rights, the International Labour Organization is a crucial institution. The ILO was set up in the wake of the social revolution that gave rise to the birth of the Soviet Union. Established under the auspices of the League of Nations, it sought to defuse an escalation of the conflict between capital and labor by calling for regulated consultations between employers and employees at the transnational level. An additional objective was the promotion of a standard model of industrial relations that would prevent unfair competition between countries marked by strikingly different modalities of waged work. These preliminary considerations were the points of departure for the tripartite formula mandated in ILO's directive: equal representation of government, employers, and employees. It was a canon that certified right from the beginning that the interests of labor would be superseded by those of the two other stakeholders.

The ILO's conventions, if ratified by member states, are guidelines for good practices at shop-floor level. Three weak spots of the ILO have to be stressed. The ILO is not only a relatively powerless organization but also reacts rather slowly to new developments. During the evolving transition to neoliberalism, the agents of government were co-opted to cater one-sidely to the demands of capital, while the trade unions that cared for the interests only of the shrinking workforce still employed in the formal economy persisted for long in looking at informal-sector workers as blacklegs. With the passing of years, the international standing of ILO has gone down. No doubt, the flexibilization of waged work is the most important reason for the erosion of ILO's mandate and agenda. All parties in the policymaking process, including the trade-union movement, have in the past decades vigorously refused to give voice to, as well as allow representation of, informalized labor in the Global South. Their vested interest in speaking up on behalf of the shrinking portion of the workforce still in the formal economy played a major role in the sustained resistance to giving a better deal to workers bereft of collective action. The wisdom of hindsight was reflected in the manifesto calling for "decent work" in 1999, but this change of hearts is nothing more than a faint effort to regain the terrain lost. The lesson learnt is that the struggle for formalization of all waged work is on the ILO's agenda. It is, indeed, a necessary although not sufficient precondition for the emancipation of the laboring classes in the world.[27]

The World Bank is another major global-development actor, with enormous financial, political, and knowledge-making power. Its strategic response to what we call the social question at the global level is "poverty alleviation," a top priority in its renewed Millennium Development Goals. But instead of tackling the structural, political, and economic sources of poverty, the bank's approach has been to reduce the problem of mass immiseration and precarity to deficient individual decision making on the part of the remaining poor, identified as a residual class to be found only in the catch-up economies. What should have been addressed as a budgetary deficit at the household level is conceived to be the lack of a predisposition to economize, self-discipline, and financial literacy of the poor, who should simply work harder to lift themselves out of poverty.[28] Applying behavioral economics to development and poverty, the policy recommendations prioritized focus on "nudging" the poor to change their cognitive and psychological predispositions and the social constraints that influence economic decision making.[29] This was essentially the logic of the World Bank's World Development Report 2015, even as the bank belatedly and reluctantly acknowledged that the trickle-down mechanism does not operate as earlier proclaimed. The report reads like a tour de force, a major reappraisal of policies not so long ago vigorously prescribed, but the recommendations are not followed up by any concrete steps to change the way the thoroughly deregulated labor market operates. Moreover, while targeting income inequality, the bank glosses over the even more striking issue of wealth disparity.

An indictment of the shortcomings of the poor harks back to the doctrine of economic dualism that in the colonial era portrayed the *homo economicus* as a creature sprouting from Western civilization, while the human gestalt in the oriental part of the world was supposed to be sadly deprived of righteous economic propensity.[30] The construction of this contrast found a sequel in the dualistic distinction made between more-advanced versus less-advanced economies in the early postcolonial era, while a new and updated version of this dichotomy does not refer any longer to civilizations or countries but is conceptualized to exist between social classes. The World Bank, in its World Development Report 2015 referred to above, sets out to comprehend penury by laying stress on the misbehavior attributed to the people entrapped in this dire predicament. Only their doings and misdoings are highlighted. Apart from the biased manner in which their inadequacy is portrayed, our objection to this simplified assessment of the problem is that the societal context of poverty remains totally disregarded.

Announcing its flagship publication, "Poverty and Sharing Prosperity" (2016), the World Bank reluctantly agrees that tackling inequality is vital to ending excessive poverty by 2030, the new signpost for what is called *sustainable development*. How to achieve this feel-good ambition? It would require a more equal income distribution, and that means a hike in the floor price at which labor is made to sell itself, backed up, in some undefined way, by employment formalization, the bank now concedes. Our contention is that the fight against income inequality will turn out to be meaningless if the divide between wealth and poverty remains unaddressed. On further reading what sharing prosperity actually implies, it seems that the policies practiced so far may not have to be reformulated at all. This far-from-surprising conclusion is reached with the argument that from 2008 to 2013, the share in income of the bottom 40 percent of the world's population has considerably gone up, and we are asked to believe that their gain in income exceeded that of the top 60 percent. It would, of course, have been setting a hopeful trend and more so, on being told that the leveling down of excessive inequality also took place at the high tide of another Great Depression of the 1930s. As usual, however, the bank's arithmetic is founded on biased and otherwise disputable statistics.

In this book, we offer an alternative analytical lens, one that shows that poverty and precarity result from loss of property—of land and other assets as well as tools and skills from the nearby or remote past—and are often compounded by dissolution or even collapse of the social fabric, state support, and the public economy. It is an argument that leads us to perceive the accumulation versus dispossession binary as processes that are not disconnected but interact in tandem. In the accelerated process of globalization, pauperism and pauperization has risen to an alarming height under the banner of predatory capitalism and has found expression in the creation of surplus people, a contingent of humankind classified as redundant to demand.[31] Emphasizing the interdependency between growing wealth and impoverishment implies that a life of human quality for all requires a fundamental redistribution of the sources of existence. It is a conclusion that stands to be rejected by the stakeholders of global capitalism. The failure of half-hearted attempts at poverty alleviation, which continue to rely on the trickle-down magic and its dismal outcome, flies in the face of the good news that the marginally reformulated Millennium Development Goals will ultimately be successfully achieved.

NOTES

1. See Robert von Pöhlmann, *Geschichte der sozialen Frage und des Sozialismus in der antiken Welt*, 3rd ed., vol. 1 (Munich: Beck, 1925).

2. Alexis de Tocqueville, *Memoir on Pauperism*, trans. Seymour Drescher, (New Haven, CT: Yale University Press, 1968); reprinted and published by Civitas (London 1997), available at http://civitas.org.uk. For the classical exposition on the spiraling of the accumulation-dispossession binary, see Karl Marx, *Capital*, vol. 1.

3. "The master 'owes' the subject something as well, not juridically, but morally. Above all—if only in his own interest—he must protect him against the outside world and help him in need. He must also treat him 'humanely,' and, especially, he must restrict the exploitation of his performance to what is 'customary.' On the ground of a domination whose aim is not material enrichment but the fulfillment of the master's own needs, he can do so without prejudicing his own interest because, as his needs cannot expand qualitatively and, on principle, unlimitedly, his demands differ only quantitatively from those of his subjects. And such restriction is positively useful to the master, as not only the security of his domination but also its results greatly depend on the disposition and mood of the subordinates. The subordinate morally owes the master assistance by all the means available to him." Max Weber, *Grundriss der Sozialökonomik, III: Abteilung, Wirtschaft und Gesellschaft* (Tübingen: J. C. B. Mohr, 1922), 682.

4. Karl Polányi, *The Great Transformation: The Political and Economic Origins of Our Times* (Boston: Beacon Press, 1944).

5. Karl Marx, "The Eighteenth Brumaire of Louis Bonaparte," (1851–52), *Marx & Engels Collected Works*, vol. 11 (London: Lawrence and Wishart, 1976), 149.

6. Marcel van der Linden, *Workers of the World: Essays toward a Global Labor History* (Leiden: Brill, 2008), chaps. 5 and 6.

7. "In the 1950s and 1960s, the labor contract for an undetermined length of time became the norm, and then served as a virtual guarantee of employment. But this stemmed only from the fact that in times of full employment, one often only hires, rarely lays off employees. As this growth [of the long boom] vanishes, however, security too disappears, and the 'indefinite' aspect of the contract reveals itself to be a simple consequence of empirical realities and not a legal guarantee. . . . This did not prevent most wage earners, during the years of growth, from experiencing their relationship in employment with the certitude of controlling the future and of making choices that take into account this future, such as investing in durable goods, taking out mortgages for construction, and so on." Robert Castel, *From Manual Workers to Wage Laborers: Transformation of the Social Question*, trans. Richard Boyd (New Brunswick, NJ: Transaction Publishers, 2003), 372–73. (Originally published in French as *Les métamorphoses de la question sociale, une chronique du salariat* [Paris, 1995]).

8. Jan Breman and Marcel van der Linden, "Informalizing the Economy: The Return of the Social Question at the Global Level," *Development and Change*, 45, no. 5 (2014): 920–40.

9. Albert Sarraut, *La mise en valeur des colonies françaises* (Paris: Payot, 1923).

10. John Walton and David Seddon, *Free Markets and Food Riots: The Politics of Global Adjustment* (Oxford: Blackwell, 1994), 46–47; Kevan Harris, "Did Inequality Breed the Arab Uprisings? Social Inequality in the Middle East from a World Perspective," in *The Arab Revolution of 2011: A Comparative Perspective*, ed. Saïd Amir Arjomand, 87–111 (Albany, NY: State University of New York Press, 2015).

11. Edward Webster and Glenn Adler, "Toward a Class Compromise in South Africa's 'Double Transition': Bargained Liberalization and the Consolidation of Democracy" *Politics and Society* 27, no. 3 (1999): 347–85.

12. See, for example, Immanuel Wallerstein, "Globalization or the Age of Transition? A Long-Term View of the Trajectory of the World System," *International Sociology* 15, no. 2 (2000): 251–67; or Wallerstein, "Capitalism as an Essential Concept to Understand Modernity," in *Capitalism: The Reemergence of a Historical Concept*, ed. Jürgen Kocka and Marcel van der Linden, 187–204 (London: Bloomsbury, 2016).

13. Thomas Piketty, *Capital in the Twenty-First* Century (Cambridge, MA: Harvard University Press, 2013).

14. See, for example, Fritz Sternberg, *Capitalism and Socialism on Trial* (London: Gollancz, 1951), 62–64.

15. Gabriel Zucman, *The Hidden Wealth of Nations: The Scourge of Tax Havens* (Chicago: University of Chicago Press, 2015).

16. Wolfgang Streeck, "The Crises of Democratic Capitalism," *New Left Review*, second series, 71 (September-October 2011); and Streeck, "How Will Capitalism End?" *New Left Review*, second series, 87 (May-June 2014).

17. See also Jan Breman, "A Bogus Concept," *New Left Review*, second series, 84 (November-December 2013): 130–38.

18. Polányi, *The Great Transformation.*

19. Michael B. Katz, *The Undeserving Poor: America's Enduring Confrontation with Poverty*, 2nd and rev. ed. (New York: Oxford University Press, 2013).

20. ICFTU, Official Report (1949), 226.

21. Sometimes they also seemed insincere. Regarding the emphasis placed by the British TUC in the 1950s on the nonpolitical nature of "proper" trade unionism, Davies has correctly observed, "Some of these sentiments sound odd in the context of the history of the British trade union movement, which

had supported a general strike, maintained a close association with the Labour Party, and in its annual congresses regularly debated resolutions on a large number of issues outside the field of industrial relations." D. I. Davies, "The Politics of the TUC's Colonial Policy," *The Political Quarterly* 35 (1964): 26.

22. Adolf Sturmthal, "Industrial Relations Strategies," in *The International Labor Movement in Transition*, ed. Adolf Sturmthal and James G. Scoville, 1–33 (Urbana, IL: University of Illinois Press, 1973), 9.

23. Ibid., 10.

24. This calculation is probably misleading. A significant, but unknown, part of the union membership consists of pensioners.

25. *Building Workers' Power, Congress Statement* (Berlin: International Trade Union Confederation, 2014), 8.

26. Andrew Herod, "Labor as an Agent of Globalization and as a Global Agent," in *Spaces of Globalization: Reasserting the Power of the Local*, ed. Kevin R. Cox, 167–200 (New York: Guilford Press, 1997), 184.

27. For further documentation on the ILO, see also Guy Standing, "The ILO: An Agency for Globalization?" *Development and Change* 39, no. 3 (2008): 355–84.

28. *World Development Report 2015: Mind, Society, and Behavior* (Washington DC: The World Bank, 2015).

29. Ben Fine, Deborah Johnston, Ana C Santos, and Elisa Van Waeyenberge, "Nudging or Fudging: The World Development Report 2015," *Development and Change* 47, no. 4 (2016): 640–63.

30. Julius H. Boeke, *Economics and Economic Policy of Dual Societies, as Exemplified by Indonesia* (New York: Institute of Pacific Relations, 1953). For an early array of criticism on the notion of colonial dualism, see W. F. Wertheim and others, *Indonesian Economics: The Concept of Dualism in Theory and Practice* (The Hague: W. van Hoeve, 1966).

31. Tania Murray Li, "To Make Live and Let Die? Rural Dispossession and the Protection of Surplus Populations," *Antipode*, 41, no. 1 (2010): 66–93. See also her anthropological monograph *Land's End; Capitalist Relations on an Indigenous Frontier* (Durham, NC: Duke University Press, 2014).

2

The Social Question in Western Europe

Past and Present

Marcel van der Linden

> *Day laborer: manual worker paid by the day. People like this make up the majority of the nation and their fate is what a good government should mainly have in mind. If the day laborer is poor, then the nation itself is poor.*
> —DENIS DIDEROT, "JOURNALIER"

The social question was a European "discovery." It was first perceived in France, after the Industrial Revolution had gone through its early boisterous phase, and after the Revolution of 1789 had run aground in the Bourbon restoration. At that time, during the 1830s, a "divorce" became visible "between a juridico-political order founded on the recognition of the rights of citizens and an economic order that carried with it widespread misery and demoralization." Pauperism expressed the social question at its clearest. It challenged "the capacity of a society (known in political terms as a nation) to exist as a collectivity linked by relations of interdependency."[1] The social question was located in the vacuum that had developed once the economic and the political spheres had gone separate ways and the economy was increasingly disembedded in the Polányian sense. Paupers were no longer integrated into society through economic ties or through political authority. They revealed the existence of a "perilous" environment, of "dangerous classes" escaping elite control.[2] After France, the dominant circles in other Western European countries would soon conceptualize the new menace in similar ways.

ORIGINS OF UNPROTECTED LABOR

Though the social question was discovered only in the nineteenth century, its antecedents were, of course, much older. Casual wage labor has existed for millennia in Europe and elsewhere. In ancient Athens, a space existed known as *kolonos agoraios* (or *ergatikos* or *misthios*), probably on the west end of the agora, where those who wanted to hire themselves out as land laborers offered their services daily.[3] If casual laborers were "free" in the Marxian ironic sense, that is, if they had no other means of existence than their bodies, then they usually enjoyed no social protection in case of unemployment, sickness, invalidity, or old age.

Casual wage labor in precapitalist societies generally remained a "spasmodic, casual, marginal" phenomenon.[4] Free wage labor often (but not always) was "an adjunct to other forms of labor and surplus appropriation, often as a means of supplementing the incomes of smallholders whose land—whether owned or held conditionally—has been insufficient for subsistence."[5] But in Western Europe, it became already important *before* the rise of capitalism. Michael Postan thought that in thirteenth-century England, "perhaps as much as a third of the total rural population was available for whole or part-time employment as wage labour."[6] Charles Tilly estimated that in 1500, about 94 percent of all European proletarians were "rural"; even in 1800, it still amounted to 90 percent.[7] The great majority of the group of "early modern" wage earners probably consisted initially of unfree wage laborers, and not of more-or-less "modern" workers.[8] Their existence signals the rapid increase of the cash economy in Europe since the High Middle Ages[9]—a process that first became clearly visible in England and the Netherlands.[10] Many were probably manorial workers, who were essentially nothing but "serf[s] to whom law denied that freedom of contract and movement which it allows to the twentieth-century labourer[s]."[11]

Alongside these unfree wage laborers, there existed an increasing number of urban and rural poor who could not find sufficient employment and became "wage hunters and gatherers" (in Jan Breman's words). We have no clue how numerous the poor were: "counts of the poor all across early modern Europe varied widely."[12] Already in the late feudal period, the authorities tried to discipline these "floaters." In Sweden, for instance,

> Liability for employment was introduced as early as in the Urban Law of King Magnus Erik's son (about 1350). Everybody who did not possess movables worth three marks was subjected to the special provisions. Since three marks was the amount of property which enabled a person to earn his living for one year, the connection of poor relief with employment-policy is here very evident. If a poor man did not accept the work offered to him, a fine was imposed upon him and he was expelled from the town. If he returned and was still unwilling to work, he was whipped and expelled again.[13]

In the eighteenth and nineteenth centuries, most wage earners in Europe were therefore not "doubly free" in the Marxian sense. Research of recent years has revealed that many so-called free workers were really *bonded* laborers, far into the nineteenth century. Master-and-servant laws, apprenticeship arrangements, and similar policies ensured that workers were tied to their employers and had significantly fewer legal rights than the literature previously suggested. In this context, there has indeed been mention of "industrial serfdom."[14] Legal historian Thorsten Keiser has even argued that in nineteenth-century Germany "multiple bonds existed, for factory workers and craftsmen as well. For grown-up industrial workers, these bonds were completely removed only around 1900, for domestics *[Gesinde]* and agricultural labourers not until 1918."[15]

Proletarianization in Western Europe went through two stages. During the first stage (roughly until 1800), the large majority of the proletariat was rural. Decentralized capital formation, with its cottage industries in rural areas plus the impoverishment of parts of the agricultural population, had the effect that even in Britain—the heartland of the so-called Industrial Revolution—for a long time only a minority of the proletarians lived in cities. When afterward, in the nineteenth and twentieth centuries, capital concentrated in cities, and rural areas deindustrialized, the proportion of rural proletarians decreased, and urban workers became concentrated in larger units of production.[16]

THE BEGINNINGS OF STATE PROTECTION

The more general proletarianization became, the larger the number of households without forms of social security. Families that depended exclusively or almost exclusively on wage incomes were extremely vulnerable; they often could not rely on a second line of defense, such as subsistence agriculture on a small piece of land or additional income through petty commodity production and trade. The larger the number of unprotected proletarians, the less effective traditional methods of charitable social assistance proved to be. Two kinds of responses emerged. First, self-organization of workers in mutual-aid societies, called Friendly Societies in Britain, *mutualités* in France, and *Hilfskassen auf Gegenseitigkeit* in Germany.[17] Second, responses from the elites, who became aware of the so-called social question. Three motives were of crucial importance.

First, the fear for the *classes dangereuses,* who were uncontrollable and brought dirt, disease, and rebellion.[18] After the July Revolution in France, in 1830, European states began to establish statistical offices, collecting demographic and economic data, and thus giving some insight into the size and distribution of social problems amongst the national population.[19] And the wave of protest that swept over continental Europe a few years later and that culminated in the revolutions of 1848 prompted the first large-scale budget surveys. In the words of George Stigler: "The agitation and violence of the working classes led to an increasing concern for their economic condition and thus to the collection of economic data, including budgetary data."[20] Studies of budgets were made in Saxony and Prussia in 1848, and in 1855 a Belgian study, by Edouard Ducpetiaux, was published with full details on almost two hundred budgets. The motive for these studies was generally a simple view of the relationship between household budgets and collective action: if the first were inadequate, the second would surely follow. But in France, the Revolution of 1848 had yet another result. Jacques Donzelot and others have shown how the defeat of that year's rebellion resulted in the beginnings of institutionalized social assistance.[21] Robert Castel has summarized the sequence of events as follows:

> [In] February, under pressure from the streets, the provisional government proclaimed at the same time the Republic, universal suffrage, and the right to work. . . . It opened the National Ateliers, which resembled more the charity workshops of the ancien régime than a genuine public system for the management of labor. The closing of these Ateliers, in June, launched the workers' insurrection and its bloody repression. The consequences of this defeat of the right to work, correlated with the awareness of the fragility of the tutelary controls exercised by the elites, opened a whole range of uncertainties that would require the development of a new conception of the social and of social policy.[22]

A second crucial factor was the concern that in the somewhat longer run, the working class might become incapable of working properly, because it would be ill nourished, physically weak, careless, and indifferent. Many of the social-security arrangements that have been realized in Western Europe since the nineteenth century were the product of these fears: reactive responses to unforeseen and threatening developments. The first Dutch law prohibiting some forms of child labor in 1863 is a good example. The liberal economist and former minister Nicolaas G. Pierson has later explained the considerations behind this initiative:

> Very often the factory-owner, who treats his workers badly, understands his own benefit all too well. Because there is sometimes a difference between what is advantageous to the entrepreneurs as a class, and what is advantageous to the individual entrepreneur. The individual entrepreneur derives benefit from everything that immediately increases his income. If he can cut down what he calls production costs by employing young children, then it is in his interest to do so, and if the consequence is that these children will later become very defective workers, then this may harm his successors, but it will be nothing to him. . . . The interests of the entrepreneurial *class* are durable interests, those of the *individual* entrepreneurs are . . . immediate interests. . . . Self-interest therefore does not only need guidance, but also curbing. . . . The state cannot quietly look on, while production is organized in a way that . . . undermines the people's productive forces. If only for purely economic reasons, which in this case are not the very best of reasons, it has to intervene.[23]

In this case, as in quite a few others, state intervention resulted from the contradiction between individual and total capital—a contradiction that creates the necessity for the state to act as an *ideelle Gesamtkapitalist*, the ideal or imaginary total-capitalist.

Capitalist competition was a third important factor. In Germany, for example, a number of big enterprisers, such as the steel- and coal-magnate Carl Friedrich Stumm, began, from the 1870s on, to ardently advocate social-insurance legislation.

TABLE 2.1. Introduction of freedom of trade and freedom of association; and founding of national trade-union confederations.

	Freedom of trade	Freedom of association	National trade-union confederations
1789	France		
1813	United Kingdom		
1824		United Kingdom	
1831	Belgium		
1839	Netherlands	Norway	
1846	Sweden		
1848		Switzerland	
1850			
1855		Netherlands	
1857	Denmark		
1859	Austria		
1860	Italy		
1864		France, Sweden	
1868			United Kingdom, Germany
1869	Germany (Prussia 1810)	Germany	
1870		Austria	
1879	Finland		
1880			Switzerland
1890		Italy	
1892			Austria
1893			Netherlands
1898		Belgium	Belgium, Denmark, Sweden
1906		Finland	Italy
1907			Finland

SOURCE: Jens Alber, *Vom Armenhaus zum Wohlfahrtsstaat. Analysen zur Entwicklung der Sozialversicherung in Westeuropa* [Frankfurt am Main: Campus, 1982], 39.

Their companies used extensive and technically refined machinery and employed highly skilled workers. But these workers were increasingly attracted by the higher wages in northern France and elsewhere, resulting in huge fluctuations of personnel. The challenge for German big employers was to develop a social-security system that would be so attractive for workers that it could compensate for lower wages and would allow for mobility between German industries. Municipal or company-based social-security arrangements tied workers to specific localities and could not achieve this. Therefore, state intervention was unavoidable. The campaign in favor of such intervention was legitimated propagandistically with reference to the supposed social-democratic "red danger."[24]

Naturally, all these trends are situated in the context of the rise of capitalism, which on the one hand reduced restrictions on trade and commerce, but on the other hand—often after stubborn resistance—resulted in the freedom of association, thus enabling the founding of local and regional and, later, of national trade unions and trade-union confederations (table 2.1).

TABLE 2.2. Emigration from Western Europe and Western European population growth, ca. 1850–ca. 1910.

	Emigration 1851–1910 in millions (A)	Population growth 1850–1911 in millions (B)	Emigration as percentage of population growth (Estimate: A/B)
Austria-Hungary	0.8	18.8	4.3
Belgium	0.07	3.1	0.2
Denmark	0.25	1.4	17.9
Finland	0.24	1.3	18.5
France	0.35	3.8	9.2
Germany	4.22	24.9	16.9
Italy	6.39	10.3	62.0
Netherlands	0.16	2.8	0.6
Norway	0.69	1.0	69.0
Portugal	1.03	2.0	51.5
Spain	2.48	-	-
Sweden	0.99	2.0	49.5
Switzerland	0.21	1.4	15.0
United Kingdom	13.29*	20.0	66.5

* Excluding 1851–52.

SOURCE: Author's calculation based on B. R. Mitchell, "Statistical Appendix," in *The Fontana Economic History of Europe*, ed. Carlo M. Cipolla, vol. 2, *The Emergence of Industrial Societies*, 747–51 [London: Collins/Fontana, 1972].

The growth of labor movements is of great importance here, because it increased the social pressure in favor of social-security provisions. A precondition of this growth and the concurrent bargaining power of sections of the working classes was the falling off of over-unemployment (that is, the number of people that are not unemployed only *temporarily*, but *permanently*). The reduction of over-unemployment (the term was introduced by Paul Bairoch) was aided by massive emigration, especially to the Americas (table 2.2).

The historical demographer Peter Marschalck summarized the German development:

> One could describe the effect of emigration as follows: it liberated the German economy for the time being from precisely that number of people that it could no longer offer jobs without depriving an equal number of employees of their resource base. German industry therefore always had an "industrial reserve army" at its disposal of which the size did not create [long-term] unemployment; social upheaval was thus avoided and industrial development was not impeded. . . . As the surplus population, i.e., the "unemployed," found possibilities to work and live across he Atlantic, emigration was an important factor in Germany's development into Europe's largest industrial nation.[25]

In Norway, "emigration absorbed about half the natural population increase, and in Norway, Sweden and Finland the population increase was a good deal smaller than the relation between their birth- and death-rates might lead one to suppose."[26] Trade unions sometimes encouraged emigration enthusiastically, as it would strengthen their power.[27]

This mass emigration probably acted as a safety valve. Albert Hirschman suspected that "the history of Europe in the 19th century would probably have been either far more turbulent or far more repressive and the trend toward representative government much more halting, had it not been possible for millions of people to emigrate toward the United States and elsewhere."[28]

During the whole "long" nineteenth century, European labor movements remained rather weak. Historian Richard Price writes about the United Kingdom in the 1870s that there was "no working-class movement in the sense of an organised presence that exercised a continuing national influence. Trade-union membership included perhaps 5%–10% of the occupied male labour force, but, as in the past, it was highly unstable and fluctuated with the local labour market."[29] On the eve of World War I, approximate trade-union density rates in Western Europe were between 7 percent in Austria and 23 percent in Britain and Denmark.[30] Apparently, the big growth of union density happened only *after* the first stage of industrialization had been concluded.[31]

From a global perspective, this reduction of over-unemployment marks a crucial difference with the contemporary Global South: in present-day Africa, Asia, or Latin America, the possibility of mass migration does not exist, and this, at least partly, may explain why informal labor has remained dominant and labor movements have mostly remained weak.

TOWARD THE "GOLDEN AGE"

From the final decades of the nineteenth century until the 1950s or 1960s, an often cumulative but planless process of reforms and changes resulted in a relatively wide spreading of the so-called standard employment relationship. These reforms and changes pertain to seven policy areas: (1) protective labor legislation, including the prohibition of child labor, safety rules at work, the prohibition of night work for women, and similar rules; (2) legalization of workers' coalitions, with the founding of employers' associations as a (delayed) response; (3) regulation of labor time through the shortening of the working day, shortening of the working week, and introduction of paid holidays; (4) introduction of obligatory insurances, such as sickness insurance, old-age pensions, invalidity insurance, and unemployment insurance (which implies the "discovery" of unemployment as a social phenomenon); (5) institutionalization of collective bargaining; (6) spread of labor contracts with unlimited duration; and (7) arrival of full employment and a high-wage economy.[32]

This is not the right place for a detailed comparative reconstruction of this planless, cumulative process in various Western European countries, but I will

TABLE 2.3. Average number of hours worked annually per person in selected Western European countries, 1950–1986.

	1950	1973	1986	1986 as percentage of 1950
Austria	1,976	1,778	1,620	0.82
Belgium	2,283	1,872	1,411	0.62
Denmark	2,283	1,742	1,706	0.75
Finland	2,035	1,707	1,596	0.78
France	1,926	1,788	1,533	0.80
Germany	2,216	1,804	1,630	0.74
Italy	1,997	1,612	1,515	0.76
Netherlands	2,208	1,825	1,645	0.75
Norway	2,101	1,721	1,531	0.73
Sweden	1,951	1,571	1,457	0.75
Switzerland	2,144	1,930	1,807	0.84
United Kingdom	1,958	1,688	1,511	0.77

SOURCE: Angus Maddison, *The World Economy in the Twentieth Century* [Paris: OECD, 1989], 132, plus calculation by the author.

briefly highlight some trends. Table 2.1 already gave a quick chronology of the *legalization of workers' coalitions. Protective labor legislation* dates from the first half of the nineteenth century at the latest. It usually focused on female and child labor.[33] From the 1880s and 1890s, the debate on more extensive protective legislation intensified and resulted in international conferences, partly motivated by the consideration that "restrictions on industrial methods intended for the benefit of the workers employed should be adopted in competing countries at the same time and in equal degree."[34]

Labor time was increasingly regulated everywhere, but the average number of hours worked declined significantly after World War II (table 2.3).

Forms of *obligatory insurance* were introduced *after* voluntary forms of insurance had become institutionalized. This happened mostly during the first three decades of the twentieth century.[35] At the beginning of the long boom of the 1950s, social-security schemes were therefore mostly in place.[36]

The next step was the tendential generalization to all citizens, or to a substantial part of all citizens—in many cases, social security became a right for all citizens, not just for wage earners.[37] Although the social question had largely been perceived as a *labor* question, its partial solution brought in its wake the tackling of other social problems, such as old-age pensions for farmers and health care for self-employed. Naturally, this process took more time and took off somewhat later, as is illustrated by tables 2.4 and 2.5.

Institutionalized *collective bargaining* is usually only possible if two conditions are met. First, incomes have to be relatively high and should be rising, "so that labor-management conflicts are mainly concerned with the distribution of the

TABLE 2.4. Coverage of health insurance in selected European countries, 1900–1990 (members as a percentage of economically active population). Figures with an asterisk (*) are estimates based on legal regulations.

	1900	1910	1920	1930	1940	1950	1960	1970	1980	1990
Austria	18	24	39	59		56	71	85	87	86
Belgium	6	12	21	33	31	57	57	92		
Denmark	27	54	97	*100	*100	*100	*100	*100	*100	*100
Finland								*100	*100	*100
France	9	18	17	32	48	60	69	96		
Germany/West Germany	39	44	53	57	56	57	67	67	84	*100
Ireland				34	44	53	58	67	78	89
Italy	*6	*6	*6	7	47	44	76	92		
Netherlands				*42	*42	54	60	74	85	*100
Norway			55	56	86	*100	*100	*100	*100	*100
Sweden	13	27	28	35	49	97	*100	*100	*100	*100
Switzerland			43	69	86	89	*100	*100	*100	99
United Kingdom			73	82	90	*100	*100	*100	*100	*100

SOURCE: Béla Tomka, *A Social History of Twentieth-Century Europe* [London: Routledge, 2013], 167.

TABLE 2.5. Coverage of pension insurance in selected European countries, 1900–1990 (members as a percentage of economically active population). Figures with an asterisk (*) are estimates based on legal regulations.

	1900	1910	1920	1930	1940	1950	1960	1970	1980	1990
Austria		2	*5	43		51	75	78	82	85
Belgium	9	29	*29	51	*44	57	89	100		
Denmark				95	*100	*100	*100	*100	*100	*100
Finland						*100	*100	*100	*100	*100
France	*8	13	14	*36	48	69	92	93		
Germany/ West Germany	53	53	57	69	72	70	82	81	91	*100
Ireland					44	55	64	71	86	*100
Italy	0	*2	*38	38	38	*39	89	99		
Netherlands			52	58	65	64	*100	*100	*100	*100
Norway						*100	*100	*100	*100	*100
Sweden			*100	*100	*100	*100	*100	*100	*100	*100
Switzerland						*100	*100	*100	*100	99
United Kingdom				82	90	94	86	83		

SOURCE: Béla Tomka, *A Social History of Twentieth-Century Europe* [London: Routledge, 2013], 168.

yearly increment of the national product rather than with shifts in the shares of different social groups in a given national income." And second, the great majority of the workers should accept "the social and political fundamentals of the society in which they live."[38] Everett Kassalow was justified when he stated that "this coming to terms . . . did not fully occur in several countries of Western Europe until the end of World War I."[39] In most Western European countries collective bargaining really took off during the interwar years, and very soon the results of this bargaining between unions and employers were extended to nonunion sectors. This method of extension had first been tried out in New Zealand and Australia around 1900 and was, after World War I, introduced in Germany (1918) and Austria (1919)—soon to be abolished by National Socialism (1934 and 1938, respectively). During the years of the Depression Britain (1934), Czechoslovakia (1935), Greece (1935), France (1936), The Netherlands (1937), Yugoslavia (1937), Luxemburg (1938), and Belgium followed.[40] The Scandinavian countries did not participate in this development.[41]

Combined with these trends, *labor contracts with unlimited duration* spread. "In the 1950s and 1960s, the labor contract for an undetermined length of time became the norm, and then served as a virtual guarantee of employment. But this stemmed only from the fact that in times of full employment, one often hires, and only rarely lays off employees."[42] At least two additional factors may have contributed to this process. First, when corporations embody large amounts of fixed capital and dominate stable markets through monopolistic competition, "a company [can] hold long term prospects, to which is linked the capability, when required, of employing workers for a long period." And, second, the more specialized employees' tasks become for the operation of these large amounts of fixed capital, the more "the worker moves from simple to more difficult jobs," through on-the-job training, and becomes indispensable.[43]

Finally, capital accumulation became, from the early 1950s on, fast and prosperous, so that unemployment rates reached "extraordinary low levels" in the early 1960s—thus stimulating the often government-driven international recruitment of migrant workers from other parts of Europe, North Africa, and Turkey.[44] Parallel to this, Western Europe came fully into the stage of "high mass-consumption."[45] These developments had also major consequences for working-class culture. The traditional labor movements—with their socialist and communist newspapers, youth organizations, theater groups, and so on—disintegrated. And more and more members of the working classes no longer defined themselves as such.[46]

The rise of the standard employment relationship by fits and starts can perhaps be interpreted as a Gramscian "passive revolution," that is, as a result of attempts of the established order to disarm antagonistic forces by partly incorporating their methods and goals, up to the point where even representatives of the antagonist are absorbed.[47] The temporary victory of standard employment was, of course, only relevant for segments of the working classes. Significant groups, such as migrant workers from Morocco or Turkey often did not share the same rights, and neither did many women entering the labor markets.

DECREASING PROTECTION

From the late 1960s, the *trente glorieuses* came to an end. The average profit rate began to fall again, and economic growth declined. As predicted by Michal Kalecki during World War II, full-employment capitalism did indeed reflect increased power of the working classes,[48] and capital had to answer this challenge. From the late 1970s, the postwar compromise between capital and labor started to break down. The case of the most important Western European economy, that of West Germany, illustrates how the turn occurred. Already during the 1950s, a shortage of skilled laborers had become visible, and this shortage had been further reinforced by the building of the Berlin Wall, which blocked the import of workers from East Germany. Working hours had, moreover, been reduced since 1956. An upward pressure on wages was the outcome. This had two consequences. Firstly, extensive growth, based on the expansion of productive capacity at the old technical level, made way for intensive growth, based on further mechanization and increasing labor productivity. And second, the labor-power supply was enlarged through the recruitment of German housewives and Turkish (and other) immigrants.[49] The first change had a stronger effect than the second and resulted, from about 1970, in a declining average profit rate, growing unemployment, and decreasing bargaining power for the unions.[50] Besides, the European economic integration since the 1960s led to a partial synchronization of business cycles, thus reducing the steering capacity of national governments.[51]

These trends, intensified by the oil crisis of 1974, led to major policy shifts. International labor migration began to fade away, while many settled immigrants initiated family reunions—a process accompanied by growing xenophobia and increasing racial harassment. An offensive of state and capital against the attainments and securities of the working population began. Four legitimations were usually given: the flexibilization of business organizations in consequence of the introduction of computerized work processes; the aging of the population, leading to higher expenditures for pensions and health care; the spreading of new family structures and new patterns of labor-market participation; and the enforced "harmonization" of social provisions in view of economic globalization and EU integration.[52]

The passive revolution more and more turned into an active counterrevolution. When the Organization for Economic Co-operation and Development (OECD) ministers decided "to move away from Keynesian demand management to a pronounced supply-side strategy, aimed at sound public finances and market flexibility,"[53] this was a crucial turning point. Wolfgang Streeck has shown how capital, with the support of national governments and supranational institutions (International Monetary Fund, World Bank) pressed its offensive through in several steps, until today.[54] This offensive implied the gradual forcing back of the working-class achievements of the 1950s and 1960s. A weakening of trade unions in most Western European countries was forced through (table 2.6).

TABLE 2.6. Union densities in selected European countries, 1920–2010.

	1960	1970	1980	1990	2000	2010
Belgium	39.3	39.9	51.3	51.1	56.2	53.8
Denmark	56.9	60.3	78.6	74.6	73.9	67.0
France	19.6	21.7	18.3	10.0	8.0	7.9
Germany/ West Germany	34.7	32.0	34.9	31.2	24.6	18.6
Italy	24.7	37.0	49.6	38.8	34.8	36.0
Netherlands	40.0	36.5	34.8	24.3	22.6	19.3
Norway	60.0	56.8	58.3	58.5	54.4	54.8
Switzerland	31.0	24.9	27.5	22.5	20.2	17.1
United Kingdom	40.4	44.8	51.7	39.7	30.1	27.1

SOURCE: ICTWSS Database, Amsterdams Instituut voor Arbeidsstudies [www.uva-aias.net/208], version 5.0, October 2015. All percentages indicate net union membership as a proportion of wage and salary earners in employment, unless these figures are not available. If data were missing, I used net union membership as a proportion of wage and salary earners in employment, as in national household or labor-force surveys.

Only in Belgium and the Scandinavian countries (countries where unions are involved in the payment of unemployment benefits) is the situation relatively stable. In parallel with the weakening of trade unions a shift from central to decentralized collective bargaining, and to individualized labor contracts occurred.

Weakened trade unions facilitated further steps, such as:[55]

- A declining wage share. In OECD countries, one can observe that "overall, real wage growth has clearly lagged behind productivity growth since around 1980. This constitutes a major historical change as wage shares had been stable or increasing in the post-war era."[56] This trend seems to have been particularly strong in continental European countries.
- The tendential replacement of permanent and full-time employment by casualized and part-time jobs. In Germany, for instance, part-time work increased from 14 percent in 1991 to almost 27 percent twenty years later.[57] This "flexibilization" is a major component of the labor contract, leading to hire-and-fire at short or no notice, withdrawal of protection against dismissal, and a progressive scaling down of out-of-work benefits. In parallel, we also see an increased role for labor mediators, for example, temporary-employment agencies.
- The increase of outsourcing and subcontracting, which is routinely resorted to in order to bring down the cost of labor, and gradually increasing multiple job holding.[58]
- Waged work is increasingly substituted by self-employment, mainly in the tertiary sector of the economy, but that trend has been much strengthened by the growing lack of waged employment. In the EU25, already one out of six workers falls into this category.
- Drastic cutbacks on secondary benefits affect social protection and social security negatively. A wide range of allowances and provisions are curtailed or withdrawn.
- The introduction of so-called activation measures, inducing the unemployed to look harder for jobs, thus implicitly reintroducing the notion of the "undeserving poor."[59]

To sum up, the Western economies demonstrate a clear trend toward informalization or precarianization of working class life.[60] A recent ILO report says:

> The past 40 years have witnessed changes to work arrangements globally. . . . Overall, the changes have been characterised by less contract duration and job security, more irregular working hours (both in terms of duration and consistency), increased use of third parties (temporary employment agencies), growth of various forms of dependent self-employment (like subcontracting and franchising) and also bogus/informal work arrangements (i.e., arrangements deliberately outside the regulatory framework of labour, social protection and other laws). The factors underpinning these changes are complex but include shifts in business/employment practices, weakening union influence and government policies/regulatory regimes to promote labour market "flexibility" and weaken collectivist regimes (where they existed). The growth of international supply chains means that work has often been relocated to countries where union presence and regulatory protection is weak or non-existent.[61]

This tendency was strengthened and accelerated by the global economic crisis since 2007–2008. In 2015, around 119 million people (23.7 percent of the population) in the European Union were at risk of poverty or social exclusion. This means that they (many of them women and first- and second-generation immigrants) were in at least one of the following three conditions: "at-risk-of-poverty after social transfers (income poverty), severely materially deprived or living in households with very low work intensity."[62] The social question seems on its way back.

NOTES

1. Robert Castel, *From Manual Workers to Wage Laborers: Transformation of the Social Question*, ed. and trans. Richard Boyd (New Brunswick, NJ: Transaction Publishers, 2003), xx.

2. Jacques Donzelot, *L'Invention du social* (Paris: Fayard, 1984).

3. Alexander Fuks, "κολωνος μισθιος: Labour Exchange in Classical Athens," *Eranos* 49 (1951): 171–73.

4. Moses I. Finley and Brent D. Shaw, *Ancient Slavery and Modern Ideology* (London: Chatto & Windus, 1980), 68. This does not exclude the possibility that sometimes small nuclei of permanent wage laborers appeared, but these were usually found among a larger group of seasonal or casual laborers. See, for example, the analysis of large Byzantine estates in late antiquity in Jairus Banaji, "Agrarian History and the Labour Organisation of Byzantine Large Estates," *Proceedings of the British Academy* 96 (1999): 198–202.

5. Ellen Meiksins Wood, *Peasant-Citizen and Slave: The Foundations of Athenian Democracy* (London: Verso, 1988), 65.

6. M. M. Postan, "England," in *Cambridge Economic History of Europe*, vol. 1 (Cambridge: Cambridge University Press, 1966), 568. Some scholars interpret this as a reason "for shifting the beginning of capitalism in England back to the thirteenth century." Heide Gerstenberger, *Impersonal Power: History and Theory of the Bourgeois State*, trans. David Fernbach (Leiden: Brill, 2007), 50–51.

7. Charles Tilly, "Demographic Origins of the European Proletariat," in *Proletarianization and Family History*, ed. David Levine (Orlando, FL: Academic Press, 1984), 1–85.

8. Alan Macfarlane suggests this was the case in England. See his *The Origins of English Individualism* (Oxford: Blackwell, 1978), 148–50.

9. Ricardo Duchesne attempts to explain this monetarization process in "The French Revolution as a Bourgeois Revolution: A Critique of the Revisionists," *Science and Society* 54 (1990): 288–320. See also Nicholas Mayhew, "Modelling Medieval Monetisation," in *A Commercialising Economy: England 1086 to* c. *1300*, ed. Richard H. Britnell and Bruce M. S. Campbell, (Manchester: Manchester University Press, 1995), 55–77.

10. See, for example, Wilhelm Weber, "Studie zur Spätmittelalterlichen Arbeitsmarkt- und Wirtschaftsordnung," *Jahrbücher für Nationalökonomie und Statistik* 166 (1954): 358–89; Kenneth D. Brown, "Introduction: Wage-Labour: 1500–1800," in *The English Labour Movement 1700–1951* (Dublin: Gill and Macmillan, 1982), 1–27; and Bas J. P. van Bavel, "Rural Wage Labour in the 16th Century Low Countries: An Assessment of the Importance and Nature of Wage Labour in the Countryside of Holland, Guelders and Flanders," *Continuity and Change* 21 (2006): 37–72.

11. M. M. Postan, "The Famulus: The Estate Labourer in the XIIth and XIIIth Centuries," *Economic History Review*, supplement 2 (1954): 23.

12. Daniel H. Kaiser, "The Poor and Disabled in Early Eighteenth-Century Russian Towns," *Journal of Social History* 32, 1 (Autumn 1998): 126.

13. Eino Jutikkala, "Labour Policy and the Urban Proletariat in Sweden and Finland during the Pre-Industrial Era," in *Aspects of Poverty in Early Modern Europe*, ed. Thomas Riis (Odense: Odense University Press, 1986), 135.

14. See, for example, Douglas Hay and Paul Craven, eds., *Masters, Servants, and Magistrates in Britain and the Empire, 1562–1955* (Chapel Hill: University of North Carolina Press, 2004); Alessandro Stanziani, *Bondage: Labor and Rights in Eurasia from the Sixteenth to the Early Twentieth Centuries* (New York: Berghahn, 2014).

15. Thorsten Keiser, *Vertragszwang und Vertragsfreiheit im Recht der Arbeit von der Frühen Neuzeit bis in die Moderne* (Frankfurt am Main: Vittorio Klostermann, 2013), 404. In a separate essay, Keiser has even argued "that the relationships of people engaged in physical work were also bonded and unfree in the German-speaking regions before 1919." See his "Between Status and Contract? Coercion in Contractual Labour Relationships in Germany from the 16th to the 20th Century," *Rechtsgeschichte/Legal History* 21 (2013): 32. The fact that this elementary fact was overlooked for a long time finds its cause, according to Keiser, in the scholarly assumption that the nineteenth century had witnessed an abrupt transition from "feudal" compulsion to market-based exploitation.

16. Tilly, "Since Gilgamesh," *Social Research* 53, no. 4 (Winter 1986): 408. One should, however, not overestimate this concentration of workers. See Ralph Samuel, "Workshop of the World: Steam Power and Hand Technology in Mid-Victorian Britain," *History Workshop Journal* 3, no. 1 (March 1977): 6–72.

17. I have written about these forms of self-help elsewhere. See Marcel van der Linden, "Mutual Workers Insurance: A Historical Outline," *International Social Security Review*, 46, 3 (1993): 5–18; van der Linden, *Workers of the World. Essays toward a Global Labor History* (Leiden and Boston: Brill, 2008), chaps. 5 and 6.

18. This point is emphasized in Abram de Swaan, *In Care of the State. Health Care, Education, and Welfare in Europe and the USA in the Modern Era* (New York: Oxford University Press, 1988).

19. Peter Flora, Quantitative Historical Sociology: A Trend Report and Bibliography," *Current Sociology*, 23, no. 2 (1975).

20. George J. Stigler, "The Early History of Empirical Studies of Consumer Behavior," in *Essays in the History of Economics* (Chicago: University of Chicago Press, 1965), 201.

21. Donzelot, *L'Invention du Social*, chap. 1; Giovana Procacci, *Gouverner la misère. La question sociale en France 1789–1848* (Paris: Seuil, 1993).

22. Castel, *From Manual Workers to Wage Laborers*, 249.

23. N. G. Pierson, *Leerboek der staathuishoudkunde*, vol. 2 (Haarlem, 1902), 79–85.

24. Rüdeger Baron, "Weder Zuckerbrot noch Peitsche: Historische Konstitutionsbedingungen des Sozialstaats in Deutschland," *Gesellschaft: Beiträge zur Marxschen Theorie* 12 (1979): 13–100, esp. 17–27.

25. Peter Marschalck, *Deutsche Überseewanderung im 19. Jahrhundert: Ein Beitrag zur soziologischen Theorie der Bevölkerung* (Stuttgart: Ernst Klett Verlag, 1973), 94.

26. Lennart Jörberg, "The Industrial Revolution in the Nordic Countries," in *The Fontana Economic History of Europe*, ed. Carlo M. Cipolla, vol. 2, *The Emergence of Industrial Societies* (London: Collins/Fontana, 1972) 378.

27. See, for example, Charlotte Erickson, "The Encouragement of Emigration by British Trade Unions, 1850–1900," *Population Studies* 3 (1949–50): 248–73; William E. Van Vugt. "Prosperity and Industrial Emigration from Britain during the Early 1850s," *Journal of Social History* 22, no. 2 (Winter 1988): 339–54.

28. Albert O. Hirschman, "*Exit, Voice, and Loyalty:* Further Reflections and a Survey of Recent Contributions," *The Milbank Memorial Fund Quarterly* 58, no. 3 (Summer 1980): 442. Fritz Sternberg, *Capitalism and Socialism on Trial,* trans. Edward Fitzgerald (London: Victor Gollancz, 1951), 62, already suggested that European mass emigration "opened up an important channel through which the European reserve armies could pour away, and it diminished social antagonisms."

29. Richard Price, "Britain," in *The Formation of Labour Movements, 1870–1914: An International Perspective,* ed. Marcel van der Linden and Jürgen Rojahn, (Leiden: Brill, 1990), vol. 1, 3.

30. Jelle Visser, *European Trade Unions in Figures* (Deventer and Boston: Kluwer, 1989), 41, 95, 151, 196, and 240; Michael Mann, "Sources of Variation in Working-Class Movements in Twentieth-Century Europe," *New Left Review* 212 (1995): 20.

31. According to economic historian Walt Rostow, the "take-off" of Western European economies started in Britain (1783–1830), was succeeded by France (1830–1870), Germany (1840–1870) and Sweden (1868–1890), and concluded by slow developers like Italy (1895–1913). In Asia, on the other hand, Japan was relatively early (1885–1905), while other countries were generally much later. Taiwan, for example, experienced its take-off in 1953–1960 and South Korea in 1961–1968. W. W. Rostow, *The World Economy: History and Prospect* (London: Macmillan, 1978), 383, 400, 407, 415, 425, 447, 540, 551, and 555.

32. I derive these seven points from Toni Pierenkemper, "Der Auf- und Ausbau eines Normalarbeitsverhältnis in Deutschland im 19. und 20. Jahrhundert," in *Geschichte der Arbeitsmärkte,* ed. Rolf Walter, Erträge der 22. Arbeitstagung der Gesellschaft für Sozial- und Wirtschaftsgeschichte 11. bis 14. April 2007 in Wien (Stuttgart: Franz Steiner Verlag, 2009), 77–112.

33. See, for example, Jane Humphries, "Protective Legislation, the Capitalist State, and Working Class Men: The Case of the 1842 Mines Regulation Act," *Feminist Review* 7 (Spring 1981): 1–33; Ulla Wikander, Alice Kessler-Harris, and Jane Lewis, eds. *Protecting Women: Labor Legislation in Europe, the United States, and Australia, 1880–1920* (Urbana: University of Illinois Press, 1995).

34. Herbert Samuel (1906), quoted in D. Shena Potter, "The Movement for International Labour Legislation," *Economic Journal* 20, no. 79 (September 1910): 353. Almost simultaneously, international conferences on the struggle against unemployment were organized, the first of which took place in Milan in 1906. See the reports by Robert Michels, "Der erste internationale Kongreß zur Bekämpfung der Arbeitslosigkeit," *Die Neue Zeit,* XXV-1 (1906–1907): 473–78, and Otto Kahn, "Der 1. Internationale Kongreß zur Bekämpfung der Arbeitslosigkeit," *Soziale Praxis: Zentralblatt für Sozialpolitik* 16, no. 6, (November 8, 1906): cols. 145–47.

35. Statistical data in Béla Tomka, *A Social History of Twentieth-Century Europe* (London: Routledge, 2013), 157.

36. The pace and sequence of the introduction of social-insurance arrangements differed from country to country, but on average, accident insurance usually came first, and unemployment insurance came last. Accident insurance was easily reconcilable with the liberal viewpoint concerning entrepreneurial liability, while unemployment insurance seemed to break with the logic of the market. Often insurances started on a voluntary basis and later became compulsory.

37. The Swedish welfare state, for example, was originally based on "the old communality between industrial labourers, agrarian smallholders and other segments of the rural population." Citizenship,

not class, became the foundation of social-security arrangements. See, for example, Sven E. Olssen, "Working-Class Power and the 1946 Pension Reform in Sweden," *International Review of Social History* 34, no. 2 (August 1989): 307.

38. Adolf Sturmthal, "Unions and Economic Development," *Economic Development and Cultural Change* 8, no. 2 (January 1960): 201.

39. Everett M. Kassalow, *Trade Unions and Industrial Relations: An International Comparison* (New York: Random House, 1969), 30.

40. Ludwig Hamburger, "The Extension of Collective Agreements to Cover Entire Trades and Industries," *International Labour Review* 40, no. 2 (August 1939): 153–94.

41. Union strength can have peculiar unintended consequences. If unions are capable of exerting direct influence, they do not have to operate through other political actors (such as political parties) and may have little interest in state regulation. An interesting analysis of this paradox is given in Patrick Emmenegger, "Maximizing Institutional Control: Union Power and Dismissal Protection in Western Europe in the First Half of the Twentieth Century," *Comparative Politics* 47, no. 4 (July 2015): 399–418.

42. Castel, *From Manual Workers to Wage Laborers,* 372.

43. Kazuo Koike, *Understanding Industrial Relations in Modern Japan,* trans. Mary Saso (Houndmills: Macmillan, 1988), 281–82.

44. Stephen Nickell, Luca Nunziata, and Wolfgang Ochel, "Unemployment in the OECD since the 1960s: What Do We Know?" *Economic Journal* 115, no. 500 (January 2005): 2; Russell King, "European International Migration 1945–90: A Statistical and Geographical Overview," in *Mass Migration in Europe: The Legacy and the Future,* ed. Russell King, 19–39 (Chichester, UK: John Wiley & Sons, 1995).

45. Rostow, *World Economy,* No. 04; HC51, R6. 1978. 270.

46. See, for example, Josef Mooser, "Auflösung des proletarischen Milieus. Klassenbindung und Individualisierung in der Arbeiterschaft vom Kaiserreich bis in die Bundesrepublik Deutschland," *Soziale Welt* 34 (1983): 270–306.

47. Antonio Gramsci, *Selections from the Prison Notebooks,* ed. and trans. Quintin Hoare and Geoffrey Nowell Smith (London: Lawrence and Wishart, 1971), 110.

48. Michal Kalecki, "Political Aspects of Full Employment," *Political Quarterly* 14, no. 4 (October 1943): 322–30.

49. Redaktionskollektiv Gewerkschaften, "Zur Intensifikation der Arbeit in der BRD (I)," *Probleme des Klassenkampfs* 4 (September 1972): 81–106.

50. Eckart Hildebrandt, "Entwicklung der Beschäftigtenstruktur und der Arbeitslosigkeit in der Bundesrepublik," *Probleme des Klassenkampfs* 19/20/21(October 1975): 41–142. For an excellent theoretical analysis, see Robert Brenner, *The Economics of Global Turbulence. The Advanced Capitalist Economies from Long Boom to Long Downturn, 1945–2005* (London: Verso 2006), esp. chaps. 2, 5, and 10.

51. Ernest Mandel, *The Second Slump: A Marxist Analysis of Recession in the Seventies,* trans. Jon Rothschild (London: New Left Books, 1978).

52. Young-sun Hong, "Social Welfare and Insurance," in *Encyclopedia of European Social History from 1350 to 2000,* ed. Peter N. Stearns (Detroit: Charles Scribner's Sons, 2001), 479–80.

53. Franz Traxler, "Bargaining, State Regulation and the Trajectories of Industrial Relations," *European Journal of Industrial Relations* 9, no. 2 (2003): 145.

54. Wolfgang Streeck, *Buying Time: The Delayed Crises of Democratic Capitalism* (London: Verso, 2014).

55. See, for example, Elke Viebrock and Jochen Clasen, "Flexicurity and Welfare Reform: A Review," *Socio-Economic Review* 7, no. 2 (April 2009): 305–31; Jason Heyes, "Flexicurity, Employment Protection and the Jobs Crisis," *Work, Employment and Society* 25, no. 4 (2011): 642–57; Jill Rubery, "Reconstruction amid Deconstruction: Or Why We Need More of the Social in European Social Models," *Work, Employment and Society* 25, no. 4 (2011): 658–74; Jason Beckfield, "The End of Equality in Europe?" *Current History* 112/752 (2013): 94–99; Lena Hipp, Janine Bernhardt, and Jutta Allmendinger,

"Institutions and the Prevalence of Nonstandard Employment," *Socio-Economic Review* 13, no. 2 (April 2015): 351–77.

56. Engelbert Stockhammer, *Why Have Wages Shares Fallen? A Panel Analysis of the Determinants of Functional Income Distribution* (Geneva: ILO, 2013), 10.

57. *Non-Standard Employment Around the World* (Geneva: ILO, 2016), 198.

58. Berndt Keller and Hartmut Seifert, "Atypical Employment in Germany: Forms, Development, Patterns," *Transfer* 19, no. 4 (2013): 457–74.

59. Markus Promberger and Philipp Ramos Lobato, "Zehn Jahre Hartz IV—eine kritische Würdigung," *WSI Mitteilungen* 69, no. 5 (July 2016): 326.

60. This is not to say though, that the precarious workers in advanced capitalist countries constitute a separate "class-in-the making," as Guy Standing, *The Precariat: The New Dangerous Class* (London: Bloomsbury, 2011), vii, has recently argued. For critiques of Standing's approach, see Jan Breman, "A Bogus Concept," *New Left Review*, second series, 84 (November-December 2013): 130–38; Ronaldo Munck, "The Precariat: A View from the South," *Third World Quarterly* 34, no. 5 (2013): 747–62; and Bryan D. Palmer, "Reconsiderations of Class: Precariousness as Proletarianization," *The Socialist Register 2014*, 40–62.

61. Michael Quinlan, *The Effects of Non-Standard Forms of Employment on Worker Health and Safety*, Conditions of Work and Employment Series, 67 (Geneva: ILO, 2015), 1.

62. European Commission, News release 3-17102016-BP, published on October 17, 2016.

3

The End of American Exceptionalism

The Social Question in the United States

Fred Block

Exceptionalism has been the dominant theme in United States history from its founding. At the time that the United States won its independence, the old nations against which the United States formed its identity were, in fact, the great European imperial powers—England, France, the Netherlands, and Spain, and the United States differed from these nations in critical ways. First, to expand and grow, the United States had no need to establish overseas colonies; it could draw immigrants from Europe and extend its territorial empire westward. It was able to create an internal colony in the American South where chattel slavery was the central economic institution. Second, it led the world in developing a democratic political system in which the right to vote was given to most adult white males. However, the tensions between slave states and free states resulted in the creation of a uniquely constrained central government.[1] Third, the combination of early democracy, the continuing inflows of both coerced and free laborers, and the richness of the American continent created a uniquely productive economy that sustained unprecedented levels of prosperity for two full centuries. Together, these elements made the trajectory of the United States exceptional.[2]

But over the last forty-five years, American exceptionalism seems to have come to an end. Werner Sombart insisted that there was no socialism in America because "all socialist utopias came to nothing on roast beef and apple pie,"[3] meaning that the material prosperity and upward mobility available to white workers in the United States precluded the kind of mass socialist movements that emerged in Europe. But for the last forty years, both prosperity and upward mobility have receded. Real wages in the United States have stagnated, and the number of well-paid manufacturing jobs has dropped precipitously. Moreover, rates of intergenerational mobility in the United States are now well below that of many countries in Europe.[4]

One of the key elements in this transformation has been the informalization of labor market arrangements in the United States. Through systematic efforts by employers, private-sector unionization rates have been falling for decades and now hover around 10 percent. When not represented by unions or protected by contract, employment in the United States is "at will," so that employees can be fired for any reason, no matter how arbitrary. Nevertheless, employers have sought even greater control over wage costs by increasing their use of contingent workers to fill job openings. This includes temporary workers, part-time workers, day laborers, and individuals who are defined as independent contractors, such as drivers for ridesharing services such as Uber and Lyft. By one estimate, contingent employment had risen to 40 percent of the labor force by 2010.[5]

Stagnating wages and rising economic insecurity played a role in the election of Donald Trump as president in November 2016. The U.S. political system has multiple barriers to block the ascendance of populist demagogues, but Trump overcame those obstacles. His slogan "Make America Great Again" tacitly recognizes the disappearance of American exceptionalism. Yet another marker of this disappearance was the strength of support for Bernie Sanders, an avowed socialist, in the Democratic primaries in 2016.

There is, of course, a global dimension to this shift. From the end of World War II to the fall of the Soviet Union in 1989, the United States used its military and economic strength to create a coherent structure of global order built around free trade and free capital movements.[6] But the ability of the United States to shape the globe has declined sharply. The failed U.S. military interventions in Afghanistan and Iraq demonstrate the limits of U.S. military power. The U.S. pressure for free capital movements and "free trade" culminated in the disastrous global financial crisis that revealed the fragility of the U.S. economic model. Moreover, global hegemony ceased to provide benefits for much of the U.S. population, as the costs of empire rose while the economic rewards were concentrated in the hands of a small oligarchic elite.[7]

This essay will, however, focus almost exclusively on the factors internal to the United States that have brought American exceptionalism to an end. The argument is that the overly ambitious extension of U.S. power globally has simply magnified these internal dynamics. The argument is organized in three parts. The first traces the arc of American exceptionalism from the nineteenth century through to the middle of the twentieth century. The second part focuses on the causes and the consequences of the right turn in U.S. politics that began in the 1970s and 1980s. The policy choices in that period created severe economic inequality and the deep social and political polarization that is currently reflected in the electoral arena. The final part examines the lived experience of polarization and shows how different social groups have responded to the crisis of American exceptionalism in sharply divergent ways.

PART 1: THE REALITY OF EXCEPTIONALISM

My argument relies on Monica Prasad's important book *The Land of Too Much.*[8] She argues that the U.S. economy was inserted into the global economy in a way very different from Europe in the nineteenth century and that that divergence channeled state building in the United States in a unique direction. Specifically, Prasad places farmers at the center of U.S. state building, in contrast to Europe, where that role was played by the industrial working class.

Prasad begins her story in the 1870s, but there are elements that started substantially earlier. Agriculture in the United States was far more productive than farming in Europe, and the industrial working class in the United States was weaker than comparable European working-class movements. Both of these elements connect back to key elements of American exceptionalism—the reality of slavery and its legacy, the early adoption of universal suffrage for white men, and the westward expansion of the United States, driven by the inflow of European immigrants. Strong demand for raw cotton from the slave plantations of the American South pushed the slave economy's westward expansion. The cotton trade generated great fortunes for Northern merchants, and the reinvestment of these profits fueled the economic development of the new nation.[9] But the economic dynamism of the new nation was also fueled by the democratic ethos in the Northern states.

Tocqueville identified several distinct ways in which democratic and egalitarian values contributed significantly to economic vitality.[10] There was a widely shared emphasis on self-improvement that led to the world's first public school system and institutions that allowed working people to improve their skills. Employees were often deeply engaged and productive at the workplace because they envisioned later setting out on their own to start a business. The importance of innovation was symbolized by the patent museum in Washington, DC, where visitors could inspect the physical models required for each patent application. This spirit was also embraced by farmers, who were eager to embrace new techniques that would improve yields and who would ultimately press for assistance from government agencies. The pattern in which the United States invested earlier than other nations in needed infrastructure, such as canals, was already well established in the early years of the Republic. This pattern was continued with Lincoln's decision to build the intercontinental rail system.

This economic dynamism allowed the United States to contest for global leadership in industrial technologies in the last part of the nineteenth century, but these legacies also shaped the peculiar development of the industrial working class in the United States. Early suffrage meant that white workers were largely incorporated into the "two-party" political system, so they were less likely to develop the consciousness of themselves as a separate class that was both economically exploited and politically excluded.[11] Moreover, the racial privilege enjoyed by white workers relative to blacks and to multiple waves of new immigrants made the construction of working-class solidarity a more difficult task than in most European nations. Finally, the vast distances in the new nation made it far more difficult to coordinate social movements than in European nations, where populations were heavily concentrated in a few major cities.

This dynamic market economy with a politically weaker industrial working class sets the stage for Prasad's argument. The U.S. comparative advantage began in agriculture, because of rich farmland and the rapid adoption of more productive technologies, but by the 1890s, a similar advantage existed in many sectors of manufacturing. To protect themselves from being inundated with imports from the United States, Europeans turned to tariffs and to economic policies that restricted wage increases to help them compete with the United States. In the second half of the twentieth century, Europeans would compensate for these limits on individual consumption by expanding public outlays for collective consumption, including old-age pensions and public services.

In the United States, in contrast, there was no advantage in protectionism or in restricting individual consumption. On the contrary, the model that was ultimately consolidated with the New Deal expanded the availability of credit, so that consumers would be able to purchase a growing share of the "too much" production. This direction began with radical agrarian pressures for greater availability of credit at reasonable rates that culminated in the Federal Reserve System and the Federal Farm Loan Act of 1916. The New Deal further expanded farm credit and created a national system of subsidized mortgage loans to facilitate mass home ownership.[12]

The last important step in Prasad's argument is that during the New Deal, agrarian interests succeeded in defeating a national sales tax. Farmers insisted that the government should rely on payroll taxes and the progressive income tax to raise revenues. New Deal social-welfare measures were created later than in Europe and were weaker because they were less universal. However, the mechanism of financing made it substantially harder to extend welfare programs in later decades because of the absence in the United States of the kind of broad-based consumption taxes that have financed welfare-state expansion in Europe.[13]

DIVERGENCES AFTER THE NEW DEAL

Prasad's framework helps us to understand the divergent trajectories of the United States and Europe in the years after World War II. Starting during postwar reconstruction, European countries continued to restrain the growth of wages to restore their competitiveness, but under pressure from a still powerful organized working class, they engaged in the progressive expansion of forms of collective consumption, including systems of national health insurance. This was financed through

BRESCIA UNIVERSITY
COLLEGE LIBRARY

the expansion of consumption taxes, as big businesses saw benefits from a more educated and healthier work force.[14]

In the United States, in contrast, the achievement of the New Deal system of agricultural price supports was the death knell of agrarian radicalism. Without its earlier agrarian allies, organized labor's political influence and power also declined. Labor-union density reached its peak level in the mid 1950s, before a relentless decline.[15] Initiatives to expand the scope of the welfare state were both more modest and more fiercely resisted than in Europe. By the 1970s, the heavy reliance of the federal government on the income tax and the payroll tax had generated a powerful opposition to increased taxation.[16]

Prasad also rejects the argument that the stinginess of the U.S. welfare state is a symptom of a lack of state capacity. Her view is that because of the importance of agrarian radicalism, U.S. state capacity developed on a different trajectory from Europe, with much more emphasis on building strong and independent regulatory agencies.[17]

U.S. government agencies were also able to nurture new industries and new technologies in much the same way that the Department of Agriculture had diffused new and more productive agricultural technologies. To be sure, this developmental side of the U.S. state was enormously enhanced by the growth of military and science spending in the Cold War era. However, starting in the 1980s, there were systematic initiatives to extend this developmental capacity beyond the Department of Defense, and these initiatives have been highly effective in maintaining the United States' superiority in technological innovation.[18]

PART 2: WEAKENING THE U.S. MODEL

Despite the historic weakness of the labor movement in the United States, the United States was still able to create a particularly dynamic version of a market economy, largely because of its strong democratic traditions and the opportunity to expand across a vast continent rich in natural resources. This was facilitated by continuing investments in public education and a responsive government that developed capacities to invest in infrastructure, regulatory, and developmental policies that gave the United States global technological leadership.

Finally, the democratic legacy opened the way for powerful social movements that have periodically been able to overcome the entrenched power of reactionary interests whose reign threatened further economic advances. Abolitionism and the Civil Right Movement of the 1950s and 1960s fit here, as does the agrarian radicalism that Prasad emphasizes.[19]

But politics in the United States took a right turn in the mid-1970s that has weakened the democratic character of the society and has fundamentally jeopardized the country's economic dynamism.[20] Piketty has highlighted the most important consequence of this right turn: the dramatic increase in income and wealth inequality that began in the early 1980s and has continued ever since.[21] From 1981, the first year of the Reagan Administration, to 2014, the share of household income going to the top 1 percent of households is estimated to have increased from 8 percent to 18 percent.

The explanation for this right turn is closely linked to the turbulent Vietnam decade, from escalation of the war in August of 1964 to Nixon's presidential resignation in August of 1974.

Faced by a powerful communist insurgency in South Vietnam, U.S. policy makers were unable to recognize the limits of U.S. military power. The obvious futility of the U.S. effort produced a sustained crisis in the United States, with the emergence of powerful left-wing social movements. There was an unprecedented public debate about the United States' global role, and there was a dramatic decline in public confidence in the political elites of both major parties.

Big business firms in the United States responded to the domestic turmoil of the Vietnam era and the failure of two presidents by reconsidering their political stance. Many previously centrist business leaders began to build an alliance with the right wing of the Republican Party, based on free-market economics and the call to roll back taxation, regulation, and labor-union gains.

At the grassroots, the turmoil of the Vietnam decade also produced significant popular backlash against the movements of the 1960s. Both in the South and in the North, many white voters were pushed to the right by escalating militancy among African Americans. Similarly, there was a strong backlash against the emergence of second-wave feminism, particularly after the Supreme Court legalized abortion in 1973. Moreover, the antiauthoritarian politics of the student movement fueled a revival of traditional values and increased mobilization among evangelical Christians. Finally, resistance to higher levels of taxation allowed all of these currents to fuse together into the strongest right-wing coalition that the nation had seen since the 1920s.

This convergence between grassroots conservatism and a turn to the right by big business led to Ronald Reagan's election as president in 1980. Reagan then set in motion a series of policies that helped generate the shifts in income and wealth inequality that Piketty has documented. The massive "supply-side" tax cuts carried out in 1981 significantly reduced the tax burden on high-income households and increased the returns to speculation in financial markets. Reagan also implemented a shift in antitrust policy that conformed to the anti-regulatory ideology of Milton Friedman's Chicago school of economics.[22] A huge increase in executive compensation followed, generally implemented through stock options and stock grants, which was justified by the ideology of shareholder value. In the same vein, the Reagan administration encouraged the consolidation of the banking sector and accelerated the financialization of the economy.[23]

Reagan fired the government employees who worked in the air traffic control system who went on strike in 1981. This sent a powerful signal, since most other working people could be replaced far more easily. Employers took advantage by forcing unionized employees to make wage concessions and increasing the use of contingent workers. Reagan also made significant cuts in spending in a range of government programs designed to aid the poor and eliminated the revenue-sharing program that had eased the fiscal strain on cities.[24]

Most of these Reagan-era policies were continued and intensified all the way up to the Wall Street meltdown in the fall of 2008. Subsequent administrations tilted taxes even further in favor of the rich and continued to encourage the rapid expansion of the financial sector. The Clinton administration was friendlier to unions and expanded a program that provided additional income to low-wage workers. However, the Clinton efforts did not halt the trend toward greater inequality.

From 1945 to 1975, the federal government had provided state and local governments with considerable support to build and repair infrastructure. This support eased the fiscal pressure on these units and facilitated increased funding of public education, including higher education. But from the 1980s onward, fiscal pressures on state and local governments intensified. Politicians became extremely reluctant to push tax increases. The end of revenue sharing and other federal cutbacks meant that states and localities had to cover a substantially larger share of infrastructure outlays at a time when such projects were rising in cost. Finally, the "war on crime," which dramatically increased incarceration rates, particularly for minority men, meant that the costs of the prison and criminal-justice systems were adding additional strain to state and local budgets.[25]

State and local governments also cut back a variety of services that had previously provided assistance to poorer households. The most dramatic impact has been the consequence for expenditures on public higher education. In the first thirty years after World War II, public colleges and universities were often tuition-free or had nominal fees that did not represent a burden for enrollees. But as a result of ongoing budgetary pressures, more and more of the cost of public higher education now falls on the students.[26] Large sectors of the population are effectively priced out of the market for higher education, and many college graduates are weighted down with tens of thousands of dollars of educational debt.

This represents a reversal of one of the longstanding patterns of American exceptionalism—greater investments in increased educational attainment than other nations. U.S. educational leadership came to an abrupt end in the last quarter of the twentieth century.[27] Other nations surged ahead of the United States with ever-larger shares of their young people directed to higher education or sophisticated apprenticeship programs. The reading, writing, and math skills of adults in Scandinavia are now substantially higher than those in the United States. This, in turn, puts U.S.-based firms at a competitive disadvantage as they try to compete in global markets.

It is still the case that large investments by the U.S. government in science and technology have given the United States an advantage in the development of cutting-edge technologies. Specifically, the U.S. global leadership in developing the internet and computer technologies has allowed firms such as Microsoft, Apple, Google, and Facebook to earn fabulous profits from their global operations. But this sectoral success has also served to mask deeper problems with the U.S. economic model.

CONSEQUENCES OF THE RIGHT TURN

Theorists of the free market insisted that policies of the right turn—such as cutting taxes, removing burdensome regulations on business, and shrinking the size of civilian government operations—would operate like a magical elixir and revitalize the U.S. economy. But the consequences of these policies have been exactly the opposite; they have undermined the historic sources of vitality in the U.S. economy.

The right turn accelerated the concentration of wealth and income in the hands of the top 1 percent. Middle-income and poor households responded to constrained income growth by taking on greater debt, and this was a major contributor to the mortgage meltdown in 2007 and 2008.[28] The concentration of income at the top also intensifies speculative activity, since those with vast fortunes have strong motivation to put excess funds into more risky investments that promise a higher return. At the same time, the ideology that corporations should be managed to maximize shareholder value has justified the shifts in corporate compensation that have allowed top managers to pocket a growing share of corporate profits.[29] The major corporations have accumulated huge cash hordes, but their investment outlays remain anemic. Finally, the concentration of income and wealth at the top, as we shall see, is a major contributor to de-democratization, as the very rich use a small share of their resources to tilt tax and regulatory policies in their own favor.[30]

The largest firms in different sectors of the economy have become entrenched, so they can avoid competition and extract unjustified rents. This is most extreme with the largest financial institutions, those that were encouraged from the Reagan administration onward to grow ever larger. And even after the government rescue, the surviving firms continue to control a more substantial share of consumer deposits.

Big pharmaceutical companies have developed few effective new medications in their own laboratories, but they have been able to leverage their ability to finance clinical trials and their access to physicians, so that smaller firms need to work with them to get their innovations to the market.[31] Similarly, the giant technology firms are able to use their vast portfolios of patents to intimidate would-be competitors from challenging their entrenched positions. They are also able simply to buy out potential competitors who are in the early stages of developing a competing technology, since such startups face such difficulties obtaining the finances to remain independent.

One of the keys to this process of entrenchment has been the relaxation of antitrust enforcement that began during the Reagan administration.[32] Corporate practices that in an earlier period might have precipitated vigorous antitrust actions were seen by the Justice Department and the courts as harmless. Economic dynamism is diminished, because many entrenched firms have too many weapons in their arsenal to blunt competitive challenges.

De-democratization goes along with entrenchment and enrichment.[33] Democratic practices in the United States have long been flawed, because elections are run by partisan local officials, numerous barriers to broad electoral participation were erected in the early decades of the twentieth century, and expensive electoral campaigns have given rich donors disproportionate influence. However, since the right turn, a series of court decisions have further weakened the voice of the people. A decades-long conservative campaign to reverse the protections provided by the Voting Rights Act culminated in a Supreme Court decision in 2013 that gave local jurisdictions much greater leeway to discriminate against minority voters.

Most importantly, the conservative majority on the Supreme Court has repeatedly held that campaign donations are equivalent to speech, so that efforts to limit the impact of big money on campaigns violates the constitution. With this logic, the court has opened the floodgates of donations by the rich and corporations and gutted regulations that were intended, at least, to force the disclosure of such contributions.

De-democratization makes the political system unresponsive to reform demands. For example, it is widely recognized that the current tax system, in which multimillionaires routinely pay taxes at a lower rate than their rank-and-file employees, is grossly unfair. However, strategic campaign contributions assure that key congressional leaders will be able to block reform legislation from coming to the floor.

The combined consequences of enrichment, entrenchment, and de-democratization has been a stagnant economy, characterized by insufficient demand and diminishing opportunities for upward mobility. Aggregate demand has been weakened by the tilting of income toward the rich, by all levels of government facing ongoing fiscal crises, and by the reluctance of wealthy corporations to invest in new projects. At the same time, for the last generation, the combination of foreign competition and technological advances have dramatically reduced manufacturing employment, significantly weakened new job creation, and have pushed a growing share of the labor force into poorly paid jobs in services and retail trade.

The impact is indicated by studies showing elevated death rates in the United States in 2014 as compared to 1999 among white men between ages of forty-five and fifty-four with only a high school education.[34] This finding goes against the general trend of declining death rates for people in midlife, and the apparent reason for the uptick is suicides and deaths related to drug and alcohol abuse. The finding is limited to white men; Hispanics and African Americans in that age group continue to show declining death rates. The logical explanation is that while Hispanics and African Americans continue to face difficult labor-market conditions, racial barriers have diminished over the last generation. But white men, who historically enjoyed an advantaged position in the labor market, face both worsening conditions and an erosion of their historic privileges.

While this represents just one piece of data, it highlights the end of American exceptionalism. The same population group—prime-age working-class white men—that through much of U.S. history did not rally to the banners of radical movements, are now experiencing increasingly difficult circumstances. Some of them are dying at a higher rate, and others are, in fact, rallying behind the banners of outsider political figures such as Donald Trump and Bernie Sanders.

PART 3: THE LIVED EXPERIENCE OF POLARIZATION

For many social scientists, it is almost a reflex to think in terms of class and jump to the conclusion that people who are in similar structural positions should respond in similar ways to economic hardship. But the reality of American exceptionalism is that class position has always been mediated through other identities, such as ethnicity, religion, generation, and region, in shaping political behavior. Different population groups have responded to parallel economic shocks with extremely divergent forms of political responses. Here, the U.S. pattern looks similar to that of Europe, where economic shocks have significantly weakened centrist political parties and have strengthened the oppositional parties of the right and the left.

The best way to conceptualize the economic dislocations is in terms of what Jacob Hacker has called, the "great risk shift."[35] Basically, the transformations in the United States since the right turn of the 1980s have significantly increased the volatility of family income. Hacker shows that by 2002, basically one household in six, headed by a prime-age adult, was likely to experience a 50 percent or greater income drop from one year to the next, and more recent analyses have shown that this volatility has continued to rise.

The most important cause is the increasing amount of turnover in the labor market. Informalization means fewer people enjoy job security. Total employment at large corporations in the United States has been falling sharply for decades, and a greater share of those that they employ work on a contingent basis.[36] Ongoing fiscal pressures have produced comparable changes for public-sector employees, who have also become increasingly vulnerable to layoffs. An ever-larger share of the labor force works at small- and medium-sized firms that are very exposed to ups and downs of the business cycle.

The second key cause is the weakening of the safety net that is supposed to protect households from this kind of volatility. Over the decades, the share of those facing unemployment who qualify for benefits has been falling; it is now at less than a quarter of all those counted as unemployed. Moreover, even for those lucky enough to receive benefits, the ratio of those benefits to the lost wages has also been falling. At the same time, a variety of state and local programs that provided cash assistance have been phased out, and the national program that was designed to protect children from poverty was effectively gutted by legislation passed in 1996.[37] Furthermore, the dramatic increases in health care costs and the spottiness of safety-net programs means that families can also be driven into poverty by either the uncompensated costs or the lost income precipitated by a severe health crisis.

In fact, the largest single cause of personal bankruptcy in the United States remains costs associated with a medical crisis. For a large portion of the U.S. population, when a doctor's visit detects a serious illness, it raises both the threat of mortality and the possibility of financial ruin. The Affordable Care Act ameliorated this problem by providing health insurance to many families that previously could not afford coverage. But families remain at risk of impoverishment caused by a health crisis. A study released in early 2016 reported that 37 percent of respondents living in households with earnings below $50,000 experienced difficulties paying medical bills.[38] This is one of the reasons why Republican attacks on the Affordable Care Act had some political traction; the law has not alleviated the public's economic anxieties about health costs.

These two primary factors, in turn, set in motion two secondary processes. The first is family breakup. Households that are strained by income instability are at greater risk of dissolution, which often means a significant income loss for some members of the original household. Second, economic stresses, including loss of income or sustained fears of an imminent loss of income, often produce anxiety, depression, and loss of self-esteem. This, in turn, can result in alcohol or drug abuse, as individuals self-medicate to manage their symptoms. However, drug or alcohol dependence can lead to arrest, job losses, and further shocks to household income.

Households in the United States have sought to protect themselves from incomes that are volatile or insufficient through increased resort to borrowing. However, this expedient frequently backfires, leaving households facing even greater economic uncertainty. During the long increase in housing prices from the 1990s through 2007, many households increased their mortgage debt. When house prices stopped rising, millions of households owed more on their mortgages than the houses were worth. The defaulted loans and foreclosures that continued for years meant that many formerly middle-class households lost whatever saving they had been able to accumulate.[39]

There has also been a vast increase in student debt over the last decade. The problem has been particularly egregious for students attending for-profit institutions, where instruction was supposed to lead to job opportunities, which failed to materialize. But as the job market has worsened in the post-2008 period, many students who attended legitimate colleges and universities have found themselves unable to find employment while they still carry loan burdens of $100,000 to $200,000. Since student debt is difficult to discharge with personal bankruptcy, it becomes a durable burden that individuals carry for years.[40] Recent reports have indicated that thousands of elderly people have portions of their social security checks withheld, because even as they reach retirement, they still owe payments on student debt.[41]

DIVERGENT RESPONSES

Those at the Bottom

Ethnographic accounts have illuminated the misery of those living at the bottom of U.S. society.[42] Edin and Shaefer document the lives of people living on $2.00 a day or less.[43] The stories are basically similar—a family is surviving on the basis of a paycheck from a low-wage job, but a conflict with a boss or a health crisis or an arrest leads to the loss of the job and a downward spiral that includes spells of living with relatives or living on the streets. Welfare is not an option either because they do not know it exists or because they are unlikely to be deemed eligible, despite desperate circumstances. Similar stories have been told by Desmond, documenting the moment at which families are put out on the street because the landlord has decided that they are no longer acceptable as tenants.[44]

But both these households that are in extreme poverty and many of those who are a single paycheck away from extreme poverty are unlikely to have any political response to their economic marginalization. Just getting by, just surviving is a full-time job, and they are unlikely to vote. Low-income households that are vulnerable to evictions or frequent change of residence are unlikely to have updated their residence information to remain eligible.

In fact, in many parts of the country, there is no longer an entity or organization that seeks to connect poor people to the political process. This role was filled for decades by labor unions, which played a role in getting their members and their members' neighbors registered to vote. But as unions have declined or disappeared in many communities, no other organizations are available to fill the vacuum. Exit polls from 2016 showed that households of all ethnicities with income below $50,000 voted for Clinton over Trump by about ten points, while most other income groups were close to evenly split. However, voters in the bottom quintile have turnout rates of about 55 percent in presidential elections, while those in the top quintile reach 80 percent turnout.[45]

Working-Class Minorities

There are many African American and Latino households who live one or two rungs up the social ladder from those living in poverty or at daily risk of poverty. Members of this group face continuing insecurity in the labor market, many of them were victimized by subprime mortgage lending, and they disproportionately face displacement, as gentrification drives them out of urban neighborhoods that have become attractive to higher-income households. Members of this group have particularly high anxieties about the prospects for their children. On the one side, repeated episodes of police violence have exposed the vulnerability of minority youths and young adults. On the other, poor schools and financial barriers to higher education create significant barriers to upward mobility.

However, men in this demographic group do not face the higher levels of mortality reported for working-class white men. The usual explanation is that minority men have long faced racial barriers and discrimination in the labor market, so they do not confront growing instability in labor markets as something new and surprising. But it might also be that a recent history of political mobilization within these communities provides an alternative to despair and self-medication.

In fact, there has been a resurgence of political engagement in these communities. Movements such as Black Lives Matter, the Fight for Fifteen—to raise the minimum wage—and campaigns for an end to deportations and a path to citizenship within immigrant communities are indicators of the potential for broader political mobilization.[46] But as we saw in the 1960s, such claims making within minority communities generates an instant backlash, provoking political figures such as Donald Trump to double down on anti-immigrant and pro-police rhetoric.

Whites without College Degrees

Here is where one sees the most divergent responses to greater economic insecurity. Depending largely upon the specific communities where they live, people in this demographic group rallied behind the very different candidacies of Donald Trump and Bernie Sanders. In a number of Northern states, Sanders won big victories over Clinton in white working-class communities. However, in the November election, non-college-educated whites favored Trump over Clinton by close to a 70 to 30 margin.[47] But this figure has to be adjusted for the regional reality that whites without a college education in the South tend to vote Republican by even larger margins. For example, white evangelical voters, many of whom live in the South and do not have college degrees, voted for Trump over Clinton by 81 percent over 16 percent.

What seems indisputable is that a slice of non-college-educated whites in midwestern heartland states, such as Wisconsin, Iowa, Ohio, Michigan, and Pennsylvania, who had been part of the Obama coalition in 2008 and 2012, crossed over and supported Trump in 2016, and that shift in those five states accounted for Trump's narrow Electoral College victory. The actual number of people who made this shift was not particularly large; it could have been as few as half a million voters, since Trump's margin in some of these states was small. However, this was enough to make the difference, given that other parts of the Obama coalition—African

Americans and young people—did not turn out to the polls for Clinton as strongly as they had for Obama.

These non-college-educated switchers in the industrial heartland had presumably voted for Obama because of his promise of significant change, but they are still hurting, and they probably voted for Trump because of his promise to bring back manufacturing jobs. For these and many other voters, Clinton was seen as an unattractive establishment figure who was unlikely to pursue a bold and disruptive agenda.

To be sure, a much larger portion of Trump's total vote came from those non-college-educated whites who had rallied to the Tea Party political insurgency that first emerged in 2009. Well-funded national right-wing organizations such as Americans for Prosperity played a key role in turning grassroots activism into a national political force. However, the movement has a very real popular base among whites, particularly in the South and in rural communities and small towns across the nation. Arlie Hochschild has explained the "deep story" of Tea Party activists with the metaphor of people patiently standing on a line stretching for miles toward a horizon of opportunity and success, but suddenly others start cutting in to the line, including minorities, immigrants, and even endangered species.[48] This story resonates both with those who have achieved some level of economic security, as well as those who are struggling to keep their heads above water.

Two of the core issues for Tea Party activists featured prominently in the rhetoric of Donald Trump. Tea Party activists were particularly mobilized by both the economic and cultural threat of immigration; they did not want immigrants coming into the United States, taking jobs and speaking other languages. Also, the iconic Tea Party slogan was "Keep your government hands off my Medicare." Activists wanted to protect their own entitlement to Medicare and Social Security while urging political leaders to cut back spending on the undeserving.[49] Trump's campaign was unusual for the Republican Party in his strong stance against cuts to both Social Security and Medicare, since the party's orthodoxy has been that the entitlement programs need dramatic retrenchment.

Some voters in this group chose Trump; and others, Sanders, because voters go with the version of economic populism that makes sense to them, given their locality and their voting history. For many voters, partisan identification is deeply held and often inherited from their parents. But what happened in places like Wisconsin, Michigan, and Ohio is that some unionized workers rejected the advice of their own unions and cast a protest vote in favor of Trump. The irony is that in all of these states, strongly anti-union Republican governors had pursued aggressive policies since 2011 to weaken trade unions. In short, these voters risked a vote for Trump knowing that the unions had been too weak to fight back successfully against the right.[50]

Whites with College Degrees

Within this demographic group, the key dividing line appears to be age. Historically, a college degree made a significant difference for labor-market outcomes, and those with such degrees experienced lower unemployment rates and a significant wage premium. The consequence was that whites with a college education have slightly favored the Republicans in recent elections. However, the same cannot be said for younger college graduates. Those who have entered the labor market over the last decade faced either a massive recession or a weak recovery. Even when jobs are available, employers often prefer to increase the number of temporary or precarious workers, who can easily be fired in the event of another economic downturn. Older employees are less likely to move on or retire, given the uncertain economic environment. Finally, many industries are facing disruptive changes that create additional pressure on employers to limit the number of relatively secure positions.

The combination of a difficult labor market and the heavy burden of student debt have pushed many young college-educated whites leftward.[51] This was a big factor in the Sanders campaign. However, the ultimate impact of this political shift remains uncertain, because young people are substantially less likely than their elders to participate in elections and some older college-educated white voters, who had been enthusiastic members of the Obama electorate, have grown disillusioned with the Democrats in recent years.

CONCLUSION

The right turn in U.S. politics that began in the 1980s has effectively dismantled some of the key structures of American exceptionalism, especially the confidence that individual initiative and hard work are sufficient to achieve upward mobility. The consequence has been growing ideological polarization, political stalemate, and the rise of new political currents, such as populist authoritarianism and socialism, that were previously restricted to the margins of politics in the United States. But this analysis also suggests that the future direction of the United States is extremely difficult to predict, since it is dependent on the complex interaction among leadership personalities, the political choices made by diverse population groups, and global events.

To be sure, the likeliest possibility remains a continuation of the status quo, with polarization and stalemate growing even worse. Since the U.S. constitution provides multiple veto points, the election of Donald Trump will likely result in continuing stalemate between Congress and the president, with few significant legislative changes. Ironically, the new administration's only significant legislative achievement—the massive tax-cut bill that was successfully pushed through in late 2017—will further intensify wealth and income inequalities, contributing to greater economic instability and rising public anger and discontent. But intensifying polarization and growing popular dissatisfaction cannot go on indefinitely. Sooner or later, the pressure for a break will become overwhelming, but that still leaves two distinct and radically different trajectories.

The first is an extended episode of authoritarian governance as domestic turbulence and perceived foreign threats are used as a pretext for suspending the constitution and giving the executive branch broad powers to impose new policies. Such a turn would probably coincide with a new hot or cold war against one or another foreign enemy or an escalation of ongoing fighting in the Middle East or Afghanistan. In both the recent and distant past, the need to defeat foreign enemies has been used as the justification for such departures from constitutional government as the internment of the Japanese during World War II, anti-communist witch hunts in the 1950s, or the use of torture against suspected terrorists after 9/11. A new authoritarianism is likely to use similar tactics.

The second possibility is another epoch of reform, comparable to the New Deal, in which a reform administration, pressed by powerful social movements, pursues an aggressive project of redistributing income and revitalizing the U.S. economy. Suggestions of this possibility lie in the broad resistance to the Trump administration that began with the huge women's marches that took place the day after Trump's inauguration in 2017 and again a year later. The Trump administration has simultaneously mounted frontal attacks on immigrants and immigrant-rights supporters, labor unions, African Americans, Latinos, Asian Americans, advocates for the environment and environmental justice, the women's movement, advocates for prison and criminal-justice reform, gun-control groups, proponents of marijuana decriminalization, defenders of an open internet, advocates for public schools, supporters of transgender rights, opponents of unlimited corporate power, and those fighting to reduce shocking inequalities of wealth and income inequality. These broad and indiscriminate attacks provide organizers with the opportunity to fuse these diverse constituencies into a powerful and majoritarian reform coalition.

However, historically even the most powerful resistance movements have found it difficult to maintain unity once they have driven their opponents from power. Moreover, in the United States, there are few signs thus far that Trump's many opponents have coalesced around a coherent reform agenda. But it is also possible that the seriousness of the threat posed by Trump's authoritarian impulses could produce a surprising level of cooperation between centrist Democratic politicians and social-movement activists.

Whether the United States moves toward authoritarianism or a new reform epoch will depend ultimately on both events internal to the United States and on what goes on in the rest of the world. Increased global disorder and mounting threats of war could strengthen anti-democratic forces. On the other hand, successful reform initiatives in other parts of the world to strengthen democratic governance while reducing inequality and environmental degradation could inspire similar efforts in the United States.

NOTES

1. Gary Gerstle, *Liberty and Coercion* (Princeton, NJ: Princeton University Press, 2015).

2. To be sure, all national trajectories are exceptional; there is no typical path. The point is that exceptionalism has loomed larger in ideology and popular consciousness in the United States than in most other places.

3. Werner Sombart, *Why Is There No Socialism in the United States?* trans. Patricia M. Hocking and C. T. Husbands (White Plains, NY: International Arts and Sciences Press, 1976), 106.

4. Timothy Smeeding, Robert Erikson, and Markus Jäntti, eds. *Persistence, Privilege, and Parenting: The Comparative Study of Intergenerational Mobility* (New York: Russell Sage Foundation, 2011).

5. U.S. Government Accountability Office, "Contingent Workforce: Size, Characteristics, Earnings and Benefits," 4.

6. Fred Block, *The Origins of International Economic Disorder* (Berkeley: University of California Press, 1977).

7. Leo Panitch and Sam Gindin, *The Making of Global Capitalism* (New York: Verso, 2012).

8. Monica Prasad, *The Land of Too Much* (Cambridge, MA: Harvard University Press, 2012).

9. Sven Beckert, *Empire of Cotton* (New York: Knopf, 2014).

10. Alexis de Tocqueville, *Democracy in America,* 2 vols., trans. Henry Reeve (New York: Vintage, 1945).

11. Ira Katznelson and Aristide Zolberg, eds. *Working Class Formation: Nineteenth-Century Patterns in Europe and the United States* (Princeton, NJ: Princeton University Press, 1986).

12. Gerstle, *Liberty and Coercion,* also emphasizes the importance of the agrarian roots of the New Deal.

13. Peter Lindert, *Growing Public* (New York: Cambridge University Press, 2004).

14. Fred Block and Margaret Somers, *The Power of Market Fundamentalism* (Cambridge, MA: Harvard University Press, 2014), chap. 7.

15. Thomas Kochan, Harry Katz, and Robert McKersie, *The Transformation of American Industrial Relations* (Ithaca, NY: Cornell University Press, 1986).

16. Isaac Martin, *The Permanent Tax Revolt* (Stanford, CA: Stanford University Press, 2008); and Isaac Martin, *Rich People's Movements* (New York: Oxford, 2013).

17. Gerald Berk, *Louis Brandeis and the Making of Regulated Competition* (New York: Cambridge University Press, 2009).

18. Fred Block, "Swimming against the Current: The Rise of a Hidden Developmental State in the United States" *Politics and Society* 36, no. 2 (2008): 169–206; Fred Block, "Innovation and the Invisible Hand of Government," in *State of Innovation,* ed. Fred Block and Matthew R. Keller, 1–26 (Boulder, CO: Paradigm, 2011); and Mariana Mazzucato, *The Entrepreneurial State* (London: Anthem, 2013).

19. Frances Fox Piven, *Challenging Authority* (Lanham, MD: Rowman and Littlefield, 2006).

20. The term was initially used as a title by Thomas Ferguson and Joel Rogers, *Right Turn* (New York: Hill & Wang, 1986). This argument is developed at greater length in Block, *Capitalism: The Future of an Illusion* (Oakland: University of California Press, 2018).

21. Thomas Piketty, *Capital in the 21st Century,* trans. Arthur Goldhammer (Cambridge, MA: Harvard University Press, 2014).

22. Brett Christophers, *The Great Leveler: Capitalism and Competition in the Court of Law* (Cambridge, MA: Harvard University Press, 2016).

23. Gerald Davis, *Managed by the Markets* (New York: Oxford University Press, 2009); and Greta Krippner, *Capitalizing on Crisis* (Cambridge, MA: Harvard University Press, 2012).

24. Many of these shifts are well documented in Jacob Hacker and Paul Pierson, *Off Center: The Republican Revolution and the Erosion of American Democracy* (New Haven, CT: Yale University Press, 2006).

25. Michelle Alexander, *The New Jim Crow* (New York: New Press, 2011).

26. Christopher Newfield, *Unmaking the Public University* (Cambridge, MA: Harvard University Press, 2011).

27. Claudia Goldin and Lawrence F. Katz, *The Race between Education and Technology.* (Cambridge, MA: Belknap Press, 2008),

28. Kurtulus Gemici, "Beyond the Minsky and Polanyi Moments: Social Origins of the Foreclosure Crisis," *Politics and Society* 44, no. 1 (2016): 15–43.

29. William Lazonick, *Sustaining Prosperity in the New Economy?* (Kalamazoo, MI: Upjohn, 2009.

30. A number of analysts have referred to a process of de-democratization, but Colin Crouch, *Post-Democracy* (Cambridge: Polity, 2004), was among the earliest.

31. Ann Case and Angus Deaton, "Rising Morbidity and Mortality in Midlife among White Non-Hispanic Americans in the 21st Century," *Proceedings of the National Academy of Sciences* (December 8, 2015): 15078–83.

32. Christophers, *The Great Leveler.*

33. Jeffrey Winters, *Oligarchy* (New York: Cambridge University Press, 2011).

34. Case and Deaton, "Rising Morbidity and Mortality."

35. Jacob Hacker, *The Great Risk Shift* (New York: Oxford University Press, 2006).

36. Davis, *Managed by the Markets.*

37. Jane L. Collins and Victoria Mayer, *Both Hands Tied: Welfare Reform and the Race to the Bottom in the Low-Wage Labor Market* (Chicago: University of Chicago Press, 2010).

38. Liz Hamel et al., *The Burden of Medical Debt* (Kaiser Family Foundation, January 2016).

39. Gemici, "Beyond the Minsky and Polanyi Moments."

40. Charlie Eaton, Jacob Habinek, Adam Goldstein, and Cyrus Dioun, "The Financialization of U.S. Higher Education," *Socio-Economic Review* 14, no. 3 (2016): 507–35.

41. Danny Vinik, "The Latest Victims of Student Debt? The Elderly," *Politico*, February 25, 2016, www.politico.com/agenda/story/2016/02/the-latest-victims-of-student-debt-the-elderly-000053.

42. Still relevant is William Julius Wilson, *When Work Disappears* (New York: Knopf, 1996).

43. Kathryn J. Edin and H. Luke Shaefer, *$2.00 a Day* (Boston: Houghton Mifflin Harcourt, 2015).

44. Matthew Desmond, *Evicted* (New York: Crown, 2016).

45. Jan Leighley and Jonathan Nagler, *Who Votes Now?* (Princeton, NJ: Princeton University Press, 2013), chap. 2.

46. Sarah Jaffe, *Necessary Trouble* (New York: Nation Books, 2016).

47. Data are from exit polls as reported in K. K. Rebecca Lai et al. "How the Presidential Election Took a U-Turn in 2016," *New York Times*, November 10, 2016.

48. Arlie Hochschild, *Strangers in Their Own Land* (New York: New Press, 2016).

49. Lawrence Rosenthal and Christine Trost, eds., *Steep: The Precipitous Rise of the Tea Party.* (Berkeley: University of California Press, 2012).

50. For a useful account of the unsuccessful Wisconsin mobilization to protect union rights, see Jane L. Collins, *The Politics of Value: Three Movements to Change How We Think about the Economy* (Chicago: University of Chicago Press, 2017).

51. Sarah Jaffe, *Necessary Trouble* (New York: Nation Books, 2016).

4

The Social Question as the Struggle over Precarity

The Case of China

Ching Kwan Lee

The modern welfare state owed its origin to the disruptive power of workers' movements and the threat of communist revolutions in Europe. Bismarck's pioneering compulsory social insurance funds in the 1880s was a response to the "worker question"—the social upheaval in the wake of proletarianization and the rising political power of organized labor. Progressive and protective social policies (insurance for sickness, pension, injuries, unemployment) gradually expanded coverage from the male proletariat to other social groups, broadening the terrain of the "social" to include workers' families, future workers, former workers, lapsed workers, thereby achieving the domestication of the working class and "regulation of the social" by the state.[1] Other European nations followed suit in the ensuing decades, with the impetus to establish full-employment capitalism reinforced by the political need to match the gains workers won in the Communist bloc during the Cold War era.[2] If the specter of Communism kept capitalism on guard, what kind of "security" was available to the working masses under Communism? And how did that system evolve to shape precarity under neoliberalism?

This chapter examines these questions through the trajectory of China's precariats from state socialism to the country's integration with global capitalism. The "social question" here refers to the multifaceted contestations, or relational struggles, over precarity. Analytically, at least three contested terrains can be identified: the *regulation* of class relation and power at the point of production, usually by the state and the law; the *social reproduction* of labor beyond wage work, or the provision of care and subsistence for maintaining and renewing workers' labor power on a daily and generational basis; and the *recognition* of labor, or the ideological and symbolic resources that members of society can use to make claims on collective security and well-being. The overall argument is that over the past seven decades, the most salient terrain for relational struggles has shifted from recognition to regulation and now to the social reproduction of labor. Notwithstanding China's spectacular economic development, the social question qua labor question remains, albeit in changing forms.

PRECARIOUS VERSUS PERMANENT PROLETARIATS UNDER STATE SOCIALISM

Notwithstanding the communist ideology of equality and protection, state paternalism during the planned-economy period was practiced on the principle of exclusivity, not universality, resulting in a hierarchy of inequality and insecurity. The famed "iron rice bowl"—permanent employment with the guarantee of cradle-to-grave welfare—was available to only one-fifth of the Chinese workforce, almost all of them urbanites.[3] The vast majority of the working population, including workers in collective industries and the even larger contingent of farmers, were categorically excluded from state-funded and guaranteed welfare. Instead, these workers depended on revenues of their own collective enterprises or communes for wages and collective benefits, which varied widely across work units, villages, and regions. The main driver of precarity in this period was the Communist state's strategy of accumulation and domination. Worker resistance was spearheaded by marginalized workers who appropriated the communist ideology of equality and proletarian leadership to demand recognition of their status and equal compensation.

Of particular importance to the Maoist regime of accumulation was the state-sponsored rural-urban divide and the concomitant unequal citizenship regime. The transfer of surplus from agriculture to industry, from country to city, and from peasants to workers could not have been possible without the *hukuo* (household registration) system, which essentially locked rural workers down in their birthplace, and the state-imposed "price scissors," which artificially devalued agricultural labor relative to industrial labor. Not guaranteed or supported by state budget, agricultural collectives (i.e., a three-level system of commune, brigade, and team from 1958 to 1979) were self-sufficient basic units of production and accounting, and depended on self-generated resources to buffer risk and provide basic medical services, primary education, and emergency relief.[4] Rural precariousness was starkly displayed during the Great Leap famine: nearly all of the estimated ten to twenty million who starved to death were rural residents. Based on data on the differential reduction in grain consumption during the famine, it was clear that the state protected urban residents from starvation.[5] Sociologist Martin Whyte calls this rigid regime of unequal citizenship a "socialist caste" system.[6]

In cities, during the first three decades of state socialism in post-revolutionary China, a "dual" labor system separated permanent workers from marginal and temporary workers, with each of these two categories marked by elaborate internal differentiation in wages, benefits, and political status. The much-touted "proletariat master" of the Communist nation, who enjoyed permanent employment, and full and free medical care, housing, and pension amounting to more than half of their former wages, represented only a small minority of the Chinese workforce at any point in time, and they were found only in the urban, state-owned, heavy-industrial sector. The split and inequality between the regular and the contract proletariat coexisted inconveniently and incongruously with the official ideology aimed at creating a united proletarian political backing for the party. The contradiction between reality and ideology—between policies geared to incentivize productivity by differential compensation and policies aimed at realizing "work according to need" and protection for all—surfaced most publicly during mass mobilization of the Hundred Flowers Campaign (1957) and the Cultural Revolution (1966–1976). The "contract proletariat" was at the forefront of labor activism, seizing these state-endorsed moments of class struggle to demand equal treatment in wages, benefits, and permanent terms of employment.

Several political economic conditions led to institutionalized inequality among Chinese workers. During the revolution, the Chinese Communist Party drew its working-class support mainly from southern skilled artisans—printers, copper fitters, metal workers, mechanics—whose guild tradition of exclusivity and paternalism found expression in the new Communist industrial order in the People's Republic. Former leaders of the Communist labor movement in Shanghai, the industrial heartland of prerevolutionary China, became top officials in charge of instituting labor insurance regulations and according trade unions with important welfare functions.

> But just as only a portion of labor had been actively engaged on the communist side during the revolution, so the fruits of struggle were enjoyed by a limited constituency as well. . . . In 1952, when the new labor insurance system was first implemented, a mere seven percent of the work force was covered by its generous provisions. By 1958, following the socialization of industry, coverage reached a high point of thirty percent. In 1978, at the beginning of the post-Mao reforms, only some twenty-two percent of the labor force could claim such benefits—a figure that remained steady throughout the 1980s.[7]

Contrary to its connotation, the "planned" economy had to deal with financial constraints, production pressure, and input shortages and fluctuation by creating flexibility in its workforce. It also depended on the deliberate use of unequal rewards to incentivize productivity among workers, spawning different kinds of polarities within the labor force, across sectors (light and heavy industries and service), ranks (seniority), occupation (skills), and ownership type (state or collective). On the eve of economic reform, there were thirteen million temporary workers (or 16 percent) in industrial employment alone.[8] A bewildering numbers of informal arrangements allocated these urban and rural residents to different kinds of temporary positions to provide necessary flexibility to state industries under the planned economy. *Temporary* workers were needed to do work permanent workers resisted doing, to pitch in during hot summer months when absenteeism of permanent workers was common, to undertake enterprise expansion or building addition, and so forth. Then there were the *apprentices,* who endured years of training at substandard wages and benefits and were often resentful of their masters. *Migrant workers* from the countryside took up contract jobs in the cities, receiving salaries without any benefits. Their numbers expanded rapidly during the Great Leap Forward. *Social youth,* a euphemistic term for the unemployed youth, usually of urban bourgeois family backgrounds, who refused to go into agriculture, were encouraged to join propaganda work to ensure their political loyalty. City governments set up labor service stations, which functioned as labor contractors and charged service fees, to help people looking for temporary jobs. In Shanghai, China's premier industrial center, as Lynn White remarked, "the social division between secure and marginal workers is as notable in a developing Communist city as in a developing capitalist one."[9]

If the state-socialist strategy of accumulation called for instituting a hierarchy of rural and urban precarity and vulnerability, its legitimating ideology directly contradicted this reality. Ironically, precarious workers under Communism developed heightened consciousness of their class position and disadvantages because official propaganda trumpeted equality and unity. Historians of Chinese labor have established that marginal workers played a disproportionately active role in responding to significant episodes of political mobilizations—the Hundred Flowers, the Cultural Revolution, and the April Fifth Movement in 1976. In 1957, after a national outpouring of labor unrest in 1956, partly spurred by popular dissent during the Hungarian revolt, labor disturbance erupted in more 587 enterprises, involving nearly thirty thousand workers. Workers in "joint-ownership" enterprises, apprentices, temporary workers, and those who had lost their permanent status through job reassignment, all resentful of their inferior conditions of service, drove the unrest.[10] A decade later, the "economistic wind" (workers demand for material improvement) during the Cultural Revolution originated among long term irregular workers and those workers who had been mobilized to go down to the countryside to support the peasants. Later, the demands of these groups spread to workers in the interior and to intellectual youths who had been part of the up to the mountain down to the countryside resettlement campaign.[11] Eventually the economistic fever infested even permanent state employees with secure urban household registration.[12] Then, in 1976, mass demonstrations and riots broke out in more than forty places across the country. Young and marginalized workers who were persecuted for their bourgeois leanings during the Cultural Revolution seized this occasion of commemorating the late premier Zhou Enlai to express their dissatisfaction with the political persecutions and injustices they suffered.[13]

In short, notwithstanding the mythology of communist egalitarianism, worker solidarity, and state paternalism, the Chinese working class under Mao was fragmented and marked by inequalities in the realms of production, social reproduction, and social status. On top of prerevolutionary cleavages of gender, skills, and native-place origins, the Communist party-state sponsored and solidified labor divisions along lines of state- or collective-ownership, core and peripheral industrial sectors, rural-urban *hukuo,* party and nonparty membership, and permanent and temporary status. The state, or its politics and policies, was the main driver of protection and precariousness, both material and symbolic. The centrality of ideological domination in the Mao era and the glaring contradictions between socialist ideology and reality fueled working-class discontents and resistance. Workers were able to seize the moments when the political opportunity structure was periodically opened up by elite struggles at the top. Relational struggles of precarity in this period pivoted on recognition targeting the state, that is, marginalized categories of workers leveraging symbolic resources offered by official ideology to make material claims on the state. Production relations in the workplace were regulated by the party-state's direct presence and bureaucratic rules. Despite its uneven distribution, the social reproduction of labor provided by either state and collective welfare or rural collective welfare was not the focus of labor strife. As we shall see, in the de-ideologized reform era, the hegemony of market competition and individual responsibility has the effect of silencing workers' recognition struggles. Regulation would become the main contested terrain as the Communist regime pursued market reform and maintained social stability through the law, the court, and related bureaucratic channels.

HIGH-GROWTH MARKET REFORM ERA: 1980–2009

If the driver of precarization during the Mao era was the state, China's reform and opening since around 1980 has ushered in global capital as an added force aggravating the social question qua labor question. To catch up with the developed world, and finding its competitive niches in the lowest nodes of the global production chains, China's industries and workers bear the disproportionate costs (razor-thin profit margins and exploitative labor conditions) of global capital's flexible accumulation. Beyond global industries, Chinese domestic strategies of growth (fixed asset investment and state-led urbanization) have also led to the rise of precarity in construction and urban services, while its strategy of domination (by monopolizing representation of worker interests) and of legitimation (market-driven trickle-down developmentalism) have seriously hampered the bargaining power of labor vis-à-vis capital. If in the pre-reform period, state domination via ideology fueled recognition struggles, in the reform period, it was labor laws that mediate and mitigate class exploitation, making regulation the pivotal contested terrain of labor precarity.

This section on the high-growth phase of Chinese reform (1980–2010) first depicts a spectrum of informal labor modalities in manufacturing, construction, and services, and discusses how their emergence is predicated on the state's economic-development strategies. While the Chinese labor literature has spotlighted the archetypical semi-proletarianized migrant worker in global factories, this section brings to light less visible (i.e., less recognized) forms of precarious labor—the self-exploited, "rush order" micro-entrepreneurs, student interns, dispatch workers, construction workers, street vendors, care workers, and others. The second part discusses the state's strategies of legitimation and its alliance with various types of capital in the making of precarious labor. Contrary to the commonplace understanding of precarious labor as the absence of state regulation, I will show that the state is actively involved in the relational struggles that define precarity in China. The third part of the discussion turns to workers' capacity, interest, and activism, a constitutive moment of precarity. As the state used the law and its elaborate bureaucratic apparatus (arbitration, mediation, and petition systems) to regulate class conflicts between capital and labor, legal mobilization also became the prevalent mode of worker struggles. When these channels failed to resolve conflicts, the state would resort to bargaining with protesting workers or selective repression to maintain social stability. The strong performance of the economy gave the state the fiscal capacity required for economic absorption of labor conflicts, and it shaped workers' interests in opting for "exit" (i.e., job hopping) as a strategy of survival. As we shall see later, in the current period of slow growth, these conditions may no longer hold.

A SPECTRUM OF PRECARITY ARISING FROM THE STATE'S STRATEGIES OF DEVELOPMENT

Global Factories, Ghost Workshops, and Shadow Workers

After the crackdown of the 1989 Tiananmen uprising, the Communist regime confronted simultaneously a legitimacy crisis and a severe economic downturn. In response, the Deng Xiaoping leadership in the early 1990s made a decisive move to hasten the pace and scope of economic liberalization and internationalization. The first casualties of urban reform were state workers in old industrial regions. But the death of the socialist working class also saw the birth of a new working class made up mostly of migrants from the countryside.[14] By then, global capital had consolidated a regime of flexible accumulation, spinning commodity chains around the world, with profits reaped mostly by multinationals in advanced core countries that specialized in design, brand, and market development. The logistical and information technology revolutions had made global sourcing and contract manufacturing the paradigmatic organizational mode of capitalist production. China found a niche as "the workshop of the world," thanks to its large, disciplined, and relatively educated and healthy rural workforce—legacies of the state-socialist period.[15] Therefore, precarious labor in the reform period resulted partly from the historical timing of China's insertion into the global economy, where it has found competitive edge in the lowest nodes of the commodity chain.

Nike, Gap, Apple, Samsung, Walmart, and the likes stand at the commanding height of many "buyer-driven commodity chains" that have extensive networks and elaborate hierarchies of contract manufacturers and subcontractors in China. The despotic factory regime that exploits and disciplines tens of millions of Chinese migrant workers has been the focal concern of China labor studies in the past two decades. In reality, hidden within and beneath this factory regime are many other modes of precarious work. For instance, since the mid-2000s, global and domestic factories have increasingly turned to a new group of vulnerable, informal workers—student interns. In Foxconn and Honda factories, interns, accounting for 15 percent to 50 percent of the workforce, are sent to work, for anywhere from two months to two years.[16] These are students enrolled in vocational schools' nursing, auto maintenance, or business administration programs, but they are sent to these factories as a mandatory part of their training. Working without labor contract or social insurance, doing tasks unrelated to their majors, these workers are not recognized as workers under the Labor Law, although they work and live like other full-time workers.[17]

What has also escaped media and scholarly attention are the layers upon layers of subcontractors working for global contractors in a wide range of industries. Buffering suppliers of global companies from market fluctuations, and concealed in shadowy workplaces are many modalities of informal production arrangements, ambiguous class relations, and precarious livelihoods that defy the binary categorization of "labor" and "capital." Chinese sociologists Huang Yan, Fan Lulu, and Xue Hong have discovered a hidden world of mobile "rush-order" workshops.[18] Kin, familial, and locality ties and trust, not legal contracts, bind workers together as "on-call" mobile but skilled work groups. They show up in subcontractor factories to fulfill particular rush orders. Some even show up in factories with their own sewing machines and production equipment, which they bought from other on-call enterprises that moved on when orders disappeared. Hence the numerous "factory-for-sale" advertisements plastered on public walls in many industrial areas.

Experienced and well-connected workers became micro-entrepreneurs toiling alongside family members in rented workshops. Lacking employment security and insurance protection, but working at an intense pace, rush-order workers reported making more money than regular factory employment, if and when orders existed. These workers and the factories that hired them seldom showed up in industrial statistics. "Most small factories like ours are not registered businesses. We do not issue invoices, so officials from Industry and Commerce Office, as well as the Tax Office, rarely come to visit. But the Labor Department does come to inspect regularly, so we do need to offer a bribe on different occasions, otherwise they will just come to check our labor agreements, pension, child labor, and etc."[19]

Many of these on-call micro-enterprises or worker cooperatives have emerged as vast networks or clusters of production: garments in Humen, Dongguan; electronics assembly in Shijie, Dongguan; leather in Shiling, Huadu District of Guangzhou; lighting fixtures in Gu, Zhongshan; footwear in Wenzhou, Zhejiang; and textiles in Shaoxing, Zhejiang. Native-place networks also bring migrant workers from particular hometowns to corner labor-market niches: workers from Hubei Province's Jingzhou City are engaged in Humen's garment industry, Jiangxi Province's Ganzhou in Dongguan's electronics assembly, and Hunan Province's Shaoyang in Huadu's leather industry.

Construction Workers

Besides China's niche in the global value chain, the centrality of state investment in infrastructure as a motor of economic growth has contributed to a three-decade-long construction boom. Between 1978 and 2008, fixed-asset investment grew from 30 percent to 45 percent of GDP, whereas household consumption dropped from 50 percent to 35 percent.[20] The $570 million stimulus package Beijing rolled out after the global financial crisis in 2008 created another infrastructure construction binge, in a sector already plagued with overcapacity.[21] In 2010, construction accounted for some 25 percent of China's GDP. A steady 30 percent to 50 percent of the 260 million–strong migrant workforce have found employment in construction, which is also the number-one industry employing male migrant workers.[22]

Worldwide, construction is one of the most informally organized industries, thanks to its project-based, mobile nature, its intricate, labor-intensive work process requiring a plethora of skills, and a long tradition of extensive subcontracting through labor brokers. Sarah Swider's book on China's construction workers differentiates three types of informal employment configurations, revealing the slave-like conditions for those workers relegated to the bottom tier of this hierarchy of informal work. The least vulnerable condition, what she calls "mediated employment" is where an employment relationship is established, mediated, and regulated through a contract-labor system based on standardized, widespread, yet informal agreement. Then there are those operating under "embedded employment," which regulates work and workers through social networks. Finally, under "individualized employment," workers find employment through street labor markets and face despotic employment relations regulated through violence or the threat of violence. While the Chinese press and the Chinese government have exposed the rampant problem of the nonpayment of wages experienced by the first two types of informal employment in construction, the blatant abuses suffered by the last category of workers have gone under the radar. Most of the time, these workers work for food and shelter rather than wages. When they get paid, they are paid at a piece rate that requires an inhumane pace of work and long hours. The main control mechanism is violence, and their main alternatives are begging or criminal activities.[23]

Service: Street Vendors, Domestic Workers, and Dispatch Workers

Besides heavy investment in infrastructure, the Chinese state's growth strategy through breakneck urbanization has also generated a sizable informal service economy in its major global and metropolitan cities. At times visible, at times not, subsistence, low-wage, or "wage-less" labor of self-employed petty commodity traders, street vendors, maids, and personal service providers of all kinds meet the cities' consumption and entertainment needs (shopping, strolling, and socializing). In 2010, there were an estimated eighteen million street vendors in China's urban areas, or 5.2 percent of the urban workforce and 16 percent of those in informal urban employment.[24] Many of them worked as street vendors of food, fruit, and consumer commodities, waste and trash sorters, cooks and servers in small restaurants, hair stylists, porters, motorcyclists, itinerant interior-decoration workers, and so forth.[25] Domestic workers, another prevalent mode of informal work, reached twenty million in 2015, according to government statistics.[26] Most of them are middle-aged female migrant workers or laid-off urban workers.

Finally, dispatch workers, or agency workers, emerged only in the late 1990s, when the government encouraged "flexible employment" in response to the mass unemployment induced by the restructuring of state-owned enterprises. By 2012, there were an estimated thirty-seven million dispatch workers, accounting for 13.1 percent of registered employees. The trend of increasing prevalence is particularly visible in the service sector.[27] Even though dispatch workers are defined and regulated by the Labor Contract Law (2008) and their protection augmented in the revised Labor Contract Law (2013), widespread violation and evasion of the law by employers are well documented. Most ironically, state-owned enterprises are found to be major users of dispatch workers.[28]

REGULATION STRUGGLES

In the period of high-growth, export-led development, relational struggle over precarity played out on the terrain of state regulation. A common conceptual error in the literature is that precarious and informal labor is caused or defined by the absence of state regulation. Quite the contrary is true in China and other places where the state is central to the structuring and reproduction of precarity through laws and government policies. Let's mention three examples to illustrate the alignment of state and capital interest in legalizing precarious labor but according them inferior rights and entitlements. First, the Labor Law and the Labor Contract Law stipulate inferior treatments for dispatch workers as opposed to regular workers by defining the dispatch workers relation to employers as one of a "labor service" relation rather than a "labor" relation. As "employees" rather than "workers," dispatch workers are legally excluded from the social insurance and other labor protections stipulated in the Labor Law.[29] Second, the state actively regulates the supply of the massive migrant population (about 250 million today). Their rights and entitlements are stipulated by local government policies in different regions, forming a variety of citizenship regimes that reflect the need of capital for a particular kind of workers.[30] Third, the supply of student interns is orchestrated by the Ministry of Education, vocational school administrators and teachers, and local education departments and is mediated by private labor agencies.[31]

Since China's first-ever National Labor Law took effect in 1995, the legal arena has become the main site of labor struggles. On paper, Chinese labor legislations set such a high standard that according to an OECD report on employment protection, in 2008 China ranked second in employment protection across ten major developing economies and exceeded the OECD average substantially.[32] The problem is that rather than submitting itself to the rule of law, the Chinese state, both central and local, uses law as an opportunistic instrument to achieve policy and political goals. This means that sometimes, some labor laws are enforced if they are in the interest of the government at various levels of the political system. A few official statistics illustrate the gaps between legal rights and actualized rights among migrant workers. In 2014, 62 percent of migrant workers still lacked written contract, 84 percent lacked pension, 83 percent health insurance, and 90 percent unemployment insurance.[33]

The pivotal role of the law is in regulating labor-market and labor relations and channeling labor resistance to the terrains of the law and related bureaucratic institutions. The state uses labor resistance as a "fire alarm" mechanism that alerts local government to particularistic and particularly egregious labor violations.[34] When the volume of labor disputes points toward certain serious abuses by the employers, the Central Government resorts to another round of legislation requiring more stringent labor protection, triggering new responses by employers to bypass new legal constraints on their use of labor. In this process, both the state and employers have common interest in preempting workers from developing collective organization capacity.

Industrial workers have been most prominent in labor unrest. In the 1990s, rust-belt workers took to the street, making moral economic claims often enshrined in state regulations about their health care and pension benefits. In the sun belt, tens of millions of young migrant workers employed in export-oriented factories waged their own struggles against exploitative labor practices and violations of their legal labor rights—nonpayment of wages, excessive overtime, unsafe workplaces, arbitrary dismissal, and dehumanizing shop-floor discipline. In both cases, labor unrest—taking the forms of street protests, public demonstrations, road blockages, strikes, and legal mobilizations—was characterized by localized, workplace-based, cellular activism, privileging socioeconomic demands, and observant of limits set by the law and the state.

On the part of the state, social stability has been maintained by a deft combination of protest bargaining (i.e., buying them off during mobilization), bureaucratic absorption (channeling workers into mediation and court procedures), clientelism (exchanging cooperation for material advantages), cooptation (recruiting workers as party members and sponsoring NGOs under official banners), and selective repression (the arrest and harassment of influential activists as warnings for all).[35] State policies and market development fragment workers' interests and identities, while repression and cooptation have largely been effective in crashing and preempting any attempt at cross-enterprise, cross-class, cross-regional, and cross-sectoral mobilization. Over time, even without institutional empowerment, the volume and persistence of worker activism has created pressure on the state to improve their lot—from the establishment of minimum wage regulations and state provision of minimum livelihood guarantee to the promulgation of various labor laws and steady increases in wages.[36]

Meanwhile, the All-China Federation of Trade Unions (ACFTU), the only legal workers' union in China, is tightly controlled by the Chinese Communist Party at the national and local levels and is dominated by management at the enterprise level. The ACFTU is deeply alienated from its 285 million–strong rank-and-file workers. Union membership typically includes management, from whom most of the union chairs at the enterprise level are appointed or indirectly elected. Unions are financed by a 2 percent payroll tax paid by the enterprise rather than membership dues.[37] Above the enterprise level, union cadres are recruited through the same civil service examination as all other government officials, and they behave and think like government officials. As Eli Friedman writes, "Union officials' first response to strikes is that of an agent of the state: intervene, 'rationally' encourage dialogue, convince the workers the make 'reasonable' demands . . . and perhaps try to persuade management . . . to meet some of the workers' demands."[38] The monopolization or appropriation of worker representation by the party-state deprives Chinese workers of a powerful leverage to bargain with capital, buttressing an institutional foundation for precarious labor to spread in China.

In the shadow of the official trade unions, grassroots labor NGOs have proliferated slowly but steadily since the late 1990s. Nationally, there are an estimated seventy-two or so labor NGOs operating semi-legally in major industrial regions to provide legal counseling, training, and recreation services to migrant workers. Reliant on foreign foundations and domestic donations, established by concerned academics, journalists, or former workers turned rights activists, these NGOs lead a very precarious existence in the legal limbo.[39] Harassment and crackdown by officials and employers, even physical assaults by thugs are commonplace. Most of them pursue a self-limiting form of mobilization: coaching individuals or small groups of workers to make rights claims against the government and thereby raising their consciousness. But once these NGOs go beyond this contained mode of mobilization to actually mobilize workers for collective bargaining or strikes, the government reacts by arresting and imprisoning their most prominent leaders and subjecting them to smear campaigns on national television, as a way to discipline the rest of the NGO sector.[40]

INTO THE VOID: AUTHORITARIANISM IN ECONOMIC DOWNTURN (2010 TO THE PRESENT)

Since the global financial crisis of 2008 and a prolonged downturn in China's traditional export markets, many internal imbalances of the Chinese economic "miracle" have been exacerbated.[41] If sustained economic growth has buttressed the legitimacy of one-party authoritarian rule for three decades, China is certainly entering unchartered waters. Concurrent with what the government has called an *economic* new normal, a *political* new normal—the state's repressive turn against civil society—has also taken roots since 2012, when President Xi Jinping took power. In this new phase of slow growth but augmented authoritarianism, labor will be hard hit. I argue that as more workers fall outside the recognition and regulatory framework of the law, the most salient contested terrain of the social question is shifting to the social reproduction of labor, or livelihood itself. Beyond exploitation, more workers are compelled into relations of dispossession, indebtedness, and exclusion. These relations may reorganize precarious labor's interest and capacity in new ways and spur labor activism to take a more disruptive and volatile turn outside institutionalized and regulated arenas. They may also prompt the state to reform its social protection policies in order to preempt a livelihood crisis for many in a period of economic downturn.

THE "NEW NORMAL"

The Chinese Government has officially announced the end of the high-growth period.[42] The Twelfth Five-Year Plan (2011–2015) recognized that the annual growth in excess of 10 percent (the average over 2003–2010) was unsustainable, and it envisaged the annual growth rate to be around 7 percent, which was further revised down to 6.5 percent in the Thirteenth Five-Year Plan (2016–2020).[43] Plagued by overcapacity in steel and coal and other "zombie" state-owned industries, the government announced in 2015 a scheduled massive laid off of five to six million in 2016.[44] Top officials in Beijing have blamed the Labor Contract Law for creating rigidity and neglecting business interests, while some local governments have frozen wage increases and reduced employers' contribution to social security accounts. The government has signaled its intention to revise the labor law to reduce protection for labor and create more labor-market flexibility in the face of economic slowdown.[45]

But the challenge for the working population is much more complicated than a sheer reduction in aggregate growth rate and lower demand for labor. Besides labor-market exclusion and precarization, I want to note the rise of two other kinds of power relations—dispossession and indebtedness—contributing to a potential crisis in the social reproduction of labor.

Dispossession

In the wake of the 2008 global financial crisis, the Chinese government rolled out an aggressive stimulus package equivalent to 12.5 percent of China's 2008 GDP, to the tune of $586 billion. This unleashed a period of debt-fueled growth whereby local governments borrowed heavily from state banks to fund transport and power infrastructure projects, build housing, and invest in rural health and education. While these measures stabilized the economy in the short run, they also exacerbated the problems of overcapacity and local debts. Local governments have since relied more heavily on selling land to repay the massive debts and interest payments, leading to rampant land grabs, which were intensified by another state policy to stimulate domestic consumption—state-led urbanization. The National New-type Urbanization Plan, announced in 2014, aims to elevate China's urbanization rate from 54 percent to 60 percent of the population by 2020. The rationale is simple: to boost domestic demand and increase consumption.

As a result of land grabs and state-enforced urbanization, a double crisis of land dispossession and unemployment is spreading among farmers, who have moved to the cities from the countryside.[46] Land grabs have happened in 43 percent of the 1,791 villages sampled in a multiyear seventeeen-province survey.[47] One recent ethnographic study depicts the grim reality for migrant workers after their land was dispossessed. In Sichuan, one of the largest labor-sending provinces in China, they became the most undesirable workers for labor brokers in the construction business. Since labor brokers have to underwrite the cost of transportation and living during workers' employment period, and laborers must survive until the end of the year for wages to be paid, landless workers are seen as too precarious for this precarious occupation. "Without land, brokers and laborers face new financial pressure. Brokers must shift recruitment to other sites where laborers hold land and are better able to withstand precarious employment."[48] In short, China's landless migrant workers, now nominally urban residents in townships, find themselves in an emerging underclass position that is even more precarious than the conventional landholding migrant workers.

Indebtedness

Just as jobless growth is a global trend, the Chinese government's response conforms to trends elsewhere—promoting entrepreneurship and the gig economy. To manage popular expectation about a prolonged economic slowdown and to create a culture of entrepreneurship rather than a culture of employment, the Chinese premier announced in his 2015 Government Work Report that "innovative entrepreneurship" is the "new economic normal" for Chinese citizens. From 2014 to 2015, three and a half million new private business entities were formed, 90 percent of them were micro-enterprises in information, software, entertainment, and services.[49] The gig economy has taken off, with a workforce estimated at sixty million in 2016.[50] Different levels of the government have set up funding schemes to encourage "mass entrepreneurship":[51] more than twenty provinces now provide loans, rent subsidies, tax reduction to encourage university graduates to set up micro-enterprises, technological incubators, and online businesses. The increase in both public debt (discussed earlier) and private debt is tantamount to deploying future resources to secure present social peace. The politics of credit will become a major arena of struggle as the debt state and the debt society compete for the allocation of credits. The Chinese government's recent national experiments with using big data to assign social credit rating to all citizens ominously portents the rise of credit as a means of authoritarian control.[52]

Disempowerment

In short, an increasing number of workers face multifaceted precarity—being excluded from the labor market (laid off, unemployed, or underemployed), dispossessed of their land as a means of social security and subsistence, and forced to incur debts in order to launch their micro-business ventures as self-employed entrepreneurs. As the economic pressures on livelihood mount, the political space for collective mobilization and self-organizing is also narrowing. The current top leader, Xi Jinping, compared to his predecessors, Hu Jingtao and Jiang Zemin, has launched exceptionally harsh, widespread, and repressive crackdowns on the human rights and NGO communities. Reversing Hu's emphasis on social harmony and Jiang's on rule of law and internationalization, Xi has announced zero tolerance for dissent and has demanded total submission both at the elite and grassroots levels in the media and education arenas. Anticorruption campaigns are used selectively to target his political opponents at the top. Arrests and imprisonment of rights lawyers and labor NGO activists have had chilling effects on worker capacity, just as some labor activists have begun taking bolder action beyond cellular and legal mobilization.

PRECARIATS' STRUGGLES FOR LIVELIHOOD

Since around 2010, economic downturns, plant relocations, and restructurings have contributed to a rising trend of strikes in the formal sector. In the wake of some high-profile strikes in foreign-invested companies making global consumer products, such as Honda, Foxconn, IBM, and Yue Yuen, some journalists and scholars of Chinese labor saw a tendency of labor empowerment. Their argument, in a nutshell, is that the second generation of migrant workers are more conscious of class and rights and savvy about social media and technology, demanding union representation in addition to increased compensation and adopting an extra-legal action repertoire. Yet closer empirical analyses of the processes and outcomes of these strikes conveyed quite a different picture. Except on the issue of wage increases, workers did not make any lasting gain in union election, security of employment, and workplace reforms. Also, action based around single factories is still the norm, and so is workers' concern to stay within the boundary of the law in their action. There is no evidence to show that second-generation workers are more prone to collective action than the first generation.[53]

A critical and new development was emerging around the time of these attention-grabbing strikes, but away from the media limelight. In the past five years, a dozen or so grassroots NGOs, after years of providing individual rights–based legal assistance to workers, sought to augment their impacts by mobilizing workers to undertake worker-led collective bargaining with their employers. With the financial support of labor groups outside of China and legal advice of rights lawyers within China, daring NGO activists built networks of worker activists across factories and recruited cross-class participation by students and academics in sustaining strikes. NGO activists coined a new term "labor movement NGOs" to distinguish themselves from their former self as service providing NGOs. They provided moral, legal, and training support to striking workers and, most impressively, liaised worker leaders from different factories to share their experience in bargaining with employers and organizing workers. Labor scholar Li Chun-yun has documented forty-two strikes in South China between 2011 to 2014 involving eleven labor movement NGOs.[54] However, in late 2015, Xi Jinping's government reacted by arresting key labor NGO leaders and orchestrated smear campaigns against them and their organizations on national television, stifling the confidence and capacity of a budding worker movement. It is uncertain whether repression under the political new normal will end up thwarting or radicalizing these NGOs.

Even as the political space for grassroots NGOs is curtailed, self-mobilized worker struggles have continued. A new tendency is that workers' demands have increasingly turned toward issues of pension, housing, and livelihood, or the social reproduction of labor. As the first generation of migrant workers approach retirement age, they have become more vigilant about employers' making the legally required contributions to their pension and housing funds. Rustbelt state-sector workers newly laid off by the state's call to reduce overcapacity also demanded en mass for the state to protect their livelihood and retirement. For informal workers who occupy the blurred boundaries between capital and labor, employed and self-employed, their demands are framed and experienced broadly as crisis of livelihood. For instance, in 2015, a wave of taxi driver strikes hit major cities in coastal and interior provinces due to the competition of on-demand app-based car services. Even though taxi drivers are self-employed—they own the means of production (taxis), pay for their own gasoline and car insurance and maintenance, and are not employees of taxi companies—they have to pay a fixed "membership fee" every month to their company in order to participate in this semi-monopolistic industry. The competition of on-demand drivers threatens taxi drivers' livelihood and survival, which is how they described the reasons for their strikes.

In cities, government encroachments on the use of the "urban commons" are increasingly depriving precarious workers a crucial resource for their subsistence economy in the Chinese cities. Street vendors' clashes with *chengguan,* a para–police force first set up in the late 1990s, at times turned violent and escalated into mass protests involving local residents resentful of official brutality.[55] In Zengcheng in 2011, the scuffle between a pregnant female street vendor and the *chengguan* turned into several days of riots by migrant informal workers, who burned government offices and destroyed police cars. In a much smaller scale, violence clashes erupted in 2013 between citizens and police after the death of a watermelon vendor who was attacked by the *chengguan* in Linwu, a city in Hunan province.[56] Such dynamics are reminiscent of the unanticipated consequences of a street vendor's self-immolation in Tunisia in January 2011, which touched off a powerful political tsunami throughout the Arab world.

Another scenario is also possible. While the struggles of precarious workers have the potential to be more violent, volatile, and less institutionally incorporated, workers can easily become more atomized and acquiescent. This is so not just because of the frequent change of jobs, depriving them of stable social relations and spatial concentration and communication. As workers cobble together various sources of incomes and resources, their interests (whether based on market or production) are also differentiated and fragmented.[57] Finally, we cannot underestimate the responsiveness of the Chinese state. Despite its autocratic politics, the state has a track record of weathering many socioeconomic crises by responding to social discontents with policy innovations in order to maintain social stability. As it has done so in the past in both rural and urban China, the state has been compelled by popular unrest to gradually develop and strengthen social and welfare policies to protect the livelihood of the most vulnerable citizens.[58] As the gig economy grows, boundaries of labor and capital are blurred, and livelihood pressures increase for the general citizenry, the regime may be compelled once again to find policy solutions.

CONCLUSION

Defining the social question as relational struggles over precarity, we can see a shift in the most salient terrain of contestation from recognition to regulation and now social reproduction of labor, as China evolved from a state-socialist political economy to one of high-growth market economy and then to a new normal of slow, job-scarce growth, overcapacity, and enhanced authoritarianism. The driver of precarity in each period also differs, shaping workers' interests, capacities, and claims. This chapter is a reminder of the tenacious salience of the social question in China, even if there is no denying that China's capitalist boom has lifted millions out of *absolute* poverty (declining from 84 percent to 16 percent of population between 1981 and 2005). Echoing a point made in the introduction, poverty reduction does not nullify the existence and politics of precarity, if only because workers everywhere experience and act on precarity in relative and relational ways. Precarity, or the social question, and the struggles emanating from and against it, should always be theorized in historical, cultural, and context-specific terms.

NOTES

1. George Steinmetz, *Regulating the Social: The Welfare State and Local Politics in Imperial Germany* (Princeton, NJ: Princeton University Press, 1993).

2. Jan Breman and Marcel van der Linden, "Informalizing the Economy: The Return of the Social at a Global Level," *Development and Change* 45, no. 4 (2014): 920–40.

3. Andrew Walder, *Communist Neo-Traditionalism: Work and Authority in Chinese Industry* (Berkeley: University of California Press, 1986).

4. Barry Naughton, *The Chinese Economy: Transitions and Growth* (Cambridge, MA: MIT Press), 182.

5. Mark Selden, *The Political Economy of Chinese Development* (Armonk, NY: M. E. Sharpe, 1993), chaps. 5 and 6; Ching Kwan Lee and Mark Selden, "Inequality and Its Enemies in Revolutionary and Reform China," *Economic and Political Weekly*, December 27, 2008.

6. Martin Whyte, ed., *One Country, Two Societies: Rural-Urban Inequality in Contemporary China* (Cambridge, MA: Harvard University Press, 2010).

7. Elizabeth J. Perry, "Labor's Love Lost: Worker Militancy in Communist China," *International Labor and Working-Class History* 50 (1996): 67.

8. Walder, *Communist Neo-Traditionalism*, 41.

9. Lynn T. White III, "Workers' Politics in Shanghai," *Journal of Asian Studies* 36, no. 1 (1976): 99–116, 115.

10. Elizabeth J. Perry, "Shanghai's Strike Wave of 1957," *The China Quarterly* 137 (1994): 1–27.

11. Jackie Sheehan, *Chinese Workers: A New History* (London: Routledge, 1998), 121.

12. Perry, "Shanghai's Strike Wave of 1957."

13. Sebastian Heilmann, "The Social Context of Mobilization in China: Factions, Work Units and Activists During the 1976 April Fifth Movement," *China Information* 8 (Winter 1993–94): 1–19.

14. Ching Kwan Lee, *Against the Law: Labor Protests in China's Rustbelt and Sunbelt* (Berkeley: University of California Press, 2007).

15. Giovanni Arrighi, *Adam Smith in Beijing* (London: Verso, 2008).

16. Jenny Chan, Pun Ngai, and Mark Selden, "Interns or Workers: China's Student Labor Regime," *Asia-Pacific Journal* 13, iss. 36, no. 2, (2015).

17. The supply of student interns as a source of precarious labor has resulted from the commodification of vocational education and the collusion between local government and powerful multinational corporations. Vocational schools have been privatized since the late 1990s, and in return for the internship programs, schools received equipment, trainers, and funding. Local governments competed with each other to lure big investors like Foxconn to move to their localities, and promised

companies a steady supply of interns. See Yihui Su, "Student Workers in the Foxconn Empire: The Commodification of Education and Labor in China," *Journal of Workplace Rights* 15, nos. 3–4 (2011): 341–62.

18. Huang Yan, "Rush Order Game beyond the Factory: The Case of Rush Production in the Pearl River Delta," *Sociological Research* 4 (2012): 187–203 [in Chinese]; Fan Lulu and Xue Hong, "The Self-Organization and the Power of Female Informal Workers: A Case Study of the Cooperative Production Team in the Garment Industry in the Yangtze River Delta," *Rural China* 14, no. 1 (2017).

19. Huang Yan, "Rush Order Game," 198.

20. Justin Lin, "Demystifying the Chinese Economy," http://siteresources.worldbank.org/DEC/Resources/84797-1104785060319/598886-1104852366603/599473-1223731755312/Speech-on-Demystifying-the-Chinese-Economy.pdf, 9.

21. Barry Naughton, "Understanding the Chinese Stimulus Package," *China Leadership Monitor* 28, May 2009.

22. Sarah Swider, *Building China: Informal Work and the New Precariat* (Ithaca, NY: Cornell University Press, 2015), 4–5.

23. Ibid., 92 and 94.

24. Huang Geng-zhi, *The Socio-Economic Roots and Spatial Politics of City Street Vendors* (Beijing: The Commercial Press, 2015), 64 [in Chinese].

25. For ethnographic depictions, see Guang Lei, "Guerrilla Workfare: Migrant Renovators, State Power and Informal Work in Urban China," *Politics and Society* 33, no. 3 (2005): 481–506; Michelle Dammon Loyalka, *Eating Bitterness: Stories from the Front Lines of China's Great Urban Migration* (Berkeley: University of California Press, 2012); and Hsiao-hung Pai, *Scattered Sand: The Story of China's Rural Migrants* (London: Verso, 2012).

26. Ma Dan, "A Labor Process Analysis of Domestic Labor in Beijing" *Chinese Workers* 2 (2015), http://images.mofcom.gov.cn/fms/201509/20150929164306092.pdf [in Chinese].

27. All China Federation of Trade Unions, 2011 report on working conditions of dispatch workers in China, [in Chinese], www.waljob.net/article/6225.html.

28. Juliana So, "Exploring the Plight of Dispatch Workers in China and How to Improve their Conditions: A Preliminary Study," *Journal of Labor and Society*, 17, no. 4 (2014); 531–52.

29. Irene Pang, "The Legal Construction of Precarity: Lessons from the Construction Sectors in Beijing and Delhi," *Critical Sociology*, forthcoming, https://doi.org/10.1177/0896920518792615.

30. Jieh-min Wu, "Migrant Citizenship Regimes in Globalized China: A Historical-Institutional Comparison," *Rural China* 14, no. 1 (2017).

31. Jenny Chan, "Intern Labor in China," *Rural China* 14, no. 1 (2017).

32. Mary Gallagher, "China's Workers Movement and the End of the Rapid-Growth Era," *Daedalus* 143, no. 2 (2014): 81–95.

33. Kevin Li, "Rising Inequality and Its Discontents in China" *New Labor Forum*, 25, no. 3 (2016): 69.

34. Gallagher, "China's Workers Movement."

35. Lee and Zhang, May 2013.

36. Dorothy Solinger, *State's Gains, Labor's Losses* (Ithaca, NY: Cornell University Press, 2009).

37. Eli Friedman, *Insurgency Trap: Labor Politics in Postsocialist China* (Ithaca, NY: Cornell University Press, 2014).

38. Ibid., 55.

39. Diana Fu, *Mobilizing without the Masses: Control and Contention in China* (Cambridge: Cambridge University Press, 2018).

40. Ching Kwan Lee, "After the Miracle: Labor Politics under China's New Normal" *Catalyst* 1, no. 3 (2017): 92–115.

41. Ho-fung Hung, *The China Boom: Why China Will Not Rule the World* (New York: Columbia University Press, 2015).

42. Keith Bradsher, "In China, Sobering Signs of Slower Growth, *New York Times,* March 5, 2012, www.nytimes.com/2012/03/06/business/global/in-china-sobering-signs-of-a-slower-growth.html.

43. "China's Priorities for the Next Five Years," *China Business Review,* July 1, 2010, www.chinabusinessreview.com/chinas-priorities-for-the-next-five-years; "The 13th Five-Year Plan: Xi Jinping Reiterates His Vision for China," http://www.iberchina.org/files/13-five-year-plan.pdf.

44. Benjamin Kang Lim, Matthew Miller, and David Stanway, "Exclusive: China to Lay Off Five to Six Million Workers, Earmarks at Least $23 Billion," *Reuters,* March 1, 2016, www.reuters.com/article/us-china-economy-layoffs-exclusive-idUSKCN0W33DS.

45. Chun Han Wong, "China Looks to Loosen Job Security Law in the Face of Slowing Economic Growth," *Wall Street Journal,* November 29, 2016. www.wsj.com/articles/china-looks-to-loosen-job-security-law-in-face-of-slowing-economic-growth-1480415405.

46. By law, every rural resident is entitled to a plot of land in her native village, owned and allocated by the village collective to which she is a member by birth and farmed by family members who remain in the village. Up until the turn of the new millennium, this family economy, while dependent on migrant workers' wage income for agricultural inputs, has absorbed the cost of the social reproduction of labor—schooling, health care, marriage, childbirth, permanent housing, subsistence during unemployment, and retirement—that would otherwise have to been borne by employers or the government. Since the 1990s, marketization of land use right and the formal preservation of collective ownership have together created a perfect storm, leading to a forceful wave of *de jure* or *de facto* land dispossession, depriving migrant workers of their most important means of long-term security. Typically, the compensation paid to affected farmers (average $17,850 per acre) amounts to just a fraction of the mean price authorities received for leasing the land (average $740,000 per acre for commercial projects).

47. Landesa, "Research Report: Summary 2011 17-Province Survey's Findings," April 26, 2012, www.landesa.org/china-survey-6.

48. Julia Chuang, "Urbanization through Dispossession: Survival and Stratification in China's New Townships," *Journal of Peasant Studies* 42, no. 2 (2015): 275–94.

49. Rungain Think Tank of Enterpreneurship, "2015 Report on China's Innovative Entrepreneurship."

50. *2017 Report on China's Sharing Economy* (Beijing: National Data Center and Center for the Study of Sharing Economy) [in Chinese], http://www.sic.gov.cn/archiver/SIC/UpFile/Files/Default/20170306164936642988.pdf.

51. "Uber to Get More Women on the Road," *China Daily,* March 3, 2016, 18.

52. Josh Chin and Gillian Wong, "China's New Tool for Social Control: A Credit-Rating for Everything," *Wall Street Journal,* November 28, 2016, www.wsj.com/articles/chinas-new-tool-for-social-control-a-credit-rating-for-everything-1480351590.

53. Ching Kwan Lee, "Precarization or Empowerment: Reflections on Recent Labor Unrest in China," *Journal of Asian Studies* 75, no. 2 (2016).

54. Li Chunyun, "Unmaking the Authoritarian Labor Regime: Collective Bargaining and Labor Unrest in Contemporary China," PhD Dissertation, Rutgers University, 2016.

55. Sarah Swider, "Reshaping China's Urban Citizenship: Street Vendors, *Chengguan* and Struggles over the Right to the City," *Critical Sociology* 41, nos. 4–5 (2015).

56. Andrew Jacobs, "Death of Watermelon Vendor Sets Off Outcry in China," *New York Times,* July 20, 2013, www.nytimes.com/2013/07/21/world/asia/death-in-china-stirs-anger-over-urban-rule-enforcers.html.

57. Wang Jianhua, "Dependent Government-Corporate Relations, Local Employment and Labor Contentions in Inland City," unpublished ms., October 2016.

58. For the spread of social assistance program in the Global South, including China, in the past two decades, see Kevan Harris and Ben Scully, "A Hidden Counter-movement? Precarity, Politics, and Social Protection Before and Beyond the Neoliberal Era," *Theory and Society* 44 (2015): 415–44.

5

Migrants, Mobilizations, and Selective Hegemony in Mekong Asia's Special Economic Zones

Dennis Arnold

INTRODUCTION

Numerous industrializing economies have failed to transition from low- to high-value-added manufacturing. In these countries, there is limited evidence that the promise of well-remunerated wage labor and comprehensive social security is likely to be realized anytime soon. Mekong (continental) Southeast Asia is one such region, in which the social question is imbricated with low-value-added accumulation models. Indeed, the potential for product or functional upgrading remains extremely limited in Cambodia, Laos, and Myanmar, while both Thailand and Vietnam struggle to "escape" the middle-income trap. Industrial centers in these countries draw on domestic and cross-border migrants, and, increasingly, special economic zones (SEZs) are being established in rural and border areas to avail of congested labor at the bottom of the rural economy. In mainstream development planning, manufacturing-led development utilizes "pro-poor" economic growth paradigms anchored in SEZs, yet local labor regimes of informality and precarity reproduce poverty rather than ameliorate it. The evident contradiction between the promise and reality of contemporary development strategies has led to disillusionment with industrial employment among affected workers and growing political tensions at sites of low-wage industrial labor. How, we thus need to ask, do states, development planners, and workers adapt to and address the failure to address pressing social concerns?

This question is addressed through case studies of border SEZs in Cambodia and Thailand. At first blush, these two economies are quite different, with Thailand's GDP at $406.8 billion and Cambodia's at $20.2 billion. The Thai economy is more diversified, with industrial exports including electronics, agricultural commodities, automobiles and parts, and processed foods. Cambodia, on the other hand, lacks diversity, and its economic "growth pillars" are restricted to textile and garment manufacturing, construction, agro-industry, and tourism. Garment manufacturing makes up roughly 70 percent of total exports, and over-reliance on this volatile sector for export revenue and employment presents a developmental challenge. The two economies are similar in that they are both characterized by low potential for value capture; low levels of firm, labor, and state stability; and a high degree of external dependency in directing strategic coupling.[1] As such, they rely heavily upon highly precarious gendered and immigrant workforces. Labor feminization and the use of migrant labor act as a powerful mechanism for controlling and disciplining the workforce, while typically favoring the spatial detachment of labor production from social reproduction and thus the spatial externalization of the costs of social reproduction to realms that are outside industrial sites.[2]

Bearing these economic development challenges in mind, the social question is analyzed through the selective hegemony lens to understanding how forms of capitalist socialization do not result in a form of hegemony that might extend to "the whole of society."[3] Rather, there is a discernable disconnect between state legitimacy derived from increases in productivity and linked economic growth, and legitimacy derived through hegemonic projects that offer (limited) concessions to particular groups linked to popular sovereignty. Faced with pressing social reproduction demands unmet through selective policies, I identify two prominent forms of workers' countermovements. The first is characterized by expanded mobility that contributes to labor shortages, and thus undermines capital-accumulation strategies, while the second is increasingly militant wage protests, which spill out of the preapproved tripartite channels.

The cases examined below highlights how the localized regimes of informality reproduce poverty and the ways in which state and international organizations selectively respond to countermovements. Prominent state responses include the introduction of social protection policies for both manufacturing and cross-border migrant workers. Social protection policies are at times utilized to acquire greater control over migrant labor forces, while in other cases they are utilized to depoliticize a dismal status of the laboring poor in light manufacturing—concessions that neither carry over to other occupations nor ameliorate pressing social reproduction concerns. A second top-down response is the proliferation of border SEZs. Zones are framed as panacea for development that couple regional economic growth with access to formal employment, yet are more usefully conceived of as spatial containers of countermovements that challenge low-value-added accumulation regimes. Zones further institutionalize poverty through informalized labor regimes that absorb congested labor at the bottom of the subregional rural economy. Far from a resolution, selective hegemony, like any hegemonic project, is fraught with tensions that, in the cases examined, scale up from border nodes to the subregional scale.

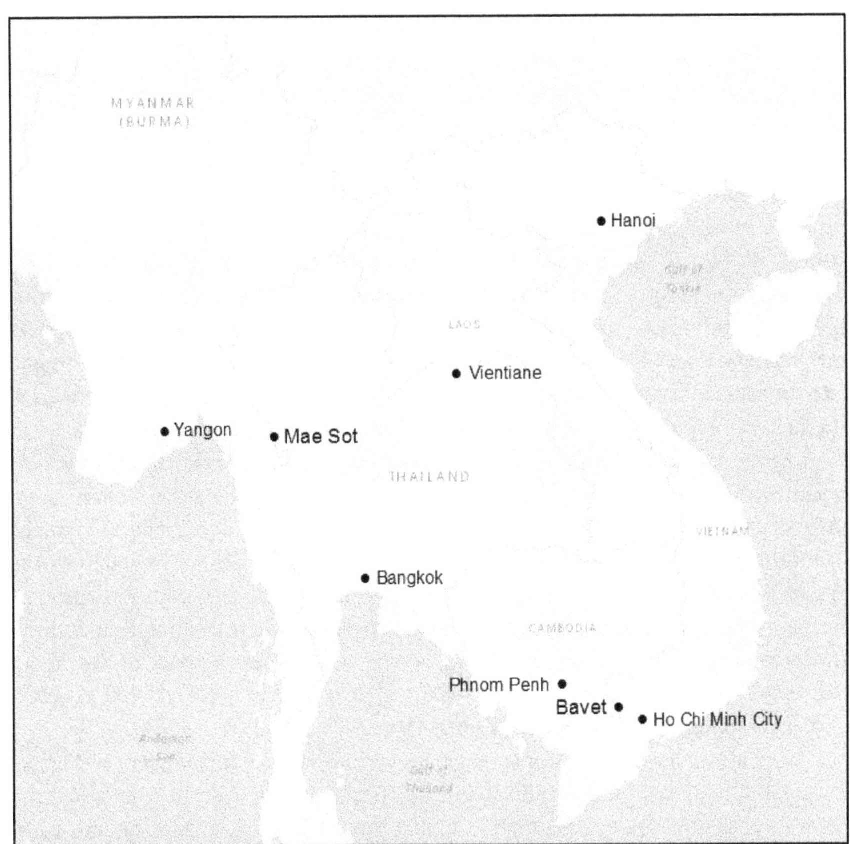

MAP 5.1. Mekong Asia.

SELECTIVE HEGEMONY AND THE SOCIAL QUESTION

Studying the social question through particular localized labor regimes of informality that are embedded in wider national and subregional political economic relations presents both methodological and theoretical challenges. To address a multi-sited, multi-scalar analysis, the relational comparison as developed by Gilian Hart is utilized to provide a conception of place as nodal points of connection in socially produced space.[4] This concept helps researchers move beyond case studies to make broader claims in a non-positivist understanding of generality. Hart asserts that "particularities or specificities arise through *interrelations* between objects, events, places, and identities; and it is through clarifying how these relations are produced and changed in practice that close study of a particular part can generate broader claims and understandings."[5] Such an approach rejects notions of global impacts on the local. The objective is not to analyze different particular cases as local or national variants of general "global" processes. Rather, it helps to focus on how particularities co-constitute the power-laden interplay between the different institutional interests and actors involved, where agendas are mediated for specific political economic objectives through a mix of distanciated and embedded actors.[6]

This approach is salient in Mekong Asia, a subregional economy in which the promise of full employment and social welfare remain far removed. It is in this context that the social question in Mekong Asia should be viewed. Social security policies in Mekong Asia are characterized by the forty-year running attention to the formal-informal economy binary, with the formal held up as a protected institutional space, and informal labor more prone to the uncertainties of the unregulated market.[7] "Inclusion" in textile-, garment-, and shoe-production networks, the primary focus of this article, is often upheld as an inherent good, with wage earning under an employer-employee contract, from one ontological position, deciding the boundary between inclusion and exclusion, privilege and marginality, prosperity and poverty.[8] Yet for the majority in Mekong Asia, formal employment is not the way out of poverty; rather, it is the informalized manner in which workers are included that reproduces poverty. Indeed, poverty is structured through formal labor markets, countering common perspectives in the region that exclude the formally employed from definitions of "the poor."[9] The existence of the laboring poor is not a policy oversight or technical error, but integral to labor regimes and development paradigms in Mekong Asia.

The continued reliance on low-wage, precarious labor informs state and international development interventions and efforts to enhance selected targets to optimize their comparative advantage in global production networks. This includes, for instance, promoting export manufacturing and the establishment of SEZs. Such targeted, spatially regulated interventions do not set out to resolve wider issues of social inequalities. Aihwa Ong's work has contributed to theorizations on such heterogeneous state spatial strategies to accommodate particular forms of globalized capital accumulation and population management that are deemed necessary to foster growth and reproduce state legitimacy.[10] The state goal, Ong explains through the China case, is to manipulate the political situation in order to achieve an implicit state-society bargain that trades acceptance of (authoritarian) political rule for sustained improvements in economic and social well-being. The state, in its multifaceted embroilment with global capital, she contends, cannot be frozen in a posture of opposition to the masses but must strategically intervene in unstable conditions, one moment acting as a draconian oppressor of workers, the next as a protector of labor against the depredations of global capital.

This approach links social space to capital accumulation strategies, implicitly addressing state practices of coercion and consent. This theorization marks the shift away from political economic regulation in which nationally bounded policy attends to a coherent body politic. In sum, Ong's approach is useful in drawing attention to state efforts that set out to enhance the comparative advantages of specific subnational zones, lead economic sectors, and laboring populations at the expense of broadly coordinated interventions across an entire national territory, thus highlighting a shift in the scale at which development is targeted. What ends up being missed from this perspective are the conflicting claims to the right and legitimacy to rule, which frustrate the unified implementation of any state projects.[11] Hence, the statecraft optic that privileges the determinative role of state and capital risks obscuring the power workers and other actors may have to reshape social relations through countermovements.

In this regard, Gavin Smith offers a useful critique of Ong's theorizations on "variegated" state effects, specifically, that she overlooks "the dialectical interplay between people and production in terms of an ongoing struggle emanating from a contradiction that becomes a perpetual preoccupation for the state."[12] Selective hegemony as developed by Smith helps in unpacking forms of consent (concessions) and coercion (violence) directed at particular groups of workers based on perceived value of their labor and/or the threat their countermovements pose. His intervention helps in understanding how forms of capitalist socialization do not result in a form of hegemony that might extend to "the whole of society." Rather, it points to the potential for disconnect between state legitimacy derived from increases in productivity and linked economic growth with legitimacy derived from hegemonic projects that offer (limited) concessions to particular groups linked to popular sovereignty, including the gradual rollout of social protection policies across the Mekong subregion.

THE CAMBODIA CASE

UN-mediated elections in 1993 signaled the end of nearly three decades of war in Cambodia. Cambodia entered the neoliberal global economy with an eviscerated state, ruined infrastructure, and social disintegration. Since that time, the ruling Cambodian People's Party (CPP) has maintained legitimacy by staving off war and facilitating rapid economic growth. Yet this has been called into question as the country continues to lag behind its neighbors in terms of life expectancy, poverty alleviation, education, and other core socioeconomic concerns.

As previously stated, Cambodia's economy currently lacks diversity. Although the country remains largely agrarian, with 70 percent of the population living in rural areas (NIS and ILO 2013),[13] Cambodia's recent urbanization rate has been one of the world's most rapid, with Phnom Penh's population tripling in the past twenty years. Across rural Cambodia, nearly one in four households has at least one working-age member emigrate, with nearly 60 percent of younger migrants moving to urban areas in Cambodia.[14] Rural-urban migrants' interests and identities remain largely agrarian in orientation, with non-farm work centered on contributing to rural household livelihoods. When factoring agricultural work,

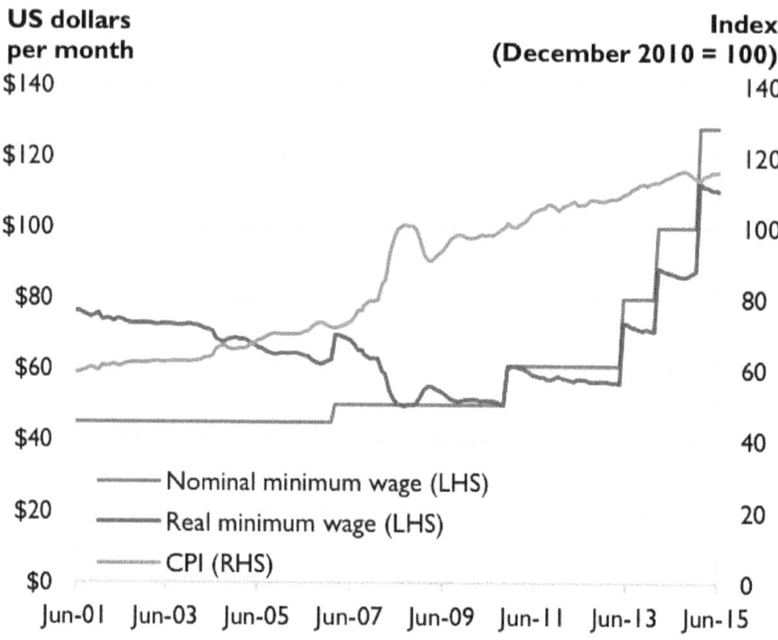

FIGURE 5.1. Nominal and real minimum wage of garment and footwear sector, 2000–2015 (US$ per month). Source: ILO 2015.

60.2 percent were in informal employment, followed by 33.3 percent in agriculture, and 6.5 percent in formal employment.[15] Although unemployment rates remain low and even fell further over the past decade, and GDP growth robust for over a decade, averaging roughly 7 percent, it has not lifted all boats, highlighting the need for comprehensive social and labor protections.

Social security initiatives

Low-value-added garment and shoe manufacturing has come to be a mainstay of Cambodia's development strategy. Employment has increased from roughly twenty thousand in 1994 to some seven hundred thousand in 2016. Figure 2 shows that real minimum wage stagnated and even declined between 2001–2013, paradoxically while the ILO and International Finance Corporation, U.S. Department of Labor, and numerous international apparel buyers have branded garment manufacturing in Cambodia as "fair" or "ethical" due to a high-profile ILO factory-monitoring regime.[16] Despite efforts to monitor work conditions in export garment factories, wages have remained low and, along with the proliferation of fixed duration contracts and excessive overtime shifts, they form the country's primary competitive advantage in global garment production networks. In other words, Cambodia's labor rights monitoring regime has aimed to repackage dead-end jobs that treat the developing-world woman's body as a site of exploitation and disposability into exemplars of the export-led development project.[17]

Cambodia's export garment industry has largely been concentrated in the Phnom Penh vicinity. In recent years there has been an explicit effort to decentralize garment production through a nation-wide SEZ program initiated in 2005. Research by the author conducted in Bavet between 2009 and 2015 points to a workforce sharing many of the same wage and working condition concerns as those employed in other parts of the country, in addition to unique features as proletarians of a particular kind. According to a 2015 survey of one hundred factory workers in Cambodia, including twenty-one in Bavet, 90 percent of Bavet factory workers do agricultural work at various times of the year, while only 12.7 percent of garment workers in the Phnom Penh vicinity report any farming activities. In Bavet, 71.4 percent of workers or their spouse own land (66 percent below one hectare, 20 percent one to two hectares), while 10 percent of Phnom Penh garment workers report land ownership (86 percent below one hectare). In Bavet, 60 percent of respondents sell over half of their agricultural produce on the market, 13 percent report selling half on the market and keeping half for personal consumption, and 27 percent consume all their crops. All of the surveyed Bavet workers' parents own land, while 70 percent of Phnom Penh workers' parents are landowners. When asked to estimate their remittances as proportion of household income—Phnom Penh workers reported, an average, 19 percent of family total, while in Bavet, it is nearly 50 percent. This can be attributed to roughly equivalent wage levels, while most workers in Bavet commute daily from the family farm/home rather than rent accommodation, as is common in Phnom Penh and vicinity. The Manhattan SEZ marketing director noted in a November 2014 interview that most workers commute at least one hour each way to and from work in the zones, while ten Bavet SEZ workers interviewed at the same time all commute two hours each way to work in the factories, noting this is quite common. Combined, the interviews and survey points to a workforce in Bavet that is literally living with one foot in the industrial and the other in the rural-agrarian realm.

Workers in Bavet are poor but not destitute; they are at the fringes of the relative surplus population. They are precariously positioned between small landholdings, with their limited livelihood potential, and low-paying work in firms in an SEZ that is struggling to maintain its grip on bottom rungs of the global economy, as discussed in further detail below. Both agrarian and industrial livelihoods could diminish or dissolve without a sufficient replacement or effective social safety net. Frustrated with limited wage gains and virtually no welfare gains in national tripartite forums, workers in Bavet and elsewhere have become increasingly militant in their demands. The number of strikes nationwide rose dramatically between 2010 and 2013—up nearly 250 percent.[18] Several strikes were met with coercion, the first of several armed responses by authorities occurring in Bavet. On February 20,

2012, Chhouk Bandith, then governor of Bavet, opened fire on a crowd of roughly six thousand protesters at the Manhattan SEZ in Bavet, outside the Kaoway Sports shoe factory, a Puma supplier.[19] Two were shot in the hand, and one nearly died after a bullet punctured her lung, barely missing the heart. Furthermore, nationwide garment workers' strikes have occurred in September 2010 and again in December 2013–January 2014, both sparked by the breakdown of national wage negotiations. The latter nationwide strike turned violent, and police armed with AK-47s fired on a crowd of protesters outside the Canadia Industrial Zone in Phnom Penh on 2 January 2014.[20] Five protesters were killed, over thirty-eight were shot or suffered other wounds, and thirteen were arrested.[21] These incidences of state violence in industrial zones and SEZs demonstrate that maintaining a docile labor force is critical to maintain investor confidence in the country's garment sector.[22]

The growing workers' movement had begun to coalesce with the opposition Cambodia National Rescue Party during the 2013–2014 protests, contributing to a reformulated position by Cambodian People's Party. First, the minimum wage has increased from US$80 per month in 2013 to $170 in 2018, which applies only to the textile-, garment-, and shoe-manufacturing sectors. Ministry of Labor and Vocational Training spokesperson Heng Sour asserted in a January 2015 interview that a range of initiatives should be considered alongside recent minimum-wage increases. Foremost, the government implemented its health care scheme in mid-2015. In the first phase, one hundred thousand workers are expected to take part, restricted to factory workers in Phnom Penh and the immediate vicinity (interview, Malika Ok).[23] According to Sour, a government survey found that, on average, workers spend 10 percent of their wage on health care. With the new health care scheme, workers and employers will each contribute 2 percent and the government 6 percent, meaning workers can save 8 percent for other expenditures. Furthermore, in early 2015, Prime Minister Hun Sen announced an initiative that aims to lower electricity costs for workers to 610 riel—they now typically pay 2,000 riel per unit (roughly $0.50) in urban areas—and in January 2015, the government increased the income tax threshold to $200. Finally, the government also promises to look into rental and housing issues—as rents typically increase along with pay raises, nullifying wage gains. Social security pensions, as specified in the Social Security Law (2002) were planned for introduction in 2015.[24] However, an ILO representative noted in a January 2015 interview that benefit provisions have not yet been developed.[25] There are no government-backed employment creation programs or unemployment programs in Cambodia, but small-scale donor-run food-for-work programs exist in rural areas. All said, according to Heng Sour's calculations, $135 is what workers are actually getting, when considering these social benefits (compared to the $128 minimum wage at the time of the interview).

While important concessions, these gains fall short of addressing core poverty concerns. protection measures—excluding minimum wages applicable to the entire garment- and shoe-manufacturing sectors—target workers in Phnom Penh and vicinity, and there is limited evidence that the pilot programs will scale up, meaning that workers in places like Bavet are excluded. In short, concessions have the effect of delimiting potentially politicized redistributive demands in urban areas that could be linked up with broad-based social movements. The hegemonic imperatives are selective in that they target only urban, formal sector workers.[26] Another shortcoming of protection policy is it does not take into consideration workers' geographic and labor-market mobility. A trade union leader estimates that workers are employed in garments, on average, for five to seven years (interview, Kong Athit, January 2015). Thus, the initiative presumes fixed occupational identity and time horizons that stretch well beyond what is the norm for a Cambodian garment worker. By selectively targeting a specific sector in Phnom Penh, the state is able to blunt criticism that it has failed to address workers' concerns, yet it does not address the manner in which poverty is structured through participation in the formal labor market. Rather, it offers insufficient wage gains and restricted social insurance that reinforce the outsourcing of social reproduction to the rural-remittance economy.

THE THAILAND-MYANMAR BORDER CASE

For over two decades, Mae Sot has been a prominent migrant-labor and refugee hub, and it is a window into Thailand's migrant-regulation practices. Burmese refugees living along the Thai border currently number over two hundred thousand. Alongside this, large numbers of Burmese have been migrating to Thailand for work, from the tens of thousands in the early 1990s to some three million today. The regional transformation from refugee to labor-migrant flows are far from linear, yet are central to understanding the place of migrants in the Thai body politic, a process in which social protection increasingly plays a role.

Mae Sot is a border district in Tak Province across the Moei River from Myawaddy, Myanmar; it is roughly five hundred kilometers northwest of Bangkok (see map 5.1). The Mae Sot regional economy remains tethered to neighboring Myanmar, where militarization and agricultural management are central to contemporary migration trends. Agricultural policies in central Myanmar, which forced farmers in areas long under military control to sell a fixed proportion of their crops to the Tatmadaw (military) below market prices, contributed to extreme poverty in the rural economy. Fujita concludes, based on case studies in Yangon and Bago Divisions (areas in central Myanmar), that peasants and farm laborers "were reduced to a bare subsistence level during the last two or three decades, and are now suffering 'absolute poverty.'"[27] Alongside this, in the 1990s the Tatmadaw consolidated control over most of the Myanmar-Thailand border areas by forcibly relocating villages, which led to rapidly increasing numbers of internal and international refugees and migrant workers.[28]

In the mid-1990s Burmese migrant workers and refugees in Thailand came predominantly from border areas.[29] In the 2000s, as the economic situation continued to deteriorate, migrant networks and recruitment expanded, and as the need for migrant labor in Thailand deepened, they increasingly came from all over Myanmar. This trend has continued seemingly unabated with the reintroduction of (partial) electoral democracy in Myanmar in 2015. Burmese migrants are located throughout Thailand and remain a critical component of the Thai economy, working in sectors including light manufacturing, agriculture, fisheries and seafood processing, domestic work, and construction. In sum, both the successive military regimes and the current National League for Democracy–led government have outsourced the financing of social reproduction across the border, with migrants' remittances propping up much of the rural economy.

Mae Sot, formally part of an SEZ from 2015, is the most industrialized of the border zones in the subregion. This has been driven by expansion of textile and garment manufacturing, with Mae Sot factories first opening in the mid-1990s, in response to declining profit rates for textile and garment firms in central Thailand and the availability of low-cost migrant labor at the border.[30] Furthermore, manufacturers' efforts to upgrade into original design or original brand manufacturing have generally not succeeded, and Thai-based regional trading companies managing value chains for global brands and retailers did not materialize as they have in Taiwan and Hong Kong.[31] The lack of indigenous technological capabilities and lead firms has compelled Greater Bangkok to take the low road to industrialization and strategic coupling.[32] These value-chain dynamics contributed to the relocation of many Bangkok-vicinity firms to Mae Sot. At its peak, approximately 470 garment factories were located in Mae Sot, employing more than 60–80,000 migrant workers from Myanmar, out of some 150–300,000 Burmese migrant workers in the area. In 2013, only 23,156 were "regular," roughly 7 percent to 14 percent of all migrants in the area.[33]

The Thai state has many years' experience in activating a multiplicity of social borders around the life and labor of Burmese migrants in Mae Sot, including racialized minimal social and labor protection practices to differentiated legal statuses that, combined, maintain a precarious workforce at the border and beyond.[34] Policing has been prevalent, with migrants lacking documentation subject to police shakedowns, harassment, as well as arrest and deportation. These authorities have made use of migrant registration schemes to regulate the labor force at the border. In turn, employers have regulated their workforces in and around the border area to prevent arrest and deportation, creating a highly precarious labor regime along the border that is characterized by policing and control. Burmese in Mae Sot have been excluded from the Thai body politic and the potential to make counter-hegemonic demands of the central state or influential employers' associations. Underemphasized in this line of analysis on deployments of migrant-labor control mechanisms has been the role of migrants' mobility in inducing recent top-down responses. Campbell asserts that migrants can be seen as "active geographical agents" who threaten the spatial organization of capital at the border and beyond.[35] Migrants pursuing work in central Thailand contribute to labor shortages in Mae Sot, generating calls from local business and state authorities to prevent migrants, even those legally registered, from "escaping" the border region. Thus, workers' mobility threatens the spatial organization of capital at the border and beyond, eliciting a different type of selective hegemony from the one outlined in the previous Cambodia case.

National and social security initiatives

Burmese migrants are critical to the Thai economy, yet they are also perceived as a national security threat. The Thai state sets out to control not only the spatial allocation of migrants' labor but also their life, and social protection policies are increasingly utilized to both ends in this biopolitical labor regime. Burmese migrants' access to social protection is predicated on formal employer-employee contracts. By linking migrant registration to as many services and facilities as possible, the security regime—security in the double sense of national and social security—closes the net around migrants, isolates them, and redefines what it means to be inside a territory by assimilating exclusion into the jurisdiction of the state.[36] Rather than de-commodify labor, Thailand's social insurance system seemingly aims to complete the commodification of migrant workers by devising a policy framework that resembles "neo-bondage," in which information on and access to social insurance is dependent upon employers will.[37] It is a state practice that extends administrative reach over migrant populations within its territory.

Thailand's constantly changing, Kafkaesque migrant registration and verification programs, first implemented in 1992, are the basis of access to social insurance programs. By law, registered migrant workers in Thailand have access to the national social security program, which includes universal health care, a child allowance, a pension, and maternity, invalidity, death, and unemployment insurance. *De jure* access to health insurance for regular migrants is significant, with over 1.8 million migrants from Myanmar, Cambodia, and Lao eligible.[38] Migrants who have completed the nationality-verification process or have entered Thailand under one of the memorandum of understanding (MOU) agreements with neighboring countries are eligible to receive benefits under both the Social Security Fund and the Workmen's Compensation Fund administrated by the Social Security Office.[39] On paper, then, migrants are covered by a range of social services also available to Thai citizens. However, in 2014 only some 10 percent of all migrants were actively enrolled in the Social Security Fund, thus policies are effectively restricted to Thai nationals.[40]

Due to the short-term nature of work contracts, with an initial legal limit of two to four years, migrant workers cannot access any long-term benefits.[41] Somkiat

Chawatsriwong, permanent secretary to the Ministry of Labor, said that migrants are only allowed in Thailand to work temporarily and not to establish a family or permanent life in the country. He also noted that migrants were not eligible for unemployment benefits, because migrants are not permitted to remain in the country for longer than seven days if they are unemployed. Furthermore, many migrants work in occupations excluded from social security coverage, including fisheries, the agro-industry, and domestic work, or are not employed continuously through the year, such as subcontracted or seasonal workers. For these irregular migrant workers—a conservative estimate being over two million—health care is generally financed through a collage of out-of-pocket payments, hospital-granted exemptions, voluntary health insurance schemes provided in some provinces, and NGO-operated migrant health programs.[42] Thailand implemented a universal health program in 2001, and even though the National Health Security Act stipulates that every person in Thailand is entitled to health services, the law is interpreted to apply only to those of Thai nationality.[43]

The benefits provided by law for regular migrants are usually out of reach in practice because of employers' reluctance to pay contributions into the funds—in some cases, colluded by migrants' own wishes to avoid salary deductions. Enrollment is optional, since there is no enforcement system to hold employers accountable if they do not enroll migrant employees in the social security system. The assumption is that employers will inform migrants of their benefits under the schemes. For those who do register, typically employers advance the cost of registration and hold onto the migrants identification papers as collateral that the advance cost would be repaid, reflecting a long-running practice among employers to keep IDs, rendering workers effectively illegal once they step outside the workplace, leaving them prone to the "policing" identified earlier.[44]

In sum, social protection programs for migrants are uncertain and becoming even more confusing. This is often framed as policy miscalculation and ineptitude on the part of the Thai government, yet it should be seen as a means of control by keeping people in state of uncertainty.[45] It is a social bordering regime aimed at the protection of Thai citizens' welfare entitlements, reproducing laboring poor status for those excluded from the citizenship regime. This reflects, as James Ferguson has argued, that such projects, even when they fail to achieve their stated goals, function to expand bureaucratic state power and embed populations more firmly within networks of governmental rule.[46] The implication is that power relations are increasingly referred through state channels, with employers' more extensive control over migrants acting as capillaries. It is selective hegemony that sets out to reinforce state control over a large migrant population that is deemed a security concern for the general Thai populace, and at the same time, it seeks to shore up state efforts to reinvigorate the lackluster economy that is dependent upon migrant labor, as addressed in the following section.

SEZS AND INSTITUTIONALIZING PRECARITY

The cases studied thus far reinforce contentions that transitions from farm to factory, country to city, informal to formal sector-led capitalist industrialization has not occurred in the same ways that it developed in the advanced industrialized countries.[47] Yet the Asian Development Bank (ADB) and related economic planners continue to line countries up along what they assume to be a linear march toward industrial-led global integration characterized by "pro-poor development" and shared prosperity enabled by "job-driven" economic growth.[48] In advancing this project, the ADB advises governments to be "wary over excessively tightening labor laws, . . . [as] rigid laws could drive an exodus of foreign firms and/or shift to more capital-intensive production that would affect long-run labor demand."[49] Indeed, the bottom of the regions' rural economy is congested, the potential for "upgrading" in global production networks is limited, thus growth led by low-value-added industries appears to be a mainstay of development planning for the foreseeable future. SEZs play a clear role in this growth paradigm, and understanding their rationale in the course of economic growth strategies in the region helps to clarify how the social question is subverted.

With global competition intensifying in labor-intensive export-oriented sectors, the ADB has been actively promoting borders SEZs, which aim to increase export competitiveness and integrate long-overlooked rural and cross-border areas to foster "sustainable, decentralized growth."[50] From the ADB's perspective, enhanced trade and transport links centered on SEZ development embedded in subregional economic corridors can facilitate integrated regional trade and structural change conducive to development, generating "a wider range of economic benefits."[51] SEZ development without regional cooperation, the ADB asserts, could lead to enclave planning with limited returns.[52] The ADB stresses that SEZs should be seen as components of an Asia-regional and global liberalization and trade facilitation project, not ends in themselves.

Border SEZs have emerged as incubators of national and cross-border economic development that set out to embed global production networks in place. From a selective hegemony lens, they are economic-planning interventions that demonstrate state efficiency and soft and hard infrastructure and logistics acumen, while further institutionalizing informalized labor regimes deemed necessary for growth. From this perspective, the social question is not marginalized from development discourse; rather, it is repackaged as part of a growth-led paradigm in which social concerns are to be addressed after the subregional geo-economic model has been institutionalized.

The Mae Sot SEZ

On May 22, 2014, the Thai military took control of the government, Thailand's third successful coup since 1991. Two months later the junta, led by former commander in chief of the Royal Thai Army and current prime minister Prayut Chan-o-cha, announced its SEZ initiative, which is central to their international trade policy agenda. The stated objectives are to attract foreign direct investment (FDI), generate employment, improve living conditions through income distribution, improve border area security, and enhance Thailand's competitiveness and boost its lethargic economy to take advantage of the ASEAN Economic Community, which took effect on December 31, 2015. Moreover, SEZ establishment will purportedly help tackle the smuggling of migrant workers and goods from neighboring countries, though it remains unclear how the Thai police and military will react, as they are central actors in Thailand's human-trafficking networks.[53]

The Mae Sot border manufacturing and trade enclave was, at a time, considered an anomaly in the broader Thai economy, and the ADB's SEZ-led development project considered a policy designed primarily for neighboring Least Developed Countries.[54] Political turmoil has negatively impacted the Thai economy, and the threat of FDI continuing to bypass Thailand for neighboring countries has contributed to a revised geo-economic strategy led by border SEZ and economic corridor planning.[55] The infrastructure, trade, and transport facilitation and logistics components of the Tak SEZs and proximate economic corridors are set to roll out by 2018.

Five SEZs in five border provinces are being implemented in project phase 1, 2015–2018 (figure 5), with five more to follow in phase 2. The Tak (Mae Sot) SEZ, at the forefront of SEZ discussions from the beginning, covers an area of 1,419 square kilometers, comprising three border districts.[56] Mae Sot is deemed a vital gateway, linking trade, investment, and tourism to Myanmar's capital, Yangon, and the proposed deep-sea port and SEZ in Dawei. It is also promoted as an emerging logistics hub, distribution center, and retail center, located in the ADB-initiated East-West Economic Corridor linking Da Nang, Vietnam, to Dawei, Myanmar. As discussed above, it has been a light manufacturing center for roughly two decades, and one that many economists and business interests hope to strategically couple with the recently opened Myawaddy industrial zone in Myanmar located ten kilometers away (interview, Tak Chamber of Commerce, December 2013). The zone is embroiled in geo-political concerns that have long held Thailand as the "natural" center of subregion, as well as geo-economic efforts to maintain low-value capture necessary as Thailand is mired in the "middle-income trap."[57] Embedding the border regions in subregional manufacturing, trade, and transport routes is an initiative that has emerged from relative discursive obscurity and ad hoc policy measures to a prominent position in national development planning.

Combined with the previous section's attention to labor control across the national territory, the pieces of a top-down spatial development planning model are moving into place. It is not yet clear whether the SEZ initiative, coupled with the social protection regime, will answer employers' calls to secure the migrant labor power deemed necessary for economic revival. It is clear, however, that the

MAP 5.2. Thailand's SEZ development. The SEZs numbered 1 are from phase 1; those numbered 2 are phase 2.

junta is tethering its beleaguered hegemonic project to the subregion by promoting border SEZs.

The Bavet SEZ

SEZ initiatives in Cambodia take on added urgency as compared to the Thailand case. Lacking advanced infrastructure and logistics capacity, and struggling to control an increasingly militant workforce, the Cambodian government is taking steps to appease uneasy investors to maintain its precarious foothold in light manufacturing. The government has approved over thirty SEZs since a 2005 SEZ decree; eleven were operational in 2014, with 145 firms employing some sixty-eight thousand.[58] One is in Phnom Penh, the rest are located at Cambodia's borders with Vietnam and Thailand and in the coastal cities of Sihanoukville and Koh Kong. Compared to Thailand's SEZs, Cambodia's are small, roughly from fifty to one thousand hectares. The central state has facilitated the privately developed and operated SEZs—indeed, all of Cambodia's SEZs are private, which reflects global SEZ trends, in contrast to Thailand's public zone administration.[59] Investment in light manufacturing, such as garment and shoe manufacturing and bicycle assembly, are most prominent. The primary logic behind Bavet border SEZs is proximity to Ho Chi Minh City and its port and manufacturing inputs, offering reduced transit and other costs compared to industrial zones further inland. Furthermore, Cambodia maintains preferential market access to the European Union under the Everything but Arms duty- and quota-free arrangement for least-developed countries. In Bavet, there are five operational SEZs employing some forty thousand local workers.

Economists indicate that improving both soft and hard infrastructure and logistics efficiency is critical for Cambodia's capacity to leverage its abundant, low-wage labor, with border SEZs deemed to be on the leading edge of such efforts.[60] Tellingly, while discussion of economic upgrading is not absent in ADB documents, spatial planning is oriented around anchoring low-value-added sectors at the borders to foster cross-border production-sharing arrangements. However, with wage gains in Cambodia between 2013 and 2016, Cambodia's wage advantage vis-à-vis Vietnam has been greatly reduced, and it is plausible that entire zones could disappear in the next round of spatial fixes. A Manhattan SEZ representative is clear (interview, November 2014), "To be honest, they [investors] come to Cambodia for low labor costs; to remain competitive, this has to be maintained." Reinforcing this view, Heng Sour of the Ministry of Labor asked, "If we want the country to grow, [we] need foreign investors, and policies to attract them. . . . To attract FDI, tell me what can we do other than low wage?" (interview, January 2015). Indeed, the viability of Cambodia's garment sector has long been under strain, and Cambodia remains far removed from upgrading into new value chains or industries such as high-value electronics or auto assembly. In this sense, Cambodia is struggling to maintain its grip on the bottom rungs of the global economy, with manufacturing centers like Bavet at the margins of global capital circuits.

There is no indication that the promise of well-remunerated wage labor with social security is likely to be galvanized by SEZ development. The ADB frames SEZ development as necessary components to address socioeconomic concerns, but there is little room to maneuver in terms of advancing workers' core concerns, as the zones themselves are predicated on a precarious labor force. State selective hegemony, as manifest in the zones, is likewise precarious, since zone workers in Cambodia are part of the body politic, and their interests cannot be marginalized as readily as is case for Burmese migrants in Thailand. In sum, zones depend upon and reproduce poverty, and the opportunities to overcome this arrangement are extremely limited. Selective hegemony in Cambodia is constrained by both investors' demands for cheap labor and workers' demands to address poverty wages.

CONCLUSION

Mekong Southeast Asia has transformed from a geopolitical territory characterized by interstate wars and conflicts to a more integrated geo-economic region that sets out to embed border SEZs into the Asia regional division of labor. These ADB-led growth logics exhibit a plurality of local labor regimes, patterns of economic development interventions and spatial administration that are paradigmatic for understanding contemporary transformations in the region. In mainstream development models, the social question has been inserted into such growth regimes, yet local labor regimes of informality reproduce and are indeed contingent upon poverty. The social question in Mekong Southeast Asia is thus delimited by a low-value-added growth model that selectively targets particular spaces, populations, and economic sectors for development.

The Cambodia case has demonstrated that the commuter laborers employed in the zones are facing land poverty, to a large extent part of the outcome of agricultural commodification processes promoted by the ADB and state actors. Formal sector employment in the zones does not ameliorate poverty; rather, it becomes a site of tension and protest that has induced state violence. These workers have responded by informally linking up with wider national-scale wildcat protest movements, and state concessions include wage increases and select social protection measures. These policies represent a small victory for workers' movements, however, the selective urban garment sector labor force orientation sets out to blunt political opposition rather than addresses workers social reproduction concerns. Thus, the potential for workers employed in border zones to access Cambodia's limited social protection program is even more restricted that those working in Phnom Penh and vicinity.

The Thailand case argues that Burmese migrants in Mae Sot have long been subject to racialized exclusions from the Thai body politic, which delimits their potential to make demands of employers and the state. Workers' mobility and subsequent labor shortages have challenged the border growth model, and irregular migrants numbering in the millions have contributed to national-scale security concerns. The Thai state has responded with a migrant labor registration scheme that utilizes social protection to cast the net over migrants. Again, these policies do not address livelihood and social reproduction concerns, rather, they extend the reach of the state. Selective hegemony targets investor concerns and a more general concern for migrant regulation, and social reproduction strategies of Burmese in Thailand remains a tenuous cross-border arrangement. This expands bureaucratic state power and embeds populations more firmly within networks of governmental rule, shoring up state efforts to reinvigorate the lackluster Thai economy heavily dependent upon migrant labor.

To understand how localized border regimes of informality act as nodes within wider subregional development trends, the SEZs' prominence in geo-economic ambitions has been presented. SEZs are key to the regional informality-mobility-poverty nexus, yet the ADB and state officials assert that SEZs are necessary components of cooperative cross-border development planning. This discourse overlooks the ways in which the zones structure poverty through labor. In this sense, the social question is not necessarily marginalized by mainstream development planning but is understood through growth logics, deferring realization of widespread benefits to a seemingly unattainable future of full employment in high-wage manufacturing. The sector-specific, selective approach creates further tensions and scales up contestations from the border zone to the region.

NOTES

1. N. Coe and H. Yeung, *Global Production Networks: Theorizing Economic Development in an Interconnected World* (Oxford: Oxford University Press, 2015).

2. Pietro P. Masina and Michela Cerimele, "Patterns of Industrialization and the State of Industrial Labour in Post-WTO Accession Vietnam," *European Journal of East Asia Studies* 17, no. 2 (2018), 289–323.

3. G. Smith, "Selective Hegemony and Beyond-Populations with 'No Productive Function': A Framework for Enquiry," *Identities: Global Studies in Culture and Power* 18 (2011): 2–38.

4. G. Hart, "Denaturalizing Dispossession: Critical Ethnography in the Age of Resurgent Imperialism," *Antipode* 38, no. 5 (2006): 977–1004.

5. Hart, "Denaturalizing Dispossession," 996.

6. J. Allen, "Topological Twists: Power's Shifting Geographies," *Dialogues in Human Geography* 1 (2011): 283–98.

7. There is no single definition or use of terms in Southeast Asia. Generally, social-protection (social security) systems in the region include social-assistance, social-insurance, and labor-market interventions. This paper is mostly concerned with social-insurance policies targeting (or not) the laboring poor, and social security, suggesting a broader set of interventions, is used interchangeably.

8. Franco Barchiesi, *Precarious Liberation: Workers, the state, and Contested Social Citizenship in Postapartheid South Africa* (Albany: State University of New York Press, 2011).

9. ILO Cambodia Garment and Footwear Sector Bulletin, issue 2, October (Phnom Penh: International Labour Organization, 2015).

10. A. Ong, "Powers of Sovereignty: State, People, Wealth, Life," *Focaal—Journal of Global and Historical Anthropology* 64 (2012): 24–35.

11. S. Campbell, *Border Capitalism, Disrupted: Precarity and Struggle at a Southeast Asian Industrial Zone* (Ithaca, NY: Cornell University Press, 2018).

12. Smith, "Selective Hegemony."

13. National Institute of Statistics (NIS) of Cambodia and ILO, *Cambodia Labour Force and Child Labour Survey 2012: Labour Force Report* (Geneva: International Labour Organization and National Institute of Statistics (NIS) of Cambodia, 2013).

14. Chivoin Peou, "Negotiating Rural-Urban Transformation and Life Course Fluidity: Rural Young People and Urban Sojourn in Contemporary Cambodia," *Journal of Rural Studies* 44 (2016): 177–86.

15. NIS and ILO, *Cambodia Labour Force and Child Labour Survey 2012.*

16. A. Rossi, "Better Work: Harnessing Incentives and Influencing Policy to Strengthen Labour Standards Compliance in Global Production Networks," *Cambridge Journal of Regions, Economy and Society* 8, no. 3 (2015): 505–20.

17. M. Wright, *Disposable Women and Other Myths of Global Capitalism,* (New York: Routledge, 2006); Arnold, D. "Political Society, Civil Society and the Politics of Disorder in Cambodia," *Political Geography* 60 (2017): 23–33.

18. Better Factories Cambodia (BFC), *Thirty First Synthesis Report on Working Conditions in Cambodia's Garment Sector* (Geneva: International Labour Office, International Finance Corporation (2014).

19. Alvin Lim, "Cambodia Rising: Neoliberal Violence and Development," *Journal of Southeast Asian Studies* 18, no. 4 (2013): 61–72.

20. The strike was sparked by a tripartite decision to increase the minimum wage from US$95 to $100 per month, short of demands for $155.

21. Asia Monitor Resource Centre (AMRC), *A Week That Shook Cambodia: The Hope, Anger and Despair of Cambodian Workers after the General Strike and Violent Crackdown* (Hong Kong: Asia Monitor Resource Centre (2014), www.amrc.org.hk/sites/default/files/FFM-Cambodia-Report-022014-amrc_0.pdf.

22. D. Arnold, "Political Society, Civil Society and the Politics of Disorder in Cambodia," *Political Geography* 60 (2017): 23–33.

23. ILO Cambodia Garment and Footwear Sector Bulletin, Issue 2. (Phnom Penh: International Labour Organization, October 2015).

24. International Labour Organization (ILO) *Toward Integrated Employment and Social Protection Policy in Cambodia* (2012).

25. Cambodia has adopted a National Social Protection Strategy targeting the poor (i.e., informal sector and rural poor), yet it remains ad hoc, donor driven, and dependent upon NGOs and international organizations for service delivery. There is, as yet, limited "bottom-up" push for such programs in the country.

26. The National Social Security Fund (NSSF) of Cambodia is lead organization on these matters with three directives: social health insurance, pensions, and employment injury fund. In 2008 it implemented the employment injury fund, currently covering some one million workers.

27. K. Fujita, "Agricultural Labourers in Myanmar during the Economic Transition, Views from the Study of Selected Villages," in *The Economic Transition in Myanmar after 1988: Market Economy versus State Control,* ed. K. Fujita, F. Mieno, and I. Okamoto, 246–80 (Singapore: National University of Singapore Press in association with Kyoto University Press, 2009), 264.

28. Campbell, *Border Capitalism, Disrupted.*

29. MAP Foundation, "Regular Rights: A Study on the Impact of Regularization of Migrant Workers from Myanmar (Burma) in Thailand," 2nd ed. (Chiang Mai: MAP Foundation, 2015).

30. J. Glassman, *Thailand at the Margins: Internationalization of the State and the Transformation of Labor* (Oxford: Oxford University Press, 2003).

31. G. Abonyi and A. Zola, "Scoping Study on Developing Border Economic Areas and Cross-border Linkages between Thailand and Its Neighbours," Prepared for the Asian Development Bank, Thailand Resident Mission, 2014, DOI: https://doi.org/10.13140/2.1.2640.5442

32. N. Coe and H. Yeung, *Global Production Networks: Theorizing Economic Development in an Interconnected World* (Oxford: Oxford University Press, 2015).

33. S. Campbell, *Border Capitalism, Disrupted: Precarity and Struggle at a Southeast Asian Industrial Zone* (Ithaca, NY: Cornell University Press, 2018).

34. D. Arnold and J. Pickles, "Global Work, Surplus Labor, and the Precarious Economies of the Border," *Antipode* 43, no. 5 (2011): 1598–624.

35. Campbell, *Border Capitalism, Disrupted.*

36. J. M. Amaya-Castro, "Illegality Regimes and the Ongoing Transformation of Contemporary Citizenship," *European Journal of Legal Studies* 4, no. 2 (2011): 137–61.

37. Jan Breman, *Outcast Labour in Asia: Circulation and Informalization of the Workforce at the Bottom of the Economy* (New Delhi: Oxford University Press, 2010).

38. IOM, "Migrant Information Note," issue no. 28 (December, 2015).

39. Huguet, "Thailand Migration Report 2014" (Bangkok: United Nations Thematic Working Group on Migration in Thailand, 2014). By the early 2010s, two primary channels to register with a passport and work permit were available (CCC and Map 2014): (1) recruitment of workers through agencies in the countries of origin—the MOU process and the Nationality Verification (NV) system for migrants who are already in Thailand with an employer, which allows them to obtain temporary passports and work permits.

40. Andy Hall, "Myanmar and Migrant Workers: Briefing and Recommendations," (Salaya: Mahidol Migration Center, Mahidol University, 2012); and Hall, "Grim Future Awaits Migrant Workers," *Bangkok Post,* February 29, 2016, www.bangkokpost.com/opinion/opinion/879616/grim-future-awaits-migrant-workers.

41. MAP Foundation, "Regular Rights: A Study on the Impact of Regularization of Migrant Workers from Myanmar (Burma) in Thailand," 2nd ed. (Chiang Mai: MAP Foundation, 2015).

42. Huguet, "Thailand Migration Report 2014."

43. V. Schmitt, T. Sakunphanit, and O. Prasitsiriphol, "Social Protection Assessment Based National Dialogue: Towards a Nationally Defined Social Protection Floor in Thailand," Bangkok: ILO, 2013).

44. Arnold and Pickles, "Global Work, Surplus Labor."

45. Hall, "Myanmar and Migrant Workers"; Hall, "Grim Future Awaits Migrant Workers."

46. James Ferguson, *The Anti-politics Machine: Development, Depoliticization, and Bureaucratic Power in Lesotho* (Minneapolis: University of Minnesota Press, 1990).

47. Tania Li, "Jobless Growth and Relative Surplus Populations," *Anthropology Today* 29, no. 3 (2013): 1–2.

48. ADB, "Sharing Growth and Prosperity: A Strategy and Action Plan for the Southern Economic Corridor" (Manila: ADB, 2010); and ADB, "Emerging Asian Regionalism: A Partnership for Shared Prosperity" (Manila: ADB, 2008).

49. ADB, "Asian Economic Integration Report 2015: How Can Special Economic Zones Catalyze Economic Development?" (Manila: ADB, 2015).

50. ADB, "Sharing Growth and Prosperity."

51. ADB, "Asian Economic Integration Report 2015," 112.

52. ADB, "Asian Economic Integration Report 2015."

53. C. Chumee and S. Poudpongpaiboon, Thailand's Special Economic Zone. Economic Intelligence Center. Siam Commercial Bank, Bangkok, 2015), https://www.scbeic.com/en/detail/product/1167; Indrė Balčaitė, A Borderless Village: Mobility and Belonging in Phlong Karen Transborder Lives between Hpa-an Area, Myanmar, and Greater Bangkok, Thailand," PhD dissertation, SOAS, University of London, 2015.

54. M. Ishida, "Special Economic Zones and Economic Corridors," in ERIA Research Project Report 2008, No 5: Research on Development Strategies for CLMV Countries, 33–52 (Jakarta Pusat: Economic Research Institute for Asean and East Asia, 2008).

55. "Thailand's Economy: The High Cost of Stability," *The Economist,* October 2014. www.economist.com/blogs/banyan/2014/10/thailands-economy.

56. Department of Foreign Trade (DFT), "Guide for Investors: Thailand Special Economic Zones" (Bangkok: Department of Foreign Trade, Bangkok, n.d.), www.dft.go.th/Portals/0/ContentManagement/Document_Mod932/thailand%20special%20economic%20zones%20eng@25590309-1637047868.pdf.

57. Thongchai Winichakul, "Trying to Locate Southeast Asia from Its Navel: Where Is Southeast Asian Studies in Thailand?" in *Locating Southeast Asia: Geographies of Knowledge and Politics of Space*, ed. P. Kratoska, R. Raban, and H. S. Nordholt, 113–32 (Singapore: Singapore University Press, 2005); Jonathan Rigg, *Challenging Southeast Asian Development: The Shadows of Success* (London: Routledge, 2015).

58. ADB, "Asian Economic Integration Report 2015."

59. Peter Warr and Jayant Menon, "Cambodia's Special Economic Zones," ADB Economics Working Paper Series No. 459, October (Manila: Asian Development Bank, 2015). Cambodian *Okhnas* (politically connected tycoons) typically own the SEZ land and either utilize the land for real estate speculation or outsource the SEZ development to foreign investors.

60. G. Abonyi and A. Zola, "Scoping Study on Developing Border Economic Areas and Cross-border Linkages between Thailand and Its Neighbour," (Prepared for the Asian Development Bank, Thailand Resident Mission, 2014), DOI: https://doi.org/10.13140/2.1.2640.5442; ADB, "Asian Economic Integration Report 2015."

6

A Mirage of Welfare

How the Social Question in India Got Aborted

Jan Breman

AN AMBIGUOUS START

The struggle for national independence was waged to gain not only freedom from foreign rule but also redemption from poverty, which held the large majority of the population captive. The development task at hand was entrusted to the vanguard of the Congress movement, which had launched the fight for autonomy against colonial domination. The constitution of the new nation prescribed equality before the law of all citizens and democracy as the organizing principle of the political order. Universalizing suffrage was an act of considerable civil courage in a society marked by hard-core social inequality. The recognition of this heritage remained veiled. The hierarchical ranking in a superiority-inferiority bind was attributed to the divisive impact of colonial policies that created contrasts and conflicts where togetherness in harmony existed. Mutuality was highlighted in the postulate of a village community founded on a division of labor in which peasant, artisan and service castes cooperated in reciprocity. It was an image strongly contested by B. R. Ambedkar. This advocate of the discriminated rearguard argued that enfranchisement of the pariah underclass would not result in their emancipation if they were not simultaneously rehabilitated to a proportionate share of economic and social rights.

India came out of colonialism with the large majority of the population living in villages and working in agriculture. Land distribution was highly skewed and the All India Congress Committee had gone on record promising "land to the tiller." To the extent land reforms were carried out, they benefitted the already better-off and not the majority of the peasants who belonged to land-poor and landless castes-cum-classes. The Gandhian model of small-scale village development was completely ignored. The pretense of a socialist blueprint to the future was foregrounded in political statements, but the bottom ranks of the peasantry, identified in official reports as Scheduled Castes and Scheduled Tribes, were often still tied in debt bondage to substantial landowners. The relationship, one of exploitation mixed with a veneer of patronage, which provided sustenance to the landless household, broke down when, in the late colonial period, capitalism gained prominence.[1] Labor became increasingly casualized, but wages remained as low as before, and the erosion of patronage inherent to the former bondage was not compensated by state-supplied social benefits at old age, disability, or bouts of unemployment. Agricultural labor was excluded from the redistribution of the surplus land that became available. Population growth went on unabated, and bringing down the high pressure on the resource base was a must. Agriculture had to be released from a low-productivity workforce redundant to regular demand. A better life was awaiting the rural underclasses in the city, where they would find steady employment in the mills that were expected to absorb and skill a huge amount of labor from the countryside. The path lying ahead was meant to repeat the urbanization-industrialization trajectory that the Global North had passed through one century earlier and for which "development" became the catchword. It was a scenario that, in the wishful thinking of India's founding fathers, would ultimately result in the creation of a welfare regime as it already existed in the advanced economies.

In the late colonial period, a city-based class of factory labor had emerged. While miners and plantation coolies in the remote hinterland constituted a much larger industrial (although unorganized) workforce, factories manufacturing textiles had emerged in urban growth poles such as Mumbai and Kolkata. Mill hands made up a tiny fraction of the total working population, but their presence was supposed to signal what the future would look like. The vanguard of the industrial times to come became organized in trade unions, which lobbied for the introduction of labor rights in legislation aimed to safeguard conditions of employment, including social security benefits and protection against adversity. Infrastructural modernization required huge capital investments, which called for state participation in the planned restructuring of the economy. The regulation of employment upgraded the welfare of the workforce engaged in what became known as the public sector. In official parlance, "labor" was understood to signify industrial work. The "workers" were identified as male factory hands in the modern economy, and their numbers would rapidly increase. The vast majority of the working population still engaged in agriculture lagged behind in backwardness and remained, beyond the care of government, stuck in deep poverty. The rural population increased from 298.6 million in 1951 to 837.7 million in 2011, respectively 83 percent and 69 percent of the total population. In this interval, the percentage of owner-cultivators in the agrarian workforce dropped from 72 percent to 45 percent, while agricultural labor doubled from 28 percent to 55 percent.[2] Guided more by fear of a growing restiveness than by the urgent need to improve the appalling plight of the rural poor, the Congress government of Gujarat finally decided in 1972 to prescribe what landowners would have to pay to agricultural labor, but the legal minimum wage failed to become effective. Mahatma Gandhi had insisted that the main worker's income should satisfy the basic needs of his household and went on public record asking for a family wage that identified the male head of the household as the sole provider. Underlying his proposal was the idea that wives should not engage in waged work but should stay at home and take care of their husband and children. In spite of his strongly biased gender leanings, the yardstick of the nation's founding father was the right to a human subsistence that included a broad package of basic needs. His subsequent reduction of a fair wage to a living wage was based on the argument that a decent reward for waged labor had to be fixed in accordance with what the employer could and should afford. However, no enterprise or industry would be allowed to operate without adequate remuneration for the labor employed.[3]

A TURN FOR THE BETTER?

In the mid-1970s a slight improvement could be observed among the subaltern ranks in the rural locations of my local-level research in Gujarat. The widening scale of the labor market facilitated daily commuting to the nearby town by bus or bicycle or going off for longer periods as migrants for the duration of the dry season. The increasing connectivity would have strengthened the bargaining position of the landless and land-poor in the village if the influx of outsiders had not correspondingly gone up at the same time. More space opened up also because of government schemes targeted on the rural poor to consolidate the vote bank, which the Congress Party required to stay in power. What became known as positive discrimination gave access to jobs in the public sector for the somewhat educated among its downtrodden constituency. Although only a forward section of Scheduled Castes and Scheduled Tribes benefited from job reservation in the public economy, it encouraged parents to send their children to primary school, in the hope that their offspring would be able to escape from the bottom of the labor hierarchy in which the victims of lifelong illiteracy remained entrapped. In my fieldwork locales, I found that toward the end of the twentieth century, two-thirds of the men and three-quarters of the women in the landless class were still illiterate, but among the age cohorts below thirty years, that proportion was much smaller. Another hopeful sign was the promotion of public health care. Primary centers were set up to cater to the low-income population in the surrounding villages with free professional help and medicine. However, the services on offer were of an inferior quality. Opening hours were irregular, while absence of competent personnel, adequate equipment, and cost-free medication added to the lack of efficiency.

Government agencies were somewhat more successful in settling the landless households in new quarters, although without giving them title deeds to their homestead plots. A major drawback was that these colonies were built on wasteland at the village outskirts and were difficult to access in the monsoon. Their shelters on their employer's land before had been self-built mud huts with overhanging thatched roofs that almost reached the ground, scattered over the locality but close to where they worked. Being clustered in compact settlements must have strengthened togetherness and a shared communal identity as tribal castes. Hidden out of sight, these jerry-built colonies without basic utilities resembled urban slums. House construction and provision of electricity came, of course, at a price but the rural underclasses expected these amenities to be uncharged public goods. Their daily wages fell already short of what they had to spend on bare survival. In the countryside, human resource development and gratification of basic needs stagnated.

The necessity to canvass votes motivated Congress politics to initiate the first social protection schemes that would reduce the threat of extreme vulnerability. In 1991, the National Commission on Rural Labour pointed out in its report that with 2.5 percent of GNP, India's spending on social security was lower than almost anywhere else in the world.[4] Moreover, that budget targeted only formally employed labor in the urban economy, one-tenth of the total workforce. Congress reckoned to make political capital out of the state pension for aged and disabled workers without adult children and without any means of their own. However, the beneficiaries turned out to be few and far between. In 1987 I came across an old woman in one of my villages of fieldwork who had once received the prescribed monthly payment of fifty rupees. She herself and everybody else saw it as an unexpected act of charity, a stroke of luck rather than a right to which she could lay claim in future. Nobody was able to tell her what to do and where to go to get her state pension.

Declaring the state of emergency in 1975, Indira Gandhi launched the Twenty Point Program to eradicate poverty and to improve the quality of life for the underclasses. The slogan *Garibi Hatao* (Get Rid of Poverty) made her a popular, even a venerated figure as *Mataji* among the masses down and out. The Bonded Labour System (Abolition) Act of 1976 decreed the end of captivity, which held workers attached in debt to their employers. The new ordinance was inspired more by the idea that bondage was an uneconomic way to utilize labor than that it degraded and oppressed the workforce exposed to it. The legal prohibition of debt bondage stemmed above all from government's desire to accelerate the pace of capitalism by doing away with an employment modality held to be a relic from a feudal past. Declaring illegal what remained widely practiced turned out to be as ineffective as it had been before. The prime minister unleashed an authoritarian regime, resorted to forced sterilization practiced on Muslims especially, but was amazingly unsuccessful in imposing a *diktat,* during her rule of emergency.

Were there no initiatives from civil society to improve the condition of the lower castes, which are also the lower classes, left behind by politics and policies? Gujarat has a proud record of what used to be called constructive work by grassroots activists. The Gandhian movement made special efforts to bring the tribal communities into mainstream society, and the landless serfs were told that they were going to be redeemed from bondage and poverty. To uplift the rural proletariat, a welfare organization was founded in 1961, but the misery in which they lived remained unaddressed. The promised progress did not materialize because its high-caste leadership refused to confront exploitation and oppression head-on. In the orthodox Gandhian mission, disputes on the terms and conditions of employment had to be solved by arbitration and compromise. Whenever relationships between farmers and laborers became tense and strikes or fights broke out, the social workers insisted on nonviolence and rushed to restore class "harmony." The Gandhian welfare agency that became part of the Congress machinery obfuscated rather than advanced the emancipation of the rural poor.

Labour Circulation

I used to trace the landless from my fieldwork localities wherever they went. Going off was due to the growing lack of demand for agricultural labor but was also inspired by a strong distaste among the younger age set to remain stuck in subordination to the local farmers. The problem land-poor and landless families face is a perpetual budget deficit. The dispossessed do not have the cash required for all kinds of expenses in the capitalist economy that has emerged. Credit expresses for the dispossessed an obligation to repay the provider of the "loan" with labor. The cash received demonstrates the supplicant's incapacity to meet basic needs without being forced to acquire part of the cost of maintenance and reproduction in advance and restricts the latitude to move around beyond restraint. Members from the land-poor and landless households are mobilized in a state of immobility. They leave home, to return only when the self-skilled and low-paid work under the open sky for which they are recruited comes to an end, many months later. When the subsistence deficit in their hamlets is at its most urgent because of lack of work and income, jobbers go around shelling out earnest money that commits their catch to depart to faraway work sites when the monsoon ends. The gangs of migrants cannot leave the destination to which they are brought until they have worked off the advance payment. Once the debt has been cleared, they should be free to leave, but their wages are held back until the end of the season. If they run away in between, they lose the net balance of their earnings. Sometimes migrants are still in arrears on departure if they have asked for a large amount in advance to cover the expense of life cycle events such as a wedding among their kinsmen or a family member's failing health, or to pay off an outstanding debt, which includes usurious interest on the loan provided.

The rural distress continues to be ignored by the government. More than half of India's workforce is still reported to make their living somehow in agriculture, but that sector's share has steadily fallen to about one-sixth of GDP. Footloose hordes roam around in search of escape from lack of income at home. In the early twentieth century, barely 5 percent of the population was urban based, and that figure remained low throughout the colonial era. That proportion went haltingly up to 18 percent in 1961 and further increased to 28 percent in 2001. A drastic change in economic policy has subsequently accelerated urban growth. But the assumption that under the regime of neoliberalism, employment would surge ahead and raise urban life standards all around is misconceived. Both housing and jobs in cities lag far behind the accelerated intrusion of rural migrants desperate to establish a firm foothold in the urban economy.

Waiting for a Bright Future

In the mega-cities that have emerged during the last half century, slum dwellers outnumber the better-off inhabitants. While the classes mired in poverty try to hang on where they have squatted down, as close as possible to where the well-established citizens live, the latter experience their nearby presence as a nuisance. Driven out from their makeshift and unauthorized shelters, the unwanted inhabitants are dumped at the city's outskirts—removed from sight but as a reserve army of labor, still sufficiently near at hand for occasional part-time and cheap usage. The spatial-cum-social divide is articulated by a change in policy to informality. The concept owes its origin to Keith Hart, who published in 1971 a pioneering paper on what he called the informal sector.[5] The term referred to a motley crowd of unskilled, low-paid, and irregular labor at the low and inchoate end of the urban economy to be found in the erstwhile third world at large. The idea was that these newcomers would gradually qualify for steady and decently paid jobs. Getting more skilled and bargaining their way up, they were going to cross the boundaries that kept them apart from formal employment opportunities.

Until the late 1970s, Congress and its leadership remained wedded to a social-democratic pathway of sorts. Progressive taxation and stringent regulation of private enterprise paved the road to what should have ultimately culminated in a welfare state. Inequality did not wither away, but neither was there an escalation of conspicuous wealth at the top end. Captains of industry, both respected and suspected, were held on a short leash. The buildup of a public economy created some space for upward social mobility. In 1947 India had fewer than ten million industrial workers, of whom only a quarter were employed in modern factories. This tiny fraction of the workforce was regarded as spearheading the new economy. Industrial employment was the shape of a future in which employers, workers, and the state would synchronize their interests for the common good. The state took a leading role in the infrastructural layout, and heavy industries were established in the public sector for the production of capital goods. The system of steady and regulated employment introduced in these enterprises helped to give labor a new dignity and was held up as the standard for private business to emulate. These workers enjoyed proper jobs and were paid a time-rated wage. In addition to their protected terms of engagement, a wide range of social benefits became statutory, bargained for by the trade unions in which the industrial workers and public sector employees were organized. This vanguard remained small in size, was reluctant to share its privileges with the overwhelming majority of workers outside of their ranks, and developed traits of a labor aristocracy. Endowed with prerogatives, the gap in life standard with the main body of the workforce, which remained stuck in agriculture and in the informal economy, escalated. Toward the end of the 1980s, the government had lost control over its agenda of development and became subservient to "liberalization," as dictated by the Washington consensus. It was a setback sealed by the collapse of a second world order that had attempted to find an alternative path to the future than the one traversed by the advanced capitalist economies. With most other third world nations, India became incorporated in a regime of neoliberalism under Western hegemony, a setting in which institutions operating under the auspices of the Bretton Woods and World Trade Organization constituted the globalized directorate. The structural adjustment policies carried out were instrumental in dismantling the public economy and blatantly announced as a poverty reduction strategy, severely cut down expenditure on social sectors such as housing, health, and education for the working classes.

INFORMALITY AS THE REMEDY

Informality turned out to be not a waiting room but an end station for the swelling workforce locked up in it. Industrialization did occur, but much more slowly than anticipated, while more and more people were being pushed out of agriculture and the village. They were mainly accommodated in construction, transport, trade, and services, or floated between them. Together these sectors far outweigh labor absorption in industry, and, as a consequence, the economic policy has radically changed course. Spurred on by the financial agencies of transnational capital, formalization of employment was not any longer the trajectory to follow. Informalization was now considered to be the solution rather than the problem. The new policy suggested that casualization would generate more and better paid jobs. By a sleight of hand, irregular, insecure, and unprotected work was proclaimed to be in the best interest of labor. Closure of the mills in the formal economy toward the end of the twentieth century meant the overnight dismissal of a massive workforce that lost, together with their regulated jobs, all labor rights and social benefits. Trade unions faded away from the laboring landscape.

In a case study, I traced the workers sacked from their mill jobs to the bottom of the urban economy, where they engaged in cutthroat competition for the trifle chores on hand.[6] It put an end to class-based solidarity. The victims did not have any other option than to fall back on their primordial loyalties for livelihood. In their search for casual work, they articulated their identity of gender, caste, and creed as the only form of social capital left to them. In 2002 a pogrom swept through Gujarat with horrendous ferocity. Hindu politics were blamed for the orgy of violence that targeted the Muslim minority in what was a politically managed and state-backed operation, but the changing fabric of the economy played a major role. Lumpenized elements were at liberty to hunt and kill non-Hindu targets in the streets, forsaking the bonds of fraternity they had shared in the mills. As a consequence to the riots, the religious minority was driven out of the neighborhoods in which they cohabited with their Hindu workmates. The communal separation has hardened and expresses the politics of apartheid dictated from above. Downward mobility was not the only fallout of informalization, but it also put in jeopardy a democratic fabric that is based on balancing the interests of all stakeholders in a spirit of proportional equivalence and social justice.

From the commanding heights one more myth percolated, maintaining that the absorptive capacity of the informal economy is infinite and pretending that newcomers are always welcome to join their swollen ranks. The premise stands corrected when one bothers to find out how these niches are watched over against uninvited intruders. The work at hand may go on day and night, but bouts of overemployment alternate with underemployment—nothing to do for days on end. A major cause for ceaseless mobility is due to the need to leave wife and children behind in the village for lack of earning capability, as well as living space. Having these dependents around would be an unbearable burden, both in terms of care and cash spent on their maintenance. Within a cycle of fifteen to twenty-five years, the harsh conditions of employment and shelter result in premature exhaustion. It means an end to their working lives, if this does not happen earlier, when they fall prey to lasting injuries or chronic illness often caused by occupational hazards. The story adds up to concluding that dislocation, labor circulation, and informality are each other's handmaiden.

Of India's workforce—at the end of 2017, roughly half a billion in a population of nearly 1.4 billion—the overwhelming majority is stuck in the informal economy.[7] Over half of the men and women in what has remained of the formal economy—a small slice estimated to hover around 10 percent of the economically active population—are also engaged on informal terms in a race to the bottom. With the upswing to neoliberal policies since 1991, labor market dualism further accelerated. In the urban economy, regular work is still the most common employment status, but in the rural economy, casual work dominates. Of the total workforce, less than half is wage dependent and more than half self-employed.[8] So-called own-account work indicates the lack of proper jobs and is often disguised waged labor of outsourced activity. Since supply of labor far exceeds demand, the income of the casualized workforce tends to remain stuck close to or below the poverty line. There can be little doubt that the drive toward informalization is in the end self-defeating. What is going to happen next? Once privatized, public space, agency, and institutions are difficult to restore. To generate solidarity rather than rank competition and individuated self-reliance is bound to be an uphill task. The public sector has shrunk and is manned by employees paid out of the country's treasury: army, police, and a corps of major and minor officials, secure in their waged prominence, and in their elevated roles safeguarding what the state is and does.

A TALE OF INCLUSION

Which policy interventions have provided relief to the laboring poor? The oldest one is the public distribution system (PDS). Having its origin in the famine of the 1940s, rationing was revived in the early 1960s to cope with acute food shortage. PDS makes subsidized food and some nonfood items available through a network of licensed fair-price shops. After decades of weak implementation, better targeting has slowly made PDS more effective. Still, wrong inclusion (of the nonpoor) and exclusion (of large chunks of the laboring and non-laboring poor) continues to be a major problem. The ration card is not valid outside the place of residence, which means that circular migrants hailing from other states remain excluded. A high percentage of adults or minors in the population at large suffer from undernourishment (one out of five) and of children underweight (close to half). Households need to provide proof of their improvidence. To qualify not only for low-priced grain but for all relief schemes, they have to be registered as being stuck below the poverty line (BPL) and are issued an identity card as testimony of their vulnerability. To be put on the list is a favor granted or withheld at the discretion of upper-caste gatekeepers, all the way from the village to higher up in the machinery of governance. I was around when, in 2002, the order from above came to close the local register to new BPL claimants.

Public housing has for many years been provided under the Indira Awas scheme: one-room tenements with brick and plastered walls, an iron-sheet entrance door, a window, and a roof of durable material. The annual quota remained low, sparingly allotted and spread over a large number of colonies, to impress a landless constituency that the Congress government was actively promoting the welfare of the underprivileged. Public health facilities were introduced in the 1970s and 1980s to provide medical care to the poor. Whatever little access to professional and cost-free expertise was made available fell short of solving their health problems. The usual practice is to stick to self-medication, and if that brings no reprieve, the next step is to consult a quack for an injection. The changeover to privatization means that over four-fifths of health expenditure comes out of people's pockets. A national health insurance scheme was introduced in 2008, limited to families officially recorded as poor. The scheme allowed for in-patient treatment in selected private or public hospitals, but it excluded coverage for many ailments and disabilities to which the laboring poor are prone.

Which measures have been taken to redeem the poor from the illiteracy in which I found them at the beginning of my local-level research more than half a century ago? Nowadays most children do go to school. It is a change for the better, to which the government contributes, with incentives such as a meal at noon, crèches for younger kids, and care for young mothers and infants by locally recruited and trained women. However, the village school has become the domain of the poor since the nonpoor send their offspring to town for private education at considerable cost. Public schools have become the domain of the working classes and are of inferior quality. At the end of their short educational track, children are able to confirm identity by writing their name instead of falling back on their thumbprint, but the teaching they have received is not enough to allow them to read even a simple form and fill it out with the required data. It means they remain cut off from all information and incentives that would connect them to mainstream society.

How to generate employment for the land-poor and landless classes in the rural economy? A time-hailed recipe has been to arrange for public works. Pressured by social activists, the Congress government launched in 2005 a scheme that offered paid work for one hundred days a year to self-selected rural households at the legal minimum wage rate on projects designed and executed by the village council. The policy makers retracted extending coverage also to the urban economy. The employment provided has to be productive in nature: land leveling, digging wells, building check dams, and improving access roads, further increasing the lead of those endowed with assets. The Mahatma Gandhi National Rural Employment Guarantee Act (in daily parlance abbreviated to *narega*) did not envisage upgrading the habitat of the rural proletariat with house construction or sanitation, let alone to arrange for care for the elderly, the disabled, and for all those unable to cope with their misery and in dire need of some support. The number of days worked are much lower than promised. Also, the clause stipulating that people who want to participate in the locally framed and managed projects should be paid the regulated wage on days no work is made available has remained ineffective. To do so would amount to an unemployment benefit, a largesse that is politically not condoned. Irrespective of these shortcomings or outright failure to achieve the targeted objectives—as, for instance, in Gujarat—the nuanced conclusion must be that *narega* has been much better handled in the southernmost states. In Kerala, in particular, where wages are above the legal minimum, the program has become a feat of female participation and assertion. But wherever pressure from below for participation remains absent, fraud and corruption are rampant: men and women listed as working on a project are simply not there; those who manage to become enlisted neither get the full wage nor do they receive it in time. An argument in favor of continuation and expansion of the scheme is demonstrated by the fierce disapproval with which local employers react to public works, because they appear to act as a lever on the going wage rate.

The plight of a workforce doomed to footloose circulation seems to defeat the idea that the global countryside has reached its maximum population and will begin to shrink after 2020.[9] In a worst-case scenario, the countryside may remain the waiting room for a reserve army of labor. A return of social Darwinism could imply closing the cities off from a further influx of surplus people in the hinterland. Locked away in villages, it would be easier to keep them in check than on the urban front. Out of sight in their rural slums, their massive presence can be ignored, and the policy of abandonment would keep them separated from the better-off citizenry. The plausibility of such a "solution" is given impetus by a bourgeois mentality aggressively antagonistic to a drift into the city of growing contingents of landless and land-poor from their scattered backyards.[10] They are seen as a dangerous class not so much because they are found to pose a threat to social and political stability, but because their polluting nearness is considered a health and safety hazard and a hindrance to civic morality.

A STATE IN DENIAL

The scale of public relief required to bridge the gap from improvidence to well-being has not been made available. Still, the pledge of successive political regimes is and remains the inclusion of all. How to realize this objective laid down in the constitution? The policy is summed up in the slogan that the poor should be helped to help themselves, even if this implies self-exploitation and a gross denial of their human quality. It is part of a neoliberal dogma that sets the government free from providing social security and protection. The drive toward self-employment, self-provisioning and self-representation is to hold people accountable for their own work and welfare arrangements. This is the marvel of Soto's brand of capitalism and its glorified success in sinking down to levels earlier unheard-of.[11] Has the magic of making the poor bankable, obliging them to stand security for each other when applying for petty loans, resulted in less improvidence? Attempts to set up to the rural landless in petty business have by and large failed, also in my fieldwork localities.[12] The wages paid out to them at day's end are instantly spent on basic maintenance, food before anything else. None of it can be saved to cope with the adversities that are an ironclad feature of their deficient subsistence. Animators of micro-credit schemes tend to portray the underclass as undeserving poor, afflicted with ailments attributed to their own defects—steadfast refusal to save up, above all—rather than to bonds of un- or underemployment and inadequate income. Refusal to pay a living wage to the rural poor, even when profits higher up continue to accrue, is accompanied by an unflagging insistence on the privatization of property. Articulation of ownership rights has led to the depletion of common resources such as access to the village wastelands. It meant the loss of communally held benefits that used to contribute crucially to the coping strategies of the rural poor and to denial of the right acknowledged in the past to squat down on unoccupied space in village or city.

Established by the government in 2004 to take stock of the informal economy, the National Commission on Enterprises in the Unorganized Sector (NCEUS) recommended the promulgation of a "social floor" of labor rights and standards: a national minimum wage and its effective payment, decent conditions of work, and the provision of social security. It would mean cost-free insurance against failing health and other benefits for the non-laboring poor. Parliament mandated in late 2008 the Unorganized Workers' Social Security Act, which sought to bring a modicum of public relief for people unable to take care of their own subsistence.[13] There is little doubt that the stony silence in the official circuit to this piece of legislation had much to do with the evidence produced that a very large portion of India's informal workforce is mired in deep poverty and that their deprivation went unabated in the first decade of the new century. This was unwelcome news for policy makers and politicians who indulged in the comfort of high-growth rates without bothering to find out at what cost. The NCEUS panel clarified its point of view that inclusion is *condition sine qua non* to progress for the masses lagging behind, an intrinsic feature of participatory involvement without which the development objective is bound to fail.

Is there no anxiety in the top echelons of society that the anguish and anger building up down below might spill over in outbursts of violence? A century ago, the notion of *la classe dangereuse* played a pivotal role in the willingness of vested interests in the Global North to accommodate the underclasses into mainstream society. While the haves in that part of the world decided to change tack and facilitate the inclusion of the haves-not and built up the welfare state, India's better-off classes appear not to be unduly bothered by the prospect of a social revolt. In contrast to the working poor in the advanced economies, who got organized in trade unions and political parties when the pace of industrialization and urbanization started to accelerate, the drive toward informalization means that the underprivileged masses are a fragmented assortment, unable to team up in collective action. The social question came up in the Global North to address the growing imbalance between labor and capital in the transition from an agrarian-rural to an industrial-urban way of life. The underlying trend toward equality in the fabric of society gave impetus to the demand for a proportional share in the distribution of economic gains. In India, the social question does not even arise in a neoliberal economy bent on favoring the well-to-do and shutting up the voices of the poor. Coming close in my fieldwork to where they live and how they make do, I have never failed to be impressed by their courage and resilience to oppose the ordeal imposed on them. However, their protest and resistance in a low-key and low-profile capacity tends to be much understated in writings on collective action, in a sphere of domination and repression very difficult to resort to.

A COURSE OF EXCLUSION

A drastic political reversal came in spring 2014 with the transfer of power from Congress to the Bajap Political Party (BJP) anxiously trying to canvass the Hinduized majority in its fold. The electoral outcome demonstrated the collapse of the Congress subterfuge and its credibility in trying to placate the underclasses while serving neoliberal interests. Popular anger in reaction to massive corruption implicating politicians and bureaucrats contributed to the defeat. Underlying what cascaded into a rout was the loss of support from underprivileged segments—Scheduled Castes, Scheduled Tribes, and Muslims—disillusioned by what had been promised but never delivered. In an ironic twist, many of the non-poor also deserted the party, which used to prioritize their well-being. The dissatisfaction of this middle- to higher-ranking segment stemmed from the proclaimed intent of Congress to spread welfare to the bottom classes. Catering to these underprivileged needs was met with strong disapproval by the better-off classes of citizens bent on remaining the exclusive beneficiaries of growth. Redistributive policies had to be pretended for reasons of political legitimacy and, if not practiced right away, then at least forecasted, in order to appease a deprived multitude that within a fabric of democracy could not be alienated. This ballot-box logic has fallen on deaf ears in a civilizational setting of stifling inequality. Bailing out the people stuck far below the poverty line is not an acceptable proposition higher up, even when that policy vow does not go beyond paying lip service to it. What has been the fallout of the new political equation?

As far as handling the social question is concerned, a definite change for the worse. Of course, this opinion is not shared by the Hindutva set of power-mongers. The former entitlement approach, never properly implemented, was replaced by a faked empowerment policy. Narendra Modi was elected prime minister with the promise that growth and development for all and sundry would be his agenda. His declared strategy is to go along with what big business wants: an infrastructural buildout at the public expense, lower taxation, and a free hand for corporate capital. This course of unrestrained capitalism, he insisted, would be in the best interest of labor, since it was going to result in a hundred million jobs. Neoliberalism never had a better advocate in India, and captains of finance and industry eagerly sponsored his campaign. From the onset, a frontal attack lined up to do away with whatever small gains labor had been able to make under Congress patronage in the preceding decades. The new budget drastically cut back on already toned down social sector expenditure—public health, housing, and education—as part of a reform meant to promote privatization in all these fields. Government expenditure on health care is 1.4 percent of GDP, lower than nearly everywhere else in the Global South. The meager budget set aside for public education makes India once more stuck at the world's rock bottom. The next step was to withdraw laws called archaic that secure and protect the dwindled contingent of workers employed on conditions of formality. In the Indian Labour Conference held end July 2015, Modi labeled such regulations as counterproductive to free enterprise.

Funding set aside for the public works program offering employment to rural households was slashed at lower levels of governance. The Food Security Act, valiantly fought for by civil rights activists, has been held in abeyance in states under BJP rule. As long as Congress was in charge, the policy makers were tardy to concretize the right to inclusion, and the promised welfare for the underprivileged did not materialize. Under the new regime, there is a brutal unwillingness to arrange for public relief that addresses the agony of the destitute underclass. The Antyodaya Anna scheme, which provided a monthly grain ration to the non-laboring poor, was phased out. It shares this fate with other benefits now scrapped as wasteful expenditure. The state-funded pension allowances are being retooled into contributory and self-financed ones. To facilitate market accessibility for the poor, a Unique Cash Transfer scheme has been announced that aims at shoring up workers in the informal economy. Equipped with a biometric identity card, a clientele deprived of state-financed largesse is encouraged to open bank accounts in which they will deposit pension payments from savings they themselves are supposed to make. It could be the running up to a Universal Basic Income (UBI) scheme, which may be experimented with as a policy ploy for self-provisioning. The beneficiaries would be kept responsible for all expenditure made by taking away much-needed subsidies on food, shelter, health care, education, and social security. In a newspeak jargon, Narendra Modi tries to cover up the reality of massive destitution. Politics of promised (though not practiced) inclusion have made way for rigorous exclusion. At the end of 2016, the prime minister suddenly demonetized high-value banknotes with the pretension to squeeze out black money. The operation completely failed to achieve this stated objective but created havoc in the cash-based informal economy, and it led to large-scale dismissal of its casual workforce and an income crunch for many months for the affected households. The introduction of a Goods and Services Tax a half year later had a similar devastating impact. Both interventions were meant to formalize the flow of capital and subject all financial transactions to state taxation while keeping labor thoroughly informalized in their condition of underpaid off-and-on employment.

What will be the fallout of the widening divide between haves and haves-not? India's constitution prescribes inclusion of all, irrespective of social identity and economic status. Politicians and policy makers of diverse ideological denominations have no option but to repeat the mantra that welfare for all remains their modus operandi. As one of the state makers, B. R. Ambedkar, popularly called Babasaheb, drew attention to the discrepancy between the doctrine of political equivalence and the brutal praxis of socioeconomic inequity. The paradox could, in his opinion, only be solved by giving the downtrodden segments access to the rights they are due as citizens. The declaration of universal suffrage and the legal imposition of the equality principle, Babasaheb argued, collided with an ingrained hierarchy that implied sustained subordination for the people at the bottom. Their status beyond the pale was reinforced by an extremely skewed distribution of the sources of existence. Mahatma Gandhi tackled the social question suggesting that the lower castes should remain under high-caste tutelage, a guardianship that would oblige the latter to raise the morality as well as standard of living of the former in a benign relationship of dependency and care. However, on the dark underside, dispossession went on unabated, resulting in a degree of poverty that spirals into pauperism, while on the shiny side, unbound consumerism whets the appetite of the better-off for ever more. In 2017, 1 percent of the Indian population owned 58 percent of the nation's wealth.[14] The idea that the more and the less well-off should be balanced in reasonable proportion to each other was never a popular credo and has faded away over time. That Gandhian wisdom of caring for the least and the last is incompatible with a predatory capitalism that drives the winners to unbridled accumulation while leaving the losers behind in misery.

FROM DEFIANCE TO ASSERTION

Does it mean that emancipation of the laboring and non-laboring poor has become unstuck? That would be a premature conclusion. First and foremost because the analysis in the preceding pages has to be nuanced since it cannot be generalized for India at large. Gujarat, where I have conducted most of my empirical research and which is one of the fastest-growing states, is at or close to the national bottom as far as wage rates for the laboring poor is concerned, an achievement that corresponds with its laggard score on the human development index. In the second place, due to an amorphous climate of defiance rather than because of concerted and collective action, even in the localities of my recurring fieldwork in Gujarat, absolute poverty is less stark than when I first came around more than half a century ago. The deprivation experienced is, in many cases, a relative one, caused by the widening gap with the better-off classes for the majority of the landless and land-poor households. Finally, the critical balance drawn fails to do justice to the social churning from below throughout the country. In some states other than the one on which I have concentrated my recurrent investigations, the underclasses appear to have acquired some more room to manoeuver.

It is not so easy to nail down the regional variation that exists and the causes of diversity. There are zones, mainly in the southern parts of the subcontinent, with moderate economic growth but more social progress, the outcome of populist politics. The so-called BIMARU states (Bihar, Madhya Pradesh, Rajasthan, and Uttar Pradesh) together with Odisha are marked by the least momentum of socioeconomic progress. Then there is a middle rank to which Maharashtra, Gujarat, West Bengal, and Karnataka belong, where, despite high industrialization and urbanization, the pace of social change is rather mediocre, and hence inequality spilling over into exclusion is very high. These regional contrasts have to be further complicated in terms of a vast divide between top and bottom ranks. In that frame, an uneven ranking is noticeable among the various communal categories of the underprivileged. Dalit assertion is spreading and has gained strength in Punjab and the Gangetic belt of North India in recent decades, but already much earlier it had surged forward in Maharashtra, Andhra Pradesh, and Tamilnad. It took longer for tribal identity to get articulated, but running through central India, covering one fourth of the country's districts, the *adivasis* are up in arms, in protest against oppression and dispossession, if not the destruction of their resources and habitat by corporate business. Sections of what are called the Other Backward Castes (that is, not scheduled in the lower ranks of identification) equipped with some assets are upwardly mobile in the informal economy and have managed to get more political clout in many states. Among Muslims, the assertion of communal profiling is least visible, clearly to avoid the risk that its manifestation might arouse suspicion of falling prey to an anti-national mindset.[15] The convoluted pattern explains the differentiation throughout the country, for instance, in wage levels, rates of literacy, as well as success (or not) in getting access to state-provided benefits. In all these struggles, whatever progress made is due not to benevolence granted from above but to claims tenaciously fought for from below. The reservation that needs to be expressed is that the prioritization of communal identities has so far not resulted in a joint action front militating for inclusion on a shared platform of common claims. Moreover, the individual or collective backlash from the higher echelons against the growing assertion from below is ferocious.

In order to upgrade conditions of work and life to a basic level of human decency and dignity three factors in particular have to be foregrounded as preconditional: the presence of social activism propelled from civil society, a clean and efficient government machinery committed to the implementation of pro-poor policies, and, finally, effective participation of the targeted beneficiaries in the struggle for welfare. Jointly, these considerations seem to have found better ground in South India. Hopeful also is an ongoing restructuring of the social order. An upsurge of a social consciousness can be detected among the lower castes-cum-classes spread over the subcontinent, manifest in their refusal to continue living in subordination. What used to be a hierarchical ranking in a relationship of proclaimed superiority versus imposed inferiority collapsed when neither the claim by the higher castes of preeminence nor professed acceptance by the lower castes of their subalternity remained the thrust of their interaction. In my perception, the lower ranks never internalized their submissiveness and refused to retreat in a culture of poverty. Entrapped in servitude in the past, they were obligated to a show of deference, but those days of a compelling need to acknowledge ritualized domination have gone. They do not any longer dwell in the shadow of the high and mighty but are settled in their own makeshift colonies in village or city. Living together has stimulated common cause. Ela Bhatt, the founding mother of the Self-Employed Women's Association, captured this notion of constituting a collectivity with her autobiography, *We Are Poor but So Many.*[16] These words convey the habitus of the rank-and-file membership that she mobilized to join her trade union for self-employed female street vendors, scavengers, cart pullers, home-based workers, and others, recruited from a gamut of Scheduled Castes, Other Backward Castes, Scheduled Tribes, and Muslims. Another recent step in the same direction is the initiative of labor activists and nongovernmental associations to formulate a charter for workers' rights in the informal economy and to get organized for representation along those lines.

The caste ranking has veered away from being spread over a vertical slope to stretching out on a horizontal plane in a frame of which inequality and not hierarchy is the most striking feature. The assertion to equivalence from down under is expressed in the claim to be included into mainstream society. But the steep inequality inherited from the past has, since 1980, further spiraled in a context of globalized capitalism. If the plunder going on does not end, and if capital is not brought under public control, the democratic fabric of politics is bound to collapse. Narendra Modi has gone on record declaring that his "Gujarat model of growth with development"—which amounted to a gross denial of the rule of law, civil liberties, social justice, ghettoization of the religious minority and not just the practice but also the principle of equality—has become the agenda for national policies. It is up to the country's citizenry at large to open the gates to inclusion. The denial to do so cannot but lapse into in a regime of naked authoritarianism, to further fracture, if not annihilate, what is left of public agency and multiclass representation. With the communalist adage that all people are unequal, but some are more unequal than others, the BJP supremo may be tempted to give this regime a more exclusionary slant. Narendra Modi was already an avid adept of a post-truth style of politics in Gujarat long before it became practiced wide and far. No doubt, the state has to be blamed for its failure to alleviate mass poverty spilling over in destitution, but the social activism fighting this remissness should not merely focus on the lapse of public governance. Beyond that, the owners and managers of capital have to be held accountable for the manner in which they treat or, increasingly, either misuse or disuse the country's massive labor force. In the globalized economy, capitalism as the hegemonic mode of production still gets away scot-free from contributing to human existence also for the down-and-out. When the social question was originally raised, labor directly confronted capital to seek a fair deal in the sharing of profit and cost. That spirit has to be brought back again in the struggle for emancipation, but not any longer at the national level only. Capital has come to operate more and more worldwide, and to engage with it at this transnational site of confrontation is going to be a major challenge for labor and its well-wishers.

NOTES

1. Further elaborated in J. Breman, *Capitalism, Inequality and Labour Bondage in India.* (Cambridge: Cambridge University Press, 2019).

2. Government of India, Ministry of Agriculture, *Agricultural Statistics at a Glance* (2015), 15.

3. S. S. Gupta, *Economic Philosophy of Mahatma Gandhi* (New Delhi: Delhi Printers, 1994).

4. Government of India, *Report of the National Committee on Rural Labour,* overview, vol. 1 (Delhi, 1991).

5. Keith Hart, "Informal Income Opportunities and Urban Employment in Ghana," Paper delivered to a conference on urban unemployment in Africa. Institute of Development Studies, University of Sussex, 12–16 September 1971. Included in R. Jolly, E. de Kadt, H. Singer, and F. Wilson, *Third World Employment: Problems and Strategy* (Harmondsworth: Penguin, 1973), 66–70.

6. J. Breman, *The Making and Unmaking of an Industrial Working Class: Sliding Down the Labour Hierarchy in Ahmedabad* (New Delhi: Oxford University Press, 2004).

7. National Commission on Enterprises in the Unorganized Sector (NCEUS), *The Challenge of Employment in India,* vol. 1, main report (New Delhi, 2009). See also J. Breman, *At Work in the Informal Economy of India: A Perspective from the Bottom Up* (New Delhi: Oxford University Press, 2013).

8. T. S. Papola and K. P. Kannan, *Towards an India Wage Report* (ILO Asia-Pacific Working Paper Series, 2017).

9. M. Davis, *Planet of Slums* (New York: Verso, 2006; reprinted 2017).

10. J. Breman, *On Pauperism in Present and Past* (New Delhi: Oxford University Press, 2016).

11. H. de Soto, *The Other Path: The Invisible Revolution in the Third World* (New York: Harper and Row, 1989); and *The Mystery of Capital: Why Capitalism Triumphs in the West and Fails Everywhere Else* (London: Basic Books, 2000; reprinted 2003).

12. J. Breman, *The Poverty Regime in Village India* (New Delhi: Oxford University Press, 2007).

13. NCEUS, *The Challenge of Employment in India,* 152.

14. F. Alvaredo, L. Chancel, T. Piketty, E. Saez and G. Zucman, eds., *World Inequality Report 2018* (World Inequality Web 2018).

15. Throughout South Asia, majoritarian politics are ferociously practiced, excluding religious minorities as hated outsiders in our midst. It is a denial of earlier statehood, which wanted to forefront secularism, as incorporated in the country's constitution, together with a culture encouraging tolerance and pluriformity. The Hindutva ideology raging in India has led to the deprivation of Muslims from citizenship rights and to their disenfranchisement in many states.

16. E. Bhatt, *We Are Poor but So Many: The Story of Self-Employed Women in India* (New York: Oxford University Press, 2006).

7

The Labor Question and Dependent Capitalism

The Case of Latin America

Ronaldo Munck

INTRODUCTION

The current debate on the social question at a global level needs to recognize very clearly the overarching structural divisions between the dominant imperialist countries and what we might call "dependent capitalism."[1] What is commonly known as "globalization" has not produced a "smooth," more equal world, as its advocates proclaimed it would, but has, rather, accentuated the inequalities between the Global North and the Global South, thus creating very different contexts for the relationship between the development of capitalism and the social question. This chapter explores, in a broad-brush manner, the particularities of the related "labor question" in Latin America, showing the inextricable links between it and various forms of the "national question." We start with a review of the National Developmental State era, running roughly from the 1950s to the late 1970s, followed by the so-called lost decade of the 1980s and after, coinciding with the heyday of neoliberal economic policies. We then review the debate around the Marginality Question, in which Latin American scholars made a somewhat neglected contribution to the formal/informal divide in labor relation that has more recently become known as the "precarity debate." The way capital interacts with labor is, of course, a two-way process, and thus we turn to the rise of significant social countermovements in the 2000s known as the "left decade" in Latin America. We note major changes in the capital/wage-labor relations and a partial reversal of the ongoing process of precarization. We conclude with some final thoughts on matters arising around the nature of the labor question under dependent capitalism following our review of the Latin American case and the global issues it raises.

The social question arguably takes a specific form in those parts of the world that were once colonized and that have since been characterized by dependent capitalist development. The structural nature of uneven development has not been surpassed by the globalized capitalist development of the last quarter of a century, and, in fact, these differences have become more pronounced.[2] In terms of the capital/wage labor relation—and what Marx called the "hidden abode of production"—a systematic form of global labor arbitrage has emerged that drives the extraction of surplus value in a "fragmented and hierarchically organized labor market" in which wage differentials create the dynamic for both labor outsourcing and labor migration. It is in this context—set by colonialism and imperialism—that labor in the South has been always-already precarious and where the social/labor question has been inseparable from the national question.[3]

Latin America is a particularly apposite region to take as a case study, given its complex position in terms of global development. In terms of Gramsci's famous East/West distinctions, Latin America could be said to be in a liminal position betwixt and between tradition and modernity, North and South, due to its particular history of uneven development.[4] Latin America has always experienced mixed temporalities, leading to multiple overlapping modernities. The most up-to-date modern technologies could be introduced in rural exporting areas while, on the other hand, traditional small-scale production and various forms of coerced labor played a key role in the industrialization process. The state also played a much greater role in the development process, and the national-popular dimension of politics prevailed over "classic" class-development patterns.

THE NATIONAL DEVELOPMENTAL STATE

During the phase of outward-oriented growth under an oligarchic state (roughly 1860 to 1930) the social question, as famously put by a minister in Brazil, was a "police matter." There was little perceived need for co-option or anything resembling a welfare state. The working class was being forged through internal but also external migration. Apart from a weak socialist current, anarchism and anarcho-syndicalism were the main ideologies at play. Unionization coincided with the main sectors of the agro-export economy—dockers, railroad workers, and miners, for example—although artisans, bakers, shoemakers, and tailors were also unionizing. While modernization required, in theory, a "free" labor force, landowners, in particular, found it too expensive and not docile enough. Thus, in many rural areas (not least in Brazil, where slavery was abolished only in 1888) relationships of personal dependency and subordination were recreated during the modernization period. Traditional patterns of labor control—including extra-economic forms of coercion—were prevalent in Mexico and the Andean countries in particular, in contrast to the more proletarianized Southern Cone (Argentina, Chile, and Uruguay).

The stock market crash of 1929 and the Great Depression of the 1930s led to a decisive shift toward industrialization based on a more inward-oriented development model. Pivotal to the import substitution industrialization (ISI) model was an interventionist or developmental state. It was the state that promoted industrialization and accelerated the social division of labor. Hand in hand with industrialization went a massive process of urbanization that made or remade the working classes. Prompted by changes in the global economy, the twin processes of industrialization and urbanization resulted in the forging of a new working class. Latin American urban growth rates in the 1950s were practically double what they were during Britain's Industrial Revolution.[5] Instead of overseas migration, it was internal rural-urban migration that, in this period, accounted for the bulk of new workers joining the work force. This was the first of Latin America's "great transformations" and one that shaped both the social relations and the politics of the era.

Import substitution industrialization was always seen by its promoters as a means to an end. This was a *national* development project, committed to the health and education of the nation's workers. The state expanded vastly in economic terms through the creation of new public enterprises and through nationalizations. It played a key role in financial intermediation and developed a synergistic relation with foreign capital. The expectation, as Garretón and his colleagues put it, "was that industrialization brought national wealth" and that "this wealth could be distributed indirectly to the population at large through government programmes."[6] This model had emerged because the old agro-export model was not viable during the recession of the 1930s, as international trade declined. While it created a new industrial bourgeoisie and working class, it did not, necessarily, confront the agrarian oligarchy. It was about creating a new model of capital accumulation that also harnessed the "old" relations of production in the rural and informal sectors to the benefit of the emerging monopoly capitalism, based on the extensive (rather than intensive) subordination of labor.

One of the key theoretical debates to emerge during the 1950–1980 period was that around "dualism" in relation to the modern and traditional sectors. Modernizers and Marxists alike agreed that the traditional sector (often associated with feudalism) was an obstacle to social progress. As with the binary logic seen in the opposition between formal and informal labor, the two sectors were seen to operate on quite distinct dynamics. In reality, as Oliveira has shown, these sectors were in a symbiotic relationship, because, as he argued, "the expansion of capitalism . . . occurred through the introduction of new relations [of production] in the archaic [sector] and through the reproduction of archaic relations in the new [sector]."[7] This critique of dualist reason may well explain the emergence of what, in Gramscian terms, we might call a "compromise state" during this period and, among other things, the failure to extend the emerging labor legislation to the rural areas.

There is, of course, no one model of the national development state that prevailed across Latin America. However, we can legitimately take Peronism in Argentina as an ideal type, with Varguismo in Brazil and Cardenismo in Mexico also sharing many of its characteristics. Peronism developed as a coalition between a nationalist military, an incipient industrial bourgeoisie, and a well-organized labor movement. Some of the profits of the agro-export sector were diverted to build up the industrial sector. Workers achieved labor dignity, but they were also expected to deliver better labor productivity. The developmentalist state promoted capitalist expansion and ensured the stable reproduction of the labor force through better education and the beginnings of a welfare state, previously neglected by the oligarchic state. The overwhelming statistic of this period is in relation to the share of labor in the national income, which went from 40 percent in 1945 to nearly 50 percent in 1955. Peronism went through many mutations subsequently, but the classic variant is emblematic of the national development state and can help explain later phenomena, such as the rise of Chávez in Venezuela.

Peronism, in many ways, encapsulates the national-popular nature of the social question in Latin America. It is often classified as populism (although this has given rise to conceptual confusion), which, as Octavio Ianni notes, "is a form of political organization of the relations of production in a period of expansion of the forces of production and internal market."[8] Populism was the form in which many of the postwar nationalist regimes incorporated the working class and generated a new expansive phase of capital accumulation. The trade unions were a key element in this process and in some cases became virtual state institutions and "transmission belts" (as in the communist model) for the populist leader. Nevertheless, many trade unions acquired during this period, and then sustained, the capacity to articulate worker demands and obtain a greater share in the national income. Favorable political conditions could allow the trade unions to engage not only in successful collective bargaining but also in political bargaining and strike actions that brought labor to the center of the national stage.

By the mid-1960s the "easy" phase of import substitution industrialization had become exhausted.[9] Part of this was due to ISI reaching technical limits in terms of what previous inputs could be substituted by locally manufactured goods. A leap into more sophisticated forms of production—both for local consumption and for export—was now called for. This would require new skills and greater levels of efficiency. There was a need for greater investment as well, something that could not be generated locally. Undoubtedly, though, it was the external environment (the debt crisis was then about to explode) that would provide the key impetus for a change of direction in Latin America, though the endogenous aspect of this transformation should not be neglected. ISI was seen as failure and the Economic Commission for Latin America (ECLA) argued that "structural heterogeneity" (dualism) had led to unbalanced growth and that the capital-intensive manufacturing sector and its modern technology had been able to absorb only a fraction of the growing workforce and thus led to the overexpansion of marginally productive activities. Labor "quality" and gender equity in employment had not been priorities, given the abundance of labor, and that now caused problems.

Later, more sober analysis, developed after the "lost decade" of the 1980s, led to a more positive overall balance sheet of this period. Various studies have concluded that the period 1950–1970 witnessed major transformations in the composition of the labor force as non-manual occupations in the secondary and tertiary sectors expanded and significant upward social mobility ensued.[10] The post–World War II industrialization had generated productive employment and, most significantly, brought a working class onto the stage and created the conditions for a dynamic labor movement.

Regardless of these arguments the horizontal expansion of capitalist relations was more or less achieved but now vertical integration was required. To achieve this, the labor process and relations of production needed to be brought fully under the sway of capital. The "formal subsumption" of labor needed to be followed by the "real subsumption" of labor to ensure the continued expansion of capitalism. Marx distinguishes between the "formal" and "real" subsumption of the labor process by capital. In the first phase of capitalist development, capital draws into its domain preexisting labor processes (for example, deploying noncapitalist techniques), markets, means of production, and workers. This Marx calls "formal" subsumption, under which the labor process as such continues much as before. Capitalism, however, cannot develop on this limited basis and is compelled to continuously transform the relations of production. The prerequisite for the real capitalist subsumption is a shift to a labor process created by capital itself. Thus capital gradually transforms the social relations until they become thoroughly imbued with the requirements of capital, and the labor process is then really subsumed under capital. The "deepening" of industrialization thus required greater labor discipline, which was a major raison d'être in the rise of military or authoritarian regimes from the 1970s onward across most of Latin America.

THE MARGINALITY QUESTION

At this point, we carry out an excursus to consider what has been Latin America's particular theoretical contribution to the study of precarity, namely the "marginality" theory of the 1960s and 1970s. It is necessary due to the growing importance of the informal sector but also as example of where Southern knowledge needs to come into play in global debates.

The origins of the term *marginality* lie in the U.S. sociology of the 1930s, at which time it referred to the psychological disorientation supposedly felt by individuals at the interface of two cultures, for example, after migration. In Latin America it was taken up by the early modernization theorists to refer to the consequences of the postwar urbanization process referred to above.[11] Various names were used to describe the informal settlements that arose around the big cities due to rural-urban migration—*villas misérias, barriadas, favelas, callampas, ranchos, campamentos,* and so forth—but in all cases, they were physically on the periphery of the city, and they lacked even the basics of communal services. Thus, *marginality* could refer to the social condition of these new urban dwellers, or, more often, it was the people who were deemed marginal in terms of their access to decent jobs, housing, or living standards. There is some common ground here with the much later European concept of "social exclusion."[12]

The most systematic Marxist study of marginality was that of José Nun as well the work of Aníbal Quijano.[13] What Nun was essentially doing was creating a new category—a "marginal mass"—to distinguish the Latin American situation from Marx's classic categories of "industrial reserve army" and "relative surplus labor." As with their modernization theory counterparts, Nun and Quijano were addressing the issue of why the postwar industrialization drive had failed to absorb the rapidly increasing labor force. Marginalization theory addressed the layer of the working population not utilized by monopoly capital, which was becoming dominant from the 1960s onward. Thus we see a category of the poor not envisaged by Marx, a relative surplus population that is not functional (or may even be dysfunctional) for the monopoly sector. The reason that it is not deemed to be functional is that it has no influence on the wages of the monopoly sector, whereas the classic reserve army of labor helped depress wages.

The positions of Nun were vigorously contested by a Brazilian think tank, the Brazilian Center of Analysis and Planning, with clear positions articulated by F. H. Cardoso and F. de Oliveira, in particular.[14] For Cardoso, the phenomenon of combined and uneven development could explain the emergence of the marginal urban population, and there was no need to go beyond Marx's original theory of relative surplus population and reserve army of labor. Oliveira's "critique of dualist reason" focused on the underlying dualism that Nun and Quijano shared with the modernization theorists. The activities of the so-called marginal sector were, in fact, both profitable and totally integrated into the overall pattern of capital accumulation. Small-scale commerce could facilitate the distribution of industrial goods, and the construction of informal settlements saved capital considerable costs. The dialectic of capital accumulation required the provision of labor and raw materials from the "backward" geographical areas and economic sectors.

The debate around marginality has continued sporadically, and its original protagonists came back to it at the end of the century.[15] It was clear that the original polemic of Nun and Quijano had been addressed to the 1960s left, which saw the shantytown dwellers as a new revolutionary vanguard. The underlying and continued mission was to distinguish what was happening in Latin America from the wage-labor society as theorized by Castel, in which most workers are salaried, there is full employment, and wage workers enjoy status, dignity, and social protection.[16] Latin America never shared this model, and even under ISI (and those countries where some form of welfarism was adopted) vast layers of the population fell outside of the capital/wage labor relation. The 1990s, indeed, saw a massive shift toward informal employment, which, to some degree, confirmed the original underlying message of the marginality thesis. The impact of structural heterogeneity, poverty, and social inequality in Latin America cannot be blamed on its victims (as the World Bank and the whole "poverty industry" still does) but requires objective and specific analysis, which the marginality writers at least tried to do.

Today we are clearly not just dealing with a debate that is of historical interest only. A symposium in 2004 entitled "From the Marginality of the 1960s to the 'New Poverty' of Today" argued that "there is now increasing evidence that although classical marginality may have lacked empirical veracity in its earliest iteration, changing economic conditions born out of the structural adjustment and austerity of the 1980s, together with the neo-liberal restructuring of the 1990s, is today creating the very conditions and cultural constructions conceived and predicted by Nun, Quijano and Lewis in the 1960s."[17] Certainly rising unemployment, generalized precarity of employment, privatization, and declining opportunities even in the informal sector had accentuated the phenomenon of marginality. What is different is a much more interventionist state in terms of social policies and a much greater degree of political participation than was possible in the conditions of the 1960s.

What is most noticeable in the current literature on precarity and the precariat is that it is almost totally Global North–centric in its theoretical frames and its empirical reference points.[18] There is a totally Global North sensibility at play here, it seems. In Guy Standing's case, it is really just Britain in the 1950s that is the model of economic and political development that he has in mind. There is hardly a reference to any part of the world outside the North Atlantic, which is simply assumed as the center and the norm that will apply everywhere. There is little cognizance that the type of work described by the term "precarity" has always been the norm in the Global South. In fact, it is Fordism and the welfare state that is the exception to the rule, from a global perspective. "Decent work," as the ILO calls it—even though it is a rather dubious term—has never been the norm in the postcolonial world. Rather, super-exploitation, accumulation through dispossession, and what might be called "permanent primitive accumulation" have by and large prevailed. From a Southern perspective, work has always-already been precarious, a basic fact that unsettles the notion that something new has been discovered. The genealogy of the concept of precarity and the precariat already shows its Southern origins, but this is never really acknowledged. While the precariat discourse exudes nostalgia for something that has been lost (the Keynesian/Fordist/welfare state), it does not speak to a South that never experienced welfare-state capitalism. The Southern experience of precarity is marked by the nature of the postcolonial state and, later, by the developmental state, where this has emerged. The changing nature of work as a result of the erosion of the welfare state is but one modality of precarity, others have been in existence for a long time in the fraught relations between workers, capital, and the state.

THE LOST DECADE

Returning now to our narrative, we will recount how the national developmental period (1950–1970) was followed by the so-called lost decade of the 1980s and the advent of neoliberalism, which was to operate a second "great transformation" in relation to capital/wage labor relations. Import substitution industrialization had been waning since the mid-1960s, but by the mid-1970s it was clearly failing as a hegemonic strategy, not least because of the changes then underway in the global economy. The horizontal expansion of capitalism had been achieved; now the vertical integration of capitalism was required. The "formal" subsumption of labor had been achieved; now what was required was the "real" subsumption of labor. The deepening of industrialization required greater labor discipline, and this gave rise to a series of emblematic military coups in Brazil (1964), Argentina (1976), and, in somewhat different circumstances, Chile (1973). The internationalized sector of capitalism—now clearly dominant—had outgrown the quite basic inward-oriented growth model and was not too concerned with the potential loss of workers as national consumers, hitherto a major factor.

The new economic model was gradually realized across Latin America under the so-called Washington Consensus, with varying degrees of brutality. Under the Orwellian title "structural reforms," these regimes implemented a coherent program of trade liberalization, labor flexibilization, and widespread privatization, designed to increase the power of capital and atomize the organized labor movement and social networks as a whole. As a systematic program of social transformation, dependent neoliberalism wielded considerable power to discipline society and the subaltern classes if they put up any resistance. The bottom line of the 1980s "reforms" was quite blunt, as expressed by Sebastian Edwards, then Latin American head at the World Bank, who stated that "in order to take full advantage of the opportunities offered by the world economy, . . . countries need a lean and dynamic labor market. Companies should be able to adjust their payrolls quickly and at low cost. This means that employment laws should be flexible and the hiring and dismissal costs should be kept as low as possible."[19] It is that subjection of labor that we now turn to.

During the 1980s, informal work and self-employment emerged as the dominant form of labor exploitation in Latin America, going up from 30 percent to 40 percent of total employment over the decade. Early definitions of informality, as used by the ILO, were not able to capture disguised forms of informality. Thus, in 2002, this definition was changed, following arguments by Portes and Hoffman, to embrace all workers not covered by social security.[20] Informal work, along with "flexibility" in the formal sector, became the drive of a new period of capital accumulation in Latin America that normalized what was before the exception to the rule. Organized labor was further marginalized after the politico-military attack it had undergone at the hand of the military regimes in the 1970s. According to Druck and Franco, in this period precarity as the dominant labor condition "takes on a central and strategic role in the logic of capitalist domination, ceasing to be something residual or peripheral [and becoming] institutionalized in all regions of the world," not least in Latin America, we might add.[21]

The dominant theories of informality, even in the 1980s tended to view it as a counter-cyclical sector taking up the labor surplus shed by the formal sector during the decade's regional crisis. In reality, we see how informality as a sector is linked closely to flexibilization in the formal workplace, which gives rise to what some authors have called a "new informality."[22] The informal sector does not exist as a separate sphere of refuge for those expelled from formal employment but is, rather, part of an integrated pattern of capital accumulation in dependent development. When we conceive of formal and informal elements as part of the same system, their dynamic becomes clearer. Thus we can see that the dramatic increase in subcontracting and outsourcing in the 1980s closely linked the formal and informal sectors. It is not that the formal economy is not able to absorb more workers—which the ECLA argued is the problem—but, rather, it is the dynamics of a system that creates increasing heterogeneity and informality as part of its continuous drive to maintain the subjection of workers and atomize their collective organizations.

At this point we need to clarify the definition and composition of the informal sector. Informal workers can be identified across a wide range of employment relationships, including own-account workers, subcontracted workers, casual day laborers, informal employees (of both formal and informal firms), and employer-owners of informal firms and unpaid contributing family members. These are all types of workers without social security or any form of legal protection, whether they work in industry, agriculture, or the service sector. Whereas this informal sector steadily declined in the ISI period, it grew steadily under neoliberal adjustment. To clarify what this meant on the ground, Portes and Hoffman have argued that "the informal proletariat is defined as the sum of own account *[sic]* workers minus professionals and technicians, domestic servants, and paid and unpaid workers in microenterprises."[23] In some countries, it was own-account workers who increased in numbers when structural adjustment reduced the number of regular jobs, while in other cases, it was domestic service or microenterprises that grew in importance.

The so-called lost decade of the 1980s led to a huge increase in informal work in Latin America as the economic and debt crisis deepened. In the 1980s nine out of ten new jobs were in the informal sector, and by 1990 the ILO estimated that 40 percent of the economically active population was engaged in the informal sector.[24] Deregulation, privatization, and trade liberalization deepened the tendency toward informality. Remarkably—as it was against all the evidence—neoliberal economists still insisted that growth would resume once the earlier inflation had been conquered and that informality was but a temporary stage on the way to modernization. In practice, labor "flexibility" was a key element in the neoliberal strategy, which took informality into the heart of the productive economy through a systematic policy of outsourcing. Legal restrictions on "atypical" contracts were removed; "standard" jobs were replaced by part-time work; subcontracting and other precarious forms of employment proliferated; there were cuts to both wages and benefits such as social security contributions; and employer contributions to payroll taxes were severely cut back in the 1980s and 1990s, more or less across the region.

Given that this era was the high-water mark of neoliberalism in ideology as much as in practice, it is not surprising that a vigorous defense of informality was mounted. Hernando de Soto became globally influential when he generalized from the case of Peru to create the image of a dynamic and entrepreneurial informal sector.[25] De Soto's social-legal discourse focused on economic activities rather than individuals or households. He showed, with ample evidence, how the poor struggle to house and feed themselves and earn a living. This was a positive reading, showing how the poor could enhance a nation's resources through their entrepreneurial skills. Their economic activities are only deemed illegal because of irrational government regulations on licensing and operational business laws. The solution was thus simple for De Soto: the unrelenting reduction of the role of the state through deregulation, de-bureaucratization, and privatization. That would lead to a win-win situation: better economic growth and enhanced social mobility for the poor. De Soto's libertarian populism attracted many international followers, but in the Peru of the 1980s, it had little impact on either economic growth or social mobility for the poor.[26] De Soto opened up an important debate but did not resolve the impasse of the ILO ideas and strategies.

During this neoliberal phase, there was a marked change in the gender composition of the informal sector. The ISI period was one that favored male employment in heavy industry and was based on the male-breadwinner model. Early studies of the urban informal sector did not disaggregate by gender and thus suffered in terms of precision and missed the impact on the changing gender division of labor. What emerged in the 1980s was a picture in which men were a majority working in the urban informal sector, but a higher proportion of women worked in the informal than in formal urban labor markets, thus shaping the majority experience of working women.[27] Not surprisingly, in terms of comparative international experience, women in the same occupational category as men earn considerably less. This is based partly on segregation (women clustered in certain occupations) but also on direct ongoing discrimination, despite gender-equality legislation, which, anyway, does not reach into the informal sector.

The gendered dimension of the economic restructuring characteristic of the 1980s and 1990s was quite marked. Sylvia Chant points particularly to women's disproportionate concentration in the informal sector leading to a fall in income and describes how the reduction in social services expenditure impacted women, particularly in relation to the household and childcare.[28] So, while in theory, economic development can enhance the position of women in the gendered division of labor, that was not the case in Latin America during the neoliberal phase. Women's participation in the workforce has increased steadily, from 18 percent in 1950 to 26 percent in 1980, and in absolute numbers, the female labor force more than tripled during that period.[29] This trend continued in the 1990s, with women's share of employment reaching 36 percent by the turn of the century. But, overall, women earned nearly 40 percent less than men and were disproportionally affected by economic restructuring, informalization, and the growing precarity of employment.[30]

THE LEFT DECADE

The crumbling of the neoliberal accumulation regime was at first gradual but then quite sudden, when Argentina's most orthodox model collapsed at the end of 2001. The illusion of the Washington Consensus as a viable development strategy had already begun to fade with so-called Tequila Crisis in Mexico in 1995.[31] Even Sebastian Edwards of the World Bank was admitting that while the region "had gone through a notable transformation, economic results were disappointing and the region's social situation showed little signs of improvement."[32] Dependent neoliberalism had been based on a mirage that convinced many (across society) that it was the royal road to modernity or, more crudely, a belief that markets + torture = modernization. Open financial systems had not led to a more stable global order, rather, it had vastly increased instability and the propensity to crisis. This issue came to a head in 2001, when Argentina, which had followed the neoliberal recipe to the letter and even tied its currency to the U.S. dollar, simply collapsed, providing the first harbinger of the 2008–2009 global financial crisis.

The collapse of neoliberalism led, in an internationally quite unprecedented way, to the emergence of left-wing, or at least progressive and post-neoliberal, governments more or less across the region from 2000 onward. The end of neoliberalism occurred not only due to its own internal contradictions but also due to the capacity of the trade-union movement (and others as well) to resist attacks (especially in the workplace) and form alliances with populist and/or socialist movements. To varying degrees—and in quite different ways in each country—the labor movement played a role in creating the conditions for the new progressive governments. The question then arises as to whether these governments were able to address the issues of poverty and inequality. Specifically, we need to consider the extent to which labor regimes were reformed and whether informality was in any way reversed. Clearly there were many constraints, not least the continued dependence on agro-mineral exports, sometimes referred to as the "new extractivism." Nevertheless, this section shows that politics matter when it comes to the social question and that the advance to precarization is not inexorable or immune to political intervention.

Far too often, the debates on Latin American politics have downplayed the role of the labor and other social movements in the process of democratization and beyond. Indeed, most of the military dictatorships of the 1980s fell precisely because the trade-union movement had kept up resistance in the workplace, along with neighborhood associations, women's groups, and new human rights organizations, which often had transnational links. Then, in terms of the rise of the left-wing governments after 2000, we need to factor in the growing importance of the labor movement in the 1990s. The progressive governments of the 2000s all signaled a widespread societal reaction against the free market policies of neoliberalism in classic Polanyian countermovement mode. They also, as Cook and Bazler argue, point toward the need to adopt a "labor lens [to] show that some left governments have jettisoned neoliberal ideas about unions. In the 1990s union power was seen as an obstacle to growth redistribution and investment. . . . In the 2000s [these] governments rejected the notion of a necessary trade-off between union strength and economic health."[33] This was a fundamental shift in the dominant discourse that would have massive social and political consequences.

There was, as would be expected, considerable variety across Latin America during the so-called left decade. For example, in Chile, while the centrist and progressive governments post-Pinochet increased social spending and expanded the social safety net, there was no decisive shift in terms of changes in labor law in the area of collective rights. In Uruguay, by contrast, the various left governments "had built up the unions' organizational resources while doing little to limit their power, and they have done so in spite of employer opposition."[34] This led a renewed role for collective bargaining between labor and capital, with only a limited role for the state. Brazil stood somewhere in between, with some more restricted elements, while the role of the trade unions in forming the governing Workers' Party gave it a certain degree of leverage. It is important to remember that the Workers' Party governments that were in office from 2003 (and longer at regional level) to 2016 were there as part of an unprecedented political project created by trade unions. In practice, these governments sought to accommodate the interests of capital—both domestic and foreign—while increasing social spending, raising the minimum wage, and shifting the balance from informal to formal employment.

Taking Argentina as an example, we can see in detail how path dependence and structural constraints regarding the social question can be altered by decisive political intervention.[35] We can recall that in the 1990s Argentina was considered the model neoliberal exemplar that should be emulated by the rest of Latin America. When the economy crashed at the end of 2001, this spelled the end of neoliberal hegemony, some years before the Northern catastrophe of 2008–2009. What emerged, after a period of great political instability, was a left-nationalist regime under the Kirchners that, to some extent, looked back at the ISI period for the inspiration. An outward-oriented growth model was moderated by a much greater orientation toward the internal market. A new labor regime began to cut down on the proportion of precarious jobs versus stable jobs. There was also a much stronger commitment to an inclusive social policy, which began to rapidly reduce the poverty and unemployment generated by the 2001–2002 economic collapse. A new decade opened up with nearly 10 percent annual growth rates, which addressed the "social debt" as a priority over the foreign debt.

The basic fact in Argentina's decisive and rapid shift away from neoliberalism toward a more inclusive social model was the proportion in the number of those registered under state security versus unregistered workers. While in 2004 the difference between the two categories was barely 200,000, by 2007 there were 2,000,000 more registered than unregistered workers: the first had gone up by 1.25 million while the latter had decreased by 0.5 million.[36] The previous labor regime characterized by precarization had been replaced by one characterized by social protection and the legal registration of employment. Where in the past the market ruled supreme, now the state took on a strongly regulatory role. Both employed and unemployed workers' associations were active players in this process whereby society seeks to protect itself from the free market, as Polanyi had predicted. In many ways acting as a model for the ECLA's strategy of "growth with equity," this model created a virtuous circle from employment to consumption to productive investment and back to employment. This had a tangible effect on the workplace—both formal and informal—and in the working-class household.

Conventionally an indicator of labor's ability to constrain the free operation of capital has been union density, that is, the percentage of the workforce covered by trade unions. Much is made of declining union density globally and in most of the North during the neoliberal era. While reliable data is hand to come by, there is enough household-sample-survey and other data for some countries to give us a general picture. In Argentina, male union membership in manufacturing stood at 50 percent in 2000, compared to 30 percent for women. In the public sector, unionization rates in Argentina were around 65 percent. In Brazil, union membership increased after 2000 to reach 30 percent across the formal private and public sectors, with male and female unionization rates being more or less similar. In Mexico, overall unionization fell in the 1990s, but there was a lot of variation, 75 percent coverage in education, but manufacturing dropping from 45 percent to 34 percent in 2000, and clerical workers going from 30 percent to 22 percent over the same period.[37] Overall, union density is moderately high by international standards, albeit with significant variations across countries and time.

Across Latin America there are many examples of the left turn impacting the tendency toward informalization and precarization. To "organize the unorganized" has always been a challenge for the trade-union movement, as these workers are less accessible, and they do not fit into standard industrial-relations bargaining structures. It is not always clear who the bargaining counterpart is when neither the state nor a capitalist employer is present. Yet the unions do recognize that they need to reach beyond the standard workplace if the working classes are to exercise their full potential power. Thus, in 1992, the powerful Central Worker's Union (CUT—Central Unica dos Trabalhadores) in Brazil sponsored the formation of the Informal Economy Workers' Syndicate (SINTEIN—Sindicato dos Trabalhadores na Economía Informal), which took up issues around micro-credit and entrepreneurship supported by the Ministry of Labor's Solidarity Economy Board. It also promoted the formation of cooperatives that would strengthen the sector in bargaining with wholesale dealers. A wide range of organizations—some more durable than others—have been formed by informal workers and street traders in Brazil and elsewhere.

In Argentina we have also seen a range of cross-sectoral labor organizations emerging, especially since the collapse of the economy in 2001. For a period of time, a retreat to a barter economy led to a flourishing of local community organizing, often led by the trade unions. The newly created layers of unemployed—often including impoverished middle-class and white-collar sectors—began to organize in a very militant way, creating the *piquetero* (picket) movement. This operated not only in the cities but also in rural areas, where there was a history of rural cooperatives. Eventually this wider working-class organizing initiative was defused by the left populist governments of the Kirchners, backed by the big trade-union leaders. Nor was it absent of contradictions, such as the mass mobilization of the Argentinian Building Workers Union (UOCRA—Unión Obrera de la Construcción de la República Argentina) in early 2002 against the presence of building workers from neighboring Bolivia and Paraguay, in a clear breach of commitments toward regional solidarity given in the past.

MATTERS ARISING

There is clearly a broad research and policy agenda emerging out of our summary consideration of the labor question in Latin America today, in the past, and in the future. It needs to be integrated, I would argue, into the broader review of the social question at a global level to the mutual benefit of both problematics. At a structural level, we need to recognize the dependent nature of capitalist development in Latin America and the impact this has had on the capital/wage labor relation. In particular, the salience of the national-popular, which cannot be reduced to facile accusations of "populism," needs to be recognized. It is also clear from the Latin American case study that we cannot reduce the scales of human activity to the global and the local domains and that we need to constantly think in terms of the national and regional. We have found that social or analytical categories developed in Europe or North America cannot be imposed on a recalcitrant subaltern reality. Above all, agency is crucial to any consideration of the social question and politics matters, to put it bluntly.

It would seem prudent, given the conventional inflation (and dubious politics) of the term *precariat,* to return to the focus on *travail précaire* as highlighted by Robert Castel in his influential treatment of the social question.[38] Precarious forms of work and precarious modalities of employment were on the rise as the Fordist social regime of accumulation began to lose its hegemony from 1970 onward (at least in the North). Employment norms were being eroded from within, and various forms of "nonstandard" working relations were coming to the fore. Precarity was probably more of a descriptive than an analytical category, and it was not regarded as a particularly new or self-contained category. Castel, in particular, placed his emphasis on *travail précaire,* not on precarity in general, and its erosion of the centrality of the wage relationship in the making of capitalist society. In the Global South, work was always-already precarious, and the wage relation was not the core element in the making of dependent capitalist countries. We should bear in mind, finally, Castel's statement that "There is a risk of confusing a phenomenon that has become more visible with a new phenomenon, or of believing that starting to assess how many people are affected by a problem marks the appearance of a new problem."[39]

In terms of the more specific current debates on the politics of labor precarity, we also have rich empirical material to consider above. In conceptual terms, we might usefully revisit the earlier Latin American debates on marginality that have somehow been airbrushed out of "global" accounts of informality. A broader issue is the problem caused by any attempt to think in terms of "standard" or normal wage relations, against which the real world is found wanting. While the discourse on labor formalization is a progressive one, there is the danger that supports a mythical non-precarious form of "decent work" that never existed in most of the world. The dichotomy between stable/protected versus precarious/vulnerable employment tends to defuse the inherently exploitative nature of capitalism. In conclusion, precarity denotes and highlights the divisive nature of capitalism and points to the need for broad economic, political, and social reforms that might reintroduce a degree of social control over capitalism and an unregulated market.

We might also consider what we mean by placing the social question at the "global level." This is not simply a question of scaling up a traditional European concern, insofar as the standard employment relationship—as deployed by the ILO and others—has never prevailed globally and only made its mark for a short period of time and in a limited sphere of the world. For the so-called majority world, capitalism was imposed from the outside, and its development remained dependent on the rhythms of development in the advanced industrial countries. The social question was deemed a "police matter" for a whole historical period, and the notion of welfarism or co-option of labor were absent concepts. In the last fifty years, however, labor has come to the fore in the majority world with massive industrialization producing a Marxist working class in the classic sense. In that sense, we do now have a "global social question," where the workers of the world are subject to similar regimes of accumulation and have common interests as they did at the time of the First International.

In Latin America, one of the main matters arising is the future role of social policy in regards to the labor question.[40] Historically, if we go back to the national-popular state period, we find around two-thirds of the working population covered by national insurance, bearing in mind that the early Latin American welfare state was based on Bismark's nineteenth-century European model. The neoliberal period changed all that, as did the rise of informality from the 1970s onward, so that only a minority of the working population was covered by national insurance. What we saw in the post-neoliberal period was the rise of the conditional cash transfers model that became the main support for nearly a quarter of the poor, providing a conditional safety net while still supporting the free market model. Latin America has always had a truncated welfare state, and the prevalence of informal work beyond labor institutions is becoming a pressing problem. While formal workers have minimal coverage, the growing informal sector does not, and conditional cash transfers are a palliative, at most. What we now see emerging is a gradual recognition that this welfare apartheid is not sustainable, and various extensions of welfare are being trialed. Whereas in the national state era workers' needs in relation to housing, health' and transport were recognized, since the neoliberal revolution, that was not the case, while at the same time, informality/marginality became the norm. The formalization of labor relations and the extension of social protection (and, of course, poverty reduction) are now key issues on the agenda. Poor workers need better jobs, but they also need unemployment, health, disability, retirement, and other forms of insurance. That is a political battle in a region where tax avoidance is rampant, and one the organizations of labor need to play a leading role in.

NOTES

1. Jan Breman and Marcel Linden, "Informalizing the Economy: The Return of the Social Question at a Global Level," *Development and Change* 45, no. 5 (2014): 920–40.

2. Giovanni Arrighi, Beverly Silver, and Benjamin Barber, "Industrial Convergence, Globalization, and the Persistence of the North-South Divide," *Studies in Comparative International Development* 38, no. 1 (2003): 3–31.

3. John Smith, *Imperialism in the Twenty First Century* (New York: Monthly Review Press, 2015), 56.

4. Antonio Gramsci, *Selections from the Prison Notebooks* (London: Lawrence and Wishart, 1970.

5. James J. Thomas, *Surviving in the City: The Urban Informal Sector in Latin America* (London: Pluto Press, 1995).

6. Manuel Antonio Garretón, Marcelo Cavarozzi, Peter Cleaves, Gary Gereffi, and Jonathan Hartlyn, *Latin America in the 21st Century: Towards a New Socio-Political Matrix* (Miami: North-South Centre Press, 2003).

7. Francisco Oliveira, "La economía brasilena: crítica a la razón dualista" *El Trimestre Económico* 40, no. 2 (1973): 36.

8. Octavio Ianni, *A formaçao do estado populista* (Sâo Paulo: Brasiliense, 1975), 135.

9. Werner Baer, "Industrialization in Latin America: Successes and Failures," *Journal of Economic Education* 15, no. 2 (1984): 124–35.

10. Joseph Ramos, Kirsten Sehnbruch, and Jürgen Weller, "Quality of Employment in Latin America: Theory and Evidence," *International Labour Review* 154, no. 2 (2015): 175.

11. Gino Germani, *La sociología en América Latina: Problemas y Perspectivas.* (Buenos Aires: Eudeba, 1964).

12. Ronaldo Munck, *Globalization and Social Exclusion: A Transformationalist Perspective* (Bloomsfiled, CT: Kumarian Press, 2005).

13. José Nun, "La marginalidad en América Latina," *Revista Latinoamericana de Sociología* 5, no. 2 (1969); Aníbal Quijano, "Redefinición de la dependencia y el proceso de marginalización en América Latina" in *Imperalismo y marginalidad en América Latina* (Lima: Mosca Azul, 1969).

14. Oliveira, "La economía brasilena"; Fernando Henrique Cardoso, "Comentario sobre os conceitos de superpopulaçao relative e marginalidade" *Estudos CEBRAP* 1, (1971): 99–130.

15. José Nun, "El Futuro del empleo de la tesis de la masa marginal," *Desarollo Económico* 38, no. 152 (1999): 985–1004.

16. Robert Castel, *La Métamorphoses de la question sociale, une chronique an salariat* (Paris: Fayard, 1995).

17. De la Rocha Mercedes et al. "From the Marginality of the 1960s to the 'New Poverty' of Today," *Latin American Research Review* 39, no. 1, (2004): 183–203.

18. Ronaldo Munck, "The Precariat: A View from the South," *Third World Quarterly* 34, no. 5 (2013): 747–62.

19. Sebastian Edwards, *Left Behind: Latin America and the False Promise of Populism* (Chicago: University of Chicago Press, 2010), 97.

20. Alejandro Portes and Kelly Hoffman. "Latin American Class Structures: Their Composition and Change during the Neoliberal Era," *Latin American Research Review* 38, no. 1 (2003): 41–82.

21. Graça Druck and Tania Franco (eds), *A perda da razão social do trabalho: Terceirização e precarização* (São Paulo: Boitempo Editorial, 2007).

22. Paulo Baltar and Cláudio Dedecca, "Mercado de trabalho e informalidade nos anos 90" *Estudos Econômicos, No especial,* (1997): 65–84.

23. Portes and Hoffman, "Latin American Class Structures," 54.

24. International Labour Organization. *Labour Overview: Latin America and the Caribbean* (Lima: ILO, 2005).

25. Hernando De Soto, *The Other Path* (New York: Basic Books, 1989).

26. Ray Bromley, "Informality, de Soto Style: From Concept to Policy," in *Contrapunto: The Informal Sector Debate in Latin America,* ed. C. Rakowski, 131–51 (New York: State University of New York Press, 1994).

27. James Biles, "Informal Work in Latin America: Completing Perspectives and Recent Debates" *Geography Compass* 31, no. 1 (2008): 214–36.

28. Sylvia Chant, "Population, Migration, Employment and Gender," in *Latin America Transformed: Globalization and Modernity,* ed. R. Gwynne and C. Kay, 226–70 (London: Arnold, 1999).

29. Helen I. Safa, "Economic Restructuring and Gender Subordination," *Latin American Perspectives* 22, no. 2 (1995), 34.

30. Martha Alter Chen, "Women in the Informal Sector: A Global Picture, the Global Movement." *SAIS Review* 21 (2001): 71–82.

31. Francisco Panizza, *Contemporary Latin America: Development and Democracy Beyond the Washington Consensus* (London: Zed Books, 2009), 156.

32. Maria Cook and Joseph Bazler, "Bringing Unions Back In: Labour and Left Governments in Latin America," Cornell University, School of Industrial and Labor Relations, Working Papers 4 (2013): 34.

33. Ibid., 24.

34. Joseph Ramos, Kirsten Sehnbruch, and Jürgen Weller, "Quality of Employment in Latin America: Theory and Evidence," *International Labour Review* 154, no. 2 (2015): 171–94.

35. Victoria Castillo, Marta Novick, and Gabriel Yoguel, "La movilidad laboral en Argentina desde mediados del decenio de 1990: el difícil camino de regreso al empleo formal," *Revista CEPAL* 89 (2006): 157–77.

36. Héctor Palomino, *El fortalecimiento actual del sistema de relaciones laborales: sus límites y potencialidades* (Buenos Aires: Ministry of Labour, Employment and Social Security, 2008).

37. Adalberto Cardoso and Julián Gindin, "Industrial Relations and Collective Bargaining: Argentina, Brazil and Mexico Compared," Dialogue Working Paper No. 5 (Geneva, ILO, 2009).

38. Robert Castel, *La Métamorphoses de la question sociale, une chronique an salariat.* Paras: Fayard, 1995.

39. Ibid., 519.

40. Santiago Levy and Norbert Schady, "Latin America's Social Policy Challenge: Education, Social Insurance, Redistribution," *Journal of Economic Perspectives* 27, no. 2 (2013); Michael Sherraden, "Social Policy in Latin America: Questions of Growth, Equality and Political Freedom," *Latin American Research Review* 30, no. 1 (1995).

8

Labor and Land Struggles in a Brazilian Steel Town

The Reorganization of Capital under Neo-Extractivism

Massimiliano Mollona

INTRODUCTION

When I started my fieldwork, in 2008, Brazil was the world's success story. In the midst of global recession, the country was growing at a rate of 8 percent, the real currency was getting stronger, and there was a self-proclaimed communist party in power led by an ex-metalworker from the poor northeast. But for more than three years now, Brazil's economy has receded, public debt and inflation are hiking, the value of the real is collapsing, and the country's investment status has been demoted to junk. The economic crisis sparked a political upheaval. In September 2016, President Rousseff was impeached, ending thirteen years of the Partido dos Trabalhadores (PT—Workers' Party) in government. The impeachment came after the investigation called "Car Wash" (Lava Jato) showed that top echelons of the PT, including the party treasury and the president of the lower house, were involved in a massive corruption scheme by Petrobras—Brazil's mighty state-run oil company, the fifth biggest oil producer in the world.

Soon after being elected president in 2003, Ignazio Lula da Silva, the former leader of the metalworkers' union, set up the massive program of poverty reduction, Bolsa Familia, which today reaches thirteen million families—one-quarter of the national population. As a result of the Bolsa Familia, the percentage of the population living below the poverty line decreased from 36 percent in 2003 to 23 percent in 2008. But in the second mandate, Lula cut welfare expenses and deregulated the labor market, which radically increased casualized work. The casualization of precarious sections of the working class went hand in hand with pro-labor policies, particularly the indexing of the minimum wage at inflation, plus GDP growth recorded two years previously. Seeing their nominal wages increase, wage earners turned to debt to finance their consumption. The radical austerity measures of Dilma put an end to Lula's pro-labor trend. Advised by Minister of Finance Joaquim Levy, a Chicago-trained economist, Rousseff radically cut social spending and credit, privatized state assets, and put together the proposal for *Lei 4330*, which, if approved, will radically deregulate Brazil's labor-relations system. According to Perry Anderson, the PT's sudden fall from grace is due to the electorate feeling "cheated" by Dilma suddenly embracing right-wing austerity policies.[1]

The cracks started to show in June 2013, when a small gathering against a rise in the cost of public transport in two weeks spread to four hundred cities and town, bringing millions of people in the streets and forcing president Rousseff to start a process of constitutional reform. The demonstrators opposed the violent relocations of favelas, increases in transport fares, the privatization of public utilities, and the proposed *Lei 4330* that the government had set in motion in preparation for the World Cup and Olympic Games. This demonstration was, according to Göran Therborn, a "movement of movements" and a cross-sectional coalition that challenged the Eurocentric model of socialism premised upon the assumption of the vanguard of the industrial working class.[2]

In this chapter I present an ethnography of the Companhia Siderúrgica do Brasil (CSB—Brazilian Steel Company), a multinational Brazilian steel company based in Volta Grande, a steel town in the state of Rio de Janeiro. The chapter shows a structural coupling between Brazil's neo-extractivist model—a mixture of financialization, labor deregulation, and extractivism—and the strategies of accumulation by dispossession by the CSB based on rent seeking, commodity export, and open conflict with the local community. Brazilian neo-extractivism is the consequence of the wider "internalization of imperialism"[3] by the Lula administration and the transformation of the Brazilian state from developer to financial investor.[4] In this chapter I show how the state-driven financialization of the economy impacts the shop floor in terms of labor deskilling and intensification and on working-class debt and conspicuous consumption. I particularly look at the impact of neo-etxractivism on three sections of the working class. In 2008, at the beginning of my fieldwork, most wage earners of the CSB considered themselves as middle-class "class C." Today, they struggle with unemployment, debts, and mortgage defaults. Another section of the working class, informal and tertiarized workers in the service and building industries, face a similarly harsh employer—the municipality of Volta Grande, which exploits their labor in the desperate attempt to develop a new economy, independent from the CSB and based on service and tourism. A third section of the working class, subcontractors and car workers, are faring better, thanks to their militant struggles against labor deregulation and their regional alliances with municipalities and local businesses. The trade union's factory-based struggles, the land activism of the civic coalition, and the legal and business activism of the new working class are different strategies of labor struggle happening at different state levels and reflecting historically and geographically diverse trajectories of capitalist development. Thus, this chapter witnesses the resilience of the Brazilian working class in the context of an epochal shift in national politics—that is, the collapse of the Workers' Party and of its model of state capitalism.

SUBCONTRACTORS ON STRIKE

In 2005 subcontracted maintenance workers led three major strikes that paralyzed the city of Volta Grande. They were striking against their employers and the steelmaker Companhia Siderúrgica do Brasil, which they held jointly responsible for their decreasing wages[5] and benefits;[6] inhuman working conditions, such as lack of air conditioning or fresh water; and stigmatization by direct workers. In that year, outsourced workers continued to lead strikes, slow-downs, and sabotages. In response, the CSB backsourced several maintenance jobs, starting a trend of re-internalization that continues today. The trajectory of subcontracted workers that I describe in this chapter goes against standard narratives of class struggle and flexible capitalism. In fact, the resurgence of working-class activism in Volta Grande came by the hands of outsourced workers, notoriously the weakest link of the labor movement. How did such a traditionally unskilled and politically fragmented section of the working class become the political vanguard of the labor movement, overshadowing even the leadership of the PT?

The CSB is the biggest steel complex in Latin America, located in Volta Grande, a steel town in the middle of a dilapidated coffee valley. The company was built in 1946 by the dictator Getúlio Vargas with American technology and money. It was the core of Vargas's developmental dream to turn Brazil into a modern industrialized country. As a state-owned enterprise, the CSB was under a mixed economy and run by generals, military personnel, and highly educated civil servants until 1992, when it was privatized. The new owner, a textile magnate from São Paulo with no experience in steel making, cut the workforce by two-thirds and turned the company into a conglomerate with diversified businesses including mining, logistics, and finance. Moreover, privatization turned the state into major stockholder of the CSB through direct and indirect shares controlled by public pension funds and the National Economic and Social Development Bank (Banco Nacional de Desenvolvimento Econômico e Social—BNDES). From the 85 thousand tons of crude steel produced in 1946, the plant currently produces 4.8 millions tons of crude steel and 4.7 tons of laminated steel. It employs 12,000 direct and 5,000 tertiarized workers. Overall, the CSB employs 22,000 direct workers and 17,000 subcontractors and is the largest fully integrated steel producer in Latin America. During the recent economic crisis, the company's profits continued to be driven by sales in crude steel fed by the government's Growth Acceleration Programs (Programa de Aceleração do Crescimento—PAC), which boosted the national construction and housing sectors. But a third of the company's profits came from its iron ore business, reflecting Brazil's extractivist model. After the impeachment of president Rousseff in 2016, PACs were suspended, and foreign carmakers fled the region, and China's economic slowdown, the main importer of CSB's iron ore, hit the company hard. Like many steelmakers in the Global South, the company is locked in a position of financial weakness and of "dependent development." Its low-value and highly polluting crude steel and tin plates production and commodity exports can hardly compete with the high-value special steel production for the automotive and aerospace sectors, dominated by EU and U.S. steelmakers. In addition to their more advanced technology, these steelmakers are backed by strong nation-states in terms of antidumping and labor deregulation.[7] Below I describe how labor law, a force emanating from Brazil's developmental state, blurs the boundaries between wage labor, subcontracting, and informal and cooperative labor and affects the workers' insurgent strategies and identities.

STATES OF LABOR

One way in which the Brazilian state has a major influence on the economy is through its labor legislation. The Labor Code (CLT) was created by the Vargas's Labor Ministry in 1943 and continues to be one of the most comprehensive labor legislations in the world. Among other things, the CLT establishes the right to a minimum wage, vacation, leave, professional training, housing, pensions, and child benefits, and it regulates trade-union affiliation, training, and education. The code made unionization de facto compulsory by establishing that only unionized workers were eligible for social benefits and nominated workers' representatives in charge of collecting trade union dues on behalf of the state. Compulsory union contribution is still in place. In the same year, Vargas's constitutional assembly created the Brazilian Workers Party (Partido Trabalhista Brasileiro—PTB), the biggest workers' party in Latin America. The CLT's generous social benefits were given based on the workers' affiliation to state-controlled trade unions and the PDT, rather than on their demands. Hence, sociologist De Castro Gomes describes the Estado Novo as an "occupational welfare state" where the working class gained political emancipation through concessions from above,[8] rather than from grassroots activism. Unlike her, French argues that the CLT empowered the working class by creating a new legal framework through which it articulated its struggles.[9] The metalworkers' union (SMSF) won the right to paid overtime and night shifts, and recreation and health and safety provisions[10] through legal challenges to the CSB and the Employer Federation rather than by top-down concessions. In Brazil, working-class formation diverges from the master narrative of working-class emancipation crafted on nineteenth-century England and based on the opposition between class struggles and identity struggles.[11] Unlike nineteen-century capitalist England, Brazil was traditionally a mixed economy based on a labor regime that mixed slavery and wage labor and where struggles for civic emancipation and struggles for economic redistribution always went hand in hand. Labor rights were heavily cut by president Fernando Henrique Cardoso, who was determined to break the power of trade unions, deregulate the labor market, and "put an end to the era of Vargas." When Lula da Silva was elected president, he passed Amendment 45 to extend the labor law to informal labor, which had peaked during Cardoso's presidency.

I have argued above that during the second mandate, Lula cut welfare expenses and deregulated the labor market. A full 94 percent of the jobs created during the Lula and Rousseff administrations are low income (1.5 times below the minimum wage)[12] and in non-industrial sectors, such as clerks, construction work, transport and general service;[13] 60 percent of these involve young people,[14] mainly women and ethnic minorities. So in the national context of decreasing levels of inequality, labor incomes are slowly converging toward a median just above the poverty line. This convergence creates political instability, because people on the same income level come from radically different backgrounds: upwardly mobile poor and downwardly mobile casualized workers. Moreover, low-income and casualized labor, as well as informal and unremunerated work, currently make up 38 percent of the labor market. But the Brazilian labor law is heavily focused on formal employment. Below I discuss how subcontracting blurs the labor forms of wage-work, informal work, and entrepreneurship—and in so doing, along with creating exploitation, it opens new forms of workers' resistance.

OUTSOURCING IN BRAZIL

Broadly speaking, there are two models of externalization of labor: subcontracting and outsourcing. *Subcontracting* refers to the practice of hiring an outside company or provider to perform specific parts of a business contract or project, and the work done by subcontractors is normally temporary. *Outsourcing* generally refers to processes that could be performed by a company's internal staff but which are contracted to outside providers working independently. For example, contracting an outside provider to manage internal technology. This model of externalization of non-core economic activities is normally associated with short-term cost-cutting, radical reorganizations (from vertical to horizontal structures) and changes in work relations (from wage contract to market exchange).

In Brazil the situation is complicated even more by the way labor informalization tends to blur with outsourcing and subcontracting. But, in fact, these are different economic practices. Informalization is a process of marginalization of laborers from the formal workforce, which, in Brazil, emerged with "dependent" industrialization from the 1940s onward. By contrast, subcontracting is a symmetrical transaction, and outsourcing is a form of precarization of the formal workforce—a more recent phenomenon concentrated in the service and IT sectors, mainly dominated by foreign corporations.

There are different kinds of outsourcing, entailing different degrees of vulnerability and precariousness. Contracts between workers and subcontractors can be permanent or temporary. Outsourced workers who are permanently employed experience a contradiction: while their contract with outsourced firms is permanent and stable, the contract between their employers and the main firm is temporary; it typically lasts between one and four years. Besides, the relationship between the main contractor and outsourced workers can be formal or informal. In Brazil, there are various forms of outsourcing: hiring autonomous workers for domestic work; subcontracting companies for supplying products, pieces, or machinery; subcontracting auxiliary and support services to specialized companies; subcontracting services within the central production area to autonomous professionals; and subcontracting to subcontractors (quarterization—*quarterização*) or cooperatives.

Subcontracting: Main contractor → subcontractor
Tertiarization: Main contractor → external company
Quarterization: Main contractor → external company → subcontractor

It must be stressed that, as yet, there is no law on subcontracting in Brazil. The main regulation on subcontracted work is Article 331 of the Labor Tribunal (now incorporated into the Labor Code), which establishes two principles. First, that the contract of outsourcing takes place between two employers (the contractor and the subcontractor) and not between employer and employee (the contractor and the subcontracted workers). Unlike direct workers, outsourced workers are not legally subordinated, and, hence, they are "juridical persons" with only civic rights. For instance, in case of their employers' bankruptcy, they have the right to their outstanding wages and pensions. Thus, subcontracting establishes a state of exception within labor law, which is active only within hierarchical relations. Secondly, the article establishes that the externalization of core ("end") activities is illegal, whereas it legalizes the externalization of marginal ("means") activities. This distinction between core and marginal activities, inherited from the corporate world, is easy to circumvent.[15] For instance, the CSB currently uses contract workers for the core maintenance operations of waste extraction, cleaning, and sealing the pig iron channels and the furnace—which were previously performed by internal workers—after the reclassification of those tasks as "not core." Article 331 had the merit to reduce the illegal and informal subcontracting of cleaners, maintenance workers and builders that spread in Brazil in the late 1980s. On the other hand, the legalization of outsourcing led to an intensification of tertiarization from the late 1990s onward.[16]

The issue of subcontracted work was one of the triggers of the public's moral outrage against Rousseff. Her proposed Law 4330, if passed, will allow firms to outsource their core activities and to operate without full-time and permanent workers. The model of the "ghost factory" adopted by some global carmakers in the region, where all core operations are outsourced, which I describe below, may become the norm. Outsourcing is a global phenomenon. It follows the flows of global finance and the patterns of commodity chains, overflowing the boundaries of nations and cultures. Yet the centrality of the legal system in Brazil and the rapidity through which it adapts to new capital reconfigurations and shapes new labor struggles is worth investigating.

OUTSOURCING IN THE CSB

This chapter focuses on outsourced maintenance workers with permanent contracts. These workers are based at the CSB, are formally registered (and hence, unlike informal workers, are covered by the Labor Law), and perform skilled tasks such as mechanical and electric repairs, welding, and refractory work. In this section, I show that the company embraced labor outsourcing during privatization in order to purge the militant and skilled workforce but that, as a consequence of the measure, the company became heavily dependent on outsourced labor. Thus, this section shows that in specific circumstances, outsourcing can increase the bargaining power of labor. Since the beginning, the CSB resorted to various forms of legal and illegal outsourcing, especially of cleaners and builders. In the late 1980s, when Brazil returned to democracy, the company started to extensively outsource maintenance workers into a separate unit (FEM), a subsidiary of the main company.

The privatization of the CSB totally restructured the company. First went the many unskilled builders, carpenters, and bricklayers, who had been employed during the recent expansion of the firm, also called "Plan D." Then, more than half of the maintenance workforce and engineers, the firm's most militant section, were outsourced and dispersed into several external, outsourced firms. This mass outsourcing was made possible by Article 311, which was approved only a few months after the CSB was privatized. Outsourcing of maintenance jobs took a pyramidal form. The CSB outsourced, via FEM, to a "smaller FEM"—*feinha*.[17] The *feinha*, in turn, outsourced to smaller subcontractors—a structure called *quinterização* (quinterization). The FEM maintained only the functions of supervision and cost accounting. The few maintenance workers who stayed in the FEM were deskilled and turned into line managers in charge of supervising a vast and often underqualified external workforce. For instance, in the coke oven, there were more than two hundred outsourced maintenance workers. Initially, outsourced workers lost all their labor rights and pensions and suffered a radical deterioration of their working condition and status. In 2002 the FEM was closed, and all maintenance operations were outsourced to two multinational firms—the Italian Comau and the Japanese Sankyu.

The CSB kept only the functions of supervision, marketing, distribution, and extraordinary maintenance, led by a small team of maintenance workers.

Subcontracted workers gained permanent positions, but their wages and working conditions worsened further. Permanent maintenance workers would describe outsourced workers as a "subrace," but, in fact, these very permanent workers were being deskilled by a managerial system, SIGMA, that standardized maintenance and embedded supervisory control into the line. This standardized maintenance system was extremely distressing for line operators. For instance, Nené, a mill operator, claimed, "This continuous attention to mechanical breakdowns is emotionally draining. Two years ago, the 'old guy' [the billet mill] broke down while I was in the control cabin. It was a traumatic experience. I felt guilty and anxious about the financial implications of my actions, about my own life, and about the future of the company. For long time I felt that my whole body was paralyzed too. . . . I lived in a state of suspension."

One of the effects of the financialization of the economy is that financial returns become more important than industrial profits in the strategic decisions of companies. The SIGMA system actualized the financial logic onto the shop floor by establishing a regime in which preventing depreciation (that is, of the value of assets) is more important than increasing productivity.

Besides, the state privatized the company right after it completed Plan D, which brought a new furnace and oxygen shop and two laminating mills on the shop floor, boosting the production capacity of the plant from one million tons to nearly five million tons. The workers remember Plan D as the company's golden age, which attracted skilled workers from all over Brazil and turned Volta Grande into a world-leading steel-making center. But they also remember that period as the dark era of privatization. Many "second-generation" workers, hired during the firm's expansion, were traumatized by witnessing the mass redundancies of colleagues, friends, and relatives. A big portion of the employees who had been made redundant, especially black and female labor, ended up in the informal and domestic labor market. Indeed, for many workers, it was difficult to understand what was really going on during privatization. The general feeling was that the firm was making new investments and expanding production capacity rather than cutting costs.

The SIGMA system had a catastrophic impact especially on the smelting shop (AF), where a third of the workforce was cut. Today, half of AF's seven hundred employees are subcontractors. In the AF, subcontractors have the harshest jobs, such as putting the molds on the furnace door or breaking the molds of slabs. But the working conditions and rights of permanent workers are often worse than those of the contractors. For instance, during the crisis of 2009, all the workers of the AF2 were immediately laid off for three months, and only some of them were reemployed when the crisis was over. For a long time, confusion reigned. Many permanent employees end up as contractors, and contractors were hired permanently. But on the whole, the company made a dramatic turnaround and from a net loss of US$749 million in 1990 went to a net profit of US$110 million in 1995. It was easy for workers to buy in to the management's narrative that these improvements were the result of labor cuts rather than of the investments that preceded them. Some workers' narratives reflect this cognitive dissonance between cuts and expansion. For instance, Bobo, a top manager, got his job at the CSB three days before the general strike of 1988. When the strike paralyzed the factory, all contracts were frozen, including his. Bobo was officially registered on the working card only one year into his job. A few years later, seeing the workforce being cut from twenty-two thousand to fourteen thousand during privatization was another life-changing event:

> Privatization came as a shock. Volta Grande entered in a state of collective hysteria. Initially I was worried too, but then the SIGMA system totally changed me. First, it made me appreciate the importance of money in my life—monetary losses of faulty set-ups, monetary gains of preventive operations, monetary cost of depreciation. Then, I had an epiphany: privatization had made employees more vulnerable as workers but more powerful as investors. I bought company shares and invested in the pension scheme. Now I think about myself in terms of ownership—ownership over my life—rather than in terms of my wage. The state and the company do not own me anymore, I am the sole responsible for my pensions, housing, and education. If this is capitalism, then, I am a capitalist.

Second-generation permanent workers like Bobo accepted privatization from a position of weakness and uncertainty. They were experiencing a historical transformation, comparable to some post-socialism transitions—from dictatorship to democracy and from mixed economy to capitalism, which they did not understand. They were in between classes and generations. Neither skilled and political connected like the older generation nor formally educated and pragmatic like the younger one; neither opposing capitalism, like the former, nor endorsing it, like the younger "wage hunters." During my fieldwork, I was always struck by their docility vis-à-vis the management and their lack of identification with their job, reflected in the way they talked about themselves as "passers-by" or a "fleeting workforce" and as *arigos* (migratory birds), even if they had permanent contracts.

In contrast to them, the tertiarized maintenance workers of the CSB have a strong occupational identity and are politically militant. From 2005, for three consecutive years, they confronted the CSB with strikes, slow-downs, sabotage, and absenteeism. Many of them were dismissed and blacklisted. In 2007 direct workers agreed to support the outsourced workers' demands for higher wages and better working conditions by halting the production line with them for one day. But at the last minute, they pulled out. As result of their activism, the contract workers' wages grew more rapidly than those of direct workers. In fact, the salary level established in collective agreements for outsourced workers became the benchmark for qualified direct workers too, which meant that they were on the same wage level of skilled engineers and technicians. Having won the right to have their collective negotiations jointly with those of direct workers, their company-related health and pensions plans, participation to profits, monthly food provisions, and salary levels were nearly in line with those of direct workers. Their health and safety standards and working environment improved radically. Moreover, maintenance workers were in high demand by the global carmakers and steel companies that had just moved to the region.

As for the China sunset workers described by Lee, the main "insurgent identity" of maintenance workers was their citizens' right to legal justice sustained by a recent change in labor law, which was achieved through the activism of left-wing judges and lawyers.[18] Going against the logic of Article 331, the new law established the principle of "subsidiary responsibility," which made the main contractors jointly responsible with their subcontractors on accidents and underpayment of wages and benefits to their employees. But, political and legal activism aside, outsourced maintenance workers won these important concessions because they were the only one left in the CSB who could run the company. When the SIGMA system was introduced, engineers and skilled maintenance workers were laid off, entirely wiping out the internal memory and knowledge of the technical system. The few internal engineers and maintenance workers left were turned into cost accountants and supervisors. But in order for the plant to run smoothly, the management needs experienced maintenance employees. The company is now dependent on those outsourced maintenance workers, often ex-CSB workers who have this knowledge. In fact, it continues to renew contracts with the same maintenance firms in the hope of winning the trust of its skilled ex-employees. Every day, gangs of subcontracted builders, mechanics, and electricians enter the shop floor, commending both respect and resentment from the direct workforce. Some small subcontractors have worked in the CSB for decades and are considered quasi-employees. Some are ex-CSB maintenance workers who set up their own business and now have higher remunerations and better working conditions that the internal workers. Both internal subcontractors and independent firms are expensive to monitor. So it is not surprising that in 2007 the CSB started a process of re-internalization (back-sourcing) of maintenance workers, as well of security and transportation workers, in the newly created General Maintenance Unit (GMU).[19] In 2010 the CSB back-sourced two-thirds of the maintenance workers previously employed by its main subcontractor, COMAU. Maintenance workers "changed their shirts back again." Direct workers cost about 150 percent to 200 percent more than outsourced workers, but they come with lower political risks. Outsourced workers are conscious of their power and knowledge vis-à-vis the company and can hit it hard through strikes, slowdowns, and absenteeism.

OTHER FORMS OF TERTIARIZATION

In the meantime, the global carmakers Peugeot and Volkswagen (VW) had moved to the region, lured by the tax exemptions, free land, and cheap labor offered by cash-stripped municipalities. These global carmakers work with a model of extreme outsourcing. The most extreme version is VW's "dream factory" in Resende, which is totally tertiarized. This so-called factory of the future pushes the Japanese lean model to its extremes. Unlike the traditional Japanese model, in which core activities are internalized, in the dream factory, all operations—both direct, such as production and assembly, and indirect, such as cleaning, transport, food, health service, data processing and logistics—are externalized to independent subcontractors operating in situ. The only core functions retained by VW are brand development and quality control. Essentially, the firm is like a merchant capitalist operating through a spatially concentrated putting-out network. The dream factory is both a market and a firm. But this extreme marketization is disguised by the fact that the subcontractors are under the same roof and share the same human resources management and VW overall—although with a fine-printed logo of their company on the front. As I mentioned earlier, this total subcontracting is against Article 331.

In 1996, when the factory opened, of a total of 1,500 workers, 1,300 were subcontracted. The situation was complicated further in 2007, when the German MAN-AG bought the factory and logistical operations were externalized to a separate firm located to the rear of the firm, adding a third level of subcontracting. The employer agreed that negotiations with all subcontractors (previously held separately) should be held in the same collective negotiations between the VW and the metalworkers' trade union (SMSF). But tertiarized ancillary workers (such as cleaners and transport workers, who represent more than half of the total workforce) and externalized logistical workers are not represented in factory councils (FC) or in collective negotiations. The "new class"[20] of car-workers is radically different from the steel workers. The majority of subcontracted car-workers are young, well educated, relatively well off, non-unionized, and loyal to their employer and their "brand"—with whom they develop trusting and long-term relationships. In 2012 50 percent of the factory's total workforce (6,000 workers) was subcontracted. For the VW management, brand management and quality control are the company's sole core businesses, and all the other activities, both direct and indirect, can be legally outsourced. Free from any legal obligation toward its workers, VW combines a tight taylorist labor regime and putting-out operations. The outsourced workers of the modular factory are of a different kind from the outsourced CSB workers. First, they are internally fragmented between ancillary workers—such as cleaners and transport workers—and direct workers. The former have a poor educational background, little experience of formal employment and political activism, and an instrumental attitude to work.[21] In spite of representing more than half of the total workforce of the factory, they are not represented in factory councils or in collective negotiations between VW and the SMSF, and they have a marginal status vis-à-vis the car workers.

Yes, in spite of their apolitical attitude, the car workers of Resende and Porto Real kept their real wages intact and avoided layoffs in a context of declining prices and profits in the industry[22] by entering in tripartite negotiations with municipalities and management[23] and reviving the early experiments of the PT in São Paulo. Car workers rescaled their action from the factory to the region and created solidarities with municipalities and workers in other industries, setting in motion a new process of class struggle. Unlike them, steelworkers focused on factory-based struggles[24] concerning wages, participation to the company's profits, and working conditions with the management and refused the cross-sectional regionalism of the car workers. This conflict between factory-based activism of steelworkers and the regional activism of car workers must be considered in relation to the ongoing tensions between the municipality and the company, an issue that I discuss in the next section.

FROM FACTORY STRUGGLES TO LAND STRUGGLES

Some studies of deindustrialized cities and rust-belt regions have argued that political decentralization, both regionalism and municipalism, may foster new forms of participatory democracy and cross-sectional alliances between the traditional working class and civic movements, including middle-class and employers' organizations. Some Brazilian scholars have used this framework in the context of deindustrialization of the ABC region of São Paulo.[25] Indeed, the cross-sectional alliances between municipalities, employers, civic movements, and trade unions against global carmakers in the industrial region of São Paulo were central engines for the raise of the PT to power. But the economic geography of Volta Grande does not match the classic profile of an industrial rust belt. The CSB is, at the same time, a global financial operator, with a globally dispersed production process; a Taylorist employer; and a powerful landowner. Historically in Brazil, industrialization coexisted with slavery and a rentier economy, and these are coming to the fore with deindustrialization. The CSB currently employs about 30.6 percent of the population, and jobs are concentrated in the service, commerce, and the public sectors.[26] Yet the company owns one-third of the municipal land and continues to control the local economy. Besides, 40 percent of the municipality's revenues come from the CSB in the form of urban rents, taxes, and environmental fines.[27] The municipality is entirely dependent on the industrial economy of the CSB, for it brings employment and income in the form of taxes, rents, and environmental fines. But in the rentier economy, the municipality and the CSB compete with each other over land, in what is described by local residents as a "mortal embrace" between the company and the town.

Indeed, the "land question" has a long history in Volta Grande. Even if the steel town was planned by the best Brazilian architects and the world's most renowned engineering company—the same that designed United Steel in the United States and Magnetigorsk in the Soviet Union—the city developed the same pattern of "predatory development" of most megalopolis in the South.[28] Since the early beginnings, the company housed only permanent workers, using most of its land for real estate speculation. In 1942 there were only 662 houses and three hotels, mostly for foreigner managers, and a total of 6,160 residents. Between 1941 and 1967, when the CSB's housing stock was privatized, the company maintained a residential deficit between 30 percent and 40 percent of its workforce. The company gave to its wage- workers two-bedroom family houses, membership to the Workers Club—a luxurious sport complex with an Olympic-sized swimming pool, three tennis courts, an Olympic-class gymnasium with a auditorium—a cinema, a hospital, and a child welfare center. The informal working class was excluded from these public provisions.

But a civic coalition developed around the municipality and led by the landed aristocracy opposed the company's monopoly over the land. In 1963 came the coalition's first success. The CSB was forced to pay seventy millions *cruzeiros* in back taxes to the municipality. In the 1970s, with the labor movement silenced by the military, a coalition of urban squatters[29] and grassroots Catholic organizations[30] led a "rights to the city" campaign, demanding the regularization of favelas, poor working-class neighborhoods, and the right to home ownership. This cross-sectional anti-dictatorship movement led to a renewal of the Brazilian labor movement famously described as "new unionism." According to Morel, this cross-sectional labor movement was facilitated by the existence of a capillary social infrastructure that the CSB had built in the city as a tool of labor control, but that, under the military, became autonomous and counter-hegemonic.[31] But privatization broke the labor movement. The company made mass redundancies and relocated the administrative departments and the central office away from the city. Its main hospital and school went under the municipality. But most of the land, as well as the leisure, cultural, and educational facilities in the city—remain under its control.[32] The focus of anti-corporate activism shifted from the plant to the land. In 1992 the PT-affiliated mayor expropriated the company from its unproductive land and forced it to pay environmental taxes in line with the new Program of Environmental Compensation (PAC). For first time in history, the company was charged R$60 million in environmental fees—a sum well above the municipality's yearly budget.[33] For the first time in history, the company was liable for land and service taxes like the any other private company.[34] The alliance between municipality and civic movements strengthened further with the establishment of a municipal body for participatory planning,[35] involving squatters, militant Catholic organizations, and women's and civic movements.

Besides, these municipal alliances extended into regional networks of social movements, trade unions, and businesses aiming at containing the power of the CSB and the global carmakers who had moved into the Sul Fluminense region. Well into the 2000s, these regional alliances were grassroots and focused on participatory planning and land redistribution. They were modeled on the cross-sectional coalitions with employers and civic movements led by the metalworkers union[36] in the ABC industrial region of São Paulo in the 1980s, which were now being displaced by the industrialization of the Sul Fluminense region. But these regional alliances slowly turned into business alliances between municipalities, new unions, and local entrepreneurs aimed at attracting foreign investors with cheap labor, as well as fiscal and environmental incentives and infrastructures. Cash-strapped municipalities waged ruthless "fiscal wars" against each other.[37] For instance, in 1996 the VW's dream factory in Resende was opened due to the generous gift—of credit and land—by the state of Rio de Janeiro. The *metalúrgicos* did not take part in these cross-sectional alliances. With their high wages and purchasing power, they kept themselves busy with conspicuous consumption of white goods, electronics, cars, and homes.[38] Ironically, at the apex of the global crisis, the working class of Volta Grande was officially ranked as "class C"—middle class. But in 2010, as the first signs of economic slowdown hit the country, local unemployment rose to 19 percent, and the steelworkers found themselves struggling with debt, unemployment, and house evictions. The company continues to lay off workers and to reclaim land from residents and the municipality through its army of private police and lawyers. The SMSF has tried to contain the most recent waves of mass redundancies. The municipality continues to seek foreign investors and campaigns against the CSB on environmental and fiscal issues in order to stay alive. In February 2016, the CSB was fined R$13 million (US$3.25 million) for failing to meet the conditions of an environmental and safety accord with the Rio de Janeiro state environmental agency to reduce air, water, and noise pollution, as well as safety risks at UPV.

BETWEEN TERTIARIZATION AND INFORMALIZATION

Privatization led to a peak in informal employment at both the national and local levels.[39] Under the PT, formal employment rose exponentially, but mainly in low-income jobs and for the female, black, and rural workers traditionally outside the formal working class.[40] These newly created low-income jobs border with the informal economy, which still makes up 40 percent of the GDP. The core of the Brazil's formal employment system is the *carteira de trabalho* (working card)—the official document containing people's employment history. Only workers with a *carteira* are entitled to pensions, social contributions, and trade-union affiliation. One obvious way to informalize wage labor is not to register the workers on the *carteira* or to register them after they have started to work for the company. It is not unusual for companies to register their employees many years after the starting date or just before they go burst. Workers lose their rights to social contributions and additional salaries for the period in which they are unregistered. Besides, in order to dodge taxes, companies keep nominal wages lower than real wages, asking their employees to declare minimum wage in exchange of a top-up in cash. Employees do not know that by doing so, they lose social contributions. It is not unusual for them to realize it only after retirement.

A third way to informalize the wage relation is to underpay overtime and hazardous work. It is also frequent for companies to outsource work to ghost companies or fake cooperatives, which they can shut down without notice, leaving the workers without wages and social contributions. At the lower end of the labor market, cleaners, domestic workers, builders, and garbage pickers work without working identification, sixteen hours per day, and on a daily salary of R$5. Domestic workers make up an astonishing 27 percent of the national population—nearly 7 million people[41]—and face the harshest working conditions. Four-fifths of these are undocumented and hence have no right to social contributions. The presence of maids, cleaners, nannies, chauffeurs, personal trainers, and security guards in the houses of the hyper-affluent families of Rio de Janeiro or São Paulo or the landowning families of the rural north is not as surprising as in the households of the steelworkers of Volta Grande. Most domestic workers are employed as day laborers *(diarista)*, paid in cash at the end of the day. The jobs of builders and garbage pickers are the most informalized. Some garbage pickers set up cooperatives or small businesses and have stable contracts with municipalities, housing associations, or condominiums. But the majority barely survives. Several garbage cooperatives, in fact—small firms dressed up like cooperatives—sell to the municipality and recycling companies the garbage that they buy at a much lower price from informal garbage pickers.

The recent construction industry boom, sparked by federal housing and infrastructural programs, boosted the building sector, where 40 percent of the workforce is informal. The biggest employer of informal workers is the municipality, which regularly tenders to illegal subcontractors working with unregulated labor. After the CSB, the municipality is the biggest "labor offender" in the city and often appears in labor courts, charged with exploiting cleaners, builders, and garbage workers. In the 1980s and 1990s this section of the working class—made up of the unemployed, informal workers, rural squatters, and community leaders—led the "right to the city" struggle against the CSB that I described above. But today, conservative evangelical organizations and neighborhood associations belonging to the municipality have co-opted them through programs of grassroots evangelization, poverty reduction,[42] popular home ownership,[43] and cultural entrepreneurship.[44]

CONCLUSION

In this chapter I have presented an ethnography of a Brazilian steelmaking plant and framed the patterns of workers' protests and identity formation that I observed on the shop floor at the urban and regional levels with the aim of unveiling the broader dynamics of dependent development, land dispossession, and state accumulation. I have argued that there is a structural coupling between Brazil's dependency in the global economy and the strategies of accumulation by dispossession by the CSB based on rent seeking, commodity export, and open conflict with the local community. In Volta Grande, the rentierist logic of late capitalism described by Harvey[45] takes a conglomerate form, encompassing global logistics, mining, steelmaking, and local landownership. In this chapter I have shown how the state-driven financialization of the economy has impacts on the shop floor in terms of labor deskilling and intensification and of working-class debt and conspicuous consumption. In 2008 wage earners like Bobo thought about themselves as capitalists. Today, they struggle with unemployment, debts, and declining purchasing power. With a powerless metalworkers' union, it is conservative evangelical organizations and loose business-citizen platforms that increasingly take up the struggles of the *metalúrgicos*. Another section of the working class, the informal and tertiarized workers in the service and building industries, face a similarly harsh employer—the municipality of Volta Grande. A third section of the working class, subcontractors and car workers, are faring better, thanks to the newly established legal principle of subsidiary responsibility. Less formally politicized than the metalworkers, car workers, subcontractors, and a growing number of IT workers have experienced first-hand the extreme tertiarization practiced by foreign corporations. Their militant struggles against labor deregulation and regional alliances take the form of legal and civic recognition. Up until the recent crisis, three sections of the working class—impoverished wage earners, the upwardly mobile urban poor, and tertiarized workers—formed a magmatic and internally divided "center" oscillating between left and right and kept together by various programs of urban development, wage indexation, poverty reduction, home ownership, and cultural regeneration. Besides, reflecting the principle of decentralization embedded in the democratic constitution, regional coalitions between municipalities, grassroots movements, trade unions, and local industrialists sprung up in the 1990s against the state which under Cardoso was quickly embracing neoliberalism. Until Dilma's impeachment, the PT administration managed to control the regional block developed around Rio de Janeiro through its strong grip over the national economy. But with the current economic crisis, the populist consensus and the fragile architecture of the financial state—after all, still subsumed to global finance—is crumbling.

NOTES

1. Perry Anderson. "Crisis in Brazil," *London Review of Books,* April 21, 2016.

2. Göran Therborn, "Class in the 21st Century," *New Left Review* 78 (November/December 2012): 16.

3. See Francisco de Oliveira, "Lula in The Labyrinth," *New Left Review* 42 (November/December 2006): 5–22.

4. See Aldo Musacchio and Sergio Lazzarini, *Reinventing State Capitalism. Leviathan in Business, Brazil and Beyond* (Cambridge, MA: Harvard University Press, 2014), 89.

5. The CSB contracted on a "man-per-hour" basis.

6. In fact, the non-monetary component of their wages was nearly inexistent, which halved the cost of their labor.

7. U.S. labor costs are 23 percent lower than in Brazil, according to a recent study by Boston Consulting Group. See Harold L. Sirkin, Michael Zinser, and Justin Rose, "The Shifting Economics of Global Manufacturing: How Cost Competitiveness Is Changing Worldwide," Boston Consulting Group, August 19, 2014, www.bcg.com/en-us/publications/2014/lean-manufacturing-globalization-shifting-economics-global-manufacturing.aspx.

8. Angela De Castro Gomes, *A Invenção do Trabalhismo* (São Paulo: FGV Editora, 1989); and for a similar argument, see also Octavio Ianni, *O Colapso do Populismo no Brasil* (Rio de Janeiro: Civilização Brasileira, 1968).

9. John French, *Drowning in Laws: Labor Law and Brazilian Political Culture* (Chapel Hill: University of North Carolina Press, 2004).

10. See Regina Morel, "A ferro e fogo: construção e crise da 'família siderúrgica': o caso de Volta Grande (1941–1968)" (PhD diss., University of São Paulo, 1989).

11. Lee makes a similar case in her analysis of labor protest in contemporary China. Ching Kwan Lee, *Against the Law: Labor Protests in China's Rustbelt and Sunbelt* (Berkeley: University of California Press, 2007), 12.

12. The minimum wage is R$700 per month.

13. Marcio Ponchmann, *Nova Classe Média?* (São Paulo: Boitempo, 2012).

14. Between eighteen and twenty-four years.

15. In 2011 the High Court of Justice (TSJ—Tribunal Superior de Justica) organized a public symposium bringing together scholars, trade unions, and employers associations to definition tertiarization and the distinction between "goals" and "means."

16. Graça Druck, "Terceirização e precarização: o binômio anti-social em indústrias," in *A perda da razão social do trabalho: terceirização e precarização,* ed. Graça Druck and Franco Tânia, 97–120 (São Paulo: Boitempo, 2007).

17. *Feia* in Portuguese means "ugly," so *feinha* would translate roughly as "little ugly."

18. Lee, *Against the Law.*

19. The GMU was closed down in 2008 due to economic crisis (72).

20. Seventy percent of them are maximum thirty-four years old, and 60 percent are married, with children; 95 percent of them have a permanent job contract; 65 percent gain between three and five *salarios minimos* (the highest wage level in the region); and 69 percent own a home, 59 percent of whom have already paid off their mortgages. See Jose Ramalho and Marco Aurelio Santana, *Trabalho e Desenvolvimento Regional: Efeitos Sociais da Industria Automobilistica no Rio de Janeiro* (Rio de Janeiro: Mauad, 2006); and Marco Aurelio Santana, "Trabalhadores e política no Sul-fluminense: a experiência de Volta Grande nos anos 1980." in *Efeitos sociais da indústria automobilística no Rio de Janeiro,* ed. José Ricardo Ramalho and Marco Aurélio Santana (Rio de Janeiro: Mauad, 2006): 159–75.

21. See Sergio Pereira "Trajetórias Individuais e Ação Sindical no Pólo Industrial do Sul Fluminense" (MA diss., University of Rio de Janeiro, 2003).

22. Jose Ramalho, Iram Jacome Rodrigues, and Jefferson José da Coinceição, "Reestruturação industrial, sindicato e território: Alternativas políticas em momentos de crise na região do ABC em São Paulo, Brasil," *Revista Crítica de Ciências Sociais* 85 (2009): 147–67.

23. The institution is called the Sectoral Chamber of Automotive Industry.

24. Ramalho, Rodrigues, and da Coinceição, "Reestruturação industrial, sindicato e território," 147–67.

25. Jose Ramalho, "Novas conjunturas industriais e participação local em estratégias de desenvolvimento," *Dados* 48, no. 3 (2005): 147–78.

26. 50 percent of the residents are employed in commerce and service, and 10 percent in public administration.

27. The IPTU and environmental fines from the CSB constitute up to 70 percent of municipal income.

28. Mike Davis, *Planet of Slums* (London: Verso, 2006).

29. Movement of Urban Squatters (Movimento dos Posseiros Urbanos).

30. Workers priests, Base Ecclesiastic Communities (CEB) and Catholic Workers' Youth Organizations (JOC).

31. See Morel, "A ferro e fogo"; and Marco Aurelio Santana and Massimiliano Mollona, "Memórias and practicas dos movimentos sociais em Volta Grande," *Dados* 19 (2013): 125–48.

32. Namely, the ETPC, the workers' and employers' clubs and the Hotel Bela Vista.

33. US$50 million.

34. Respectively, IPPU and ISU.

35. Committee for Urban Planning (Conselho Municipal de Desenvolvimento Urbano—CMDU).

36. Led by Ingacio Lula Da Silva until the early 1990s.

37. Glauco Arbix, "Guerra Fiscal e Competição Intermunicipal por Novos Investimentos no Setor Automotivo Brasileiro," *Dados*, February 10, 2018, www.scielo.br/scielo.

38. The scheme My House My Life (Minha Casa Minha Vida—MCMV) expanded homeownership to low-income families through lease-to-own agreements in which the poorest families contribute as little as 5 percent of their monthly income.

39. At the national level, between 1991 and 1997, privatization led to a 30 percent reduction of waged employment and 10 percent increase of informal labor mainly among women and black workers. See DIEESE (2000) Departamento Intersindical de Estatística e Estudos Socioeconômicos.

40. Thirty percent of the total new jobs created since 2000. See Marcio Ponchman, *Nova Classe Média?* (São Paulo: Boitempo, 2012), 32.

41. Ibid., 32.

42. Bolsa Familia.

43. Minha Casa Minha Vida.

44. Programa Pontos de Cultura.

45. David Harvey, *Rebel Cities: From the Right to the City to the Urban Revolution* (London: Verso, 2012).

9

From Poverty to Informality? The Social Question in Africa in a Historical Perspective

Andreas Eckert

INTRODUCTION

Jan Breman and Marcel van der Linden argue that "the real norm or standard in global capitalism is insecurity, informality or precariousness."[1] If this is the case, then Africa in the twentieth and early twenty-first centuries could be seen as a model case for global capitalism. Much of the history of the continent during this period was characterized by poverty, precarious labor relations, and the absence of state or company welfare measures, as well as the failure or the lack of efforts to challenge precariousness. This paper analyses the social question in Africa since the colonial period with a focus on social (in)security and labor against the backdrop of a related research literature that largely ignores the continent. In the rich field of social sciences' studies of the welfare state, Africa does not feature prominently, to say the very least. Esping-Andersen's famous typology of welfare states completely ignores Africa.[2] In the index of the more recent, authoritative *Oxford Handbook of the Welfare State,* Africa is only listed twice, and these references are related to trade unions and unemployment insurance. When we look at the referenced pages, we learn only that unionization rates are lowest worldwide throughout much of Africa and that Africa is the weakest area of social insurance development.[3] For a long time, Africa seems to have served as the epitome of "otherness," not only in the history of welfare and labor but also in much Western scholarship. A Europe- or West-centered perspective still often places Africa at the other end of the developmental spectrum—a clear instance of a region that simply does not fit the patterns familiar to a North Atlantic framework. However, as will be argued here, the history of the social question in Africa has a great many lessons to offer to those who are interested in tracing the historical connections between regions and in critically engaging with the idea of the North Atlantic world as "normal" and the rest as "exceptional" and "in need of explanation." If our historical analysis of the social question has to transcend the notion of a single telos modeled after the example of the West that is supposed to be achieved everywhere, or if we are to go beyond the conception that the non-realization of this telos represents somehow a "lack" or a "lag" in those societies to understanding their specific examples coevally—to echo Johannes Fabian's insight[4]—with that of the West, then we must take the different social forms in Africa seriously in all their complexity and all their linkages with welfare and labor forms elsewhere.

This paper chronologically discusses the social question with a focus on sub-Saharan Africa and emphasizes a context in which capitalist production regimes have not led to employment relations typically characterized by stable and protected wage labor.[5] While often drawing from examples from specific regions, it attempts to provide a broad historical view on larger trends and transformations of the social question in Africa, referring to a literature that tackles questions of welfare, social security, and social marginality within a wide array of topics such as labor, state, or urbanization.

WHITES ONLY: COLONIALISM AND WELFARE BEFORE WORLD WAR II

Until World War II, the colonial state and European private employers delegated the field of social security and poverty care more or less completely to what they labeled "traditional African solidarity," occasionally also to a few private and especially church welfare institutions. There is little detailed information about related initiatives.[6] In 1931, for instance, the Holy Ghost Fathers alone managed 132 orphanages and 176 hospitals or dispensaries in sub-Saharan Africa. During the following year, 648 people passed through the poor asylum run by the Sisters of Cluny at Walezo in Zanzibar. Missionaries also provided most of the rapidly expanding institutional care of leprosy. In some parts of Africa, mostly in the settler colonies, the Salvation Army undertook some welfare work among Africans. The Red Cross, the world's first international secular charity and the first to establish itself in Africa, mainly worked among European communities in French and Belgian Congo. In British colonies, local governments made little provision for the poor beyond some general services such as famine control, free (but very limited) public health services, or rudimentary urban sanitation.[7]

In his influential *African Survey*, published in 1938, Lord Hailey, the great theoretician of British colonial rule, praised the practice of "externalizing" systems of social security. He stated that "it is clear that by treating the native reserves as reservoirs of man-power, there is, in effect, a saving in that outlay on social services which in other circumstances might have to be incurred on behalf of industrialized labor."[8] Thus it is no wonder that until World War II, the few measures in the realm of social policy benefited Europeans almost exclusively. Programs associated with the "modern" welfare state were first and most comprehensively introduced in South Africa, where noncontributory, means-tested old-age pensions were created for elderly people classified as "white" or "colored." For the National Party and Labor Party—partners in the coalition Pact Government of 1924–1929—noncontributory old-age pensions were a crucial pillar in the "civilized labor" policies designed to lift "poor whites" out of poverty and reestablish a clear racial hierarchy. Welfare reform was thus, in significant part, a response to the *swart gevaar*, or menace of black physical, occupational, and social mobility.[9] Programmatic provision was extended to the disabled, poor mothers with children, and the unemployed. By the late 1930s, South Africa had a comparatively well-developed welfare state for its white and colored citizens. Similar noncontributory old-age pensions were introduced for white residents in Southwest Africa and Southern Rhodesia. The construction of welfare states in these settler societies reflected a combination of elite ideology, shaped both by racist and progressive elements, and democratic politics within the enfranchised white and colored population.

In other parts of Africa, it was only in the field of health where, after 1900, some colonies like German East Africa (which became Tanganyika after World War I) introduced decrees concerning industrial law that were relevant to a small minority of African workers.[10] In 1909 the governor of German East Africa issued a "decree concerning the rights of indigenous workers" that introduced the duty of employers to guarantee medical care of their employees. However, this measure was seldom put into practice. In 1923 the British passed the Master and Servants Ordinance, which provided for small compensation to be paid by employers in the case of industrial accidents. African government clerks were initially classified into lower administrative ranks with neither pension rights nor other employers' contribution. The Provident Fund (Government Employees) Ordinance, issued in November 1942, introduced a fund also for lower ranks that provided for at least small payments in the case of retirement or premature inability to work.[11]

Right from the beginning of colonial rule, access to labor was crucial to European colonizers in Africa. However, before World War II, this importance was reflected neither in the administrative order nor in colonial archives. Until the mid-1930s there was hardly any African colony with a "labor department." In its prewar heyday, colonialism, even when administered by relatively democratic governments in the home context, evaluated its African subjects essentially as primitive and ineffably "different" tribesmen with a patriarchal and rural mold. The conservation of an ossified tribal Africa coupled with the extraction of unskilled seasonal or casual labor was common wisdom. The debates of the day were about the necessity for forced labor and the extent to which Africa was becoming diseased and depopulated due to colonial labor demand. Dynamism in this system was confined to white settlers or energetic Levantine and Asian traders.[12] Against this backdrop, colonial officials found it convenient to leave agricultural production to former slave owners and chiefs, or enlist their aid to supply the labor required for public, and even private, purposes. Moreover, desperate to make their territories economically viable, they resorted to various devices for mobilizing unfree labor themselves, including forced labor, conscription into the army or police forces, and the recruitment of contract labor by all kind of dubious means. The Portuguese colonies were particularly notorious for relying on forced labor, and parts of Portuguese-ruled Africa fell at the far end of a spectrum of brutality of labor practices. However, at least until the 1940s, institutionalized violence to extract African labor was by no means solely a Portuguese approach.[13]

After World War I, the newly founded League of Nations took up this issue. The debates culminated in the Forced Labor Convention of the International Labor Organization of 1930.[14] The realities on the ground in Africa were much more complex, and the hierarchies and forms of exploitation much more subtle than what the discussions about forced labor in Geneva addressed. Moreover, neither the missionary critics who asked "Africa: Slave or Free?" nor League of Nations investigators questioned the premise of colonial rule itself; consequently, the resulting debate sought only to draw distinctions among labor policies considered acceptable and not acceptable in a European-dominated Africa. Officials in the colonies wanted to use the labor of Africans as much as they could, but at the same time, they firmly believed in the necessity of stable African communities under the control of male elders. European administrators saw mining towns or cities as sites of labor, but not of the reproduction of the labor force. Those Africans who had left this imagined traditional village life and permanently settled in the cities were labeled "detribalized."[15]

During the Great Depression, the first substantial debates about the problem of unemployment emerged. According to John Iliffe, "the great novelty of the depression was tropical Africa's first serious experience of unemployment."[16] In the formal sector, in branches where Africans worked under contracts, a rapid decline of working places took place during the early 1930s. Between 1930 and 1933, the copper mines in Katanga reduced their African workforce from 73,000 to 27,000.[17] However, only a small portion of the African population was officially "working" and thus qualified for appearing in statistics. In French West Africa, 120,000 people were in official employment in 1933, plus 39,000 migrant peanuts laborers in Senegal, 1.1 percent of the population.[18] The Inspecteur du Travail of French West Africa remarked in 1934 on the absence of unemployment but had a circular definition of it: since the African family took care of its members and had access to land, only the most detribalized Africans, notably urban artisans, could be unemployed. Such an argument is "indeed a telling instance . . . of how belief in the peculiar nature of African society could define an entire problem out of existence."[19] One example of this circular argument comes from a report of 1936: "There are no unemployed in French West Africa. Anyone who so desired could go back to the soil and any worker who does not prefers to vegetate in the city which he only will leave at the last extremity. There is thus constituted a floating urban population of 'sans-travail' of a particular nature, seeking daily labor without enthusiasm, living most often at the expense of more favored brethren." A year later the Inspecteur du Travail indicated that he did not believe that African workers were quite like other workers. He opposed unemployment compensation, saying, "I am not a partisan of unemployment indemnities in a country where the soil can nourish those who wish to cultivate it."[20]

DECOLONIZATION AND THE SHORT SUMMER OF THE WELFARE STATE

These assumptions began to be challenged in the 1930s, first by minority voices and then, as one approaches the 1950s, on a broader front. For this, there were various reasons, not least the realization that such policies led to semi-stagnation in a world where development became more and more an imperative.[21] The suddenly manifest capacity of African workers to organize and throw a wrench in the works of the extractive economy was, however, also of fundamental importance.[22] Arguments mounted that African workers needed to be treated as workers, not as Africans. They should be permitted to form trade unions, critically, a strategy of containment and boundedness. And they should benefit from a social welfare system. The colonial state tried to conceptualize structures that would allow for a stable detribalized urban working class in towns, focused on a European family model. "By the mid to late 1940s," Fred Cooper writes, "influential officials wanted Africa to have a working class, to separate an identifiable group of people from the backwardness of rural Africa, attach its members to particular jobs and career ladders and over time make them into a predictable and productive collectivity."[23]

Over the following decade, colonial administrators and experts worked on a new labor policy that was called "stabilization." This term referred to the fact that in the eyes of the Europeans involved, the task in Africa was not to make wage labor the basic form of production, as in ideal-type capitalism, but to separate a domain of wage labor from a domain of traditional production. Above all, colonial administrations had to be insured that the reproduction of the wage-earning class would take place uncontaminated by the "backwardness" that apparently lay outside it, in the villages. In many reports, a vision of a male African appeared who was weaned from dependence or nonwage income and lived with his wife and family in an urban location, sending his children to school and, over time, becoming acculturated to industrial and urban life. The gender bias in all of this was too self-evident for much contemporary discussion. Throughout the colonial period, employment and unemployment were overwhelmingly associated with men. For long, women had entered urban centers and, with waged employment deemed appropriate for them being restricted, had made a significant contribution to sectors outside the realm of wage work. However, no one at the time commented on the fact that the definition of the worker in the Code du Travail for French West Africa—the result of intense debates between French officials and African trade unions and accompanied by numerous strikes—placed the kind of tasks that women most often did outside the law's conception of work. That women were crucial to the commerce of West African cities or that they performed a great variety of income-generating activities did not enter into the discussion of any aspect of the code.[24]

The rising global importance given to social security after World War II is reflected by the UN Declaration of Human Rights of 1948, which stated that "everyone, as a member of society, has the right to social security." Already four years earlier, a declaration had emerged from the ILO conference in Philadelphia that announced that "labor is not a commodity" and called for international effort for the "common welfare." Furthermore, it sought measures "to provide a basic income to all," for regulation of working hours, for collective bargaining, and for measures to improve public health, housing, nutrition, education, child welfare, the status of women, and public services. The last paragraph of the document emphasized that the principles listed were "fully applicable to all people everywhere"; it called specifically for "their progressive application to peoples who are still dependent, as well as to those who have already achieved self-government."[25] Soon after, the ILO began to develop its "social policy in dependent territories," which set out to globalize its "standards" on work regulations, housing, education, health, and family life. ILO resolutions were weak on supranational enforcement mechanisms and did not mandate the colonial powers in Africa to act in a particular way, but legitimized and delegitimized certain policy strategies. In some ways, Britain and France thought that the "social" direction put forward by the ILO was consistent with their reformed postwar colonialism and even celebrated the 1952 ILO convention "Minimum Standards of Social Security" as the "internationalization" of their respective social policies. However, the standards soon hit a wall. The British held the view that their African colonies should raise the revenues necessary to pay for social security themselves. Given the financial situation of their territories, the implementation of substantial social security systems was delegated to a distant future.[26]

In 1958 the ILO published the *African Labour Survey*, which made some reflections about the state of social security as part of the stabilization project on the continent. The authors saw "evidence of the interest of the authorities in Africa in the possibility of introducing social security measures and their awareness of the urgency and growing importance of the question." However, they also listed the factors that, according to them, militated against the successful introduction of social security, for instance "the instability of the labour force, the low level of wages, the inadequacy of population registers, polygamy, the illiteracy of workers and even of small employers in rural areas, poor communications and the difficulty of supervising migrant workers who, at times, disappear, never to be heard of again." Still, they happily acknowledged that "it is generally accepted that one way of stabilising labour is to give workers effective protection against occupational and other risks."[27]

Admittedly, this new approach was often expressed in a restrained manner, as in 1952 in the Tanganyika Standard: "The average African labourer has sprung from generations of men content to sit under the shade of the nearest tree and do little or no work whatsoever. . . . But, the African, while inherently lazy, is by no means beyond redemption. . . . If he can adapt himself to regular employment under conditions where food, accommodation, medical and other amenities are available, he can and does become worthy of his hire."[28] Still, in contrast to prevailing low-wage, labor-extensive forms of employment, from the 1950s, increased skill levels were rewarded with higher salaries. Paradoxically, this increase in wages formed a prime cause of growing urban poverty. According to John Iliffe, it "attracted people into towns, encouraged employers to replace workers by machinery, and bred the unemployment, overcrowding, and ancillary problems which the authorities had intended to prevent."[29] A background context profoundly shaping the phenomenon was demographic change. Rapid African population growth from the mid-twentieth century, alongside a diminishing resource-to-population ratio, resulted in a shift from famine-related "epidemic starvation for all but the rich . . . to endemic undernutrition for the very poor."[30] One of the most prominent forms in which this "structural" poverty manifested itself was the growth of urban joblessness. In the context of rapid urbanization, the problem of a reserve army of unemployed or jobless young men observable in towns caused increasing attention.

In a number of African colonies, a set of social institutions was created for relatively small groups of formal-sector workers. One striking aspect about social welfare measures in late colonial Africa is, however, that unemployment insurances were never seriously discussed. In the 1950s, unemployment in urban Africa was recognized and discussed by contemporaries, but belittled by colonial officials.[31] The Code du Travail for French Africa from 1952 contained no fewer than 241 articles and provided for a comprehensive arsenal of welfare measures. However, there was no mention at all of unemployment compensation.[32] The ILO in its *African Labour Survey* observed "considerable underemployment" on the continent, but concluded that "unemployment, except in a few towns in the form known in highly industrialized countries, exists only to a limited extent; there are usually more offers of employment than applications for jobs."[33] In most late-colonial labor laws, unemployment compensation was held to be particularly undesirable, because most officials would not acknowledge that the African wage earner who was not working was, in fact, a worker. One also has to emphasize the gendered way in which the "unemployment problem" was interpreted. In the official imagination, it was once more male youth who constituted a potentially insurrectionary unemployed class, who were more visible "loitering" on urban streets. The absence of female unemployed in surviving commentary reflects the gendered occupation of urban space. In contrast to young men, whose street presence has remained a concern up to the present, women were more restricted to the home and/or the workplace. Or they simply did not constitute a threat in the eyes of the male colonizer.[34]

Especially in the French African colonies, the main instruments in social welfare policies were family allowances. After long and controversial debates, and due to massive pressure from African trade unions, on January 1956, family allocations went into effect in French West Africa, six months later in French Equatorial Africa. In Senegal, a family would receive 4,800 francs "allocation du foyer" for the birth of each of its first three children; each pregnancy would bring the family 3,600 francs prenatal allocation and 4,800 francs maternity allocation; in addition, 400 francs per month would be paid as the basic family allowance for each dependent child, through the end of his or her schooling. The 400 francs per month would be around 8 percent of the minimum wage; the maternity allocation, around a month's minimum pay. Such allocations would make a considerable difference to the life of a worker. The decrees provided support for the children of female workers as well as of male; there was even a special provision for benefits for wage-earning women who gave birth. But the expectations of the planners were that of the male worker and the female child-care provider. In the studies on which these cost estimates were based, the surveyed population in industry included 25,357 African males, but no females; in commerce, there were 14,045 males and 105 females. The language in which officials addressed the burdens of raising children on a worker's salary was comfortably masculinist, and officials allocated, using their workforce data, minimal funds for working mothers.

The implementation of family allowances got off to a slow start. One reason was that the administration had the utmost difficulties to put these schemes into practice, because the required information, such as documentations of birth, was difficult to obtain. Still, by 1956, family allocations had been extended to the entire wage-labor force of French West Africa, and officials now embraced them for much the same reason that they rejected them earlier—the peculiar nature of the African family. But now it was a question of weaning workers away from its debilitating effects, of creating family norms that resembled those presumed to predominate in Europe, of insuring the reproduction of a working class on the basis of workers' earnings and within the milieu of the workplace.[35]

In many ways, the dualism imagined by the colonial administrators and experts of a small, restricted modern African working class separated from the "traditional rest" was a mere fantasy. African workers in regulated jobs did not cease to be African; they did not cut themselves off from the wider range of social and cultural relationships in their lives, including their home villages. They regularly opted to live in a family arrangement rather than that of the monogamous male breadwinner with his dependent wife and children. They began to invest in the education of their children and to accumulate savings and pension rights toward retirement. However, they did not necessarily simply accept the notions of the European welfare state, but often used part of their wage resources to invest in social networks and rituals to foster their patriarchal authority.[36] African trade-union leaders were rather successful in using European officials' hopes for a productive, "modern" working class in order to make claims. They argued that if the Europeans wanted Africans to produce like a European working class, then Africans should be paid like their counterparts in Europe. Wages increased considerably, especially in key industries, in the civil service, and for vulnerable areas like railroads and ports. These increases were by no means uncontested but rather the result of protests, strikes, and negotiations.[37]

In effect, the colonial state could not respond to demands for increased benefits and rights from organized labor—which would put its members on par with metropolitan workers—without dismantling the justification of colonialism. There is an ironic charm—but also a kind of Pyrrhic victory—in the African success in defeating European developmentalist logic. One could view the decision by Europeans to accept unionist demands that African laborers be treated on the same basis as their European counterparts as a mutual failure to comprehend the African social reality. It was a consequential failure, since the cost of providing European-scale wages and benefits under African economic conditions could not be borne by either colonial or postcolonial regimes. European governments were thus encouraged to withdraw from Africa, while their local successors co-opted some of the labor leadership but rather quickly suppressed the unions as an autonomous force. The leaders of the newly independent countries, former trade-unionists among them, were acutely aware that they lacked the resources to ensure that the demands of the citizenry would be met. Many of them build up relations of patronage with power brokers inside the nation but also clientelistic networks with former colonizers. By this, they undermined democratic processes and the kind of social movements, such as labor movements, that had helped them get into power.[38]

HOPES AND DISILLUSION: INDEPENDENT AFRICA AND THE RISE OF THE INFORMAL

Around 1960, when many African colonies gained independence, numerous observers thought that with population growth having accelerated after 1945, and with the urban population growing faster than the rural, a class of landless manual workers would be created, and Africa would reproduce European patterns. But wage laborers made only a small percentage of the overall working population in Africa, both in colonial and postcolonial times. It was, however, exactly this small group of miners, dockworkers, factory workers, and railway workers that constituted the focus of African labor historiography between the 1960s and 1980s. The academic focus on wage labor went hand in hand with the assumption that Africa was becoming "proletarianized"; its working class was growing and becoming better defined and more self-conscious.[39] From the late 1950s to the 1970s, many African countries experienced at least modest economic growth, life expectancy rose considerably, and education became more accessible. The emergence of elements of a welfare state raised considerable expectations. State employees, workers in copper mines, or railway workers, for instance, had reasonable hopes that they could get something out of participation in economic activities. But these decades proved to be not a mid-point in a natural "transition" from a nonwage-labor to a wage-labor economy in a welfare state. While it is difficult to count precisely, it is clear that the number of hired workers in sub-Saharan Africa was vastly greater by 1960 than it had been in 1900, and is much greater today than it was around the time of independence. Yet labor markets since the end of colonial rule are characterized much more by short-term hiring and a high turnover of workers than by long-term, stable employment. Precarious labor prevailed, both in the formal and in the informal sector.[40]

The seemingly reasonable aspirations of millions of Africans of turning jobs—especially stable, unionized jobs, with pension funds promised at the end—into careers proved unrealizable. The mining sector in the Zambian copper belt initially promised steady material rewards—a salary and health and retirement benefits—as well as other, more ineffable rewards in terms of cultural cachet and social status. That pathway to working-class stability and respectability soon came to an end with the oil crisis, structural adjustment programs, and the fluctuating global prices of copper. What meager resources these miners kept for their old age came not so much from the formal institutions of modern welfare capitalism—social security, pensions, medical insurance—or the contractual gains won by trade unions, but from sets of personal relationships that ex-miners could draw on or forge.[41] Petty trade, access to farmland through social relations in a village of origin, or support of kin-networks became necessary to survive in the context of a contracting regulated wage-labor sector. The notion of being a "big man," an element of men's self-esteem that had been given a new dimension by wage earning, increasingly had to confront the fact that women engaged in urban marketing and other activities were contributing more to the family economy and providing the stability that male wages could not. The bureaucratized world of work had not been eclipsing the world of social relations; if it had done so, the collapse would have been even more deadly than it was.

Today, young men whose social power long rested on their ability to earn wages increasingly find themselves in a more precarious position. In turn, others, notably women and pensioners, acquired new powers and possibilities. This transformation is partly due to the relative expansion of work in service industries that are more open to women than the blue-collar industrial jobs of the past.[42] The increasing instability of economic prospects in many African countries today has also changed migration patterns. Seasonal labor migration, which was central to African economies in the first half of the twentieth century, has been overtaken by more permanent rural-urban migration and by large-scale labor migration to Europe and beyond. Africans are more likely to travel longer distances in search of employment. In the twenty-first century, many African countries have apparently become increasingly dependent upon the productive activities and remittances of their citizens who live abroad in other African countries or in Europe, Asia, the Gulf States, or the United States.[43]

By the 1970s, the ILO began to use the evocative but sloppy term "urban informal sector" for the urban dimension of what did not fit inside national labor legislations and a bounded, stabilized working class. The term points to the continued—indeed, growing—importance of forms of work that lie outside the form of labor legislation that African countries inherited at independence and outside the limits of the imagination of policy makers who thought they were modernizing Africa.[44] Although some Africanists insist that "African economies are the most informalized in the world," nonwaged economic activities, unregulated by law and unprotected by social regulations or services, have become increasingly visible in many parts of the world, including the North Atlantic region.[45] The discovery of the "informal" went in hand in hand with the observation that full-time wage labor with relatively good social benefits over the course of an entire career was not a global norm, but rather the exception in many parts of the world, the contingent product of a particular conjuncture in twentieth-century world history.

A critical literature seems to agree on the inadequacy of the term "informal" but has failed to produce alternative terminology.[46] I would argue for an understanding of "informal labor" not as a residue of earlier and obsolete modes of socially organizing labor. Rather, it should be understood as a contemporary and adaptable sociopolitical category that distinguishes a heterogeneous and unstable set of transformed and new "informal," mainly socially regulated labor forms from an equally diverse and malleable set of "formal," predominantly state-regulated labor forms. These two sets of labor forms are mutually constitutive and interdependent, and they have assumed diverse features and proportions over the course of historical time, as well as in different local and territorial contexts. The social content and the interrelationship of "informal" and "formal" labor is shaped and persistently transformed by economic and social policies, business strategies, and social conflicts. Accordingly, the politics of informal labor is often connected to efforts at the resolution of crises of capitalist over-accumulation, including efforts to solve such crises by way of spatial expansion and relocation. It is crucial to emphasize the political character of formal/informal divisions in the contemporary world of labor across the continents, as well as to reconstruct the historical genesis of this divide. It is not by accident that as an academic and political concept, "informal labor" gained currency in the course of the 1970s, the middle of that decade being a crucial chronological marker for a major shift in the pattern of economic and social policies, business strategies, and social conflicts the world over. In fact, the career of the term "informal sector" may be linked to the rise of the political and ideological formation that is commonly referred to as "neoliberalism." Thus, it would be important to study more carefully the political and social processes that had rendered the informal/formal division conceivable. Finally, many activities labeled "informal" are not relatively new and exclusively spawned by neoliberal reforms and structural adjustment programs of the 1980s. Such assertions would overlook the deep roots of African productive systems and the relationships that contemporary skilled workers and craftsmen share with older services and forms of fabrication. Indeed, one of the shortcomings of studies on informality is that they often present snapshots of specific activities and processes, but they do not necessarily locate them within larger trajectories of historical change.[47]

While the term "informal" might be problematic and not sufficiently differentiated as an analytical tool, it refers to processes crucial to the social question in Africa. When the world economic recession of the 1970s hit Africa hard, most governments were forced to seek aid from the International Monetary Fund and other international institutions, which, in turn, enforced the destruction of much that could be considered "social." The right to education, medical care, and a livable wage were undermined in the name of financial rigor. Cutbacks in the public sector and in social programs eroded the number of waged employees. Households were forced to diversify their sources of income, and people involved in informal activities increasingly suffered from their work's uncertain juridical status and the volatility of their finances. Small-scale workshops were often characterized by low surplus and strong competition and were usually not more than severely undercapitalized and unskilled businesses. Market women particularly suffered, as they faced the falling incomes of poor and working-class customers, and more and more they had to compete with men who began working as street vendors after losing their waged jobs.[48] What also could be observed was "dividing a given activity in ever-finer morsels."[49] As Fred Cooper emphasized, "a young man, who in the 1970s would have sold tiny packets of peanuts in the streets of Dakar or in the 2000s low-denomination phone top-up cards, finds a niche because his labor is worth so little that an entrepreneur can employ him to sell things to people too poor to spend a significant sum of money at a time."[50] This reality on the ground stood in stark contrast to celebratory statements of the World Bank or NGOs highlighting the energy and skill of the small-scale entrepreneur. There is the bitter irony that empowerment through informal enterprise so cherished by neoliberal commentators was undermined by neoliberal politics that drastically weakened the very institutions—such as family, education, and basic safety nets—upon which informal entrepreneurship is based.[51]

CONCLUSION: PRECARIOUS AFRICA?

The terrifying leviathan "assumes more and more the traits of a milk cow," the conservative German philosopher Arnold Gehlen stated some forty years ago in his polemic against mass democracy and the welfare state. In the meantime, we see that politicians in the industrialized countries prescribe various diets and fitness training for this milk cow. The situation is very different in Africa, however. Because of the low importance of formal, institutionalized labor markets, state-sponsored systems of social security were never widely spread south of the Sahara anyway. During the twentieth century, these state systems had only very limited and socially selective spheres of operation, which, after a peak in the 1960s and early 1970s, constantly diminished over the last decades. On the other hand, those institutions, practices, and resources of "welfare production" that were not under state management enjoyed great importance. In this context, government officials, development experts, and scholars alike usually referred to the "traditional solidarity" of African families and communities. Already in the colonial period, European administrators returned to this "solidarity," because it was supposed to arrange what to colonial officials—despite all rhetoric—seemed far too expensive: absorbing, at least partially, the manifold risks of working life.

African independent states inherited a complex and potentially explosive combination of authoritarian governance, high expectations for improved living conditions, a limited extent of formal employment, and already fragmented trade unions. Thus, even before the devastating impact of the oil crisis, followed by structural adjustment programs, wage labor was never available as the foundation of an egalitarian and democratic society. Labor coercion and personal dependence did not disappear; it was often facilitated by poverty at all levels. The colonial discourse of development that began in the 1930s and continued after independence relabeled work that otherwise could have been classified as forced labor as "voluntary work," "self-help," or "human investment." In this process, certain sections of African labor were rendered invisible as workers and instead constructed as "beneficiaries," "participants," and "volunteers."[52] The issue of forced labor continued to be debated after independence. In 1962, the ILO Committee of Experts on the Application of Conventions and Recommendations criticized a number of recently independent African countries, such as Guinea and the Ivory Coast, for having set up new forms of forced labor in the form of compulsory labor services for young people. As Daniel Maul points out, "To be accused of a 'classically colonial crime' such as forced labour was particularly hard for the postcolonial nations to stomach," and they reacted bitterly.[53] The problem of "un-freedom" never went away: it is diffused and can be found in many sectors or embedded in various labor relations. In 2016, the ILO estimated that "there were a total of over 9.2 million victims of modern slavery in Africa."[54] Immigrant workers from Africa are part of this number. The question is how to label all those Africans who, by their own initiative, cross the Mediterranean Sea to Italy or Spain, or the Atlantic to the Canary Islands, to seek wage labor? Those Africans who, between the sixteenth and nineteenth centuries, were sent across the Atlantic to work on slave plantations in the Americas were coerced, and they were called "slaves." Today's migrants, however, are in some ways the freest of the free: "they not only agree to leave Africa for Europe, but they go to great effort and great risk to do so."[55] Often people with some means and education dare the dangerous and expensive trip, with the idea to make some money in Europe in order to support the family back home. Those Africans who make it to Europe, usually after a traumatic voyage via the desert and the Mediterranean, definitely work under conditions that deserve the label "precarious." Their ideas about a Europe full of opportunities soon vanish. They are mostly *sans papiers* and thus subject to deportation or exploitation by employers who misuse their vulnerability.[56]

It would be misleading to see informal and precarious work only as a new phase in capitalism in which workers in many parts of the world, and most notably in Africa, have become unnecessary, disposable. Multinational capital might still need many workers from Africa, as long as they are cheap, particularly to reach customers of modest means.[57] Moreover, precarity could be seen as a constitutive feature of capitalist labor, inasmuch as uncertainty and instability have always been inherent characteristics of wage labor, in Africa as elsewhere.[58] Yet political mobilization of and collective bargaining for precarious and informal workers remain a challenge. In West Africa, for example, the share of informal employment ranges from 76 percent (in Senegal) to 93 percent (in Benin) of the labor force; the total unionization rate was 12.8 percent in 2007.[59] However, given the ongoing increase of "land grabs," with states helping to alienate land to both foreign and domestic capitalists, in combination with the increasing pressure of the population on land and on soil fertility, it is not unlikely that landlessness will supersede the lack of labor power as the major source of poverty in Africa.

NOTES

1. Jan Breman and Marcel Van der Linden, "Informalizing the Economy: The Return of the Social Question at a Global Level," *Development and Change* 45, no. 5 (2014): 920.

2. Gosta Esping-Andersen, *The Three Worlds of Welfare Capitalism* (Princeton, NJ: Princeton University Press, 1990).

3. Francis G. Castles, Stephan Leibfried, Jane Lewis, Herbert Obinger, and Christopher Pierson, eds., *The Oxford Handbook of the Welfare State* (Oxford: Oxford University Press, 2010), 209, 434. For some recent attempts of social scientists to look at the social question in Africa from a historical perspective, see Alex Veit, Klaus Schlichte, and Roy Karadag, "The Social Question and State Formation in British Africa: Egypt, South Africa, and Uganda in Comparison," *European Journal of Sociology* 58, no. 2 (2017): 237–64; Carina Schmitt, "Social Security Development and the Colonial Legacy," *World Development* 70 (2015): 332–42. For a recent state of the art volume on African labor history that includes numerous references to the social question, see Stefano Bellucci and Andreas

Eckert, eds., *General Labour History of Africa: Workers, Employers, and Governments 20th–21st Centuries* (Woodbridge, England: James Currey, 2019).

4. Johannes Fabian, *Time and the Other: How Anthropology Makes Its Objects* (New York: Columbia University Press, 1983).

5. For a useful conceptual history of the term *social question*, see Holly Case, "The 'Social Question,' 1820–1920," *Modern Intellectual History* 13, no. 3 (2016): 747–75. The crucial role of the working class in twentieth-century struggles around the social question is emphasized by Breman and Van der Linden, "Informalizing the Economy."

6. For the following examples, see John Iliffe, *The African Poor: A History* (Cambridge: Cambridge University Press, 1987), 195–200.

7. See Ulrike Lindner, "The Transfer of European Social Policy Concepts to Tropical Africa, 1900–1950: The Example of Maternal and Child Welfare," *Journal of Global History* 9, no. 2 (2014): 208–31. For a broad view on the British Empire, James Midgley and David Piachaud, eds., *Colonialism and Welfare: Social Policy and the British Imperial Legacy* (Cheltenham: Edward Elgar, 2011).

8. Lord Hailey, *An African Survey: A Study of Problems Arising in Africa South of the Sahara* (Oxford: Oxford University Press, 1938), 710.

9. Jeremy Seekings, "'Not a Single While Person Should Be Allowed to Go Under.' *Swartgevaar* and the Origins of South Africa's Welfare State, 1924–29," *Journal of African History* 48, no. 3 (2007): 375–94. See also the chapter by Ben Scully in this volume. The exclusion of black Africans from welfare measures went hand in hand with conceptions of native work ethics that did cast blackness as an antagonistic other, usually associated with images of indolence and work avoidance. See Franco Barchiesi, "The Violence of Work: Revisiting South Africa's 'Labour Question' through Precarity and Anti-Blackness," *Journal of Southern African Studies* 42, no. 5 (2016): 875–91.

10. Andreas Eckert, "Regulating the Social: Social Security, Social Welfare and the State in Late Colonial Tanzania," *Journal of African History* 45, no. 3 (2004): 473–74.

11. John Iliffe, *A Modern History of Tanganyika* (Cambridge: Cambridge University Press, 1979),

12. Frederick Cooper, *Decolonization and African Society: The Labor Question in French and British Africa* (New York: Cambridge University Press, 1996), chap. 2.

13. Eric Allina, *Slavery By Any Other Name: African Life under Company Rule in Colonial Mozambique* (Charlottesville: University Press of Virginia, 2012); Alexander Keese, "Searching for the Reluctant Hands: Obsession, Ambivalence, and the Practice of Organizing Involuntary Labour in Colonial Cuanza-Sul and Malange Districts, Angola, 1926–1945," *Journal of Imperial and Commonwealth History* 41, no. 2 (2013): 238–58. For a nuanced study of the connections between migrant labor and forced labor in a later period, see Zachary Kagan Guthrie, *Labor, Mobility, and Colonial Rule in Central Mozambique, 1940–1965* (Charlottesville: University of Virginia Press, 2018).

14. See J. P. Daughton, "ILO Expertise and Colonial Violence in the Interwar Years," in *Globalizing Social Rights: The International Labour Organization and Beyond,* ed. Sandrine Kott and Joelle Droux, 85–97 (Houndsmills, U.K.: Palgrave Macmillan, 2013); Frederick Cooper, "Conditions Analogous to Slavery: Imperialism and Free Labor Ideology in Africa," in *Beyond Slavery: Explorations of Race, Labor, and Citizenship in Postemancipation Societies,* by Frederick Cooper, Thomas C. Holt, and Rebecca Scott (Chapel Hill: University of North Carolina Press, 2000), esp. 132–34. One important text voicing contemporary concerns about abuses in labor recruitment was Raymond Leslie Buell, *The Native Problem in Africa,* 2 vols. (New York: MacMillan, 1928). For the broader context of the rise of international organizations and most notably the role of the League of Nations during the interwar years, see Patricia Clavin, *Securing the World Economy: The Reinvention of the League of Nations, 1920–1946* (Oxford: Oxford University Press, 2013); Susan Pedersen, *The Guardians: The League of Nations and the Crisis of Empire* (Oxford: Oxford University Press, 2015).

15. Cooper, "Conditions Analogous to Slavery," 129. Note that in this context also women participated in migratory initiatives in order to get away from patriarchal authority. See Marie Rodet,

"Forced Labor, Resistance, and Masculinities in Kayes, French Sudan, 1919–1946," *International Labor and Working Class History* 86 (2014): 107–23.

16. Iliffe, *The African Poor*, 155. Some authors refer to the fact that in some parts of Africa, unemployed labor was already an issue at the beginning of the century. For instance, in 1905 unregulated settlements of about twenty thousand unemployed were reported in Entebbe. See Thomas Fuller, "African Labor and Training in the Uganda Colonial Economy," *International Journal of African Historical Studies* 10, no. 1 (1977): 84.

17. Bogumil Jewsiewicki, "The Great Depression and the Making of the Colonial Economic System in the Belgian Congo," *African Economic History* 4 (1977): 158. More broadly on the effects of the depression on Katanga miners, see John Higginson, *A Working Class in the Making: Belgian Colonial Labor Policy, Private Enterprise, and the African Mineworker, 1907–1951* (Madison: University of Wisconsin Press, 1989), chaps. 4–6; Julia Seibert, *In die globale Wirtschaft gezwungen: Arbeit und kolonialer Kapitalismus in Kongo (1885–1960)* (Frankfurt: Campus, 2016), part 3.

18. Cooper, *Decolonization*, 43. More generally on the wage labor sector in Senegal before World War II, see Babacar Fall, *Le Travail au Sénégal au XXe Siècle* (Paris: Karthala, 2011), 71–132.

19. Cooper, *Decolonization*, 42.

20. Quotes in ibid., 485, n. 67.

21. The history of the development concept and related practices have been intensely studied over the last two decades. See, among the numerous publications, Frederick Cooper and Randall Packard, eds., *Development and the Social Sciences: Essays on the History and Politics of Knowledge* (Berkeley: University of California Press, 1997); Joseph Hodge et al., eds. *Developing Africa: Concepts and Practices in Twentieth-Century Colonialism* (Manchester: Manchester University Press, 2014); Hubertus Büschel and Daniel Speich, eds. *Entwicklungswelten: Globalgeschichte der Entwicklungszusammenarbeit* (Frankfurt am Main: Campus, 2009).

22. The history of strikes and labor movements constituted an important part of African labor historiography, but it was rarely conceptualized within the paradigm of social movements. See Andreas Eckert, "Social Movements in Africa," in *The History of Social Movements in Global Perspective. A Survey*, ed. Stefan Berger and Holger Nehring, 211–24 (London: Palgrave Macmillan, 2017).

23. Cooper, *Decolonization*, 14.

24. Frederick Cooper, "African Labor History," in *Global Labour History: The State of the Art*, ed. Jan Lucassen, 91–116 (Berne: Peter Lang, 2006); Cooper, *Decolonization*.

25. The International Labour Organization Declaration Concerning Aims and Purposes (May 10, 1944), http://avalon.law.yale.edu/20th_century/decade15.asp. On the Philadelphia declaration, see Alain Supiot, *The Spirit of Philadelphia: Social Justice versus the Total Market* (New York: Verso, 2012); Frederick Cooper, "Social Rights and Human Rights in the Time of Decolonization," *Humanity* 3, no. 3 (2012): 473–92.

26. Daniel Maul, "The International Labour Organization and the Globalization of Human Rights," *Human Rights in the Twentieth Century*, ed. Stefan-Ludwig Hoffmann (New York: Cambridge University Press, 2011): 301–20; Cooper, "Social Rights."

27. International Labour Office, *African Labour Survey* (Geneva: ILO, 1958).

28. Quoted in Andrew Burton, "Raw Youth, School-Leavers and the Emergence of Structural Unemployment in Late-Colonial Urban Tanganyika," *Journal of African History* 47, no. 3 (2006): 372–73.

29. Iliffe, *The African Poor*, 171.

30. Ibid., 6.

31. The Labor Department in Tanganyika is a good example for how the problem of unemployment was downplayed by officials. In order to meet the protests of African trade unionists about growing unemployment in the country's urban centers, a government official suggested: "I can't help feeling it's a problem on which we ought to be better informed, if only to show that we know what we are talking about if we say the problem is not serious." Quoted in Burton, "Raw Youth," 375.

32. See Omar Guèye, *Sénégal: histoire du mouvement syndical—la marche vers le Code du Travail* (Paris: L'Harmattan, 2011); Cooper, *Decolonization,* chap. 7.

33. ILO, *African Labour Survey,* 404.

34. On gendered images of youth, see Andrew Burton and Helène Charton-Bigot, eds, *Generations Past: Youth in East African History* (Athens: Ohio University Press, 2010). For by now classic studies on the economic roles of women in colonial urban Africa, see Claire Robertson, *Sharing the Same Bowl: A Socioeconomic History of Women and Class in Accra* (Bloomington: Indiana University Press, 1984); Luise White, *The Comforts of Home: Prostitution in Colonial Nairobi* (Chicago: University of Chicago Press, 1990).

35. Cooper, *Decolonization,* 305–20. By contrast, the British subcommittee on wage fixing and family responsibilities rejected the concept of family allowances in 1953, not the least on political grounds. It argued that in "British Colonial territories the amount of any family allowance would be likely to be a greater proportion of a wage-earner's total income than in this country, and therefore, if family allowances were introduced, government would have a say in fixing a significant percentage of a man's total income. The workers could then reasonably conclude that their interests could be better advanced by political agitation than by action in the industrial field" (quoted ibid., 331).

36. Lisa Lindsay, *Working with Gender: Men, Women, and Wage Labor in Southwest Nigeria* (Portsmouth: Heinemann, 2003), shows this with the example of Nigerian railwaymen; see also Cooper, "African Labor History," 113.

37. Cooper, *Decolonization.*

38. Frederick Cooper, *Africa since 1940: The Past of the Present* (Cambridge: Cambridge University Press, 2002); Paul Nugent, *Africa since Independence: A Comparative History* (Houndsmills, U.K.: Palgrave MacMillan, 2004).

39. See Bill Freund, "Labor and Labor History in Africa: A Review of the Literature," *African Studies Review* 27 (1984): 1–58.

40. For statistical data, see John Sender and Sheila Smith, *The Development of Capitalism in Africa* (London and New York: Methuen, 1986). Their claim that "by the end of the colonial period, capitalist labor markets had become predominant, and that a working class had emerged as a major social and political force" (129) seems difficult to sustain. For the development in South Africa after the end of Apartheid, see Franco Barchiesi, "Wage Labor and Social Citizenship in Post-Apartheid South Africa," *Journal of Asian and African Studies* 42, no. 1 (2007): 39–72; and Scully, this volume.

41. James Ferguson, *Expectations of Modernity: Myths and Meanings of Urban Life in the Zambian Copperbelt* (Berkeley: University of California Press, 1999); Alastair Fraser and Miles Larmer, eds., *Zambia, Mining, and Neoliberalism: Boom and Bust in the Globalized Copperbelt* (New York: Palgrave Macmillan, 2010); Jonas Kreienbaum, "Der verspätete Schock—Sambia und die erste Ölkrise 1973/74," *Geschichte und Gesellschaft* 43, no. 4 (2017): 612–33.

42. For the South African context, see, for example, Franco Barchiesi, *Precarious Liberation: Workers, the State, and Contested Social Citizenship in Postapartheid South Africa* (Albany: State University of New York Press, 2011). Among the fast-growing literature on other parts of Africa, see Aili Mari Tripp, *Changing the Rules: The Politics of Liberalization and the Urban Informal Economy in Tanzania* (Berkeley: University of California Press, 1997); Dmitri van den Bersselaar, "Old Timers Who Still Keep Going: Retirement in Ghana," *Österreichische Zeitschrift für Geschichtswissenschaften* 22, no. 3 (2011): 136–52; also James Ferguson, *Give a Man a Fish: Reflections on the New Politics of Distribution* (Durham, NC: Duke University Press, 2015), 52.

43. Christian Nsiah and Bichaka Fayiassa, "Remittances to Africa and Economics," *The Oxford Handbook of Africa and Economics,* vol. 2: *Policies and Practices,* ed. Celestin Monga and Justin Yifu Lin (Oxford: Oxford University Press, 2015): 711–26.

44. Keith Hart, "Informal Income Opportunities and Urban Employment in Ghana," *Journal of Modern African Studies* 11, no. 1 (1973): 61–89; Cooper, "African Labor History."

45. Kate Meagher, "The Scramble for Africans: Demography, Globalization and Africa's Informal Labor Markets," *Journal of Development Studies* 52 (2016): 485.

46. Franco Barchiesi, "Casual Labor and Informal Economy," *Sociology of Work: An Encyclopedia*, vol. 1, ed. Vicki Smith (Thousand Oaks, CA: Sage, 2013), 74–78; Ferguson, *Give a Man a Fish*. A good summary of the literature is offered by Kate Meagher, *Identity Economics: Social Networks and the Informal Economy in Nigeria* (Woodbridge, England: James Currey, 2010): 11–16. The following paragraphs profited much from discussions with Ravi Ahuja (Göttingen).

47. Emily Lynn Osborn, "Work and Migration," *The Oxford Handbook of Modern African History*, eds. John Parker and Richard Reid (Oxford: Oxford University Press, 2013), 196. An illuminating case study for this context is found in Trevor H. J. Marchand, *The Masons of Djenné* (Bloomington: Indiana University Press, 2009).

48. Gracia Clark, *Onions Are My Husband: Survival and Accumulation by West African Market Women* (Chicago: University of Chicago Press, 1997).

49. Ferguson, *Give a Man a Fish*, 106.

50. Frederick Cooper, "From Enslavement to Precarity? The Labour Question in African History," in *The Political Economy of Everyday Life in Africa: Beyond the Margins*, ed. Wale Adebanwi (Woodbridge, England: James Currey, 2017), 139.

51. Franco Barchiesi, "Precarious and Informal Labour," in *General Labour History of Africa*, Stefano Bellucci & Andreas Eckert, eds. (Woodbridge: Boydell & Brewer/James Currey), 45–76.

52. Benedetta Rossi, "What 'Development' Does to Work," *International Labor and Working-Class History* 92 (2017): 7.

53. Daniel Maul, *Human Rights, Development and Decolonization. The International Labour Organization, 1940–70* (Houndmills, U.K.: Palgrave Macmillan, 2012), 265. For a case study that emphasizes continuities of forced labor into the period of independence, see Romain Tiquet, *Travail forcé et mobilisation de la main d'oeuvre au Sénégal, Années 1920s–1960s* (Rennes, France: Presses Universitaires de Rennes, 2019).

54. International Labour Organization (ILO), *Regional Brief for Africa. 2017. Global Estimates of Modern Slavery and Child Labour*, https://goo.gl/9MEqM7.

55. Cooper, "From Enslavement to Precarity?" 140.

56. For a useful account on this complex, see Peter Tinti and Tuesday Reitano, *Migrant, Refugee, Smuggler, Saviour* (London: Hurst, 2016). In a recent book, widely acclaimed by European politicians and heavily criticized by scholars (especially demographers), the journalist Stephen Smith (*La Ruée vers l'Europe: Le jeune Afrique en route pour le Vieux Continent*, Paris: Grasset, 2018) predicts a "stampede for Europe" and argues that the scale of migratory pressure from Africa will submit Europe to a trial without precedent.

57. Meagher, "Scramble for Africans," 487.

58. Breman and Van der Linden, "Informalizing the Economy."

59. Craig Phelan, "Trade Unions, Democratic Waves, and Structural Adjustment: The Case of Francophone West Africa," *Labor History* 52, no. 4 (2011): 461–81.

10

The Social Question in South Africa

From Settler Colonialism to Neoliberal-Era Democracy

Ben Scully

INTRODUCTION

The classical social question of the nineteenth and early twentieth centuries is usually thought to pertain to Europe and North America, where the expansion of capitalist production brought social dislocation and political upheaval, especially in growing urban industrial centers. Yet South Africa experienced similar processes of industrial expansion and rapid urbanization in roughly the same period. Coupled with this, colonial occupation and racialized restrictions on land ownership dispossessed significant portions of the rural population from the land, precipitating a simultaneous crisis in the traditional agrarian economy, which the majority still relied on as a main source of livelihood. As a result, South Africa had its own version of the social question, the history of which provides a lens for rethinking the social question on a global scale.

In the Northern capitalist countries, conflict over the inequality and immiseration produced by capitalism led to the rise of labor movements as major political forces in many countries in the late nineteenth and early twentieth centuries. In many cases, labor movements were key actors in expanding formal democracy. This democratization can be thought of as one aspect of the Northern response to the social question, and it was followed by, in most places, the expansion of labor market protections and welfare provisions. By the mid-twentieth century, some form of a welfare state had been established in almost all advanced capitalist countries.

South Africa followed a different trajectory, which could be considered as a settler colonial response to the social question. Rather than an opening of a democratic political space, the late nineteenth and early twentieth centuries were marked by an institutionalization of racial inequalities that expanded citizenship for the white minority and restricted it for the majority. Long-standing practices of segregation and racism came to be codified in law, as the state attempted to accommodate organized white workers whose demands for protection from the vagaries of the market included a demand for protection from labor-market competition with the black majority. During this period, South Africa's political movements pushing for democratization and economic justice usually framed demands in terms of anti-racism and anti-colonialism rather, or in addition to, anti-capitalism. The rejection of the state's legitimacy forestalled demands for state social protection, and social policy implemented in the Apartheid era was often looked upon with suspicion.

Despite this history, South Africa is not just a negative example for thinking through the social question. The country achieved democracy in 1994, when the influence of neoliberal ideology was at its height. The new government faced the task of replacing the racialized social compact it had inherited at precisely the time when the mid-twentieth-century model of welfare states was coming under pressure in much of the rest of the world. In response to this challenge, South Africa has come to be a site of innovation both in policy and in scholarly debates on new forms of social protection.

This chapter will trace the changing meanings of and responses to the social question in South Africa. I concentrate on two key moments of state policy formation. The first part describes the settler colonial response to the social question, which emerged in the late nineteenth century and culminated in the formalized Apartheid system from the middle of the twentieth century. During this period, the expansion of capitalist development and colonial dispossession created crises of poverty and landlessness among the indigenous majority, as well as among a section of the white working class. However, the state's response was to define the social question as the "poor white problem." The policies that were implemented in this era aimed to protect white workers not only from the market in general but especially from competition with the black majority in the labor market. By giving white workers privileged access to the labor market, much of the work of social protection was accomplished through private employment, and explicit social policy was necessary only as a safety net to protect the few whites who could not gain security through wage work. This "solution" of the social question intensified the already established link between race and citizenship rights in the country.

The second part of this chapter will discuss the post-1994 democratic period, in which the contradictory forces of neoliberal ideology (at both the local and global levels) and a political and ideological imperative to expand access to social welfare for the previously excluded black majority have produced a new, neoliberal-era response to the social question. The liberalization of the economy from the 1990s led to increasing informalization of work and rising unemployment. This meant that the labor market could not provide security to the majority in the post-Apartheid period as it had in the middle of the twentieth century for the minority. As a result, state-provided social protection became more important, but its growing role had to be reconciled with the neoliberal ideology that shaped economic policy after 1994.

The third and final section of the chapter draws on my own research and secondary literature to show how gaps in the state's response since 1994 put pressure on households and other social connections, which highlight the continued relevance of the social question today.

THE SOCIAL QUESTION IN THE SETTLER COLONY

The nineteenth century as whole, even before the diamond and gold rushes, had been a period of conflict and dispossession across what is today South Africa. However, widespread, permanent landlessness remained a rarity, as did concentrated urban poverty. The Europeans' discovery of diamonds and gold in the latter half of the nineteenth century transformed the economy and society of southern Africa, creating widespread urbanization and proletarianization for the first time. The new demand for labor led to a number of policies that were aimed at undermining the economic security of the rural African population in order to compel them to seek wage labor. Subsidies for white farmers ensured that new opportunities for commercial farming afforded by growing urbanization would not be captured by the African peasantry.[1] The 1913 Native Land Act went further by preventing Africans from owning or renting land outside of the 13 percent of the country set aside as "reserves." The group who were most affected by this restriction were Africans who had been operating under sharecropping arrangements on white-owned farms outside of these reserves. Such arrangements were banned in the Orange Free State and severely curtailed elsewhere. In total, one-fifth of the five million Africans in South Africa at the time were proletarianized by the act.[2]

The late nineteenth and early twentieth centuries also saw class differentiation among rural whites, with small-scale farmers being pushed out by larger enterprises. As a result, newly proletarianized African workers were joined in the urban labor market by growing numbers of landless Afrikaners. These two groups entered primarily into low-skilled wage work in the mines and related industries, like construction and transportation. The new mining industries also attracted skilled immigrants with mining experience in Europe and the gold-producing areas of North American and Australia. These workers formed the core of the first trade unions to develop in the urban centers. By the last decades of the nineteenth century, urban slums were a feature of almost all South African cities. John Iliffe notes that although these concentrated areas of urban poverty were multiracial spaces, "South Africa's rulers identified multiracial poverty as the Poor White Problem. Although destitute white men had long been numerous, they were first seen as a social problem—rather than as a victim of their vices—during the 1880s and 1890s, when new European notions of poverty as a social phenomenon mingled with South Africa's growing concern with racial categorization."[3]

Already in the 1890s city leaders in Johannesburg established a public works program and relief fund for poor Afrikaners.[4] In 1906, also in Johannesburg, a group of white workers organized around the identity of the "unemployed," demanding support from the state. In response to these workers' protests, the city established a public works program to absorb the labor of unemployed urban whites.[5] Despite these developments, social protection remained piecemeal and uncoordinated at a national level.[6]

In the first decades of the twentieth century, trade unions began to emerge a serious political force. Major strikes, especially among white workers in the mines, but also including black dockworkers in Cape Town and Asian sugarcane workers in Natal, made industrial conflict a central issue of the early Union government. One outcome of these early strike waves was the emergence of private pensions and other forms of company-backed social protection, almost exclusively for white workers. Initially, however, the state's role remained limited.

In contrast to welfare provisions, labor law was coordinated by the state at the national level, and this period saw increasing attempts to formalize a legal system of industrial relations for the first time. National workers' compensation insurance was implemented in 1914. The Mines and Works Act of 1911 instituted basic protections for workers, including setting a limit on working hours, outlawing child labor, and giving government inspectors the ability to monitor and sanction safety violations. However, this law is most remembered not as an early example of workplace safety legislation, but rather for the fact that it was the first legal implementation of a color bar, which allowed skilled jobs to be reserved for white workers.

The juxtaposition of safety protections and legalized racial discrimination in the same law is emblematic of the way in which settler colonialism shaped South Africa's response to the social question. In this same period, in parts of the Global North, burgeoning labor movements were forcing reforms that mitigated both absolute poverty and the growing inequalities that accompanied capitalist growth. In South Africa, by contrast, both the politics of organized workers and the state's response to them served to deepen settler colonialism's pattern of racialized inequality. The African labor force had been created, in part, by undermining the security of African peasants, and the approach to labor and social protections did little to reverse this impact.

Early labor legislation barred black workers from striking (the 1911 Native Labour Act) and from participating in collective bargaining (the 1909 Industrial Disputes Prevention Act). White workers' demands for protection were frequently couched in racial terms. The first major strike on the gold mines, in 1907, was led by white workers fighting the use of Asian immigrant labor. Among the first agreements signed, once the mines recognized the white workers' union in 1918, was one that sought to halt the mines' practice of replacing skilled white workers with cheaper black workers, demanding that the ratio of seventeen black workers to every two higher-paid white workers—the earlier status quo—be continued. In

1922, the Rand Revolt, a major general strike that spread into a mass insurrection against the government, was carried out under the slogan "workers of the world, unite and fight for a white South Africa."

Two years after the Rand Revolt, South Africa passed its first comprehensive industrial-relations legislation. The Industrial Conciliation Act of 1924 aimed to recognize trade unions in all industries and to formalize wage negotiations and dispute settlements between workers and employers. However, the law only applied to white workers, meaning black workers' wages and working conditions continued to be the prerogative of employers, and any improvements in the conditions of black workers relative to that of their white counterparts could be resisted in collective bargaining by white unions. Black trade unions were not illegal during this period. In fact, one of the most celebrated black trade unions in the first half of the twentieth century, the Industrial and Commercial Workers Union (ICU), reached its peak membership in the late 1920s. But the prohibition on black workers striking, and their exclusion from the institutions of collective bargaining, made organizing a challenge, as exemplified by the collapse of the ICU by the early 1930s.[7]

As more white workers were absorbed into privileged positions in the labor market, the workplace became increasingly important as a location of welfare provision. A means-tested national social pension was introduced in 1928 for white and colored workers, but it affected a relatively small portion of the white population, most of whom tended to have access to higher-value private pensions through their workplaces.[8] In 1933 the state established the first national social welfare agency. The agency was initially situated within the Department of Labor, signifying the association between poverty and wage work. In 1937 Social Welfare was made an independent government department. Its primary programs were pensions and child welfare, but it also promoted the introduction of a limited unemployment insurance, which was instituted for white workers in 1945.[9]

These developments left South Africa with a widespread social welfare system for white workers, even before the 1948 victory of the National Party that ushered in Apartheid as official state policy. Apartheid made explicit the racialized definition of the society that the state and social policy should serve. Whites were provided exclusive access to superior education, various basic state services, democratic representation, collective bargaining institutions, and institutions of social protection. Nonwhites were restricted, with inferior education; pass laws, which limited their physical movement (especially to cities); forced removal from areas designated for exclusive white residence; and a range of other forms of institutionalized disadvantage. In short, the state's response to the social question was bifurcated between protection for whites and repression for nonwhites.

However, the Apartheid government did give increasing attention to the social and economic lives of black South Africans, especially as a widespread crisis of social reproduction was developing in rural parts of the country as a result of the decline of rural economy that followed the 1913 Land Act. The government's main concern with this crisis was not the moral imperative to protect citizens, but the economic and political implications that would result from a collapse of rural economy. The centrality of "traditional" rural spaces to the social and economic lives of black people was a fundamental tenant of Apartheid ideology. The official justification, for example, of excluding black people from the state pension system was "the assumption that Native custom makes provision for maintaining dependent persons' in rural areas."[10] The rural area was seen not only as a source of social security for black South Africans but also as important to the profitability of urban mining and industry. Mine companies openly argued that migrant workers' access to rural income allowed them to be paid lower wages in the cities.[11]

This idea of a rural source for black workers' social security was likely always little more than a convenient assumption on the part of employers and the Apartheid state, and it became increasingly difficult to reconcile with reality throughout the twentieth century. The Land Act and subsequent forced removals from "white" areas put enormous population pressures on the black rural areas, as the growing black population was restricted to the 13 percent of the land set aside as "native reserves." This led to overstocking of pastures, soil erosion, and other problems that undermined the viability of the reserve economies. Charles Simkins estimates that already by 1918, the agricultural production of the reserves could meet less than 50 percent of the food requirements of residents. This proportion declined significantly, especially after 1950.[12]

It is noteworthy that some of the main sources of data on the crisis of the reserve economies are reports and studies from the South African state itself. State officials were concerned with maintaining the reserves both as a source of labor for urban industry and as a viable place of residence for the African majority, who were legally prevented from permanently settling in cities. One response of the government was to promote industrial development in or near the reserves. For African residents, this policy offered an alternative to decreasingly viable agricultural activity. Concurrently, for the white government, this policy offered an alternative to the politically untenable relocation of African residents to main urban centers. From the 1950s, cities in and near the reserves were identified as "growth points," and businesses were offered tax breaks and subsidies to relocate production to these places.[13] This support for the economies of the reserves was the flip side of the state's repressive answer to the social question for black South Africans. The developmental thrust of "separate development" was an attempt to preserve, and even strengthen, the self-sufficiency of the reserves, which was necessary to underpin the settler colonial response to the social question.

SOCIAL QUESTION IN A NEOLIBERAL-ERA DEMOCRACY

The settler colonial resolution to the social question was remarkably successful for the white citizens who were its primary beneficiaries. By the latter part of the

TABLE 10.1 Key aspects of the policy base of racialized inequality under Apartheid.

Policy Sphere	Metric of Inequality	Description
Education	Spending per Pupil	Spending levels per pupil were ten times higher in white schools than in schools for black Africans.[1]
	Teacher-Student Ratio	"In 1987, whereas the student-teacher ratios for whites was 16 to 1, that for blacks in so-called white areas was 41 to 1, and for KwaZulu [a Bantustan or reserve area] primary schools was 53 to 1 and KwaZulu secondary schools 37 to 1."[2]
Labor Market	Collective Bargaining Rights	Collective bargaining was established for white workers in 1924. Black workers were prevented from participating in bargaining and were excluded from agreements reached until the 1980s.
	Job Reservations/ Color Bar	Through a range of legislation, occupational categories in a number of industries were segregated by race, with black workers restricted to low and semi-skilled positions while skilled and managerial positions were reserved for whites.
Social Policy	Pension Levels	When pensions for black South Africans were first introduced, in 1944, their levels were set at one-tenth the level of white citizens' pensions. Although racial disparity in pensions decreased through the Apartheid era, levels of pay were not uniform until 1993.[3]
	Unemployment Insurance	A nonracial unemployment insurance scheme was established in 1947, just before the Apartheid government came to power, but was amended in 1949 to exclude black workers[4] who did not gain access to unemployment assistance again until the late 1970s.[5]

[1] Edward B. Fiske and Helen F. Ladd, *Elusive Equity: Education Reform in Post-Apartheid South Africa* (Washington, DC: Brookings Institute Press), 5.

[2] J. Keith Chick, "Safe-Talk: Collusion in Apartheid Education," in *Society and the Language Classroom*, ed. H. Coleman (Cambridge: Cambridge University Press, 1996), 33.

[3] Van der Berg, "South African Social Security," 488.

[4] Iliffe, *The African Poor*, 141.

[5] Van der Berg, "South African Social Security," 491.

twentieth century, absolute poverty was virtually eliminated among the white population. Whites had enjoyed many decades of state policy aimed at advantaging them over nonwhite South Africans in the areas of education, land, employment, health, and security (see table 1). A testament to the Apartheid state's success in this regard is the durability of whites' advantages, even after two decades of explicit policy aimed at reducing racial inequalities.

However, while the system was successful for its white beneficiaries, its unraveling was, at least in part, a result of its failure to answer the social question of the black majority. Waves of protests from workers and students in the 1970s marked the beginning of a sustained anti-Apartheid protest movement, which eventually achieved the victory of nonracial democratic elections in 1994. This was the height of the period of neoliberal economic ideology. While neoliberal ideas shaped social pacts across the world, South Africa is a uniquely complicated example of a state tackling the social question under neoliberalism. The political moment of the new democracy compelled the state to deliver tangible improvements in the lives of the black majority, but the promises of freedom had to be realized within the constraints of a neoliberal global political economy.

As the previous section showed, labor and welfare policy were building blocks of white advantage in the pre-Apartheid period of rapid industrialization and urbanization. However, between these twin pillars of racialized social policy, it was labor laws that gave the strongest support for a white advantage. In the context of sustained economic growth through the mid-twentieth century, the labor market became the primary engine of inequality, while the welfare state acted as a buffer for white workers who fell through the cracks. In the democratic neoliberal era, labor and welfare policy remained the primary levers of addressing the social question, this time for all citizens. However, their relative importance was reversed. The informalization of wage work and the decline of the manufacturing sector in the face of global competition meant that the state had limited ability to deliver on its election promise of "a better life for all" through the labor market. It was, however, able to expand the already significant welfare state that it had inherited from the Apartheid government.

This is not to say that the post-Apartheid state has not been concerned with labor law or the world of work. One of the first major pieces of legislation passed by the democratic government was the Labour Relations Act (LRA) of 1995. This act made a firm commitment to collective-bargaining institutions and promoted co-determination in the governance of workplaces. However, the hopeful vision behind the law has never been realized. Collective bargaining has been implemented in unionized sectors, but it has done little to move workers out of the "Apartheid wage structure" that confines a significant portion of the employed working class to poverty.[14] For the majority of workers who are not covered by collective bargaining, there have been even fewer improvements. A recently introduced national minimum wage is a recognition that these workers have not been able to improve their own situation through bargaining, and unions have expressed disappointment with the low level at which it has been set (R3,500, or roughly US$250 per month).

The failure of the new industrial relations system to improve workers' situations is partially explained by the growth of precarious forms of labor since 1994. The 1980s had already been a period of economic crisis for the Apartheid state. The immediate post-Apartheid economic policy, inspired by the neoliberal orthodoxy of the time, tended to exacerbate, rather than alleviate this crisis.[15] South Africa has experienced a transformation of its labor market, with declining absolute levels of employment in both mining and agriculture; the only significant employment growth has taken place in the retail sector, which is dominated by precarious work.[16] While levels of employment have remained steady in manufacturing, there has been a major trend toward precaritization. Some formally unionized manufacturing industries have been decimated by the removal of tariff protections, with clothing and textiles being the most dramatic example.[17]

This situation has led some scholars to talk about a growing "representation gap" in the private sector, where increasing sections of workers don't have the associational power necessary to utilize the bargaining structures, which were set up with a very different workforce in mind.[18] A further blow to the functionality of the legal system of industrial relations has been the crisis within the Congress of South African Trade Unions (COSATU), the country's largest union federation, which has been plagued by factionalism and splintering. This situation gives little hope that the labor market can play the same role for the neoliberal-era social question that it did in the settler colonial period. As a result, the importance of welfare and social policy has been magnified. Because of the power of neoliberal ideology when South Africa achieved democracy, a major expansion of state-provided social welfare was unlikely to gain widespread support. However, the democratic government was fortunate to inherit one of the more widespread social welfare systems among middle-income countries. Since 1994 there has also been the introduction of new forms of state social support, but not without debates and resistance, which serve clarify the contours of the neoliberal-era social question.

A major plank of the post-Apartheid welfare system, the old-age pension, was actually put in place by the outgoing Apartheid government on the eve of democratic elections. The pension first introduced for white and colored workers in 1928 was expanded to all races by the 1940s, although at much lower levels for nonwhites. As the Apartheid system came under political siege in the 1970s and 1980s, the state began to move toward eliminating racial biases in an attempt to gain some legitimacy.[19] Throughout the 1980s the value of pensions for black South Africans was increased while the value of whites' pensions was decreased, and by 1993 pension levels were equalized across races. The democratic government has largely maintained the pension system. It has even increased the value of pension in real terms after 1994; and in 2008 the pensionable age for men was lowered from sixty-five to sixty (making it equal to the age for women).

Yet other aspects of the inherited welfare system could not simply be maintained and expanded. The second largest social grant program of the Apartheid era, the support for poor mothers with young children, remained skewed toward white beneficiaries. While the law did not explicitly set different grant levels based on race, a number of logistical challenges were put in the way of nonwhite women (in particular, rural black women), who would otherwise qualify for the grant. The most significant barrier was that the grant required a court judgment to be obtained that demonstrated that the mother had no other sources of support. Rural black women had far less access to courts than did their urban white counterparts.

In 1996, recognizing the racial bias of the grant, the new government established a commission to look into reorganizing the grant for children. The main concern of the state was that simply expanding access to the majority of the citizens at given benefit levels would be exceedingly expensive. Therefore, the commission's proposal, which eventually was implemented, was to expand access, but at a significantly reduced grant value. However, COSATU was strongly against this solution, and their resistance prompted a brief but important debate about the appropriate form of a post-Apartheid welfare state.

COSATU was not against the child grant itself, but the federation pointed out the virtual absence of a system of protection against long-term unemployment in a country that had one of the highest unemployment rates in the world. Rather than simply a "piece-meal tinkering with the elements of the inherited, fragmented social security network,"[20] COSATU argued for "restructuring the social welfare system."[21] COSATU's position highlighted the inadequacies of a welfare system set up by the Apartheid government in the mid-twentieth century for a democratic country in a neoliberal global economy. In particular, COSATU called for new forms of protection for the unemployed, which had been poorly developed in the Apartheid era.

The Apartheid state had used labor market tools to ensure that unemployment was no more than a residual social problem among the population who were included in the settler colonial social compact. The national Unemployment Insurance Fund, which had been first introduced in the 1940s, was aimed a short-term cyclical unemployment.[22] This had little effect in a post-Apartheid situation, where unemployment fluctuated between 25 percent and 30 percent. Furthermore, this unemployment was, in part, a legacy of Apartheid-era social policy. The restriction of education and job mobility for black workers before 1994 left South Africa with a workforce dominated by low-skilled workers. The liberalization of the economy after 1994 put these workers in competition with much cheaper low-skilled workers elsewhere in the world.[23]

One of the solutions that COSATU proposed for rethinking the welfare state in light of the post-Apartheid unemployment crisis was the introduction of a Basic Income Grant (BIG). The BIG was to be a universal monthly payment that, although small in value, would take a step toward decommodifying livelihoods in an environment where the labor market had proven to be an insufficient at regulating access to basic needs. Some of its supporters called it a "solidarity grant"[24] and trumpeted it as a form of "'citizen's income' that acknowledges a kind of nationwide membership and solidarity that would go beyond such (often empty) political rituals as voting to include rights to subsistence and consumption."[25] In this sense, the debate about reformulating the welfare system was a debate about the way in which social policy would structure social inclusion and citizenship in the neoliberal era.

The proposal for a BIG received widespread support from unions, churches, and other sections of civil society. It was even recommended by the government-appointed Taylor Commission, which was established to evaluate the post-Apartheid social policy framework. Yet the proposal was never implemented and never even received the backing of the ruling ANC party.[26] Instead, the government went ahead with the reforms to the child grant, which is now the second largest social grant in terms of value and the largest in terms of recipients. The ANC government's skepticism of the BIG reflected an enduring commitment to the idea of wage work and to the labor market as a key vehicle of social inclusion, even in a situation where work was not able to serve this function for a significant section of the population.[27]

An adherence to market logic has also shaped the expansion of access to basic government services. One of the most onerous legacies of Apartheid that the post-1994 government had to address was the extreme imbalances in the provision of housing and services. Large sections of both urban and rural areas where black South Africans lived were not provided with national and municipal services such as water and electricity. While the new government has achieved a significant expansion of connections to both water and electricity, the provision of these services has been marketized, meaning that many poor households remain unable to access these basic needs, despite being connected to national and municipal infrastructure.

Apartheid policies that limited urban housing construction, in an attempt to slow urbanization, also left an enormous housing backlog, estimated by the government to be between 3 and 3.7 million houses in 1999.[28] Since 1994 the government has undertaken an enormous project of building new low-cost housing for the poor, and by 2010 it had completed between 2.3 and 2.8 million houses.[29] Unlike water and electricity, government houses are usually provided free of cost.

The ANC government's solution to the neoliberal social question has established access to services and grants as a defining feature of citizenship for poor South Africans. It has come to be understood as a right, with social movements and community protests often explicitly linking the demand for social welfare provisions to the act of voting. For example, beginning with the Landless Peoples Movement's campaign for a boycott of the 2004 national elections (under the slogan "No Land! No Vote!"), calls for election boycotts have become a standard tactic of social movements. In 2009 the Durban shack-dwellers movement Abahlali baseMjondolo used the slogan "No Land! No Houses! No Vote!" and the Anti-Privatisation Forum of Johannesburg included demands for electricity and water in their boycott campaign.[30]

COOPERATION AND CONFLICT: SOCIAL PROTECTION BEYOND POLICY

The expansion of grants and access to services has built a relatively extensive system of social welfare in South Africa in comparison to other middle-income countries in the Global South. However, the system remains inadequate to meet even the basic needs of the country's poor. A major portion of the burden of protection has fallen onto the households of the masses of unemployed and working poor in the country. Households have become an important social space in which the neoliberal-era social question is addressed. However, in contrast to Apartheid-era assumptions about traditional forms of social protection among African families, households are not simply sites of altruism and communalism. The pressures that poverty and unemployment have placed on households has fueled conflict as much as cooperation. This section will discuss the household-level social protection that has become so important. It will also touch on other non-policy social spaces in which the social question is present, namely, spiraling personal debt, patronage and protest at the level of local government, and xenophobic violence.

The most significant gap in the post-Apartheid social policy framework is the lack of significant direct support for the working-age unemployed. As table 2

TABLE 10.2. Structure of state social protection in post-Apartheid South Africa.

Vulnerable Group	Programs in Place	Eligibility	Approximate Number of Beneficiaries	Coverage of Total Eligible Population
The Elderly	Old Age Pension	People over sixty-five who live in households that meet a means test.	3.25 million	Covers the vast majority of older people, including 80 percent of age-eligible black Africans. Technically means-tested, but in practice, this only excludes a small portion of age-eligible recipients.[1]
Children in Poor Households	Child Support Grant	Caregivers of children under eighteen who live in households that meet a means test.	12.02 million	A means-tested grant. There are some problems with means and age eligible recipients not applying,[2] but overall, an estimated 85 percent of poor children are covered.[3]
The Disabled	Disability Grant	People with disabilities whose spouses meet a means test and who do not receive another grant for themselves.	1.08 million	Coverage difficult to estimate because of ambiguities in the definition of *disabled,* but a much larger portion of disabled people are covered now than under Apartheid.[4]

(Continued)

Vulnerable Group	Programs in Place	Eligibility	Approximate Number of Beneficiaries	Coverage of Total Eligible Population
The Unemployed	Unemployment Insurance Fund	People who lose their job and who have previously contributed to the fund can claim for a period based on their previous contributions.	Approximately 100,000–200,000 at any given time[5]	As few as 1.3 percent of the unemployed are covered.[6]
	Expanded Public Works Programme	Unlike the other programs, EPWP eligibility is not a right. There are no clear guidelines governing where projects are implemented and how beneficiaries are selected.	Approximately 1 million per year[7]	In 2015 there were 1.1 million beneficiaries of EPWP[8] who got short-term (four to six months) part-time jobs against 7.4 million unemployed.[9]

[1] Anne Case and Angus Deaton, "Large Cash Transfers to the Elderly in South Africa," *The Economic Journal* 108, no. 450 (1998): 1330–1361; Justine Burns, Malcolm Keswell, and Murray Leibbrandt, "Social Assistance, Gender, and the Aged in South Africa," *Feminist Economics* 11, no. 2 (2005): 103–115; Margaret Ralston, Enid Schatz, Jane Menken, Fransisco Gomez-Olive, and Stephen Tollman, "Who Benefits—Or Does Not—From South Africa's Old Age Pension?" *International Journal of Environmental Research and Public Health* 13, no. 85 (2016): 1–14.

[2] Department of Social Development, South African Social Security Agency, and UNICEF, *The South African Child Support Grant Impact Assessment* (Pretoria: UNICEF South Africa, 2012).

[3] International Labour Organization, "South Africa's Child Support Grant: A Booster for Poverty Reduction," April 14, 2016, www.ilo.org/global/about-the-ilo/newsroom/features/WCMS_468093/lang--en/index.htm.

[4] Gabrielle Kelly, *Regulating Access to the Disability Grant in South Africa, 1990–2013*, CSSR Working Paper 330, Centre for Social Science Research (Cape Town: University of Capetown, 2013).

[5] Haroon Bhorat, Sumayya Goga, and David Tseng, "Unemployment Insurance in South Africa," Africa Growth Initiative Working Paper 8. (Washington, DC: The Brookings Institution, 2013), 11.

[6] Geeta Kingdon and John Knight, "Unemployment in South Africa: The Nature of the Beast," *World Development* 32, no. 3 (2004): 5.

[7] Department of Public Works, *Annual Report 2014/2015* (Tswane Central: Republic of South Africa, 2015).

[8] Ibid.

[9] Stats South Africa, Quarterly Labour Force Surveys, www.statssa.gov.za.

shows, coverage is reasonably good for the elderly, poor children, and the disabled. However, for the unemployed, there are only two programs available, the Unemployment Insurance Fund (UIF) and the Expanded Public Works Programme (EPWP). Both cover only a small portion of the total unemployed. The UIF is available only to those who previously had formal work and paid into the fund, and even then, the duration of benefits is limited. UIF is not available to those who have never been employed, workers in the informal sector, government employees, and the long-term unemployed.[31]

Given this gap, other social grants, and the old-age pension in particular, have become a de facto safety net for the long-term unemployed and underemployed. These grants reach the working-age unemployed through household and familial connections. A range of studies drawing on different data sets have shown that one of the most common strategies for coping with unemployment is to join or remain in the households of grant recipients in order to have some access to income.[32] The informal welfare system of the household is a gendered one. Women's pensions have been shown to have a positive influence on the health of children in poor households, an effect that does not extend to pensions paid to men.

Grants are often used as a base from which to develop other income sources. Contrary to the common view that social grants disincentive wage work, the South African old-age pension has been shown to be positively associated with both migration and employment of working-age household members.[33] This is evidence of what might be called "reverse remittances." In the Apartheid era, young male migrants would send remittances to support family who remained in rural areas. However, in the present, older grant recipients often use their grant to support younger family members migrating to urban areas. Because unemployment and short-term informal work are so prevalent, rural-to-urban migrants might have to be supported for some time, often years, before they can find work.

However, to say households are important is not to suggest that they are a panacea to the challenges of poverty and precarity. The increased significance of resource allocation within the household leads, in many cases, to increased conflict.[34] Fakier and Cock have described a "crisis of social reproduction" that has developed within poor households, in which the female household members who bear the burden of caregiving are unable to compensate for the inadequacies of the labor market and basic service provision.[35] Individuals and households do draw on mutualistic ties of solidarity at the community level, but even these are put under strain in situations of extreme poverty.[36] Erik Bähre has described mutualistic savings societies in Cape Town as being characterized by "reluctant solidarity," which is as conflictual as it is cooperative, based not on "extensive unifying bonds of comradeship, but [on] small bonds fraught with social tension."[37]

In addition to the social connections of the household and community, formal debt has become an increasingly central feature of the economic lives of many South Africans. Poor households often rely on informal lenders, who charge very high interest rates, sometimes reaching triple figures.[38] Social grant recipients are often the most reliable customers of informal lenders, since they have a more regular source of income than the precarious and informally employed. It is not unusual for grant recipients to pay a significant portion of their payment to lenders on a monthly basis. However, the most heavily indebted are not the most poor, but the lower middle class, especially civil servants and low-level salaried employees whose access to a steady wage allows them to gain credit with formal lenders.[39] The primary causes of debt for these borrowers are payments for major life events, such as marriage, funerals, or higher education for their children.[40] The student protests that swept the country in the latter part of 2015 demanding free tertiary education highlighted the enormous anger and anxiety over the financial barriers to universities, which are seen as gateways to some level of financial security and stability.

Karl von Holdt, in a study of protest and violence around local government across South Africa, has argued that these struggles are, in part, marked by contestation over the meaning and content of citizenship. The most extreme form of this contestation is both individual and collective violence, which has led von Holdt to characterize South Africa as a "violent democracy."[41] Community violence in South Africa takes place at multiple levels. On the one hand, there is the upward-oriented violence against the state, which explicitly advances demands for protection and inclusions. This is often intertwined with horizontal violence against political opponents, which seeks to gain or protect access to the state for particular individuals or groups. Finally, there is downward-oriented xenophobic violence, which has become a feature of South African struggles in recent years. In 2008, a wave of attacks against foreigners across the country killed sixty-two people and displaced thousands. In the years since then, periodic smaller waves of attacks have been a regular occurrence, as is the daily reality of a widespread popular resentment of non–South Africans among a significant portion of the country's citizens. The xenophobic violence is an explicit expression of subaltern contestation over the boundaries of inclusion.

The violence and conflict that is present in so many social spaces in South Africa is evidence of the degree to which the neoliberal response to the social question has pushed the burden of insecurity into the social spaces of households, communities, and the market. However, even in these private spaces, the informal systems of protection bear the imprint of state policy. Grants, connections to local government, and the identity of "citizen" are all resources that are drawn upon, and contested, in the livelihood strategies of poor South Africans.

CONCLUSION

South Africa's history provides a microcosm of the social question when considered at a global scale. The initial dislocations of capitalist growth led to a system of citizenship-based protection for a privileged minority, while the demands of the majority were dealt with through a combination of repression and developmentalism. Eventually, contestation from below opened up new democratic space, which was accompanied by new forms of generalized social protection. However, the social benefits of democracy were limited by changes in the labor market, which had been a primary vehicle of protection for the privileged minority of the past, but now came to be marked by widespread insecurity and exclusion. As a result, families and communities have become spaces of informal social protection and conflict.

At a global scale, the contemporary situation has made clear what was always obvious in the South African context: twentieth-century answers to the social question are inherently exclusionary and cannot be universalized across the world. However, the contemporary limits of the neoliberal-era social question are not set in stone. The neoliberal economic orthodoxy that constrained South Africa's policy options in its early years of democracy were thoroughly discredited by the 2008 financial crisis. South Africa is one of the many places where welfare protections have been expanded and new types of provision, not linked to the labor market, have been debated (for example, the BIG) or implemented (the child grant) over the past twenty years. At the same time, demands for seemingly "old-fashioned" social protection, such as a national minimum wage and increased access to affordable health care, stand beside new visions, such as basic income protection.

An important factor in whether and how these new directions are pursued is the protection and extension of democratic spaces. Earlier answers to the social question were accompanied by limited expansion of democracy. In the neoliberal era in South Africa, as in many countries around the world, the social benefits of democracy were limited by the global constraints that neoliberalism placed on state actions. In the current moment, it seems possible that such limits could be challenged, as evidenced by contemporary debates in South Africa such as those raised by recent student protests, which raise possibilities that extend significantly beyond the limits of neoliberal orthodoxy. However, an equally plausible possibility is that the limited gains of democracy lead to frustration and disillusionment with the state, leaving space for corruption, empty populism, and other political forces that are unlikely to push forward answers to the still-pressing social question of contemporary global capitalism.

NOTES

1. Sampie Terreblanche, *A History of Inequality in South Africa, 1652–2002* (Scottsville, South Africa: University of KwaZulu-Natal Press, 2002), 259.
2. Terreblanche, *History of Inequality*, 262.
3. John Iliffe, *The African Poor: A History* (Cambridge: Cambridge University Press, 1987), 116–17.
4. Ibid., 118.
5. Charles Van Onselen, *New Babylon New Nineveh: Everyday Life on the Witwatersrand 1886–1914* (Johannesburg: Jonathan Ball, 2001), 338–41.
6. Iliffe, *African Poor*, 118.
7. Philip Bonner, "The Decline and Fall of the ICU: A Case of Self-Destruction?" in *Essays in Southern African Labour History*, ed. Edward Webster, 114–20 (Johannesburg: Raven Press, 1978), 116–17.
8. Servaas van der Berg, "South African Social Security under Apartheid and Beyond," *Development Southern Africa* 14, no. 4 (1997): 486.
9. Bonner, "Decline and Fall of the ICU," 116–17.

10. Social Security Committee, cited in van der Berg, "South African Social Security," 487.

11. Harold Wolpe, "Capitalism and Cheap Labour-Power in South Africa: From Segregation to Apartheid," *Economy and Society* 1, no. 4 (1972): 434.

12. Charles Simkins, "Agricultural Production in the African Reserves of South Africa, 1918–1969," *Journal of Southern African Studies* 7, no. 2 (1981): 256–83.

13. Hermanus S. Geyer, "Industrial Development Policy in South Africa—The Past, Present and Future," *World Development* 17, no. 3 (1989): 380.

14. Neil Coleman, "Towards New Collective Bargaining, Wage and Social Protection Strategies in South Africa-Learning from the Brazilian Experience." Global Labour University Working Paper, 2013.

15. Giovanni Arrighi, Nicole Aschoff, and Ben Scully, "Accumulation by Dispossession and Its Limits: The Southern Africa Paradigm Revisited," *Studies in Comparative International Development* 45, no. 4 (2010): 410–38.

16. Abhijit Banerjee, Sebastian Galiani, Jim Levinsohn, Zoë McLaren, and Ingrid Woolard, "Why Has Unemployment Risen in the New South Africa?" *Economics of Transition* 16, no. 4 (2008): 724.

17. Sarah Mosoetsa, "The Consequences of South Africa's Economic Transition: The Remnants of the Footwear Industry," in *Beyond the Apartheid Workplace: Studies in Transition,* ed. Edward Webster and Karl Von Holdt, 317–34 (Scottsville, South Africa: University Of KwaZulu-Natal Press, 2005).

18. Edward Webster and Rahmat Omar, "Work Restructuring in Post-Apartheid South Africa," *Work and Occupations* 30, no. 2 (2003): 194–213.

19. Van der Berg, "South African Social Security."

20. COSATU, "Audit of COSATU Positions on Social Security," 2000, www.cosatu.org.za/show.php?ID=2167.

21. COSATU Oral Submission to Portfolio Committee on Welfare, Regarding Proposed Changes to the System of Child Support Benefits Arising from the Report of the Lund Committee on Child and Family Support," Cape Town, April 21, 1997, www.cosatu.org.za/docs/subs/1997/childsupportbenefits.pdf.

22. Van der Berg, "South African Social Security under Apartheid and beyond."

23. Arrighi, Aschoff, and Scully, "Accumulation by Dispossession and Its Limits."

24. Guy Standing and Michael Samson, *A Basic Income Grant for South Africa* (Cape Town: University of Cape Town Press, 2003).

25. James Ferguson, *Expectations of Modernity: Myths and Meanings of Urban Life on the Zambian Copperbelt* (Berkeley: University of California Press, 1999), 158.

26. See Leila Patel, *Social Welfare and Social Development in South Africa* (Cape Town: Oxford University Press, 2005), 141–43, for an overview of these debates.

27. Franco Barchiesi, "Wage Labor and Social Citizenship in the Making of Post-Apartheid South Africa," *Journal of Asian and African Studies* 42, no. 1 (2007): 39–72.

28. Kate Tissington, "A Resource Guide to Housing in South Africa 1994–2010: Legislation, Policy, Programmes and Practice" (Johannesburg: SERI, 2011).

29. Ibid.

30. "No Electricity, No Vote, Say Protesters," *Mail and Guardian,* October 30, 2008. https://mg.co.za/article/2008-10-30-no-electricity-vote-say-protesters.

31. Haroon Bhorat, Sumayya Goga, and David Tseng, "Unemployment Insurance in South Africa: A Descriptive Overview of Claimants and Claims," DPRU Working Paper 13/160. Development Policy Research Unit, 2013, https://ideas.repec.org/p/ctw/wpaper/13160.html.

32. Stephan Klasen and Ingrid Woolard, "Surviving Unemployment without State Support: Unemployment and Household Formation in South Africa," *Journal of African Economies* 18, no. 1 (2009): 1–51.

33. Cally Ardington, Anne Case, and Victoria Hosegood, "Labor Supply Responses to Large Social Transfers: Longitudinal Evidence from South Africa," Working Paper, National Bureau of Economic Research, September 2007, www.nber.org/papers/w13442.

34. Sarah Mosoetsa, *Eating from One Pot: The Dynamics of Survival in Poor South African Households* (Johannesburg: Wits University Press, 2011).

35. Khayaat Fakier and Jacklyn Cock, "A Gendered Analysis of the Crisis of Social Reproduction in Contemporary South Africa," *International Feminist Journal of Politics* 11, no. 3 (August 18, 2009): 353–71.

36. Mosoetsa, *Eating from One Pot.*

37. Erik Bähre, "Reluctant Solidarity: Death, Urban Poverty and Neighbourly Assistance in South Africa," *Ethnography* 8, no. 1 (2007): 52.

38. Mosoetsa, *Eating from One Pot.*

39. Deborah James, "Money-Go-Round: Personal Economies of Wealth, Aspiration and Indebtedness," *Africa: The Journal of the International African Institute* 82, no. 1 (2012): 20–40.

40. Ibid., 20.

41. Karl von Holdt, "South Africa: The Transition to Violent Democracy," *Review of African Political Economy* 40, no. 138 (2013): 589–604.

11

The Social Question in the Middle East

Past and Present

Kevan Harris

In 1840, a coalition of European powers decided to take on an alarming problem to their south. The Albanian-born governor of Ottoman Egypt, Mehmed Ali, had spent the past two decades building up a formidable industrial and military capacity among his assigned territories. A veteran of the Napoleonic wars, the Wahhabi revolt, and the Greek rebellion, Ali administered Egypt as a province of the Sublime Porte in name only; in reality, he was forging a Mediterranean Prussia. Ali's troops marched on Palestine, Syria, and then Greece, claiming territory and stationing men. The Ottoman sultan could do little about it. Eventually, the British and Austrian navies cut off Egyptian supply lines and entered Alexandria's waters. Ali signed a series of capitulations under duress that opened Egyptian markets, dismantled its manufacturing base, and defanged its military. Egypt experienced rapid underdevelopment, becoming an exporter of raw commodities and an importer of European manufactures for the next century.[1] It was not until the rule of Gamal Abdel Nasser that such statist attempts would occur again in North Africa, to be met again with external military response. Today, not coincidentally, Egypt lags behind other middle-income states in industrial capacity, and it is the world's largest importer of wheat.

Amid these mid-nineteenth-century efforts of geopolitical renewal, writers such as the Egypt-based intellectual Rifa'a al-Tahtawi attempted a synthesis of Islamic political thought and European political economy.[2] Qasim Amin's *The Liberation of Women* and *The New Woman* appeared not long after. Though the actors have changed since al-Tahtawi and Amin paid heed to the emerging social question in relation to state building, the debates over the prospects for regional order, popular cohesion, and political rejuvenation remain largely unaltered. To chart the historical terrain, this chapter provides a survey of social regulation and political economy for states in Middle East and North Africa (MENA), amid changing political-economic conditions, across five broad chronological periods: the tail end of the Ottoman and Persian Empires, the colonial interlude, the era of political independence, the *infitah* years of economic opening, and the current upheaval of unrest and militarization.

EMPIRES UNRAVELED

Notwithstanding the lack of a settled conceptual or geographic definition for the region itself, few zones of the world have been placed in opposition for so long than Europe and the Middle East. Mostly recently, the institutional turn in economics has produced attempts to explain anew the divergence between them. These accounts focus on the persistence of "bad" institutions in MENA areas over the longue durée—lack of primogeniture, for instance, or dominance of state rulers over local elites.[3] Yet economic historians of the region counter that institutional pluralism, not uniformity, was the rule. Land-tenure patterns ranged from small peasant holdings to tax farming by notables to imperially administered estates. Commerce and credit tended to flow through and between urban locales, overcoming or bypassing religious dictates against usury through flexible interpretations of scripture; women's and religious minorities' roles as traders were not insignificant. Nomadic tribal confederations ranged across large swaths of the region, coexisting within and around agrarian empires and their urban metropoles. The "gunpowder empires" of the early modern period—as Marshall Hodgson termed the Ottomans and Safavids—more successfully centralized a ruling apparatus and market penetration over large territories compared to previous centuries. Long before Western colonialism, the internal and external borders marked out by these and subsequent warring empires laid the foundations for twentieth-century state-building in the MENA region.

As elsewhere, the internal authority of these empires was irregularly exercised. By the end of the eighteenth century, merchants, artisan guilds, and religious endowments tended to administer most social aid and welfare in imperial urban zones. Charitable giving was, of course, an Islamic injunction. Through the pooling of donations and assets under religious endowments, Hodgson noted, "various civic essentials and even amenities were provided for on a private yet dependable basis without need or fear of the intervention of political power."[4] Yet the few studies that exist show that inequality was quite high in West Asian empires. The Gini index during the eighteenth century for sampled records in Cairo and Damascus hovered around 0.75, while northern Anatolian locales stood at 0.60.[5]

There was no generalized effect from increased commercial trade with the capitalist world economy and penetration by European merchants and militaries in the region. The variation of peasant tenure patterns, merchant-state relations, and artisan-guild politics widely differed, based on relations between local elites and imperial centers. Hardly the paragon of "Asian despotism," Ottoman capacity for state regulation was, in fact, limited and reached its apex in the sixteenth century. Most revenues were kept by tax-farming notables, while merchant entreaties against foreign competition from European trade went largely unheeded.[6] The recentralization of the Ottoman bureaucracy through nineteenth-century reforms brought the state back into social regulation and class formation, most notably in Mehmed Ali's Egypt and the wealthier Ottoman provinces.[7] The Persian Empire under the Qajar dynasty fared worse at fiscal-military centralization, as evidenced by a series of famines during the 1860s and 1870s. During these catastrophes, an imperial ban on cereal exports was mandated but unenforceable. Most of the famine aid came from European missionaries, not the imperial government in Tehran, and was directed toward religious minorities.[8]

Given the unevenness of state penetration combined with social deprivation, it is not surprising that unrest broke out. The nineteenth century witnessed a wave of uprisings on MENA imperial peripheries that Eric Hobsbawm would have instantly recognized as led by primitive rebels: the Sudanese Mahdi, the Daghestani Imam Shamil, the Shirazi Bab (precursor to Bahaism), the Sokoto's Usman dan Fodio (across the Sahara along the Niger), or the Somaliland's Mohammad Abdullah Hassan (the original "Mad Mullah"). These were generally millenarian movements that devised radical worldviews and appealed to social justice under the guise of Islamic tradition. Whether quickly extinguished or successfully converted into proto-states, their presence was often the pretense for intervention of Western colonial armies.

The inability of MENA empires to confront external and internal challenges spurred urban intellectuals to argue for more radical social and political measures to be carried out by the state. Along with other agrarian empires, such Russia, India, and China, the Ottomans and Persians underwent anti-imperialist revolts at their urban centers in the early twentieth century. The dynamics were similar: elites attempted to redirect their remaining imperial resources toward military upgrading, popular mobilization, and nationalist myth-making, often combined with a degree of emancipation for women of the elite, at least.[9] It is not a coincidence that the first successful attempt occurred at the heart of West Asia's imperial arena: Kemalism. The MENA social compacts of the mid-twentieth century owed much to its example.

THE COLONIAL INTERLUDE

The exercise and profile of European power in the Middle East and North Africa varied by subregion. The British pushed Napoleon's army out of Egypt, but the restored Bourbons entered Ottoman Algeria in the 1830s and forcefully integrated territory into the French state. For most of the region, in contrast with sub-Saharan Africa, inter-imperialist rivalries slowed the formal usurpation of power. The British viewed a contained Ottoman empire as a useful bulwark against Russian expansion. Tunisia fell to French gunboats only in the 1880s; Morocco, which had always maintained independence from the Ottomans, was partitioned into French and Spanish protectorates in the 1910s. The priority of British imperial policy in the MENA expanse was geopolitical control over travel routes to South and East Asia. The Persian Empire slowly lost territory during the nineteenth century to Russian and British incursions, but never formal independence, largely for this reason.[10] In fact, there was only one direct colony established over two centuries of European imperialism in the region—the port of Aden on the Yemeni coast, ruled as part of British India.

European capital was less hobbled. French and British banks financed Ottoman state reforms in the mid-nineteenth century, which put them in sound position after the Ottomans defaulted. Eventually a European consortium took over Ottoman finances in the late nineteenth century, an arrangement that was, unsurprisingly, favorable to creditors.[11] The vehicle of debt arrears furthered British machinations for control over the Suez Canal and indirect rule in Egypt and Sudan. As with Iran, the Maghreb region from Morocco to Egypt was racked with famines in the 1870s. A prime culprit lay partly in the shift to monocropped agriculture—usually wheat and cotton exports—which had suffered from American competition and declining terms of trade during the global depression of the late nineteenth century.[12] Yet even amid minor British and French imperial efforts at fostering plantation agriculture, a small landholding peasantry persisted throughout most of the Ottoman empire into the early twentieth century.

A crucial analytic point for the MENA region, then, is that European imperialist penetration of political and social structures was highly uneven. So was Ottoman rule, of course—some stretches of the Libyan coast were limited to trading posts for warding off Bedouin raids. After the Ottoman Empire shattered in World War I, some areas were ruled by mandate administration, others in an indirect fashion, and other areas won formal independence through rebellion. Though vogue, it is hyperbolic to believe that a Franco-British colonial order created the modern Middle East; such an order rather cobbled together structures of rule out of a diverse Ottoman-Persian imperial zone. As this zone collapsed on itself during the early twentieth century, elite-led nationalist movements of both minority and majority varieties—such as Greeks, Serbs, Armenians, Kurds, Turks, Arabs, and Maronites—maneuvered among the ruins.[13] Some of these intelligentsias converted into state rulers; others formed the transnational diasporas that today reside in Western metropolises.

The interwar period drew together the challenges of external colonial imposition and domestic political rejuvenation in contradictory relation to the social question. In British and French administered territories such as Egypt or Syria, nationalist elites mobilized on social as well as political grounds. In areas where the colonial question was largely settled, as in interwar Turkey or Iran, splits appeared earlier between nationalist elites and labor movements.[14] Unlike Latin America, where the interwar years provided a spur toward industrialization, in European-controlled MENA the emphasis was on regulating the safe flow of goods through the region. Early oil discoveries in Khuzestan, Baku, and Kirkuk added to such imperatives.

Though the geopolitical priority was control over transit, inter-European rivalries allowed for acquisition of capital goods in trading zones. Industrial production finally resumed as another world war loomed, leading to increased proletarianization in mandate-administered urban centers. The irony is that, while a Bismarckian state-led development project had commenced under the guise of an anti-imperialist push for independence in the newly forming nation-states of Turkey and Iran, similar processes were occurring under British and French colonial administration. Unlike independent states, however, less was spent on welfare and public works by colonial elites, and nascent industrial drives remained based in enclave areas.

The period from the 1900s to the 1940s forged another of the great ironies of modern Middle Eastern history. Amid crises of domestic authority, transnational networks of intellectuals—religious and secular, liberal and communist—created a common set of frameworks for nation building, myth making, and postcolonial citizenship (industrial Japan was a widely held exemplar). Their eventual success in forming coherent nation-states out of imperial clay would result in the erasure of the memory of their own roles. The transmissions of pamphlets, laborers, and revolutionaries along the paths of Istanbul-Tabriz-Baku-Tashkent or Cairo-Damascus-Baghdad were possible only in a late imperial milieu of cosmopolitanism. Bolstered by armed uprisings and mass organizations, these energies poured into the containers of the state over subsequent decades. Yet once the actual work of state building commenced, political theory was not easily translated into practice. If there is a common lesson for MENA states in the interwar and postwar periods, it is the failure of elitist liberalism and the success of popular mobilization for the purposes of state building. With a freer hand, Kemalist Turkey and Pahlavi Iran had already engaged in such efforts during the 1930s. The Wafd (delegation) Party in Egypt achieved popular appeal while under British protectorate status, but it focused doggedly on independence at the expense of a radical mass agenda. European interwar left movements were of little help—the 1936 French popular-front government refused independence to Syria, Lebanon, and Algeria.

Once decolonization set in, however, a region-wide social compact began to coalesce. To map out its contours, a contrast with Latin America is useful. During the 1930s rise of populist states in Brazil, Argentina, and Mexico, public goods and social citizenship were extended de jure to the entire citizenry. Latin American elites crafted nationalist appeals to *mestizaje* or racial democracy, which attempted to reverse the stark colonial legacies of ethno-racial classification under slavery and indigenous servitude. Yet de facto distribution of these public goods tended to fall along preexisting hierarchical lines of social distinction. Unequal access to basic health care, education, and infrastructural improvements led to the notoriously high inequality observed within much of twentieth-century Latin America.[15] In the MENA region, the opposite occurred, due to the postwar configuration of state formation though corporatism.

THE POSTWAR CORPORATIST COMPACT

Initially welcomed by newly independent states, postwar U.S. hegemony was doubly edged in the MENA region. On the one hand, the lack of major U.S. corporate interests compared to Latin American markets meant that U.S. policy makers largely encouraged import substitution and aided state-led development during the 1950s and early 1960s. On the other hand, U.S. geopolitical strategy of securing favorable access to oil resources through informal alliances laid the foundation for a subsequent direct militarization of vital MENA areas. The Cold War context and its coalescing divides masked a widely shared approach to social compacts in the postwar era. No matter the ideological sheen, state-led planning amid scarcity of capital ruled the day. This was the context for nationalization projects from Nasser in Egypt to Mossadeq in Iran. Resources could be mobilized through maneuvering among Cold War alliances, but claims of a distinctive model of "Arab socialism" were partly aimed at warding off or co-opting the growing power of left-wing movements.[16]

The Turkish example loomed large. In response to the chaos of Ottoman collapse and radical domestic upsurges, the Kemalist Republic forged its own authoritarian version of Polanyi's double movement in the 1930s and 1940s: Soviet-inspired five-year industrialization plans, Italian-inspired corporate labor control, and U.S.-inspired distribution of state lands to middle peasants and large landowners. As a result, the decentralized land-tenure patterns in Ottoman Anatolia were, even into the 1960s, preserved.[17]

For the new nation-states of the MENA region, this corporatist model of industrialization allowed a newly emergent political class to undercut the power bases of economic and social rivals. Iran's Pahlavi monarchy built up a military and bureaucratic corps in the 1930s, a concentrated industrial class in the 1960s, and only afterward began to force landowners to divest their holdings of village lands. The shah compared what he labeled Iran's 1960s "White Revolution" with the examples of Meiji Japan and Bismarckian Prussia.[18]

Other countries took the same approach in speedier fashion, thus appearing all the more radical. Unlike Anatolia, in Egypt, Iraq, Tunisia, and greater Syria, land enclosures by tribal chiefdoms and landlords had intensified during the early-twentieth-century imperial breakdown. The longevity of new Arab states, therefore, was connected to how their leaders dealt with the social question in the countryside. Sixty percent of the Egyptian peasantry was landless in 1950, the same ratio existed in Syria, and Iraq's tribal areas were racked with peasant revolt. In Algeria, an extreme case of proletarianized rural wage labor policed by colonial arms remained in existence.

These were not traditional social structures inherited by postwar states, but rather a product of rapid consolidation by local agrarian elites that dislocated segments of the population. As Hanna Batatu explained, "Extensive tracts of state domain and communal tribal land passed into the hands of new men of capital, European *colons,* ex-warring shaykhs, or retainees of ruling pashas, often through forced purchases or without ground of right or any payment whatever."[19] Under this politics of notables, sometimes with liberal democratic guises, peasants were displaced from kinship networks and communal mechanisms of social reproduction. Amid these fraying ties, the revolutionary Arab state promised to step in—Egypt in 1952, Tunisia in 1957, Iraq in 1958, Algeria in 1962, Syria in 1963, and Libya in 1969, not to mention revolutionary guerrilla movements in Oman, Lebanon, Yemen, and Jordan from the late 1960s onward. To a large extent, the social origins of this new power elite were rural or provincial men who had risen up through military and other state institutions. The goal was not a peasant revolution, however, but a Kemalist revolution to be carried out by bureaucrats from above. Democracy was largely seen as a divisive distraction from the task of state consolidation.

These processes are often jumbled together under an umbrella category of clientelist rule or neo-patrimonialism, sometimes claimed to be a fixed legacy of Ottoman sultanism in Arab lands. But as James Gelvin notes, this line of argument tended to reveal more about mid-twentieth-century historians and social scientists than the actual region itself.[20] As Gelvin saw it, Arab corporatism was a form of class warfare. Not between capital and labor, but between the new state elite and the old oligarchical landed classes. To some degree, the repressive apparatus of many MENA states stem from this rapid and stealthy capture of political power by men of rural lower-middle class backgrounds, such as Nasser and Hafez al-Assad. Forever paranoid of retaliation by enemies, real or conjured, these men first deployed security forces against the "feudal" elite and the same apparatus was subsequently marshaled against any perceived threat of ouster.

The incorporation of peasant, worker, and professional strata into state-linked bodies provided a countervailing social base from which to break up landholdings and dismantle mercantile networks. As a result, rural peasants were not emancipated as a class, but many of their children ended up in public employment in the city. A key outcome of the corporatist model—ideological patinas about rule of the masses aside—was the provision of rapid upward social mobility for select individuals. As Gilbert Achcar stressed, "the state went so far as to largely substitute itself for the private sector by means of both far-reaching nationalization programs and massive public investment."[21] The average annual rate of manufacturing growth among MENA states was 13.5 percent in the 1950s and 10.6 percent from 1960 to 1973. In the realm of social protection, non-state charities and philanthropies of the liberal interwar period—schools, workshops, clinics—were eventually taken over by the state and homogenized.[22]

The social compact involved a huge push in credentialing citizens through education and high status professional-technical employment. The Nasser period in Egypt (1954–1970), for example, saw primary school enrollment rise by 234 percent and higher education by 325 percent.[23] Education was the path of least resistance for many of these states to reduce preexisting class privileges and reorder status hierarchies. It also was a tried-and-true method of creating loyal citizens who identified with the nation-state's imagined community more than its competitors.

Once in place, the MENA state-led social compact had an impressive impact on livelihoods over the next three decades. The World Bank deemed the model as "rapid growth . . . and generous transfers to large parts of the population." From 1960 to 1985, Arab states outperformed all other Third World regions except East Asia in income growth with equitable income distribution. Infant mortality was cut in half, life expectancy increased by ten years. As far as we can trust internationally comparable poverty lines, MENA became a relatively low-poverty region in the Global South: 5.6 percent of the population lived under the $1 per day purchasing power parity (PPP) line in 1990 versus 14.7 percent in East Asia and 28.8 percent in Latin America.[24] The same can be broadly said for internal inequality. Though household surveys in MENA tend to measure consumption, not income, Gini levels of inequality in the region floated around 0.35 to 0.50, well below the extremes faced in Latin America. As shown below with a set of non-income development indicators in table 11.1 and figure 11.1, a generation of social leveling arguably took place in the postwar era, with positive trends lasting into the subsequent neoliberal period.

As a social compact, however, corporatism contained at least three contradictions that intensified over time. First, a sharp urban bias sat at its core. Even where living standards rose in the countryside from land reforms, rural migrants flocked to cities in search of higher wages in the form of cash income. With the rise in population due to investments in public health, urban bias led to a relative depeasantization of the region. The increasing scale of subproletarian life in urban areas was impossible to absorb into the state and semi-state apparatus, much less govern in a systematic manner. The response by MENA states was to implement systems of subsidies and price ceilings for staple goods and fuel. Inefficient in structure and regressive in absolute terms of total distribution, but progressive in terms of household consumption effects, subsidies were the only universal social policy in the Middle East other than primary education. They were blunt but effective forms of social protection—an understandable approach by states that did not possess the capacity to make their populations "legible" enough to target with anti-poverty

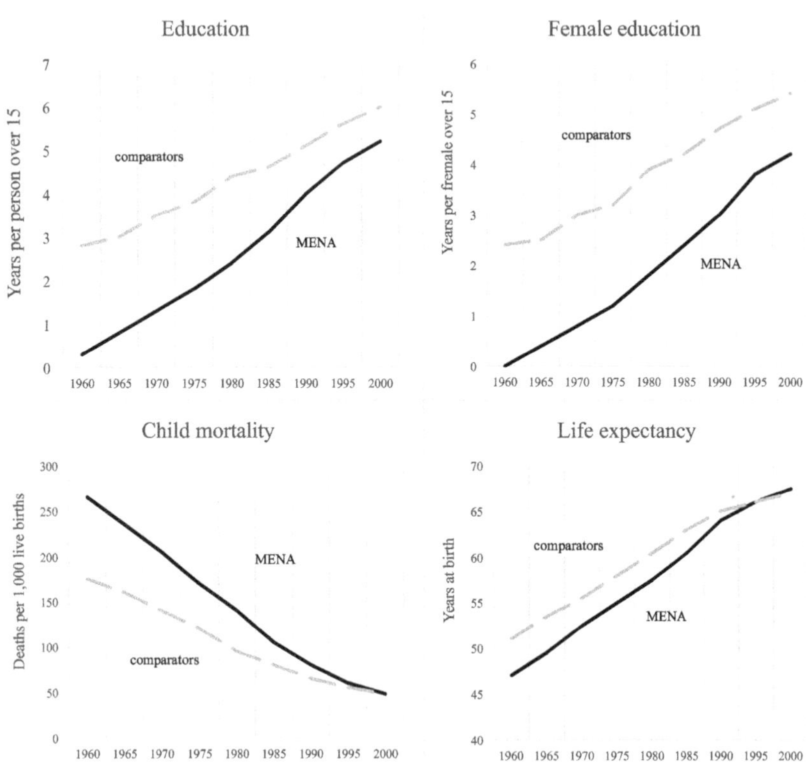

FIGURE 11.1. Comparative trends in human development indicators, Middle East and North Africa, 1960–2000. Data from combined averages of ten MENA states (Algeria, Egypt, Iran, Jordan, Lebanon, Libya, Morocco, Syria, Tunisia, and Yemen) and thirty non-MENA comparators (defined as middle-income countries in 1980).
SOURCE: Farrukh Iqbal, Sustaining Gains in Poverty Reduction and Human Development in the Middle East and North Africa (Washington, DC: World Bank, 2006), 24.

TABLE 11.1 Human development indicators for MENA 10, 1960–2000. (Data from combined averages of ten MENA states—Algeria, Egypt, Iran, Jordan, Lebanon, Libya, Morocco, Syria, Tunisia, and Yemen. See Farrukh Iqbal, *Sustaining Gains in Poverty Reduction and Human Development in the Middle East and North Africa* (Washington, DC: World Bank, 2006), 23.

Indicator	1960	1980	2000
Years of education (average per person over fifteen)	0.9	2.6	5.5
Years of education (average per female over fifteen)	0.5	1.8	4.6
Child mortality (deaths per 1,000 births)	262	138	47
Life expectancy	47	58	68

programs. After a generation, low prices for commodities became understood as citizenship rights, not state privileges. As population and urbanization increased, the relative weight of subsidies in state budgets also increased.[25] Here lay the social setting for the so-called International Monetary Fund riots in Egypt and Tunisia of the late 1970s and early 1980s, when these states attempted and then balked at raising prices on subsidized goods. Eventually, most MENA states would open up the countryside to capitalist agriculture after the 1980s, which pushed another generation into the cities.[26]

Second, staple subsidies and import substitution industrialization put increasing pressure on MENA states' balance of payments. There was no single source of stable foreign exchange with which to buy capital goods from wealthy countries: migration remittances, oil-money transfers, and agrarian surpluses were all too volatile and dependent on cyclical fluctuations in the world economy. The easy phases of manufacturing, from textiles to consumer goods to auto assembly, had pushed up against the demand limits of the domestic market. The OPEC price hikes of the 1970s could have, hypothetically, produced the capital to fund a campaign to sustain a region-wide diversified industrialization strategy. That capital, however, largely ended up in the hands of financiers in London and New York, with Beirut as a secondary beneficiary, due to its regional entrepôt function.

Third, even with the exclusionary form of corporatism practiced by MENA states, wherein entry to formal-sector employment was limited, middle-stratum beneficiaries began to protest. If the corporatist social compact was limited on the outside by the extent of public-sector expansion, it was limited on the inside by the empowerment of middle-stratum workers and professionals who demanded the democratization of that social compact. This resulted in a regional wave of "unruly corporatism." In countries where "authoritarian elites have attempted to force associational life into a tighter state corporatist mold their regimes have been deeply shaken or overturned by unanticipatedly powerful oppositions."[27] From Iran to Egypt to Syria to Algeria, these oppositions took secular *and* religious forms—or sometimes an amalgam—but they all shared similar social bases. In short, MENA corporatism produced its own gravediggers through the twin processes of proletarianization and professionalization. Hardly the stabilizing "authoritarian bargain" pronounced by Western analysts, by the late 1970s the social compact was being reassessed by elites and masses across the region.

What of the smaller oil-producing states (and city-states)? Though Saudi Arabia had won its independence in the 1930s, some of the littoral Gulf states had come into formal sovereignty only by the 1970s, such as the United Arab Emirates or Qatar. In most of these territories, an oligarchy of mercantile chiefdoms had long ruled, with migrant labor utilized in the pearling and portage industries. British patronage and preference led to the rise of selected families as state rulers by the late 1930s. Yet unlike in West Asia and North Africa, the Arabian Peninsula was penetrated earlier by U.S. corporate capital, though limited to select sites. In Saudi Arabia, labor regulation was borrowed not from the Kemalist model of Turkey, but from the racialized model of the United States. U.S. firms such as ARAMCO exported labor practices from U.S. mining and oil sectors to the Gulf oilfields, with hierarchical tiers of pay and benefits for white versus nonwhite labor. The same practices occurred in U.K.-established oil-company towns in southern Iran and Iraq, but in those areas, nationalization put an end to racial stratification of labor. Not so in the Arabian Peninsula, where state-led development codified a tiered racial citizenship in key zones of production well into the 1960s, underpinned by a hard gender division of labor. As the Gulf increased in political and economic relevance during the late twentieth century, this citizenship regime spread as a peninsular model.[28] These states' legitimacy rested on a combination of invented tradition and spectacular forms of outwardly displayed modernization. Kinship lineages became vital for bounded citizenship and informal networks of capital accumulation that spilled over into large Arab states in the 1970s. The Gulf sheikdoms are not tribal throwbacks by any means, but a subcategory of semi-peripheral state formation.[29]

By the late 1970s, then, the social compact in most MENA states appeared similar irrespective of ideological persuasion. Its outlines were a relatively large public sector with corporate linkages to various subaltern groups, an expansion of primary health and education to most of the population, a subsidization of staple goods and services for urban classes, and a piecemeal land reform tailored toward strategies of import-substitution industrial growth. Each of these segments underwent partial liberalization from the 1980s onward. In Arab states, the overall approach was labeled *infitah:* openness.

The Infitah Years

Asserting that the Middle East's main dilemma is neoliberalism—that this was the cause of the 2011 Arab uprisings, for instance—tells us little about the key dynamics of recent decades. During this period, the MENA region was not subject to external or internal pressures of neoliberalization to the extent that occurred in most of sub-Saharan Africa or Latin America. Arab states did not actively dismantle their welfare systems as much as let them ossify. Non-state entities moved into these states' widening gaps of service provision. Turkey and Iran expanded their social compacts due to intra-elite factional politics and continued reliance on popular mobilization. Gulf monarchies, lastly, cordoned off access to social citizenship while actively regulating flows of disposable migrant labor.

Two factors help explain why the region was less subject to the dictates of the neoliberal wave of the 1970s–2000s. First, after the Sino-U.S. détente and denouement of the Vietnam War, the main theater of military buildup, geopolitical conflict, and mass warfare shifted from East Asia to the MENA region. For most MENA political elites, and no matter the side of the conflict, war and war preparation served as a useful excuse to fight off technocratic efforts to shrink the state's budget and privatize national "mother" industries. When state elites did eventually engage in such activities, they did so dragging their feet, a half-hearted neoliberalism at best.

Second, even though many MENA states were not oil producers, the commodity bubbles of the 1970s generated sufficient intra-regional transfers of capital, which enabled states to keep segments of corporatist welfare systems in place. These capital flows, coupled with new sources of external finance for MENA states, prevented the deep balance-of-payments crises that Latin America and sub-Saharan Africa experienced in the 1980s and 1990s and allowed for the continued use of the public sector as a provider of employment and status attainment. Jordan's public sector, for instance, employed more people in the 2000s than in the 1980s. Egypt's public-sector salaries rose, rather than fell, over the same period.[30] To this must be added U.S. flows of military and development aid that buffered political elites in U.S.-friendly states, such as Egypt and Jordan, from ever being removed, no matter the internal situation. Neoliberal elites abound in the Middle East, well received among the chattering classes of Northern countries. But they arguably never held the reins of power for a long period in anywhere but Turkey, and there were no crises deep enough to allow the takeover of Arab states and purging of old guards until the 2011 protests.

Given that many of these states' association with a hazy secular-left discourse was embedded in the popular imagination, Islamist movements could more easily take advantage of oppositional politics as disillusionment with these states' social compacts mounted. The main beneficiaries of the postwar MENA social compact were the middle urban strata created by and linked with state-led development. As states began to experiment with piecemeal liberalization, cleavages within these middling groups appeared. Political Islam in most Arab states was a phenomenon with middle-class roots, often linked through university and professional associations. Rarely developed within the seminary traditions of teaching jurisprudence, political Islam largely originated outside of existing religious institutions. Lay individuals who had amassed prestige in other social spheres also laid claim to the application of spiritual knowledge toward social and political reform. Though traceable back to the late nineteenth century, political Islam in the late twentieth century possessed divisions homologous with its radical secular cousins. There were Leninist-type institutions, vertically organized and based on seniority, the most successful (and exportable) being Egypt's Muslim Brothers. And there were more anarchic, cellular organizations, often revolving around a charismatic spiritual guide, which appeared from mid-century onward.[31]

Arab states' relations with these Islamists were instrumental at best, often seen as a tool to harass or compete with the left. When the 1979 Iranian revolution produced an Islamic-garbed state to replace a crucial ally of the United States, political Islam received a wave of prestige among many who knew little about Iran or Shi'a

Islam at all. The Soviet invasion of Afghanistan produced another "international" of Islamists whose varying ideological persuasions collectively cascaded toward a Saudi-supported salafism. These two waves of rebellion sometimes flowed in tandem, but occasionally crashed into each other.[32] Yet the main driver of Islamist success was discontent with the status quo and existing alternatives, given the failed communist rebellions in the MENA region. As an amorphous framework that could equally glom onto Third International Marxism, Third Worldist nationalism, or High Street banking, political Islam gave the added benefit of providing a regional touchstone to the nativist promise of a region-wide renewal.[33]

These intellectual streams circulated while Arab states slowly peeled away layers of the public sector. Instead of applying shock therapy, Arab states shuffled off state sectors in piecemeal fashion. The result was a long decline in public investment with no concurrent uptick in private investment. Since 1985, the ratio of fixed investment/GDP in MENA states has remained between 20 percent and 25 percent. East and South Asian investment rates matched and then surpassed the MENA region in the 1980s and 2000s, respectively.[34]

The OPEC "revolution" that washed Gulf states in capital did not produce a deluge of investment toward populous MENA countries. Under a different geopolitical order, perhaps, after the 1967 and 1973 Arab-Israeli wars these incoming revenues could have been converted into a regional equivalent to the Marshall plan. The real sink of Gulf capital was, however, Euro-U.S. financial markets, part of which then flowed back to Third World countries in the form of Wall Street private lending.[35] The Gulf capital that did travel to MENA states was targeted toward activities that barely distinguished it from Western capital—namely, finance and real estate—thus evading state clutches and making it harder to repurpose for state-defined developmental goals. The form of business enterprise attached to Gulf capitalism, the diversified business conglomerate, was often portrayed as a traditional monarchical throwback. This trope hid the fact that family-held holding companies and state-linked conglomerates were the *most common* form of capital accumulation across the North and the South, globally thriving in neoliberal habitats.[36]

Amid the din, the hidden success story of Arab MENA states during the global neoliberal turn was a marked continuation in improvement of non-income welfare levels at a pace commensurate with the postwar statist period. This occurred while, relative to wealthy Northern states, per capita income levels stagnated and then declined. Between 1985 and 2000, the World Bank reported, MENA "developing" countries outperformed other middle-income regions in the Global South in their improvement of schooling years, literacy levels, child mortality, and life expectancy. This occurred, the World Bank puzzled, "despite a considerably slower rate of output growth and a decline in levels of public spending."[37] In fact, compared to countries at similar income levels, MENA states performed far more poorly in terms of income growth from 1980 to 2000, but their non-income welfare indicators *caught up* with comparators (shown above in table 11.1 and figure 11.1).

It is indeed puzzling, and the development literature on the region itself contains no consensus to account for the data. The convergence of MENA with other regions on non-income welfare indicators is observed even when controlling for levels of income and public spending.[38] A provisional explanation is that the *differentia specifica* of the region for its non-income basic welfare successes was the absence of full-throttled neoliberalism. An ossifying yet intact public sector was arguably better than one subject to neoliberal strictures. In a weak state system such as that of Lebanon, private spending on health and education was the norm even in the postwar years. Yet in those Arab states with a legacy of large public sectors, private spending did not serve as a replacement for public services. Given the deepening underinvestment in the state, however, two glaring fissures appeared. The quality of service suffered, leading to increased private welfare spending on top of existing social provisions. Also, access to advanced health care, as in most countries, was limited to those with social insurance—mainly public-sector workers and the wealthier elite. The welfare institutions of the previous era were never upgraded or expanded.[39]

For Iran and Turkey, a breakdown in postwar elite rule—by the 1979 revolution and the 1980 coup, respectively—resulted in a process of unstable intra-elite competition. For all the well-known differences between the two countries, one common fact stands out. This elite competition allowed for newly mobilized social groups to force demands onto the state. Turkey's Justice and Development Party (AK Party) was the most successful actor of them all, wielding a long-curated popular mobilization to eventually transform the political structures of the Kemalist republic. In the process, the uneven corporatist pillars of the welfare system were remolded into a broader—though more fragile—social protection regime that mixed market, state, and non-state actors.[40] In Iran, continual jockeying within a fractious postrevolutionary elite resulted in the proliferation of new welfare organizations and inclusionary social provisions. Yet the inability of the state to robustly enforce such regulations has produced a mixed welfare regime where casualization occurs alongside expanding social insurance protection.[41] Nevertheless, in both cases, there has been a marked change in social protection systems over the past decade, as new segments of the population have been provided access to state welfare.

A TIME OF MONSTERS

Given the positive trends mentioned above, why did the Arab uprisings occur? Improvements in non-welfare indicators are not incommensurate with political unrest. Indeed, coupled with lack of income convergence with the wealthy North, especially in light of the rapid economic growth in other Southern regions and growing inequality between MENA subregions, grievances were plenty. Given increases in health and education, as well as a concurrent demographic transition toward nuclear household sizes, exit and voice were prevalent strategies among those who felt blocked from pathways of upward mobility available to previous MENA generations. A common option was, as always, migration. Yet North African migration to southern Europe as well as the Gulf increasingly came under harsh constraints—"fortress Europe" in the former, a switch to South Asian labor under the latter. The classic political safety valve of migration was, for these countries, increasingly obstructed.

Some of the social grievances highlighted in the 2011 Arab uprisings, however, stem from problems that arose from earlier successes. Mass primary education and basic health care were pro-poor interventions by the state. From 1975 to 2010, Arab MENA states enjoyed the fastest rate of growth of average years of schooling of any region. Fertility rates declined and spending per child increased in households. As a result, the subsequent generation's horizons toward education were starkly different than that of their parents. Yet on the tertiary level and in the labor market, class inequality was reproduced. Quantitative gains in educational attainment masked the qualitative avenues of elite status distinction that reduced the returns on so-called human capital. Even more structural factors were at play. The baby boom of the 1970s–1980s meant that the number of youth entering the working age circa 2010 was four to six times that of people reaching retirement age. The ossification of public investment channeled the search for employment toward private forms, usually informal. Reservation wages tended to be higher than other Southern countries, with little incentive for foreign capital to hire skilled or technical labor.[42] These particulars lay under the relatively high formal unemployment rates for youth in the region when compared to other Southern countries. As a result, many young individuals faced a "failure to launch."

This social stratum is awkward to classify in theoretical terms. Carrie Wickham has labeled such individuals in Egypt as the *lumpen intelligentsia,* a "professional underclass" with "graduates unable to find permanent white-collar employment . . . not unemployed so much as forced to accept jobs they perceived as beneath the dignity of someone with a university degree."[43] While the 2011 uprisings had roots in earlier formal-labor protests, this new stratum was present throughout the initial protest wave across the region.[44]

Fortunately, on account of questions added to the 2011 Arab Barometer Survey in Tunisia and Egypt, survey data exists that details some of the contours of unrest in these two best-known cases. Protest participants in both countries tended to be mostly male, with above average income and education levels. Forty-six percent of surveyed protestors in Egypt, for instance, had at least some university education, compared to 19 percent of the population as a whole. Unemployment was not a predictor of protest, nor was youth, but protestors disproportionately possessed professional and skilled vocational backgrounds compared to the rest of the population. More unskilled workers protested in Tunisia than in Egypt, the surveys found, but in both cases, there was a disproportionately high rate of protest participation by government employees. Women who did participate tended to be active in the labor market. The younger the age of the protestor, the more likely he or she was to identify economic grievances or corruption rather than civil and political freedoms as the key motivation for participation.[45] Snapshot surveys cannot capture questions of timing and process in the two countries' uprisings, but they do give some weight to the *lumpen intellgentsia*'s role as compared to the formalized proletariat or informal sub-proletariat.

As a sop to the poorest strata, MENA Arab states did not fully liberalize their subsidies on staple goods and fuel. The increasing trend, in line with other regions, has been to replace segments of the subsidy system with new "targeted" anti-poverty programs. Unlike in Latin America, these are relatively new, small-scale, and disconnected from party mobilization. Along with decreased spending on public housing and infrastructure, the erosion of the previously established social compact has contributed to the informalization and casualization of the domestic labor force, including disguised female labor.

If there is an overriding factor determining the trajectory of MENA states, however, it is not neoliberalism as much as militarism. While sporadic wars had taken place in the region after 1948, since the 1970s there has been a long cascading war with multiple sub-currents. At least three varieties can be distinguished. First are national-expansionist projects under U.S. protection—Israel in Palestine, Lebanon, Syria, the Sinai; Iraq into Iran; Saudis in Yemen; and Iranian soft expansionism in Afghanistan and Iraq. Second are national-expansionist projects without U.S. protection—Iraq into Kuwait. Third, and most widespread, are conflicts with a popular-war dynamic, where social discontent has combined with national anger—Palestinian intifadas, Yemeni oppositions, Hezbollah, the Kurdish Workers' Party, and Sunni militias in Iraq—which often become entangled with internal security struggles and temporary external alliances. This semipermanent state of war and increasingly direct intervention by U.S. military forces set the stage for a series of counter-revolutions after 2011 to contain the wave of mass uprisings.

The other outcome of this war cascade was to push the political and economic leadership of MENA states toward the Gulf monarchies. The Gulf model attempted to create a costless, codified capitalism: social citizenship for elite kinship minorities, imported professional and working classes, and territorial security subcontracted to the American superpower. Celebrated by sycophants and held up as an obverse to state-led development, the model is under strain on all three fronts. Young Gulf Arabs are growing tired of being cloistered and pampered without career trajectories, leading the monarchies to pursue a half-hearted policy of "nationalization" of the workforce, with increased costs in tow. The long-term circulation of South Asian and North African labor throughout the Gulf has built up local communities with their own resources of social solidarity. Hidden resistance is still the norm, but costs of containing labor unrest are increasing. The U.S. protection umbrella, as the royals are now grumbling, is looking more like a protection racket. But if the Gulf monarchies had to protect themselves, they would also have to enter into a more ordinary balance of power in the region where Iran, Turkey, and other possible competitors could claim a veto irrespective of American or Israeli wishes. This has occurred to some extent anyway, making the Gulf model even more precarious.

Like the 1848 revolutions, the 2011 uprisings brought forth a reactionary wave of violent containment, as well as bargained co-optation. Yet if authoritarian retrenchment were again the main outcome, the situation would be less dire. In the decade and a half since the U.S. invasion of Iraq, segments of the postwar MENA political order shifted back toward the politics of notables, local social formations, and transnational flows of pamphlets, laborers, and revolutionaries. In the previous iteration of this, in the early twentieth century, it took waves of anti-elite, anticolonial mobilization, as well as radical political state-building projects, to produce order from the mayhem. For the time being, however, the chances of a repeat look rather slim.

Instead, as occurred in Afghanistan during the 1980s and 1990s, coherent and crafted political systems along the Maghreb and Levant are being pulverized into a set of rump chieftaincies. The labor reserves that had been accumulating during the shrinking of the state—unskilled proletarians and skilled professionals alike—are now the uprooted migrants that sit in the shatter zones of the old geopolitical order. As reported in the *London Review of Books,* "The mobilisation techniques used in the Arab Spring, which brought thousands of demonstrators to a given place, were now being used to organise the new waves of migration."[46] Increases in health and educational attainment produced in postwar social compacts are being reversed for a generation. It remains to be seen if outstanding regional powers can prevent their own further entanglement or if additional conflagrations will arise.

If some form of cold peace comes to the region after further population resettlement, new social questions for the MENA region might revolve around centers of state power and capital accumulation, their exploited peripheries of inclusion, and the excluded remainder. Competitive spheres of influence are not necessarily anti-developmental, if order is established and new cadres are developed. Any stability might come in the region only when states build political and social compacts that not only incorporate wider segments of the population but also significantly reshape their life chances. It is unlikely, though, that emulating the developmental models of the present will create a solid compact for MENA states. Processes of urbanization and depeasantization that were corollaries of MENA state formation meant that rural reserves of semi-proletarian labor of the sort that fueled rapid growth in East Asian markets and lured in Western capital are today nowhere to be found. The rural subsidization of social reproduction cannot be re-created. As Faruk Tabak insightfully pointed out, access to plantation labor attracted Western capital flows in the late nineteenth century, while access to rural networks of semi-proletarian labor in East Asia supported the manufacturing activities in which global capital invested in the late twentieth century. The Ottoman Empire lacked the former, and today the Middle East lacks the latter.[47]

NOTES

1. Ian Lustick, "The Absence of Middle Eastern Great Powers: Political 'Backwardness' in Historical Perspective," *International Organization* 51, no. 4 (1997): 653–83.

2. Juan Cole, "Al-Tahtawi on Poverty and Welfare," in *Poverty and Charity in Middle Eastern Contexts*, ed. Michael David Bonner, Mine Ener, and Amy Singer (Albany: State University of New York Press, 2003), 225.

3. Timur Kuran, *The Long Divergence: How Islamic Law Held Back the Middle East* (Princeton, NJ: Princeton University Press, 2011); Lisa Blaydes and Eric Chaney, "The Feudal Revolution and Europe's Rise: Political Divergence of the Christian West and the Muslim World before 1500 CE," *American Political Science Review* 107, no. 1 (2013): 16–34.

4. Marshall Hodgson, *The Venture of Islam*, vol. 2 (Chicago: University of Chicago Press, 1974), 124.

5. Historical calculations of the Gini coefficient—zero representing perfect equality and one representing perfect inequality—are rough proxies for the concept of social inequality but still can function to compare across space and time, as long as the underlying data is put into context. For these particular measurements, see Colette Establet, Jean-Paul Pascual, and André Raymond, "La mesure de l'inegalite dans la societe ottomane: Utilisation de l'indice de Gini pour Le Caire et Damas vers 1700," *Journal of the Economic and Social History of the Orient* 37, no. 2 (1994): 171–82; Boğaç Ergene and Ali Berker, "Wealth and Inequality in 18th-Century Kastamonu: Estimations for the Muslim Majority," *International Journal of Middle East Studies* 40, no. 1 (2008): 23–46.

6. Şevket Pamuk, "Political Power and Institutional Change: Lessons from the Middle East," *Economic History of Developing Regions* 27, no. S1 (2012): S41–56.

7. Mine Ener, "The Charity of the Khedive," in *Poverty and Charity in Middle Eastern Contexts*, ed. Michael David Bonner, Mine Ener, and Amy Singer (Albany: State University of New York Press, 2003), 185–201.

8. Xaiver de Planhol, "Famines," *Encyclopedia Iranica*, online edition, 2012, www.iranicaonline.org/articles/famines.

9. Cemil Aydin, *The Politics of Anti-Westernism in Asia: Visions of World Order in Pan-Islamic and Pan-Asian Thought* (New York: Columbia University Press, 2007).

10. The 1812 Anglo-Persian treaty stipulated that Persia would oppose any European army that attempted to invade India via Central Asia.

11. Sükrü Hanioglu, *A Brief History of the Late Ottoman Empire* (Princeton, NJ: Princeton University Press, 2008), 89–92.

12. Faruk Tabak, "The Middle East in the Long Twentieth Century," in *The Long Twentieth Century: The Great Divergence: Hegemony, Uneven Development, and Global Inequality*, ed. Jomo Kwame Sundaram (New Delhi: Oxford University Press, 2006), 146–47.

13. Michael Reynolds, *Shattering Empires: The Clash and Collapse of the Ottoman and Russian Empires 1908–1918* (Cambridge: Cambridge University Press, 2011).

14. Joel Beinin, *Workers and Peasants in the Modern Middle East* (Cambridge: Cambridge University Press, 2001), 77–80.

15. See James Mahoney, *Colonialism and Postcolonial Development: Spanish America in Comparative Perspective* (Cambridge: Cambridge University Press, 2010).

16. Cyrus Schayegh, *The Middle East and the Making of the Modern World* (Cambridge, MA: Harvard University Press, 2017).

17. Eighty-five percent of Turkish agricultural holdings in 1963 were owner-operated, most of which were family farms under ten hectares (24.7 acres), up from 73 percent in 1950. Beinin, *Workers and Peasants in the Modern Middle East,* 122.

18. Eric Hooglund, *Land and Revolution in Iran, 1960–1980* (Austin: University of Texas Press, 1982).

19. Hanna Batatu, *The Egyptian, Syrian, and Iraqi Revolutions: Some Observations on Their Underlying Causes and Social Character* (Washington, DC: Georgetown University Center for Contemporary Arab Studies, 1984), 3.

20. James Gelvin, "The 'Politics of Notables' Forty Years After," *Middle East Studies Association Bulletin* 40, no. 1 (2006): 19–29

21. Gilbert Achcar, *The People Want: A Radical Exploration of the Arab Uprising* (Berkeley: University of California Press, 2013), 69.

22. See Beth Baron, "Islam, Philanthropy, and Political Culture in Interwar Egypt: The Activism of Labiba Ahmad," in *Poverty and Charity in Middle Eastern Contexts,* ed. Michael David Bonner, Mine Ener, and Amy Singer (Albany: State University of New York Press, 2003), 239–54.

23. Carrie Wickham, *Mobilizing Islam: Religion, Activism, and Political Change in Egypt* (New York: Columbia University Press, 2002), 25.

24. Nemat Shafik, *Claiming the Future: Choosing Prosperity in the Middle East and North Africa* (Washington, DC: World Bank, 1995).

25. For instance, Egypt spent 20 percent of the total budget on food subsidies alone in the late 1970s. Farrukh Iqbal, *Sustaining Gains in Poverty Reduction and Human Development in the Middle East and North Africa* (Washington, DC: World Bank, 2006), 57–69.

26. Habib Ayeb and Ray Bush, "Small Farmer Uprisings and Rural Neglect in Egypt and Tunisia," *Middle East Report* 272 (2014): 2–11.

27. Robert Bianchi, *Unruly Corporatism: Associational Life in Twentieth-Century Egypt* (New York: Oxford University Press, 1989), 25.

28. See Robert Vitalis, *America's Kingdom: Mythmaking on the Saudi Oil Frontier* (Stanford, CA: Stanford University Press, 2006).

29. Nadav Samin, *Of Sand and Soil: Genealogy and Tribal Belonging in Saudi Arabia* (Princeton, NJ: Princeton University Press, 2015).

30. Oliver Schlumberger, "Opening Old Bottles in Search of New Wine: On Nondemocratic Legitimacy in the Middle East," *Middle East Critique* 19, no. 3 (2010): 245–46.

31. Carrie Wickham, *The Muslim Brotherhood: Evolution of an Islamist Movement* (Princeton, NJ: Princeton University Press, 2013); Hazim Kandil, *Inside the Brotherhood* (Cambridge: Polity, 2014).

32. See the final comments by Suleiman Mourad, "Riddles of the Book," *New Left Review,* II, no. 86 (2014): 15–52.

33. Thanks to James Gelvin for this point; also see Sami Zubaida, *Beyond Islam: A New Understanding of the Middle East* (London: I. B. Tauris, 2011), chap. 4.

34. Achcar, *The People Want,* 38–40.

35. Giovanni Arrighi, *The Long Twentieth Century: Money, Power, and the Origins of Our Times* (London: Verso, 1994), 333–35.

36. Adam Hanieh, *Capitalism and Class in the Gulf Arab States* (New York: Palgrave, 2011).

37. Iqbal, *Sustaining Gains,* xix.

38. Iqbal, *Sustaining Gains,* chap. 2.

39. See the essays in Ragui Assaad and Caroline Krafft, eds., *The Egyptian Labor Market in a Time of Revolution* (Oxford: Oxford University Press, 2016).

40. In a comparative frame, Turkey looks most like southern European welfare regimes. See Ayşe Bugra and Aysen Candas, "Change and Continuity under an Eclectic Social Security Regime: The Case of Turkey," *Middle Eastern Studies* 47, no. 3 (2011): 515–28.

41. Kevan Harris, *A Social Revolution: Politics and the Welfare State in Iran* (Oakland: University of California Press, 2017).

42. Djavad Salehi-Isfahani, *The Role of the Family in Social Integration in the Middle East and North Africa* (DIFI Family Research and Proceedings, 2013), 5.

43. Wickham, *Mobilizing Islam*, 54.

44. See the contribution of labor unrest in the long left tail of the protest curve in Joel Beinin, *Workers and Thieves: Labour Movements and Popular Uprisings in Tunisia and Egypt* (Stanford, CA: Stanford University Press, 2015).

45. Mark Beissinger, Amaney Jamal, and Kevin Mazur, "Explaining Divergent Revolutionary Coalitions: Regime Strategies and the Structuring of Participation in the Tunisian and Egyptian Revolutions," *Comparative Politics* 48, no. 1 (2015): 1–24.

46. Ghaith Abdul-Ahad, "Some Tips for the Long-Distance Traveller," *London Review of Books*, October 8, 2015.

47. Tabak, "Middle East in the Long Twentieth Century," 165.

12

Post-Socialist Contradictions

The Social Question in Central and Eastern Europe and the Making of the Illiberal Right

Don Kalb

Jan Breman and Marcel van der Linden have provocatively claimed that the Global South is coming to the North, rather than the other way around.[1] Not "development" toward Northern modernity, but the informalization and flexibilization of the North, as in the South. They see the global economic agenda as hijacked by capitalist interests that seek the precariatization and stepped-up exploitation of the world's laboring populations. Global agencies duplicitously present this agenda as one of employment generation and poverty reduction—and therefore representing the "general interest." "Rigidities" stemming from the old language of labor cannot be allowed to derail this. The language of labor is a particularist trick on behalf of "rent seekers," "insiders," and "oligopolies of labor." The rhetoric of global institutions has perhaps been changing slightly since the financial crises of 2008–2014. Global economic technocrats consider social inequality now evidently as a negative. But the demand for "structural adjustment" and all that it entails in terms of precariatization and the flexibility of labor remains pervasive, from the IMF to the OECD to the ECB. And then there are "the markets" with their imperious judgments and their rejection of inflation. There is no reason to believe that a new era has arrived.

But as they are making this claim, Breman and van der Linden are sharply aware of differences and differentiations worldwide. There is no implication of global homogenization around a zero point of social dumping. But the overall direction they picture is globally shared, and it is useful that they state it without further ado. Until the recent revolt of "angry white labor" in the provinces—a symbol and figure of speech, of course, not a simple reality—social democrats and center-liberals of the "varieties of capitalism" school would certainly have responded to such a provocation with incredulity. Capitalism, in their vision, is an assortment of significantly diverging national varieties, to be chosen by major actors, not a unifying global historical complex with various systematically nurtured articulations.[2] They will point to ongoing investments in "complex manufacturing" in new spaces, such as Brazil, Mexico, China, and central and eastern Europe. Such new spaces of "high-end" accumulation tend to be associated with upward regulation rather than any downward trends. One could also point to the Bolsa Familia in Brazil, the recent income-support schemes in India, and the officially sanctioned upward pressure on labor and social standards in China as other examples of opposite tendencies.[3] There is space for a more dialectical vision in their overall approach, of which they are aware. But, once more, it is useful that they state their main thesis of capitalist precariatization and social dumping straightforwardly.

Central and eastern Europe (CEE) has been powerfully re-industrialized in the years after 1995, though unevenly. It now serves as the premier mass-manufacturing site for the European Union and hosts various branches in transnational services such as call centers, retailing, media, software, and finance. The "Visegrad countries" of north-central Europe, plus Slovenia, have been reintegrated into western European—above all, German—supply chains. The Czech Republic, Slovakia, and Hungary are now more open to trade and are more export-dependent than they ever were before and more so than most western countries. Until the mid-2000s they had also received broadly similar amounts of foreign direct investment per capita as China. With 70 percent of GDP generated through international trade, the smaller post-socialist countries close to the EU heartland now even beat historical champions of economic openness in the West such as Belgium and the Netherlands. They are proportionally among the top exporters worldwide, including in such branches as automotives and electronics. Since 2005, countries like Romania, Bulgaria, and Serbia have also acquired more complex manufacturing industries. The employment structures of the "successful" CEE countries therefore tend to be more industrial than those of western or southern Europe, with around 30 percent of the labor market in manufacturing. So, against this background, what about Breman and van der Linden's universal precariatization thesis?

THE VIOLENCE OF A TRANSITIONAL RECESSION WITH MERE SHALLOW POVERTY

By 2000, the Visegrad countries (Poland, Hungary, the Czech Republic, and Slovakia) and the Baltics were slowly extricating themselves from what experts in "transition economics" (a deeply neoliberal field) had disingenuously called the "transitional recession." That so-called transitional recession—the name suggests ephemeral qualities—was, in reality, the largest, most devastating and protracted social crisis that any part of the modern world had ever experienced. Greece after

2010 comes close in purely economic terms, but aggregate economics was only a part of the post-socialist crisis, and Greece did so at a much higher level of wealth. There had been an average reduction of real wages with around 30 percent, followed by a long stagnation of median incomes; consistently high inflation of basic prices; a durable reduction of formal employment of some 20 percent across the board; and a slide of real GDP anywhere between 20 percent and 50 percent.

This economic devastation coincided with a fundamental restructuring of social relationships and social institutions; a swift dwindling of state power and authority; ongoing panic about "the law" and security; the threat of open, collective violence in many places, serious social and cultural tensions everywhere, and actual civil wars in the least fortunate spaces; dramatic reversals in male mortality, as males died from alcohol and the cold; and even, over time, declines in literacy. In the more "successful" post-socialist countries, those losses would be evened out sometime between 2000 and 2008; others had to wait a decade or more. Just when some modest optimism was emerging, the Wall Street and Euro crises caused serious hits.[4] It was no wonder that the new governing elites in CEE in the early 1990s had been terrified that the liberal transition they were overseeing might be undone by popular rage.

In the early 1990s, two broad social policy designs resulted from those elite fears for popular havoc: (1) Relatively generous pension and disability benefits for people above fifty years old, meant to cushion mass redundancies; and (2) unemployment and family benefits, much less generous, to help younger working families stay out of absolute poverty.[5]

With some initial exceptions—the Czech Republic, Slovakia, and Romania—most countries settled on a dual policy path combining fast economic liberalization and privatization with a flanking social policy to cushion the mass exit from the labor market and forestall destitution and mass revolts. By the late 1990s the upshot for labor had become clear. (1) A massive reduction in formal employment throughout the region from some 70 percent to 50 percent of the working population. (2) Consistent medium to high levels of unemployment (in Poland, for example, the level was 18 percent for roughly a fifteen-year period). (3) The stabilization of median wages at a very low level that endangered family social reproduction (fertility declines everywhere). Prices rose quickly to western European levels. Apart from Slovenia and the Czech Republic, median wages were stuck anywhere between two hundred and five hundred euros per month even by 2015, despite two decades of economic growth. (4) There was a proliferation of informal forms of social reproduction, including migration (circular, seasonal, and definite), self-provisioning, petty entrepreneurship, moonlighting, and double and triple jobs. (5) The spread of complex practices of income pooling within domestic groups, households, and kinship networks, including the income from public transfers such as pensions and social benefits. (6) The labor market had become radically deregulated in practice. (7) Politics was characterized more by "exit" and voting with the feet than by "voice."[6] Electoral participation hovered generally around a low 50 percent.

Taken together, these downward spiraling processes were inevitably leading to the making of substantial relative and absolute surplus populations, in particular outside metropolitan spaces. The Roma were among the most identifiable of victimized groups. The sheer duration and extent of their poverty inevitably produced sharp segregation; illicit economies; violence; harsh competition for space, work, and benefits; ethnicization; and the predictable moral panics among local working and middle classes, including raw political attacks.

But it has always been deeply misleading to equate social expendability in CEE with visible ethnic markers—the liberal "transition lie" par excellence. Large populations in the provinces all over CEE, even in the Czech Republic, were turned into semi-surplus populations and ostensibly written off. Many poorly educated people in CEE found themselves durably caught in a poverty and precarity trap, particularly those in regions that were locked into long-term spirals of decline. Many people felt squeezed between those with access to the few good jobs and a hold over local politics, on the hand, and the ethnicized absolute surplus populations on the other. In some areas in the 1990s, a majority of actually employed or self-imagined working people, the working poor, were coping with household income levels around two hundred to three hundred euros per month and were structurally dependent on benefits, remittances, and *in natura* support from kin. The household surveys done by a team of urban geographers led by Alison Stenning in Nowa Huta, Poland, and Petrzalka, a suburb of Bratislava, show that this was true even for households in the boom cities of the mid-2000s, as well as when local unemployment was very low.[7] In those relatively well-off urban neighborhoods, if your education was poor or of the wrong type, and if you had young children, you were very likely to be in structural poverty. Existential insecurity was widespread. This was the case amid economic growth and ostentatious consumption by the few and in a context where politicians were more interested in pointing at the latter than caring about the former. In the absence of a credible left, this would come to haunt the region in the form of a slowly building politics of anger and resentment.

POLARIZING SOCIETY, FUELLING CULTURE TALK: THE CLOCKWORK OF HIERARCHY

Why did labor fail to defend itself against the neoliberal onslaught? This has understandably been a key question in the literature. Most authors have resorted to a "labor weakness" explanation.[8] But if labor was indeed so weak, where did its weakness lie or come from? Was it weak on the shop floor, in the national public sphere, in post-socialist ideology? Scholars have pointed to subdued labor unions under socialism, unions that were mere parts of the administrative apparatus, with no experience of mobilization—but in Poland, the opposite was the case. Other authors have pointed to the negative ideological reputation of class politics and labor rhetoric after socialism. I have come to doubt the intuitive validity of these answers. My own answer has emphasized that labor was sometimes surprisingly strong on the shop floor, often decidedly stronger than in the West, but not so on the national level—either within the bargaining structure of "tripartism" or on the level of public ideas. While labor was not a unified national force, it was an important local factor in many places, in companies, and in local politics. Every weakness it had seems to have emerged from the disconnect between those levels.

More fundamentally, the weakness of post-socialist labor, I have claimed, was a "weakness within."[9] It sprang from the crumbling of socialist solidarity between those who stood to gain from capitalism and were—amid stagnation and serious economic threats—hoping to finally get a fair price for their labor, and those who were seen as going to fail the test of the new value regime. In other words, in anticipation of capitalism's coming, labor fractured between the skilled, flexible, and efficient workers who had often formed the labor aristocracies of socialist production and those perceived as the spoilers of the coming efficiency drive. Thus, capitalism magnified and pushed into the open the status conflicts that had been obscured under socialism. It set a competition in motion, desired as well as real and inevitable, among the self-ascribed deserving and those they deemed undeserving, and it cracked open the always smoldering but repressed hierarchies of labor under socialism. It was this internal conflict within labor—fueled to the utmost by an intellectual state class that had made its reputation in the fight against socialism and, therefore, in the context of the global slide toward capitalist restoration, was always already liable to smoothly embrace neoliberal imaginaries—that ultimately explained the "emptiness" of labor as a political category.

Ethnographies have often reported of labor activists being jubilant about the coming fairness of the market. Labor organizers were certainly ready to advocate social protection for laid-off workers, and they were sometimes also ready to fight—hard—to defend local employment. But, avowedly, not for everyone. Annoyance about supposedly pervasive slacking often broke through. There was sometimes open satisfaction that those slackers were going to be punished. Ideologically, many workers tended to see the market as their opportunity to finally overcome an overbearing socialist mediocrity. The market was seen as the fair and transparent "culturally arbitrating" institution that would finally set them free from the socialist slackers, as well as from the socialist bureaucrats.[10]

The labor-weakness account is thus both problematic and more culturally complex than is usually assumed. A realistic relational approach should focus on those accelerating social cleavages and emergent hierarchies within labor itself. These served to disable collective action by workers as workers. A logic of de-solidarization was rolling through the region and transforming the potential collectivist politics of class into the myriad identity politics of culture and hierarchy.

Jan Breman, writing about the global context, has recently called this the return of social Darwinism. The return of such social Darwinism in post-socialist Europe—a desire for a natural and meritocratically justified hierarchy—was not entirely unlike that in the West itself. But in CEE, it came in a pressure-cooker version in a peripheral and dependent capitalism that was going down the road of de-industrialization in the 1990s much faster and much more pervasively so than anything seen in the West. Nor was there the compensation of fast growth in professional and consumer services characteristic of the metropolises of the core. The singular reality of CEE was the collapse of a full-scale urban industrial modernity—indeed, a labor-based and labor-driven modernity. After the collapse, only an uneven rebirth took place amid the culture-talk of deservingness and un-deservingness.

Such hierarchical desires emerging "from below" were magnified by a public sphere that was openly condescending toward common workers and peasants. The whole higher stratum of intellectuals and professionals in eastern Europe, including trade union experts and labor representatives themselves, stood to gain significantly from capitalist state making and market expansion, and they sensed it. Many of the leading intelligentsia and dissidents turned themselves from pro-labor advocates into aspiring state classes almost overnight, clamoring for the proliferating jobs and consultancies within the new central bureaucracies—administrations that, in fact, grew in numbers everywhere after socialism. The second echelon of apparatchiks and managers, meanwhile, were busy transforming themselves into the privatizers of assets that had belonged to the socialist commons or setting themselves up as political leaders.[11]

These social divisions became openly expressed in a new public vocabulary of cultural hierarchy from above. Intellectuals and professionals began to identify themselves boisterously as middle class and civil. Those just below desperately aspired to become part of that same enchanted circle. And all were impatiently awaiting the advent of a magical "Europe." Occidentalism took such a flight that, inevitably, the "East" became now often openly associated with an unsophisticated red-brown populist despotism of an imagined Asiatic type. While the new self-appointed middle classes were righteously claiming their place near or in the advanced West, their neighbors without such cultural elevation were expressly relegated to the supposed wastelands of the Orient. Rude Asiatic despotisms were seen as rightly befitting uneducated workers and peasants "who could not take care of themselves and were used to following orders"—*Homo sovieticus* types of persons.[12] Their politics was seen as reflecting precisely this: unruly peasant and worker demonstrations were rejected as a form of uncivil and irresponsible "claiming behavior" that had to be rooted out. No respect for the subaltern here. Michal Buchowski has called this syndrome "internal orientalism."[13]

In such discourses, productivity and efficiency were not seen as abstract properties of national economies or production processes. Rather, they were perceived as deeply personal characteristics, key indexes of personal worth—thus organically anticipating and internalizing the tenets of the emergent neoliberalism.[14] Those who failed to live up to the capitalist value regime, those literally described as the "losers of transition," were imagined to also dress, talk, and smell differently. And they were seen as only having themselves to blame. They were felt to be a dead weight on national productivity and dignity, a fifth column against the global success of newly sovereign and utterly deserving nations: traitors, embezzlers, slackers, hooligans, and drunkards. And it was felt that those who were now going to be surplus populations had always already been inappropriately shielded by "really existing socialism." Socialist rulers, it was said, had sought, unforgivably in the eyes of many, the alliance with the unruly and the unskilled, thus consigning their nations to an embarrassing mediocrity.

In a nutshell: what may have been crucial for the "defeat of solidarity" was how the local labor aristocracies felt about the less skilled.[15] Labor aristocracies were essential for the running of socialist economies.[16] These were rather tightly knit local working-class groups that were sometimes, as in Poland and Yugoslavia, de facto running the factories, including the associated social funds and affiliated labor unions and sports associations. By 1989 in Poland, they were sometimes even nominating their own directors on the managing boards, as had been commonplace in Yugoslavia. Also in Hungary or Romania, directors used to be "men of the people," since they could not rule without the people and, often, not so easily against them. But these core groups of workers were increasingly exposed to drastic economic pressure and the threat of total social failure. In this life or death economic context—a context of fear and ontological insecurity—they were not against turning the slackers and the unruly among the unskilled workers into a relative surplus population. My interviews with workers in Wroclaw in the late 1990s were full of such thoughts, internal dialogues about the rightfulness of the impatiently awaited restoration of meritocratic hierarchy. Powerful capitalist pressures thus helped to unravel the possibility of solidarity among working classes upon which socialism as a form of rule had tenuously rested. The emergent informal capitalism of the 1980s, and then the quickly accelerating formal capitalism of the 1990s, cracked open the can of worms of repressed but visceral cultural hierarchy and inequality that state socialism had tried to compress and keep together against the odds.

The longer historical perspective is essential here. Socialism had installed itself in the first half of the twentieth century in a backward region. It was overwhelmed by this backwardness. In the absence of a "world revolution," Soviet socialism was, after 1923, pushed into political isolation by a vengeful West. "Socialism in one country" was incapable of escaping the logic of uneven and combined development in Russia, as well as later in central Europe. The low level of urbanization; the prevalence of large, undifferentiated, and underdeveloped agricultural spaces; the persistence of large post-feudal latifundia, semi-serfdom, debt peonage, and illiteracy—these were ominous starting points for a socialist modernization by and on behalf of workers and peasants. In the aftermath of Stalin's counterrevolution of 1928, agricultural collectivization, planned industrialization, and industry-driven urbanization were designed to overcome such backwardness. They were crucial for defeating Hitler. But the consequences of the prior underdevelopment, combined with the contradictions of socialist accumulation itself, put steady limits on what could be achieved.[17]

For one, socialism kept featuring a significant under-urbanization. Aggregate urbanization in the 1950s and 1960s was fast, but it brought semiskilled industrial jobs to people in new provincial towns rather than concentrating both people and jobs in metropolitan centers.[18] Agriculture was at best only partly efficient. Scarcity regularly reappeared, and agricultural prices remained high. Sharp uneven development within the region, mostly going from west to east, was also never redressed. But even in the more advanced socialist urban districts in western areas, such as around Wroclaw (Breslau) or Györ—successful cities in the German and Habsburg Empires—a majority of workers in the local light engineering industries, even in the 1980s, would only have a primary school education. Commuting peasant workers were a large and economically essential category in socialist countries. Many urban households would share kitchens, toilets, and bathrooms. During the famous and funny Kitchen Debate between Nikita Khrushchev and Richard Nixon in 1959, Khrushchev had boasted that in ten years time Soviet workers would enjoy the same comforts as their American counterparts. Instead, after one more round of urbanization and industrialization in the early 1960s, Eastern European socialism ran up against its limitations and would struggle for another twenty years—and ultimately, it would not undo those limitations but rather bury itself instead. It had produced an illiberal provincial industrialism of 1930s–1950s type. It was unable to switch, like the West, to an education- and consumption-driven accumulation that would export its blue-collar jobs overseas and sweep up agricultural productivity.

So, in the context of the imposition of the capitalist value regime and the consequent fears and uncertainties, there were discourses of personal value, deservingness, and un-deservingness; cultural hierarchy; and "civilization" among common workers too, discourses that sought to separate the worthy from the unworthy. This was the powerful cocktail of forces (geostrategic, political, economic, social, cultural, and psychological) that served to silence, delegitimize, disorganize, differentiate, and then divide the eastern European working classes—*despite* their strong position on the local shop floor, despite high union membership, and despite sometimes very capable union leaders.

NEOLIBERAL CONSOLIDATIONS: UNEVEN, COMBINED, CONTRADICTORY

From 1998 to 2008, the post-Soviet world bifurcated into a set of unevenly neoliberalized and differentially transnationalized and financialized spaces.[19] The question of labor and its relation with the illiberal Right is part of these territorial differentiations within one universalizing, capitalist space-making process. Relative distance to the operational core of capitalism in the West was a key differentiating property, changing with time. The social policy outcomes ranged from very neoliberal in the urban republics of the Baltics to much less so in social democratic Slovenia, though, over time, differences were evening out as the financial crises and austerity hit.[20] Subsequently, the rise to power of illiberal populist forces in Hungary and Poland, and then elsewhere in the region, produced new differentiations in the direction of workfare and family benefits. Overall, integration into the European Union produced growth and reindustrialization as well as dispossession and disenfranchisement.

The average wealth outcomes, in fact, resemble pre–World War I positions vis-à-vis western Europe: Slovenia and the Czech Republic, once the most industrial parts of the Habsburg Empire, are now close to the EU average in wealth and productivity, on a par with Portugal and Greece (with some 50 percent to 60 percent of median incomes of "the West"); Hungary, Slovakia, and Poland remain below 40 percent. The rest of the region sticks to some 20 percent to 30 percent. Out-migration, *the* response to dispossession, was facilitated by the European Union and the Schengen agreements and has been substantial, significantly reducing unemployment in Poland, the Baltic republics, Romania, and Bulgaria, countries that now occupy top positions in the world out-migration and remittance rankings.[21] All CEE countries have some 20 percent to 30 percent of GDP in the informal economy, making some households less poor in pecuniary terms than they appear on paper.

In a highly financialized and globalized environment, hard-pressed post-socialist states transformed into Schumpeterian "competition states."[22] In the competition to attract mobile capital, they began subsidizing foreign investments, reducing capital's tax bill, and putting downward pressure on wages and legal protections, all on behalf of international competitiveness.

In this context, social and economic policy outcomes were intensely contradictory. One tenacious path dependency from socialism seems to stand out: large constituencies never bought into the neoliberal idea that one is expected to simply take care of oneself. The notion that families with children, in particular, have a right to a minimal standard of social reproduction, including public health and education, is popular everywhere in CEE.[23] What emerged, then, in the bargain between electorates and neoliberalizing states was the oxymoron of a quaint "neoliberal paternalism," an unstable compromise erected upon a fragile fiscal base geared to subsidizing transnational capital from the taxation of poor domestic labor.

Labor codes, for example, became increasingly neoliberalized over time, with the Polish and Slovak codes of the early 2000s unleashing a wave of region-wide anti-labor regulations. Romania's 2013 labor code went perhaps the furthest in allowing unlimited hours, hardly any regulation of hiring and firing, hardly any legal redress—a code obscenely offered to lure foreign capital in the midst of the euro crisis. Global capital was consistently in favor of downward regulation of labor codes, domestic capital sometimes less so.

EU accession, thus, became a contradictory and confusing experience for labor. On the one hand, it appears that the *acquis communautaire* has helped to strengthen the de jure legitimacy of central bargaining and tripartism. But in reality, that tripartism remained overly weak. CEE states such as Poland and Romania kept a whole array of repressive legal measures in place against labor, including severe legal punishment of labor leaders if a strike was not first approved by a judge. The EU environment does help in singling out such measures for some public opprobrium. But policy competition among states to attract foreign capital, the deeper driver of the process, is all but hard-wired in the European Union and is further magnified in the CEE context. It has also driven the liberalization of the labor market below what was common even in the mid-1990s.[24]

Policy competition also explains the dramatic slide toward an upwardly redistributional flat rate all over the region. Latvia introduced its flat tax of 13 percent in 1993, pushed through by a government of Latvian-American return-migrant entrepreneurs and libertarian adventurers. It spread soon through the Baltics and was copied by Slovakia in 2003 under Dzurinda's notoriously neoliberal catch-up government, which then caused a chain reaction. Almost overnight, Slovakia was turned into a world champion of export-driven car manufacturing—the introduction of the euro helped too, taking away foreign-exchange risk. By 2010 all CEE nations with the exception of Slovenia had introduced flat taxes. They are anywhere between 9 percent and 20 percent for both labor and capital, but rates for capital have been declining further. The actual taxation of capital has dwindled even below the nominal flat rates. There is little transparency on this, as everywhere else. The effective average taxation of capital in Hungary has been estimated at not more than 3 percent.[25] Neoliberal paternalism is paid for by labor itself, including big subsidies for capital.

In spite of these downward pressures on the finances of CEE states, neoliberal governments have not succeeded in radically entrenching or privatizing the welfare systems that were introduced in the early 1990s, despite continuous advocacy to that effect by the World Bank and the European Bank for Reconstruction and Development. Without exception, post-socialist electorates refused to give up their public pension systems and family benefits; nor were they persuaded that privatized health would overall be good for them. Where such neoliberalizations were driven through, mostly by social democratic governments, large popular mobilizations emerged, often supportive of right-wing nationalist parties that condemned such policies. Populist right-wing governments in Poland and Hungary after 2010 have reversed earlier pension privatizations. In 2016 the Polish Law and Justice government drastically increased the benefits for families with children and lowered the pension age—defying the neoliberal current. The rise of "illiberal" right-wing governments, such as Orban's in Hungary and Law and Justice in Poland, is largely explained by the popular rejection of the dismantling of the post-socialist commons by neoliberal social democrats. Illiberal nationalist parties rhetorically and sometimes factually celebrate the protection and well-being of the working poor.

CLASS STRUGGLE WITHOUT CLASS

In the context of the defeat of Europe's labor-based modernity, Göran Therborn has posed a pertinent question about possible "class compasses" for the global twenty-first century.[26] What sort of ideological frameworks might class struggle without class generate in the twenty-first century? Karl Polanyi's work perhaps suggests an answer.[27] Polanyi wrote about "countermovements to protect society" against the planned imposition of transnational "free" markets (the "double movement"). In contrast to class movements, these could be on either the Left or the Right. He was writing with the central European experience of the interwar period as backdrop: fascism and Nazism. The "protection of society" against planned marketization in a context of class struggle without class can well take the form of the re-articulation of endangered "traditional" hierarchies. The post-socialist experience offers a contemporary illustration. In a first phase, dominant until the financial crises, neoliberalization and marketization are imposed in a "planned" way. In a second, the countermovements that emerged in the first phase become dominant, later even regionally hegemonic.

On closer scrutiny, this scheme is too neat. The phases are far less ontologically opposed in reality than the Polanyian reading suggests. Both phases of the double movement are, in fact, about creating social hierarchies. But they do so differently and with a different ideology. The neoliberal marketization phase invited a strong undercurrent of consent from the upper segments of labor, as from the governing elites, who wanted to believe that their desires for a deserved meritocratic hierarchy would be realized through fair markets. The second, illiberal phase, can be understood as emerging out of the realization among common people and workers, as well as provincial bourgeoisies, that this supposed association of markets with meritocratic fairness is an illusion. Hence, in the 1990s, there was the tenacious public narrative in the region that real capitalism never arrived, that it was always already corrupted by former communists or the secret services now playing the democratic game. In the next phase, an authoritarian state was now brought in to reassert the interests of deserving working families and provincial bourgeoisies.

In fact, we have, then, two contemporary varieties of social Darwinism. Both are striving toward a justified natural hierarchy, the first through markets and efficiency, the second through protective nationalist states. The first is a neoliberal Darwinism; the second, a national-socialist *(stricto sensu)* Darwinism. These varieties do not represent a hard bifurcation or opposition. Both seek a hierarchy and support the market, though the first trumpets the global market and cosmopolitanism and employs a liberal state machine, and the second embraces nationalist regulation and illiberalism. They are, then, two observable strains within one broadly right-wing thread, one seeking economic inequality, the other cultural hierarchy, to coin a phrase.

Neoliberal Darwinism is primarily middle-class driven and cosmopolitan, in factual as well as imaginary ways, though it does gain substantial working-class consent for a while. It deploys notions of meritocratic hierarchy interwoven with a glorification of capitalist discipline and efficiency against poorer and weaker classes of citizens, and it is ready to turn such citizens into undeserving surplus populations.

The national-socialist variant may also be middle-class driven but is more provincial, rather lower-middle class, literally and stylistically. It rhetorically cherishes the deserving national working classes, which are strictly separated (symbolically, ritually, and in policy) from the undeserving segments. Indeed, it needs and summons deserving workers as a vital and mobilized electoral constituency. It projects a protection of deserving working members of majority ethno-nations against a greedy and disloyal cosmopolitan capitalism, on the one hand, and the "criminal" *classes dangereuses,* the surplus populations, on the other.[28] Both strains, the neoliberal as well as the national-socialist, are driven by the politics of class struggle without class and articulate a vindictive politics of culture and hierarchy.

How did the rise of illiberalism unfold within CEE? Hungary has served as a laboratory for the national-socialist form: a right-wing super majority that allowed for a new constitution and the construction of an illiberal state with universal welfare rights definitively switched off. It was first driven by the rise of a radical faction organized around the Jobbik party. This radical right-wing party flirted openly with paramilitary exercises in Roma settlements, the harassment of NGOs, and a pro-Putin—even pro-Iran—foreign policy, all combined with a rhetorical attack on foreign finance, foreign capitalists, the European Union, and the "plebeian" enemies: the ethno-nation, immigrants, and the Roma. The Polish Right does not march far behind. It features a stronger labor-contingent than the Hungarian Right and has accordingly claimed stronger positions on child benefits, family benefits, and pensions. With this program, it won the Polish presidential and parliamentary elections in 2015. Taking programmatic inspiration from Orban's illiberal revolution in Hungary, it is similarly disposed against the Roma, migrants, Muslims, gays, Jews, transnational capitalists, and the European Union (though it is ready to arm itself against Putin's Russia and is decidedly more misogynistic than Jobbik). Putin himself has mobilized the Russian workers of the provinces in an illiberal alliance against the big cities, the gays, the NGOs, and the West. He purposefully marshaled them against the "creative classes" of Moscow and other big cities who rallied against his usurpation of power in 2011–2012. In Slovakia,

Romania, and Ukraine, waves of public attention to issues of deservingness/undeservingness have focused on majority/minority relations, often mobilizing the nation against poor Roma (if and where they have been "available" for such purposes) or finding others to take the place of the Roma—from Jews and gays to communists (the Polish and Ukrainian Right).[29]

In contrast, the Baltics have produced a strong vernacular neoliberal Darwinism. These countries have again turned into city-states, singularly dominated by foreign finance, real estate, entrepreneurial "creative classes," and associated inputs into higher education. Russian speakers, located in the mining provinces close to the Russian border, have been seen as the cultural fifth column.[30] Russian-speaking miners are the local substitute for the Roma.

The Bulgarian experience of 2013 shows how shifty the class bases and orientations of these angry populisms can be. During a cold February, a nationalist-protectionist uprising in the provinces, driven by "common Bulgarian people" protesting against poverty and the high cost of basic utilities—privatized to transnational capitalists—led to the immediate abdication of a neoliberal right-wing government. The post-socialist social democrats won the subsequent election but made (characteristic) errors with personnel choices. They were immediately confronted with a months-long Sofia-based "Bulgarian middle-class" mobilization, kept up day after day over the summer, seeking to keep the nation out of the hands of the "red oligarchs and their alliance with the uneducated poor." It claimed that Bulgaria had to be run on behalf of "the productive Bulgarian bourgeoisie" and not for "the parasites on welfare." Protestors in Sofia literally demanded "quality versus quantity."[31] For a taste of context, it might be added that in Bulgaria—the European Union's poorest nation—85 percent of income was spent on basic necessities, including utilities. A local journalist remarked dryly that the Bulgarian "productive middle classes" who were protesting in Sofia, and who were supposedly beyond such dire straights, earned, on average, not much more than four hundred euros a month, far below any poverty line in the West of the continent. The outcomes of elections in both Bulgaria and Romania in late 2016 suggest, further, that the national-socialist politics of class without class in southeastern Europe might, in contrast to Poland and Hungary, be carried forward by social democratic parties.

LABOR, POLANYIAN COUNTERMOVEMENTS, AND THE MAKING OF THE ILLIBERAL VISEGRAD BLOC

Most westerners first learned about the "Visegrad Bloc" in late 2015 as it loudly refused to share in the reallocation of Middle Eastern refugees over EU space. The bloc, driven by the avowed "illiberal democracies" of Hungary and Poland, was adamantly nationalist, celebrated its national cultures as European *fines fleures,* and declared that it would defend these national cultures and, indeed, Europe itself against a multicultural, cosmopolitan European Union.

The Visegrad Bloc, however, was not at all new. It had existed as a formal collaboration between Poland, Hungary, Slovakia, and the Czech Republic from 1993 onward. But as CEE states turned into neoliberal competition states to lure global capital away from each other, there was little to discuss among them. Synchronization worked on automatic pilot toward a low point of neoliberalization and social dumping. National-socialist *(stricto sensu)* mobilizations—first in Poland in the early 2000s, then in Hungary after 2006, and again around the elections in Poland in 2015 and in Slovakia in 2016—transformed this bloc into a boisterous illiberal *affront* against a cosmopolitan European Union.[32] Neoliberal cosmopolitanism was meeting its "other" in neo-nationalist electoral mobilizations driven by the politics of class without class, endorsed by the "white working classes" of the provinces.

As I have argued, we need to place the dynamics of the bloc's making squarely within the relationships between capital, states, labor, and the politics of value. While this is not the place to work this out in detail,[33] here is a basic outline, offered as a coda.

First, an elite campaign of public condescension of workers and peasants took place in the 1990s. The "illiberal revolution" should be understood as the popular and populist counterpunch. Now the symbolic East had found its voice and spoke back in a biting tone against civil society and other idols of the 1990s. The rise of illiberalism was the political outcome of the making of the "eastern scale." I use this as a metaphor for the "orientalized" losers of the transition, as well as a reference to the geographic location where they assembled their critical mass—an electoral bloc of the self-declared disenfranchised of the poor eastern provinces, just as the Visegrad Bloc itself assembles the "eastern scale" for the European Union as a whole. The illiberal transformations in CEE are driven by electoral mobilization processes in the east of the East, in eastern Hungary, eastern Poland and eastern Slovakia—in other words, in those territories where the social reproduction of labor has stagnated more lastingly than in the new industrial spaces in the western manufacturing corridors and around the capital cities. They express the unevenness of capitalist dynamics—the stagnation, humiliation, and disempowerment of wide strata of labor—and the spread of relative and absolute surplus populations.

Second, the "eastern scale" came into its own as a veritable Polanyian countermovement. It reacted against transnational marketization and the social abandonment associated with the "competition state" syndrome. It emerged as a classical Polanyian "protection of society," substituting itself for the absent capacity of labor to confront capital and the state directly.

Third, this Polanyian countermovement came in three phases. The first phase played itself out in the late 1990s and early 2000s in Poland and was labor driven. Constituencies with a history of radical confrontation with the state—first in the context of Solidarnosc and later in the context of privatization, transnationalization, and consequent neoliberal dispossessions and disenfranchisements—developed an organic angry politics of resentment against the liberal state classes who had driven the moral assault on workers and peasants. This ushered in the first Kaczynski government (2005–2007), which went under in chaotic symbolic politics and intense infighting. It would depend on the next Hungarian phase of illiberal mobilization for the Polish Right to develop a more coherent program.

The second phase played itself out in the northeastern Hungarian districts.[34] Instead of labor, it focused on social reproduction. It came into being as a reactionary popular mobilization against what was perhaps the first genuine social democratic government in Hungary and CEE at large (2002–2006), which sought to extend universal social rights at the municipal level in Hungary, including a guaranteed social minimum through family and child benefits and the reintegration of Roma children into mainstream primary education. This was a program explicitly meant to reintegrate the surplus populations. In a context of media-driven moral panics around "gypsy crime," local constituencies rebelled. In their eyes, the social democrats were elevating the undeserving and unemployed Roma to the standards of the Magyar "working poor," from whose taxes the subsidies were paid. They refused to subsidize the social reproduction of large and unruly Roma families and the desegregation of municipal schools. Relative surplus populations were being mobilized against the absolute surplus population. This was nationalist hierarchy in action.

This second phase can be understood, however, only in the context of the weakness of the Hungarian state in relation to global capital. This was the deeper cause behind the failure of the push toward more universalist welfare-statism and the subsequent self-destruction of Hungarian social democracy. Mutual competition meant that CEE states failed to tax capital. The social democratic government in Hungary financed its new politics of social redistribution largely by selling state debt to the financial markets, markets that were flush with liquidity in the early 2000s. The Hungarian national bank also allowed Swiss franc– and euro-denominated private mortgages with low interest rates (compared to the local currency) to substitute for lacking wage growth. A consumer bonanza was launched with the Hungarian private housing stock as collateral. The social democrats exploited, in other words, the opportunities of transnational finance to make up for the weakness of domestic labor and the state vis-à-vis transnational industrial capital.

What happened next destroyed social democracy in Hungary and opened the gates for an assertive, hierarchy-seeking neo-nationalism. In 2006, with the financial crisis approaching, global investors told the social democrats that new loans would not be forthcoming. Ferenc Gyurcsáni, the prime minister who had just won the 2006 elections from Viktor Orban with his program of universally extended social redistribution, conceded in a leaked post-election speech before his own activists that he had "lied night and day" and that his promises had to be withdrawn immediately. The escalating right-wing rebellion of the working poor against universal welfare in northeastern Hungary now rolled into the streets of

Budapest. Months of huge and angry mass demonstrations followed, leading to the abdication of Gyurcsáni.

Worse came when the financial crisis broke in the fall of 2008. After 1989, Austrian finance had gradually reoccupied the paramount position in southeastern Europe that it had lost in the crisis of the 1930s. But in late 2008, in the midst of the credit crunch, Viennese financiers panicked. Loans to Hungary and other states had been based on global securitization, not on limited Austrian savings. Austrian bankers feared that the credit crunch would prevent the rollover of those international loans. Outstanding credit to eastern Europe would have to be called in, bankrupting millions of households and states in CEE, or, alternatively, they would have to allow the bankruptcy of the Austrian banks. The rumor alone led to immediate and uncontrolled devaluations of the local currencies, further increasing CEE indebtedness in real terms. Hungary was the largest Austrian liability. The Viennese treasury now intervened by calling in the IMF—an episode not widely reported in the western media—which decided to offer "preventative credits" to CEE states, meant to buffer the local currencies and make a pool of public credit available in case Austrian loans were not to be rolled over. Hungary was offered a twenty-five-billion-dollar credit line, on the order of magnitude of Argentina's state debt (per head).

The then IMF president, the French socialist Dominique Strauss Kahn, explained that old-style IMF conditionality was not on anymore. That turned out not quite to be true. The recently introduced "thirteenth month," which had been the ultimate symbol of "growth" for many workers, was cancelled; health was further privatized; and serious cuts were made in pensions and public salaries. The social democrats were committing nothing less than collective suicide in front of the public. The radical Right Jobbik party and its affiliated Magyar Garda began exploiting small local conflicts in the East to destroy the social democratic base in the eastern provinces, pushing Orban's Fidesz party further to the populist Right. The outcome, in 2010, was the arrival of the most popular radical right-wing government in Europe. It set about using its two-thirds majority in parliament to transform Hungary's rights-based constitution and welfare state into an "illiberal national workfare state." In the process, it attacked the autonomy of the Hungarian National Bank and the Constitutional Court; it renationalized the privatized pension system; it attacked the transnational banking sector, as well as the transnational media and utilities, and forced them (via new taxes and mandated price discounts) to sell out to Hungarian corporations; it nationalized the Budapest stock exchange; and, above all, it created a punitive regime against the Roma and other surplus populations, institutionalizing the Jobbik-driven moral panics of the 2010s into a permanent zero-tolerance workfare regime. The nation re-created its "natural" ethno-hierarchy, both domestically in the governing of populations and transnationally in the relation to foreign capital. In 2014 it paid off its IMF debt.

In the third phase, this "illiberal democratic" program was taken over by Law and Justice in Poland, which in October 2015 won the largest electoral victory of any party in Poland since 1989—once again significantly based in the mobilization of its eastern constituencies. Now, with a national-socialist right *(stricto sensu)* actively creating new illiberal state forms in the two key states of CEE, the Visegrad Bloc began presenting itself as the "eastern scale" within the European Union. For the first time since 1989, it began to speak with a unified political voice, condemning "western-imposed multiculturalism" and confronting the European Union on civil society, human rights, democracy, and immigration, and doing so on behalf of nothing less than the protection of "deserving" domestic labor and for the support of the even more deserving national bourgeoisie and its domestic accumulation.

The contradictions of social reproduction, in particular of working families, until then violently obscured under the mantra of economic growth and "successful transition," returned to haunt the European Union with a vengeance. Cultural hierarchy on behalf of the deserving majority-nation had finally become the new good sense. Internally divided labor, state weakness, dispossession, and disenfranchisement explain why—the multi-scalar narrative presented here as a coda narrates how.

NOTES

1. Jan Breman and Marcel van der Linden, "Informalizing the Economy: The Return of the Social Question at a Global Level," *Development and Change* 45, no. 5 (2014): 895–919.

2. Dorothee Bohle and Bela Greskovits, *Capitalist Diversity on Europe's Periphery* (Ithaca: Cornell University Press, 2012); David Lane and Martin Myant, eds., *Varieties of Capitalism in Post-Communist Countries* (Basingstoke, U.K.: Palgrave Macmillan, 2007); Peter Hall and David Soskice, eds., *Varieties of Capitalism: The Institutional Foundations of Comparative Advantage* (Oxford: Oxford University Press, 2001); Bob Hancke, Martin Rhodes, and Mark Thatcher, eds., *Beyond Varieties of Capitalism: Conflict, Contradictions, and Complementarities in the European Economy* (Oxford: Oxford University Press, 2007).

3. James Ferguson, *Give a Man a Fish* (Durham, NC: Duke University Press, 2015).

4. Gareth Dale, ed., *First the Transition, Then the Crash: Eastern Europe in the 2000s* (London: Pluto, 2011); Srecko Horvat and Igor Stiks, eds., *Welcome to the Desert of Post-Socialism: Radical Politics after Yugoslavia* (London: Verso, 2015); more ethnographically, see David Kideckel, *Getting By in Postsocialist Romania: Labor, the Body, and Working Class Culture* (Bloomington: Indiana University Press, 2008).

5. A. Cerami and A. Vanhuysse, eds. *Post-Communist Welfare Pathways: Theorizing Social Policy Transformations in Central and Eastern Europe* (Basingstoke, U.K.: Palgrave Macmillan, 2009); M. A. Orenstein, "Postcommunist Welfare States," *Journal of Democracy* 19, no. 4 (2008): 80–94.

6. Bela Greskovits, *The Political Economy of Protest and Patience: East European and Latin American Transformations Compared* (Budapest: Central European University Press, 1998). Guglielmo Meardi, *Social Failures of EU Enlargement: A Case of Workers Voting with Their Feet* (London: Routledge, 2011).

7. Alison Stenning, Adrian Smith, Alena Rochovská, and Dariusz Świątek, *Domesticating Neo-Liberalism: Spaces of Economic Practice and Social Reproduction in Post-Socialist Cities* (London: Wiley-Blackwell, 2010).

8. David Ost, "Illusory Corporatism Ten Years Later," *Warsaw Forum of Economic Sociology* 2, no. 1 (2011): 19–49; Stefan Guga, "Fordism in the Periphery," (Phd thesis, Central European University, 2017).

9. Don Kalb, "Conversations with a Polish Populist: Tracing Hidden Histories of Globalization, Class, and Dispossession in Postsocialism (and Beyond)," *American Ethnologist* 36, no. 2 (2009): 207–23; Don. Kalb, "'Worthless Poles' and Other Post-Socialist Dispossessions," in *Blood and Fire: Toward a Global Anthropology of Labor*, ed. August Carbonella and Sharryn Kashmir, 250–87 (New York: Berghahn Books, 2014).

10. Guga, "Fordism in the Periphery."

11. Gil Eyal, Ivan Szelenyi, and Eleanor Townsley, *Making Capitalism without Capitalists: Class Formation and Elite Struggles in Post-Communist Central Europe* (London: Verso, (1998); J. Staniszkis, *The Dynamics of the Breakthrough in Eastern Europe: The Polish Experience* (Berkeley: University of California Press, 1991).

12. A good example is Vladimir Tismaneanu, *Fantasies of Salvation: Democracy, Nationalism, and Myth in Post-Communist Europe* (Princeton, NJ: Princeton University Press, 2009).

13. Michal Buchowski, "The Specter of Orientalism in Europe: From Exotic Other to Stigmatized Brother," *Anthropological Quarterly* 79, no. 3 (2006): 463–82.

14. Don Kalb, "Regimes of Value and Worthlessness: How Two Subaltern Stories Speak," in *Work and Livelihoods*, ed. Victoria Goddard and Susana Narotzky, 123–36 (London: Routledge, 2016).

15. David Ost, *The Defeat of Solidarity: Anger and Politics in Postcommunist Europe* (Ithaca: Cornell University Press, 2005).

16. Michael Burawoy, *The Politics of Production: Factory Regimes under Capitalism and Socialism* (London: Verso, 1985); Katherine Verdery, *What Was Socialism and What Comes Next?* (Berkeley: University of California Press, 1996).

17. Eszter Bartha, *Alienating Labour: Workers on the Road from Socialism to Capitalism in East Germany and Hungary* (New York: Berghahn Books, 2013); Alina-Sandra Cucu, *Planning Labour: Time and the Foundations of Industrial Socialism in Romania* (Oxford: Berghahn Books, 2019).

18. Ivan Szelenyi, *Urban Inequalities under State Socialism* (Oxford: Oxford University Press, 1983).

19. Martin Myant and Jan Drahokoupil, *Transition Economies: Political Economy in Russia, Eastern Europe, and Central Asia* (London: Wiley, 2010). Bohle and Greskovits, *Capitalist Diversity on Europe's Periphery*; S. Haggard and R. R. Kaufman, "The Eastern European Welfare State in Comparative Welfare State," In *Post-Communist Welfare Pathways: Theorizing Social Policy Transformations in Central and Eastern Europe*, ed. A. Cerami and A. Vanhuysse, 217–36 (Basingstoke, U.K.: Palgrave Macmillan, 2009); Cristiano Perugini and Fabrizio Pompei, eds., *Inequalities During and After Transition in Central and Eastern Europe* (London: Palgrave Macmillan, 2015).

20. Bela Greskovits, *The Political Economy of Protest and Patience: East European and Latin American Transformations Compared* (Budapest: Central European University Press, 1998).

21. Guglielmo Meardi, *Social Failures of EU Enlargement: A Case of Workers Voting with Their Feet* (London: Routledge, 2011).

22. Jan Drahokoupil, *Globalization and the State in Central and Eastern Europe: The Politics of Foreign Direct Investment* (London: Routledge, 2008); Bob Jessop, *The Future of the Capitalist State* (Cambridge: Polity Press, 2002).

23. Cerami and Vanhuysse, *Post-Communist Welfare Pathways.*

24. Linda Cook, "More Rights, Less Power: Labor Standards and Labor Markets in East European Post-communist States," *Studies in Comparative International Development* 45 (2010): 170–97.

25. Gabor Scheiring, "The Political Economy of Democratic Backsliding" (paper presented at a conference of the European Sociological Association, Prague, 2015).

26. Göran Therborn, "New Masses? Social Bases of Resistance," *New Left Review* 85 (2014): 7–16.

27. K. Polanyi, *The Great Transformation: The Political and Economic Origins of Our Time* (Boston, MA: Beacon Press, 2001), originally published 1944.

28. See also K. E. Friedman and J. Friedman, *Modernities, Class, and the Contradictions of Globalization: The Anthropology of Global Systems* (Lanham: Altamira Press, 2008); K. E. Friedman and J. Friedman, *Historical Transformations: The Anthropology of Global Systems* (Lanham: Altamira Press, 2008).

29. Nicolette Makovicky, "'Work Pays': Slovak Neoliberalism as 'Authoritarian Populism,'" *Focaal: Journal of Global and Historical Anthropology* 67 (2013): 77–90; Cristina Rat, "The Impact of Minimum Income Guarantee Schemes in Central and Eastern Europe," in *Post-Communist Welfare Pathways: Theorizing Social Policy Transformations in Central and Eastern Europe,* ed. A. Cerami and A. Vanhuysse, 217–36 (Basingstoke, U.K.: Palgrave Macmillan, 2009).

30. Eeva Keskula, "Reverse, Restore, Repeat! Class, Ethnicity, and the Russian-Speaking Miners of Estonia," *Focaal: Journal of Global and Historical Anthropology* 72 (2015): 95–108.

31. Georgi Medarov, "Is Liberal Populism Possible?" (paper presented at the conference "The Sources of Populism in the Balkans," Marija Bistrica, October 2014).

32. Don Kalb, "Upscaling Illiberalism: Class, Contradiction, and the Rise and Rise of the Populist Right in Post-Socialist Central Europe," *Fudan Journal of the Humanities and the Social Sciences* 11 (2018): 323–39; Gabor Halmai, "(Dis)possessed by the Specter of Socialism: Nationalist Mobilization in 'Transitional' Hungary," in *Headlines of Nation, Subtexts of Class: Working-Class Populism and the Return of the Repressed in Neoliberal Europe,* ed. Don Kalb and Gabor Halmai, 113–41 (New York: Berghahn Books, 2011); Kristof Szombati, *The Revolt of the Provinces: Anti-Gypsyism and Right-Wing Politics in Hungary* (New York: Berghahn Books, 2018).

33. For a more complete discussion, see Kalb, "Upscaling Illiberalism."

34. Szombati, *The Revolt of the Provinces.*

13

The Social Question in Russia

From De-Politicization to a Growing Sense of Exploitation

Karine Clément

Despite the dramatic social shock that has traumatized millions of Russians after the fall of the communist system, the social question is, strangely enough, almost absent from public discussions, intellectual debates, and even social movements.[1] Social problems are a topic in everyday conversations; there are not a political issue. It is striking that in a country where social and labor precariousness is so high and where attacks on social security are so harsh, the social question does not exist as articulated or explicit preoccupations or demands. In this paper, I will try to assess the roots of the depoliticization of the social question in post-Soviet Russia and to interrogate whether there are some changes taking place in the ways people experience their precarious social and labor conditions today, almost thirty years after the end of the communist regime.

In order to explore the problem, I will examine the trajectory of the social question issue in post-Soviet Russia from three perspectives: social-economic transformations since the fall of the Soviet regime and the evolution of public discourses on social problems, the subjective and social experience of precariousness and informality, and the place of social grievances in claims addressed to the state. The analysis is based on primary data from field research on labor relations[2] and social movements[3] carried out by the author and colleagues in several regions and organizations from 1995 to 2012, and more recent data come from field research on everyday nationalism in contemporary Russia, conducted in 2016–2017.[4] The paper will argue that concerns about social rights and social consciousness, after a long period of collapse, tend to develop among large parts of the society, and that they arise from a growing sense of exploitation. The politicization of this social consciousness, however, remains problematic.

MARKET CAPITALISM AND THE "SOVIET-STYLE NEOLIBERALISM"

The most radical capitalist and neoliberal reforms were made just after the breakdown of the communist regime, leading to social disorientation, impoverishment, and precarization of a large majority of the population. However, that neoliberal course has not changed, even up to today. The only thing that has changed is the rhetorical packaging of the reforms. The ultraliberal tone of the 1990s, when Boris Yeltsin was in power, has been replaced by the populist and patriotic discourse of the Putin's government.

Ultraliberal Policy of the 1990s and Weak Resistance to It

Ultraliberal reforms were launched in early 1992 with the price liberalization and continued with mass privatization of enterprises, the state withdrawal from economy, and the minimization of its social functions. As a result, the income of the majority of population plummeted. According to Russian government statistics, in 1992 real incomes fell by 43.7 percent compared to 1991, then grew a little, and after the 1998 default, fell again by 42.5 percent compared to 1991. They recovered their pre-reform level only in 2005. Throughout the 1990s, most people depending on wages and social payments were brutally impoverished. They faced the problem of wage and pension reduction, non-payments, or delays in payment. Savings vanished because of ultra-inflation and default. Most of the population was living in poverty, whereas a small, notorious, and hated segment of the population—referred to as the "oligarchs"—was becoming richer and richer. Ben Judah describes it thus: "the 'wild 1990s' is a synonym in Russian for a decade that left practically every family with stories of deprivation, unpaid wages, economic humiliation and diminished status."[5]

The Soviet welfare system guaranteed free medical care, free education, job security, and a stable salary, as well as a pension. Under the Soviet system, social services were mostly provided by enterprises, which took care of their "social sphere" (kindergartens, schools, sports equipment, health and housing services, or gas and water supply). These enterprises got rid of this "social burden" soon after the fall of the wall, leading to a deterioration of the social protection and utilities system. Another feature of the Soviet social welfare system continued to exist: the system of "categorical benefits," whereby certain categories of the population (such as the disabled, war veterans, and large families) received in-kind benefits *(lgoty)*, such as free or subsidized public transportation, discounts on residential utilities, and free medication. Although the system was highly criticized by international financial organizations as inefficient and contrary to market logic, it continued to be developed under Yeltsin's presidency. Indeed, the system was a popular and cheap way for state authorities to offset hardships.

Except for the system of in-kind benefits, the Soviet welfare system broke down after the 1991–1992 ultraliberal reforms. Most people found themselves deprived of social security and any certainty of what tomorrow would be like. Neither the federal state nor local authorities took on the responsibility of providing social protection. Instead, they delegated social care to each individual and his or her close relatives. As a well-known Russian folk saying goes, "the salvation of those who are drowning is the business of those who are drowning"—meaning that one is expected to save oneself. Meanwhile, most workers, in all types of sectors and types of ownership, continued to rely on the enterprises' social sphere, going to their workplace even without being paid in order to have at least some protection—or at least the illusion of protection. This explains the low level of unemployment.[6] The problem in post-Soviet Russia is not unemployment, rather unpaid wages, compulsory leaves, low-wage jobs.

Thus, the first stage in the formation of Russian capitalism (the 1990s) led to a sharp economic downturn, a health crisis, the rise of social inequality, and the impoverishment of the majority of the population. Between 1989 and 1994, life expectancy declined by more than 6.7 years in men (from 64.1 years to 57.4) and 3.4 years in women (from 74.5 years to 71.1), such a gender gap being linked to the stronger stress experienced by men who had lost their role as breadwinners.[7] After the 1992 economic reforms, official statistics show the poverty rate rising to 33.5 percent and remaining at a high level all through the 1990s. A large percentage of the population lived with incomes not much higher than the official poverty line, while a minority monopolized national wealth. A key feature of Russian poverty—which endures until now—is that it is not limited to specific groups (although the disabled, families with many children, single-parent families, and retirees are among the most vulnerable categories), but also affects a lot of workers, skilled and nonskilled.

However, instead of revolting and rising up against power holders and oligarchs, people rejected politics and activism and retreated into their private lives and households. There were a couple of reasons for this. First, most of them had to survive, and that meant holding multiple jobs, being involved in subsistence and petty commodity production, and experiencing despair and exhaustion. Second, the dominant neoliberal or consumerist ideology led to self-criticism. Impoverished and precarized people tended to blame themselves, painfully enduring privations and passively hoping for state protection or economic restoration. The "tsunami of third-wave marketization," as Burawoy calls the Russian transition to the market,[8] led to the prevalence of commodification, economic decline, impoverishment of the majority, and stigmatization of blue-collar workers, poor people, and others who did not succeed in "adapting" to the market. The market reform of the 1990s thus did not lead to mass mobilization and resistance. Social struggles mostly broke out in a spontaneous and disordered fashion and were not part of an ongoing mass movement. Industrial disputes occurred, but they were scattered and limited, with a few exceptions, like the miners' strikes and blockades of the Trans-Siberian Railway in May–June 1998, in which a broad range of people participated—not only miners, but also machinists, teachers, and municipal-services workers.

The Economic Revival of the 2000s and the Development of Grassroots Social Movements

The socioeconomic situation started to improve in the 2000s after the 1998 default and devaluation of the ruble. Real wages and pensions recovered, and poverty fell by half.[9] Many people no longer had suffered from the day-to-day struggle for survival, and they got a firmer foundation under their feet. However, a new stage in neoliberal reforms began in 2004, when the Putin administration aimed at restructuring the social welfare system. The neoliberal logic of these reforms is not as visible as it was during the 1990s, since the rhetoric changed and the "antisocial" reforms were complemented by other "social" ones.

At first, it seems that the government opted for a strict neoliberal course. A flat income taxation (13 percent) was introduced in 2001. The new labor code implemented in 2002 strengthened employers' positions while weakened the employees' ones, especially concerning the possibility for organizing in independent trade unions and for striking. Later in the 2000s, legislation on housing, urban, and ecological issues was reformed, which increased the cost of utilities and housing maintenance due by residents while opening the path to the privatization of communal and housing services and lands. The course chosen by the government, under the influence of the World Bank and World Trade Organization, focused on price deregulation and privatization.

However, people had recovered from the shock of the 1990s, and new antisocial reforms launched by Putin's government gave rise to protest. In 2004, Putin's government attacked the social benefits system and faced the most massive protest movements post-Soviet Russia has known.[10] The mass social movement of winter 2005 was directed against a reform known as the monetization of in-kind benefits *(lgoty)* that threatened the social benefits of a number of specific professional categories, but which, in practice, affected most of the population, particularly retirees, but also school children, students, the disabled, Chernobyl survivors, Great North workers, victims of political repressions, and so on. Protest actions began on a small scale and focused on concrete issues: following altercations on buses and trolleys, retirees objected to having to pay for their tickets. From bus stop to bus stop, indignation spread, as retirees shared their anger in familiar public spaces. The news spread like a wildfire, fanned by feelings of indignation, injustice, and contempt.

The movement quickly gained traction: only a few days after the monetization law went into effect, on January 1, 2005, thousands of people, led by the retirees, demonstrated in the street to demand the law's repeal. During the month of January, the movement mobilized more than half a million people in 97 towns and 78 regions across the country. In February, national action days were organized to demand that the federal government and Vladimir Putin withdraw the law. The national campaign ultimately achieved a partial repeal of the reform—but that was a rare occurrence in contemporary Russia.

After this concession, the social policy course seems to have been corrected in order to demonstrate the state concern for social care. Federal programs in health, housing, and education were launched with great publicity. Special aid was granted to young families and mothers through the popular "maternity capital" program, which also aimed at demonstrating the state concern for the birthrate. These programs had a brief positive effect, improving access to affordable housing or increasing education and health care workers' wages. However, the economic crisis of 2008–2009 and the recession that began in 2014 have stopped the improvement of families' social situation and living conditions. Currently, the problems of wages arrears, diminution of real wages, and impoverishment have made a dramatic comeback, while social inequality has been reinforced.

Since the 2005 movement against the monetization of social benefits, the most massive mobilization has been a grassroots movement that is scattered, local, and rooted in the daily lives of its participants, and that seeks to address particular but narrow social problems (school or hospital closures, increases in transport or communal charges, problems of urban construction and so forth). These social demands are usually not translated in terms of welfare state or social redistribution.

As a whole, social movements, because of their local and spread-out character, tend to be largely ignored by the media, whatever their ideological orientation, and underestimated or delegitimized by the intellectuals for their egoism or narrow materialism. This is one explanation of why it has been so difficult for a nation-wide social justice movement to develop. Another explanation is the lack of mobilizing structures, the high degree of atomization, and the loss of the sense of social belonging.

One of the few nation-wide organizational structures is the trade unions, but they are not very powerful in mobilizing. In practice, relations between rank-and-file workers and the management in factories are strongly unbalanced, because of the weakness of the trade union movement. The movement remains dominated by former official Soviet unions, renamed the Federation of Independent Trade Unions of Russia (FNPR), and this group collaborates with management in most cases. The alternative or free trade unions more frequently focus on the defense of labor rights and confrontations with employers, but they face difficulties gaining recognition and support among workers.[11] This situation explains the high level of distrust toward trade unions in general.

Up to now, the labor movement remained one of the weakest social forces. There was a small wave of strikes in 2007–2008, especially in profitable and foreign-owned enterprises, with workers confronting managers with demands for higher pay and better working conditions. Then the global economic downturn in 2009–2010 led to a wave of spontaneous street protests that were focused on individual crises (for example, fighting the threat of an enterprising closing entirely or conducting mass lay-offs). The crisis of the Russian economy, which began at the end of 2014, has generated a new wave of labor protests in manufacturing industries and in the public sector. However, these protests are scattered and poorly organized, and they have not led to any movement for the improvement of the workers' condition as a whole.

Local protests usually do not address the social question as such. The national protest most widely covered in the media, the 2011–2012 movement "For Fair Elections," did not raise the social question. As some commentators have pointed out,[12] the protest was over moral issues, as illustrated by the most popular slogan: "against the party of crooks and thieves." Still there are some exceptions, mostly in movements emerging from local grassroots initiatives located far from the wealthier centers, and especially in labor conflicts, such as the month-long strike at a Ford plant (Vsevolozhsk, in the St. Petersburg region) in 2007 or the wave of protests for the survival of industrial "monotowns" (towns that were built around a single local industry) all around the country in 2009. In some cases, timid voices can be heard that raise the issue of social justice; however, they do not demand expressively a new social policy. In most cases, social inequalities, dispossession, and impoverishment are experienced as social ills that are beyond the reach of grassroots local activists. They fight against unpaid wages, the increase of the housing utilities' prices, the closure of factories, or against the local government. They do not fight for social justice or welfare entitlements as such.

The Displaying of the Social Question in the Public Sphere

The evolution of social policy is reflected in the way influential political actors have displayed or silenced the social question over time during the post-Soviet period. In the dominant discourse of the 1990s, the social question was not a matter of concern. In the mass media, people who needed social protection were portrayed as old, reactionary, or incompetent people who failed in adapting to the market and deserved their miserable existence. The tone of "democratic" media was particularly disrespectful and ironic while reporting protest actions for the payment of wages: protesters were depicted as lazy or reactionary, fools or extremists. Older people and blue-collar workers were among the most stigmatized. The former for their nostalgia for the Soviet Union ("A new misfortune fell down on Russia: fools show the way").[13] The latter for their laziness ("They work only three days per week, but they are still discontent and participate in protest actions").[14] Government officials and liberal intellectuals actively participated in the stigmatization of those who needed or demanded social security from the state. They were "losers" by their own fault, because they lacked the personal qualities needed in the modern, democratic market era.[15]

Thus, the market capitalism ideology predominated in the 1990s in the public discourse in the media, intellectual circles, and institutional politics. State intervention in the economy was considered as bad for economic growth. Social welfare was a sign of state paternalism and demands for social rights a sign of the infantilism of people unable to take care of themselves. Social inequality was good, and equality associated with the Soviet *uravnilovka,* "equalization." Because of the rejection of state-imposed communist ideology, critic of capitalism was taboo and class language rejected, even by the workers themselves.

In Putin's Russia, this rhetoric has radically changed, while the neoliberal politics has remained the same. Especially after the massive protests against the monetization of social benefits in 2005, the Putin administration accentuated the discourse of government concern for the people and the rejection of the neoliberal reforms of the 1990s. Thus, one can argue that under Putin a "Soviet-style neoliberalism" has developed[16] that is a neoliberal politics coupled with populist and nationalist values and the ostensible opposition to the 1990s-era economic reforms that were so traumatizing to most of the population. The rhetoric is appealing, since it was accompanied by economic growth and concrete demonstrative measures, such as the war on oligarchs controlling Russia's exporting companies in the sectors of oil, gas, and metals (the most famous case being the one that led to Michail Khodorkosvky's imprisonment) and the strengthening of the state authority. In his populist rhetoric, Vladimir Putin turns back to the "hard-working" and "conscientious" "ordinary folk," and primarily speaks to "ordinary citizens" and "people who work" and "love Russia."[17]

Thus, many impoverished and stigmatized people during the 1990s had their self-esteem restored thanks to the change in official public discourse. It is not surprising, then, that many of them support Putin, at least passively. Indeed, the liberal and democratic opposition, for its part, continues to use the rhetoric of the 1990s. Moscow intelligentsia considers "mass post-Soviet people," especially poor people from the regions, as "paternalistically minded," authoritarian, and interested more in materialistic stuff than in democracy and cultural or ethical values.[18] However, if welfare claims in post-Soviet society were long delegitimized as sign of the old-fashioned Soviet "paternalism," recent studies indicate the development of a social consciousness. More people, especially from the lower classes, are beginning to raise the issue of socioeconomic injustice and to claim for more social guarantees and redistribution. This change goes along with the change in public discourse, the growing level of socioeconomic inequality, and the return of socioeconomic hardships. As paradoxical as it may seem, the Kremlin's nationalistic and populist discourse offers new clues to perceive social cleavages and to identify with the ones who are exploited and despoiled by the economic and political elites. To a certain extent, the rising popularity of the opposition leader Alexei Navalny and the mass participation in the all-Russian protest days against corruption that he initiated in March and June 2017 provide evidence that concerns for social problems and inequality are developing. Interviews conducted by sociologists during these mobilizations (including by myself and colleagues from the Laboratory of Public Sociology)[19] demonstrate the strength of social and economic motives. Interviews and videos from demonstrations in regional towns show that people took to the streets not so much to protest corruption or support Navalny, but rather to voice their discontent with the state of public services, health care, public education, culture, or roads. They were pushed to protest by their dissatisfaction with wide social inequalities between the small group of the rich at the top and the poor majority, between the prosperous central cities and the neglected and remote regional towns.

Capitalism Pervading Informal Coping Practices

The social question was difficult to embrace in Russia because of its informal character, which rendered invisible social insecurity, precariousness, uncertainty, and isolation, these being characteristic features of neoliberal capitalism.[20] There were no available and trustable statistics on informal practices for the 1990s, because the Russian State Statistical Agency (Rosstat) did not gather information on it at that time. Informality was considered a side effect of the transition toward capitalism—and it was expected to soon disappear. The most representative sociological survey, the Russian Longitudinal Monitoring Survey of the Higher School of Economics (RLMS-HSE), started to measure informality in the early 2000s and relies on the respondents' willingness to admit their participation in informal activities. Using different data sources (the Rosstat statistics as well as the RLMS-HSE data), Gimpelson and Kapelyushnikov estimate the informal-sector employment within the range of 20 percent to 30 percent in the 2000s.[21] Vinogradova, Kozina, and Cook make similar estimation, but add non-standard work arrangements that encompass more than 40 percent of the enterprises.[22] However, not all forms of non-standard work arrangements are informal and not all of them are experienced by the workers as precarious.

Formal and informal practices are intertwined,[23] and this does not facilitate the evaluation of informality. Most frequently, informal activities develop inside formal economic organizations and in response to the formal order. The most widespread such practice was the second, informal job that workers, formally employed by registered enterprises, were performing during the 1990s because of the nonpayment or underpayment of their wages. Another illustration can be the informal work that most workers have to perform in order to do their work—for instance many workers must repair the machines they work on before using them—because of the disorganization of the labor process in the 1990s, and, later, because of the increasingly high and practically unfulfillable formal targets required by the management in the 2000s.

The social question was difficult to grasp for ordinary people because of the overwhelming informality surrounding it. Precariousness, for instance, tended to be just coping practices of ingenious people who tried to take care of themselves by themselves. Social public services were provided without clear rules and visibility. In-kind benefits, for example, were provided covertly and consisted of things like free access to public transport or minimal healthcare, the providers of which were not refunded by the state budget. Access to public services of better quality could be gained through the payment of small bribes or an informal social network. The state encouraged the development of these informal tactics of coping for providing social care.

This is changing now, with the new capitalistic logic that the government has been pushing in the social sphere and public sector since the second part of the 2000s. A new trend toward formalization tried to make the public sector—particularly healthcare, education, and housing—conform to the capitalistic logic. This worsened social, educational, and medical care available to the poor, disabled, seriously ill, or rural people. Neoliberal reforms of the 2000s led to the retrenchment of the state from social welfare, to the institutionalization (formalization) of a reduced state commitment to the provision of social care, and to the introduction of neo-managerial principles in the public services sector. In turn, this led to the exclusion of large categories of social services from state budget funding and to stronger control over workers in the fields of health, social services, and education. Being underdeveloped and under growing state control, nongovernmental voluntary or philanthropist organizations cannot effectively supplement state social welfare. Private profit-based services are not affordable for the majority. Thus, in interviews about everyday life, many people complain about the degradation of the health care, education, housing, and transport system.[24] This is certainly one of the explanations for why more people are beginning to address the social question now, at least in terms of blaming socioeconomic inequality and the state's inaction on promoting social equity and social welfare guarantees.

THE EXPERIENCE OF PRECARIOUSNESS: FROM DESUBJECTIVATION TO THE GROWING SENSE OF EXPLOITATION

In this section, I shall trace the everyday experiences of precariousness and informality and show how desubjectivation dynamics (the loss of some sense of the self and agency) tend to be overcome in recent time.

Desubjectivation

Precariousness was maybe nowhere so widespread and all-pervading as it was in the 1990s in Russia. Blue-collar and industrial workers were among the first victims of the new labor regime, because of deindustrialization, the loss of the previous symbolic significance of the mythicized Soviet proletariat, and the weak mobilizing potential of their organizations. In the 1990s, they lost two-thirds of their average real wages; most of their social benefits and protections, including guaranteed employment; as well as their social image as the leading class of Soviet society. However, workers stood by relatively passively in the face of such a loss. Quiescence resulted from their—successful or unsuccessful—adaptation to the social transformations that were taking place. Given the degree and scale of these transformations, adaptation often meant complete human flexibility, the ability to bend and distort oneself without breaking. Some people did break (the men's life expectancy fell dramatically during the 1990s). Others did not break but lost their sense of self in the course of constantly adapting to changing conditions. Most of them lost points of reference and their orientation in life; they had trouble identifying themselves and the society they lived in. The field studies I conducted in the 1990s among industrial workers led me to describe their life's precarization as a process of *desubjectivation*.[25] Many talked about themselves in derogatory terms: "a small screw in the soulless machine," "nothing," "unneeded people," "cattle," or "slaves." My conclusions are supported by the ethnographic study conducted by Sarah Ashwin who explained workers' "endless patience" by alienation, atomization, and workers' reliance on individual survival strategies.[26]

Although more affected by it, industrial workers were not the only ones to be shaken by precarization, which pervaded all spheres of human living and took a thousand faces. The predominant feature of precariousness was and remains informality, that is to say, the bypassing of the law and the formal (established and collectively recognized) rules.

Informality: From Destabilization to Inhabiting

Although some scholars at the time argued that informality was a legacy of the Soviet system that would disappear as soon as market capitalism developed, informality has not decreased over time. In fact, it has sharply increased in times of crisis. Thus, the socioeconomic crisis that began in 2014 because of inflation, the collapse of the ruble, decreasing oil prices, and Western sanctions has led to a decline in economic growth and income levels, a rise in unemployment, and an increase in poverty. The extent of informality and precariousness has increased, as testified by the rise of nonpayment or delayed payment of wages, flextime, "voluntary" dismissals, and so forth.

The 1990s were the triumph of informality, since all formally existing institutions and laws fell apart or split in the face of the new conditions of life that they could no longer constrain or sustain in any way. The only rule was to survive, to cope, or to make it work, by any means necessary. Informal practices at the workplace embraced all aspects of the labor regime.[27] Payments varied according to the situation, as well as interpersonal relations. There were widespread wage arrears, nonpayment, or unofficial payments (so-called envelope wages). The amount and mode of calculation of wages were unclear and flexible, as the employers had the ability to increase or decrease wages by modifying the amount of workers' monthly bonus, which often constituted a large part of their wages. Hiring and firing were discretionary and depended on informal arrangements. Although legislation was and remains rather stringent concerning workers' dismissals, it was (and continues not to be) not a problem to get rid of anyone—the only condition was to obtain the formal agreement of the worker himself or herself. The labor organization was chaotic and changing, because of the deterioration of equipment, irregular provision of raw materials and tools, incoherence of the production policy, and arbitrary in human resources management. The tasks workers had to fulfill might change daily and went far beyond their formal labor requirements. Compulsory overtime was widespread. Workstations and tasks were often distributed according to interpersonal relationships between the worker and the supervisor. Rights and obligations at work changed according to individuals' interpretation of them—from relaxation of discipline (a supervisor might look the other way regarding small pilferages or smoking or drinking at the workplace in exchange for some services or because of a particular worker's indispensableness) to the strengthening of discipline, in case of interpersonal hostility or disloyalty. Interpersonal relationships also played a major role in the informalization of work. It could take the form of informal arrangements or bargaining, informal networks of coping inside and outside the enterprise, patron-client relations, or parallel business networks within the enterprise. The work schedule could be ultra-flexible—from absenteeism, tardiness, or leaving early to unpaid overtime or compulsory shortening of the workweek with wage cuts or even forced furloughs.

Sometimes these practices could provide self-confidence and reasons to be proud of oneself. Sometimes they attenuated social insecurity by giving workers ways of coping with material difficulties. In most cases, however, the personal and social cost of these practices was quite high. Negative consequences on the character and solidity of relationships included the uncertainty of what the next day would bring and the impossibility of long-term commitments, the implosion of the workers' collective, the lack of trust and solidarity, the withdrawal into oneself, and the impossibility to rely on anything but one's own ability, cleverness, and inventiveness. Informality as an everyday life experience meant destabilization and devaluation of labor.

A trend toward more formalization unfolded during the 2000s thanks to the economic and social improvements, but informal practices never disappeared, and they made a massive comeback with the 2014 crisis. However, changes have happened in the ways workers experience informality and precariousness. Instead of suffering or bending, some of them have begun to deal with precariousness and informality in other ways. Although it may look like resilience or the process of never-ending individual adaptation to hardships, it is rather a striving to get some satisfaction or enjoyment from life. Striving to make one's life livable and even comfortable instead of binding oneself to the neoliberal demands of individual adaptation or market achievement. This can be grasped as a process of "inhabiting"—what Morris, studying working-class people in a Russian monotown, calls "the striving for mundane comfort and ordinariness."[28] *Inhabiting* means living one's life despite insecurity and uncertainty; it means finding it normal, ordinary, even good. *Inhabiting* is "making habitable the inhospitable and insecure space of lived experience."[29] This is one of the new trends countering the dynamics of desubjectivation prevailing in the 1990s, since inhabiting one's everyday life, including its precarious characters, provides some grounds for gaining self-confidence and opening to others and the larger world.

Informality Pervaded by Power Relations and Formal Control

The importance of informal networks (reflected by the Russian term *blat*) has been pointed out by many students of the Russian transition.[30] Informal networks are the relatives, friends, and acquaintances one turns to (instead of formal institutions) in order to get help, borrow money, find a job, and so forth. However, informal networks have changed since the 1990s; they now form a more symbiotic relation with formal institutions and rules. Most people continue to rely to a significant degree on informal practices and relationships in everyday life, while dealing also with the state institutions and private agents.[31] The strengthening of the state and market capitalism has led to a new imbalance between informal and formal relationships in favor of the latter. Horizontal relations based on kinship or friendship have weakened, to the advantage of hierarchical power relations. In other words, informal networks have been perverted by formal power relations and social inequality. It has become more difficult for poor or subordinate people to rely on informal help from relatives or friends.[32] Because of the strengthening of the market logic and the orientation toward profits, unpaid social care and simply helping others tends to lose any attraction for people who must focus on building a successful career or who are struggling to comply with new and constraining formal requirements in their jobs (for example, teachers or health care personal). Russian gender studies gives some empirical evidence of marketization's destructive influence on social care and social or kinship relationships.[33]

Since the 2000s, a new process of formalization has developed that has not led to the disappearance of the informality but is aimed at controlling it. The process of formalization has taken place because of four circumstances: the pressure of international financial institutions for new reforms, Putin's stated policy of reestablishing the "rule of law," the policy of increasing state control, and the need to sustain predatory capitalism. Pressures toward formalization have strengthened since Russia entered a new economic crisis in 2014, aiming at redirecting money flows toward the state budget and economic and political elites. In a wide range of sectors (such as labor, taxes, housing, and the social sphere), legislation, codes, and regulations have been modified in order to better fit the reality of informality and to control the use people from below could make of it. Informal practices and rules are still part of the labor experience, because they are often necessary in order to fulfill formal requirements and bureaucratic control procedures. However, they have become more risky. If needed (in cases of disloyalty, budget cuts, changes in leadership, political or administrative pressures), the set of formal rules and regulations can be implemented, and those workers who have resorted to informal practices can be punished. Informality has become a more precarious line of behavior, at least for the subordinates. Instead of being one of the means accessible to them for coping with precariousness, informality became one of the means available to the dominants for controlling, bending, and punishing, thus accentuating precarization. The formal order is indeed becoming so constraining that it is hard to comply with its requirements without informal arrangements, but that makes it easy to fall into the trap of the formal control. Thus, the oppressive side of informality becomes more graspable.

Gaining the Sense of Exploitation

An important point to add about informality is that it implies some kind of work—unstable, precarious, or flexible—but still work. Most of the practices mentioned above include physical, social, emotional, or cognitive work. This means a life invaded by work that is not recognized as such and thus not paid, and work that is performed without any labor or social guarantees. Moreover, this work is often not recognized and not experienced as such even by the performers. They therefore engage in a kind of self-exploitation and cannot demand any formal recognition or retribution for that work.

However, this is changing. Surveys confirm a growing sense of social cleavage and inequality,[34] findings also made in our ongoing research on everyday nationalism in Russia.[35] In-depth interviews with people about their everyday lives show a high proportion of them blaming the rising social inequality. One of the most widespread views from below on the Kremlin nationalist project is social critical. The critique is addressed to the patriotic state propaganda and to the unpatriotic behavior of the economic and political elites. The critique is social in its contents, people denouncing the antisocial aspects of the policy, especially compared with the official discourse of government concern for the people. In interviews, many people address claims on the state for welfare protection. They demand recognition for those who really work for the good of the country, and they blame the theft of the state by oligarchic elites who have stolen the wealth of the nation and continue to steal money from the people through taxes, low wages, and the rising cost of public services and utilities. Below are some typical quotations to provide some empirical evidence.

A pensioner, male, St. Petersburg, May 2016: "I cannot figure out how is it possible that people live so poor in such a rich country."

A cook, female, St. Petersburg, April 2017: "What kind of patriotism is it to force people to work for peanuts?"

A young high-skilled blue-collar worker, St. Petersburg, Jan. 2017: "I love my job—I really enjoy it. And I want to earn money from it. However, it turns out to be without any value. Human labor is not valuated anymore. . . . Those fat assholes—sorry—who sit in their chairs in the Duma don't do anything and earn half a million, [and they] are considered far more useful. . . . And what about the pensioners? They have worked all their lives for the good of the country! And they still have to work in order to survive, instead of traveling and enjoying life, like foreign pensioners. It's a shame! . . . And the regions, all these little towns where people live without jobs and money. Why did all factories close?"

A businesswoman, Astrakhan, June 2016: "What is the Crimea for? I don't need it! Increase wages and give our children good education! No! They don't give us anything, only take everything from us!"

A blue-collar worker repairing the roof of an apartment building, Astrakhan, June 2016: "Nothing will never change in Russia in our lives. What can change? Everything has been seized. It's business; it is profitable for them—do you understand?—it's profitable to take everything from the workers, to pay them so little. . . . They say, 'love the motherland and be hungry.'"

A collective interview in a courtyard in Astrakhan, June 2016 (all working-class women between the ages of thirty and sixty).

—"[Putin] lifts the country up? Not our country, maybe Syria or Crimea."

—"You know, I don't think he lifts our country up, nor Crimea and Syria."

—"Yes, he lifts up the well-offs."

—"All the money is offshore. . . . Nothing remains in Russia."

—"Yes, he works for the rich."

—"Banks also do well—our welfare funds go to the banks."

—"What did Putin do for the pensioners? What? Nothing! Nothing! Only empty words."

—"They live very well, and we struggle to survive."

From the analysis of recent data on everyday life experience, I draw the conclusion that a growing sense of exploitation is developing, through which people raise the social question, demanding social protection and decent wages for working people who work for the welfare of the nation far more than the exploiting oligarchic elites controlling the government. A clear social cleavage appears in conversations that separates those who work in earnest for the good of the country, who do something useful or productive (or have done, if speaking of pensioners), and those who only talk or live at the expense of the genuine workers.

CONCLUSION

Striking social changes are unfolding now in Russia, in a direction opposite to the atomization, alienation, and desubjectivation dynamics that developed in the 1990s among people impoverished and precaritized by the liberal capitalist restructuring. Thirty years after the breakdown of the communist regime, a social sense of exploitation is emerging through which the social question is being raised. This means that the social question is not so much claims on the state for social care as it is the social critique of the state belonging to the oligarchs and of the political and economic elites exploiting working people.

This trend is especially widespread among the lower classes, although it's not restricted to them. The awakening of a sense of exploitation is linked to the stabilization of life experience many people experienced in the 2000s, as well as to the process of inhabiting one's social and material environment that gives some of them rootedness in their quotidian life experience and allows them to grasp the rising social inequality and exploitation. This process is fueled by the feelings of outrage that arise from the contradiction between the patriotic state propaganda and their everyday life experience. The main issue at stake is the assertion of the commonwealth, which has to belong to those who deserve it by their work or their real acts for the good of the country. This is a social critical version of nationalism. The problem is that this standpoint does not lead to mobilization, except maybe through the Navalny anti-corruption campaign. In most cases, social criticism and the sense of exploitation are accompanied by a strong sense of powerlessness: people do not have any confidence in their ability to change things and to force the economic and political elites to stop exploiting people.

In the end, I would interpret the changes occurring now in Russian society as a revival of a certain class-based perception of social inequality relying on an unexpressed, and maybe unconscious, Marxist frame for grasping the social reality around them. I am encouraged to make such an assertion by my empirical findings and by recent ethnographic studies that also stress "vernacular Marxism"[36] as a strong framework for the understanding of everyday Russian world. Maybe it is time for scientists to come back to Marxism as a theory useful for grasping the deep structural constraining process of social changes, as well as the way people, more or less consciously or actively, arrange with them.

NOTES

1. Another version of this paper was already published: K. Clément, "Social mobilizations and the question of social justice in contemporary Russia." Globalizations (Special Issue ed. by A. Gunvald Nilsen and K.Von Hold, "Rising Powers—People Rising: Neoliberalization And Its Discontents In The BRICS Countries") (2018). 1–15.

2. On labor relations, see Karine Clément, *Les ouvriers russes dans la tourmente du marché* (Paris: Syllepse, 1999); Karine Clément (K. Kleman), "Formal'nye i neformal'nye pravila: kakov optimum?" [Formal and informal rules: what balance?], in *Stanovlenie trudovyh otnošenij v postsovetskoj Rossii*, ed. Vladimir Yadov, Joan De Bardeleben, and Svetlana Klimova, 135–92 (Moscow: Akademičeskij Proekt, 2004); Karine Clément (Kleman), "Fleksibil'nost' po-rossijski': očerk o novyh formah truda i

podčineniâ v sfere uslug" [Russian flexibility: essay on new forms of labor and submission in the sphere of services], *in Sociologičeskij Žurnal* 4 (2007).

3. On social movements, see Karine Clément, "Unlikely Mobilisations: How Ordinary Russian People Become Involved in Collective Action," *European Journal of Cultural and Political Sociology* 2 (2015); Karine Clément, Andrey Demidov, and Olga Myriasova, *Ot obyvatelej k aktivistam: zaroždaûŝiesâ social'nyê dviženiâ v nynešnej Rossii* [From ordinary people to activists: Emerging social movements in contemporary Russia] (Moscow: Tri kvadrata, 2010).

4. "Everyday Nationalism," research under the author's supervision. Part of the project "Living Together: Issues of Diversity and Unity in the Modern Russia; Historical Legacy, Modern State and Society" (2016–2017), supported by the grant of the Foundation for Support of Liberal Education.

5. Ben Judah, *Fragile Empire: How Russia fell In and Out of Love with Vladimir Putin* (New Haven, CT: Yale University Press, 2013), 13.

6. The unemployment rate (by ILO definition) has never been very high in Russia (it was only 3.7 percent of the active population in 1996, rose to 13 percent in 1999, and then decreased slowly). The unemployment rate was 5.8 percent at the beginning of 2016.

7. Sarah Ashwin and Tatyana Lytkina, "Men in Crisis in Russia: The Role of Domestic Marginalization," *Gender and Society* 18, no. 2 (2004): 189–206.

8. Michael Burawoy, "Ethnographic Fallacies: Reflections on Labour Studies in the Era of Market Fundamentalism," *Work, Employment and Society* 27 (2013): 532.

9. Anders Åslund and Andrew Kuchins, *The Russia Balance Sheet* (Washington, DC: Peterson Institute for International Economics, 2009).

10. For more on this, see Karine Clément, "Civic Mobilization in Russia: Protest and Daily Life," *Books and Ideas* (2013). www.booksandideas.net/Civic-Mobilization-in-Russia.html.

11. Sarah Ashwin and Simon Clarke, *Russian Trade Unions and Industrial Relations in Transition* (New York: Palgrave Macmillan, 2003); Graeme Robertson, *The Politics of Protest in Hybrid Regimes: Managing Dissent in Post-Communist Russia* (Cambridge: Cambridge University Press, 2010).

12. Lev Gudkov, "Social'nyj kapital i ideologičeskie orientacii" [Social capital and ideological orientation], *Pro et Contra* 16 (2012); Alexandre Bikbov, "The Methodology of Studying 'Spontaneous' Street Activism (Russian Protest and Street Camps, December 2011–July 2012)," *Laboratorium* 2 (2012).

13. From the "democratic" newspaper *Segonya, March* 3, 1997; caption under a picture of an aggressive toothless babushka in a protest demonstration.

14. Television channel ORT, Vremya, April 8, 1998, on Voronezh aircraft plant's workers who suffered from administrative reduction of their work week and received only two-thirds of their already miserable salary.

15. Elena Danilova, "Neoliberal Hegemony and Narratives of 'Losers' and 'Winners' in Post-Socialist Transformations," *Journal of Narrative Theory* 44 (2014).

16. Julie Hemment, "Soviet-Style Neoliberalism? Nashi, Youth Voluntarism, and the Restructuring of Social Welfare in Russia," *Problems of Post-Communism* 56 (2009).

17. Quotations from Putin's speech at the rally held on February 23, 2012 at Luzhniki in Moscow against the "For honest elections" movement

18. Gudkov, "Social'nyj capital."

19. The Laboratory of Public Sociology can be found at www.facebook.com/PublicSociologyLaboratory.

20. Richard Sennet, *The Corrosion of Character: The Personal Consequences of Work in the New Capitalism* (New York: W. W. Norton, 1998); Luc Boltanski and Eve Chiapello, *Le nouvel esprit du capitalisme* (Paris: Gallimard, 1999); Guy Standing, *The Precariat: The New Dangerous Class* (London: Bloomsbury Academic, 2011); Jan Breman and Marcel van der Linden, "Informalizing the Economy: The Return of the Social Question at a Global Level," *Development and Change* 45 (2014).

21. Vladimir Gimpelson and Rostislav Kapeliushnikov, *Between Light and Shadow: Informality in the Russian Labour Market* (Bonn: Institute for the Study of Labor, 2014), https://ssrn.com/abstract=2462711.

22. Elena Vinogradova, Irina Kozina, and Linda Cook, "Labor Relations in Russia: Moving to a 'Market Social Contract?'" *Problems of Post-Communism* 62 (2015): 193–203.

23. Jeremy Morris and Abel Polese, *The Informal Post-Socialist Economy: Embedded Practices and Livelihoods* (London: Routledge, 2014); Alena V. Ledeneva, *Can Russia Modernize? Sistema, Power Networks and Informal Governance* (Cambridge: Cambridge University Press, 2013).

24. Research on Everyday Nationalism (2016–2017) under the author's supervision.

25. Clément, *Les ouvriers russes dans la tourmente du marché.*

26. Sarah Ashwin, "Endless Patience: Explaining Soviet and Post-Soviet Social Stability," *Communist and Post-Communist Studies* 31 (1998).

27. Clément, "Formal'nye i neformal'nye pravila: kakov optimum?"

28. Jeremy Morris, *Everyday Post-Socialism: Working-Class Communities in the Russian Margins* (New York: Palgrave Macmillan, 2016), 8.

29. Ibid., 236.

30. Alena V. Ledeneva, *Russia's Economy of Favours: Blat, Networking and Informal Exchange* (Cambridge: Cambridge University Press, 1998); Richard Rose, "Uses of Social Capital in Russia: Modern, Pre-Modern, and Anti-Modern," *Post-Soviet Affairs* 16 (2000): 33–57; Snejina Michailova and Verner Worm, "Personal Networking in Russia and China: Blat and Guanxi," *European Management Journal* 21 (2003).

31. Morris and Polese, *The Informal Post-Socialist Economy.*

32. ISRAN, *Bednost' i neravenstva,* 48.

33. Svetlana Yaroshenko, "'Ženskaâ rabota' i ličnoe blagopolučie: tehnologii isklûčeniâ v post-sovetskoj Rossii" ["'Women's work' and personal well-being: technology of exclusion in post-Soviet Russia], *Èkonomičeskaâ sociologiâ* 14 (2013).

34. Levada Centre, *Points of Disagreement in the Society* [Press release in Russian] (2016); Svetlana Mareeva and Natalya Tikhonova, "Public Perceptions of Poverty and Social Inequality in Russia" [in Russian]. IS RAN (Institute of Sociology of the Russian Academy of Sciences), *Mir Rossii* 25, no. 2 (2016): 37–67.

35. The fieldwork consists of twelve observations of everyday interactions and 220 in-depth interviews on their everyday life experience with people from six regions with different social and professional profiles.

36. Anna Kruglova, "Social Theory and Everyday Marxists: Russian Perspectives on Epistemology and Ethics," *Comparative Studies in Society and History* 59, no. 4 (2017).

Postscript

The Social Question in Its Global Incarnation

Jan Breman, Kevan Harris, Ching Kwan Lee, and Marcel van der Linden

The social question emerged during the first decades of the nineteenth-century in Europe, when the rise of capitalism led to low wages, long hours, miserable housing, unemployment, diseases, and social insecurity for the working classes. Trade union–led struggles and the well-understood self-interest of elites resulted in a comprehensive body of labor rights that gradually led to more inclusive and generous public support, culminating in the welfare state. Still, the social question never lost its initial meaning of aiming at the emancipation of the working class. The case studies collected in this volume bear witness to the diversity of the nature and handling of the social question in different eras and different regions of the world, due, first, to the variety in historical trajectories these regions passed through; second, to the plurality in the character of the social forces and their dynamics; and third, to the differences in the shaping of politics and policies that either supported or ignored welfarism within the national context. Rather than highlighting the heterogeneity found across the first, second, and third worlds—terms that anyway have rapidly lost their relevance—we have in our introductory chapter focused on the commonality that exists in the way the social question is mutedly raised and why it remains in limbo in the era of globalized capitalism.

For a number of decades, especially after World War II, it seemed as if the social question had more or less been solved in the privileged part of the world. Advanced capitalist and so-called socialist countries apparently had defeated (or at least marginalized) insecurity and unemployment. Public housing, health care, and education facilitated upward mobility and were important markers of a trend toward more equity and equality. But this proved to have been a temporary and geographically localized success. With the globalized switch to the credo of neoliberalism in the last quarter of the twentieth century, a turnabout that coincided with the dissolution of alternatives to capitalism, the social question made a comeback with a vengeance. This has also happened in first world countries where universalized welfare policies were, for a couple of decades, successfully implemented. In these better-off parts of the planet, the state has retreated from securing welfare and protection against adversity to all who can claim citizenship rights. As discussed in the introductory chapter, the large majority of humankind remained deprived of public benefits aimed at the economically inactive (because of old age or disability) and least so in case of cyclical inactivity (because of unemployment or underemployment among able-bodied workers). The emancipatory momentum failed to spread and slowly faded away where it existed. It meant that the already skewed balance between capital and labor further spiraled in subsequent decades.

The return of the social question worldwide is documented in our regional profiles as a labor issue first and foremost. The Global South, in particular, is experiencing a crisis of exceptional proportions. Voices from civil society are fully justified in saying, "Living wages and decent work for the world's workers are fundamental to ending today's inequality crisis. All over the world, the economy of the 1% is built on the backs of low paid workers, often women, who earn poverty wages and are denied basic rights."[1] But the social question is not an issue only for the South. It is returning to those parts of the world that appeared to have largely solved the problem. The tempestuous economic growth of the 1950s and 1960s created the impression that capitalism had at last become "social." The average income level grew with an unprecedented speed, and the level of consumption increased so fast that many social scientists began to believe that the old class society had elevated itself to a higher level and that work had lost its central place in social development. When the southern European dictatorships collapsed in the 1970s and eastern European "actually existing socialism" imploded around 1990, many believed that the victory of a liberal and social capitalism was final. The "end of history" seemed to have arrived.

Nothing could have been further from the truth. In the "old" capitalist countries, the average profit rates had—despite some interruptions—been declining since the 1960s. The shipbuilding and textile industries were the first to move many of their production sites to East Asia and other regions with low wages. The entry of the People's Republic of China, the former Soviet Union, and a liberalizing Republic of India caused a true "labor supply shock," doubling the total number of workers producing for the world market and thus globally reducing bargaining power of the working class. Full employment disappeared as the standard to adhere to. In line with the prescribed recipe from the directorate of neoliberal capitalism, the IMF and World Bank, the economy became increasingly informalized. The shift to labor-market flexibilization led to the phasing out of regular as well as regulated employment. In the Global South, the much-awaited transition from informality to formality had only haltingly taken place when the switch back to informality emerged as a firm trend—in the Global North as well as the South. After the 1980s the trajectory leading to development, which had postulated that the Rest would follow the West—began to turn in the opposite direction.

Both in the advanced capitalist and the former "socialist" countries, attainments such as the "standard employment relationship," high wages, and social security arrangements came increasingly under attack. Already since the 1980s "nonstandard employment relationships" had become more common. Contingent, precarious, and temporary jobs are becoming the norm. The outbreak of the global economic crisis since 2007 has accelerated this downward trend enormously. It is now for all of us to see that "social capitalism" was only a temporary interlude before unrestrained market capitalism. The insecurity and poverty that have always been with the large majority of the world's population are now becoming endemic in the Global North. The demolition of social capitalism confirms an insight in a long-term trend that the philosopher István Mészáros expressed as follows: "The objective reality of *different rates of exploitation*—both within a given country and in the world system of capital—is as unquestionable as are the objective differences in the *rates of profit* at any particular time. . . . All the same, the reality of the different rates of exploitation and profit does not alter the fundamental law itself: i.e. the *growing equalization of the differential rates of exploitation* as the *global trend* of development of world capital."[2] The fierce competition between capitals has a clear downward effect on the quality of life and work in significant parts of globalized capitalism.

Unemployment and underemployment have remained a massive challenge for the developing world. In the 1990s, economic historian Paul Bairoch estimated that in the Global South "total inactivity amounts to around 30 to 40 percent of the potentially active time."[3] In subsequent years, the situation is unlikely to have improved and may even have become worse. According to the *World Employment Social Outlook 2017*, vulnerable forms of employment are expected to remain above 42 percent of total employment, accounting for 1.4 billion people the world all over. In developing countries, the proportion of workers employed in vulnerable forms of labor rose to four out of five workers. Living on less than $3.10 per day in purchasing power terms, which is the ILO's yardstick for coping existence, nearly half of the laboring poor in South Asia and two-thirds of them in sub-Saharan Africa were stuck in moderate to extreme working poverty in 2016.[4] The countries of the South today differ from the advancing countries during the nineteenth century in two fundamental ways. In the nineteenth century, average unemployment rates were far lower in the cities of the currently developed countries. Ranging from merely 4 percent to 6 percent, it indicated the labor-intensive character of the urban-industrial transformation process at that time. And most importantly, the unemployment was cyclical, that is, essentially concentrated in the years of economic adversity, whereas in the Global South, unemployment is structural.

The crisis that has kept the world in its grip for the last decade has immensely intensified the struggle from above for lower wages and less social security. And since the attainments of the working classes have been based to a significant extent on the redistribution of income within the working classes, within and between countries, this also implies that huge sums of money are channeled away from the workers' total wage fund (of which deferred wages in pension funds are also a major part) and are transferred to capital. The reversal indicates the return of the social question also on the agenda of the rich countries. To carve out a niche through self-employment, self-provision, and self-representation is endorsed and hailed, but it is the socioeconomic policy of the last resort for a globalized workforce bereft of proper jobs and decent income. The multitudes that do not manage to find waged employment are not supposed to be out of work; they are listed as own-account workers, with the added warning that the state won't help people who can't help themselves. The predicament of the laboring poor in the catch-up economies is aggravated by the ongoing substitution of labor for capital, resulting in a rapidly growing reserve army unable to make a fair living. They fail to find steady engagement, are hired and fired in quick succession, and have no access to contributory social protection. Held captive in a regime of neoliberalism that has, over the years, acquired a punitive streak, their dire plight resembles the label attached to the erstwhile "non-deserving poor." As victims of exclusionary politics, they are blamed for the progressive disuse made of their labor power. The problem as stated is not absence of gainful work per se but adamant unwillingness to scratch around and source it.

In the light of the extremely uneven development in the world at large, it comes as no surprise that more and more people from the Global South try to escape and settle in the better-off zones of the world. Between 2000 and 2017 the number of international migrants living in the North increased from 82.4 million to 146 million, while this fraction of the population from elsewhere residing in high-income countries rose in the same period from 9.6 percent to 14 percent.[5] In September 2016, a summit of the United Nations discussed the worldwide issue of refugees and migrants. The report observed, "Member States noted that poverty, including the lack of access to health care, education, labour markets and essential services, were key drivers of voluntary migration. . . . The lack of economic opportunities for youth was identified as an important driver of migration."[6] The people who have become footloose beyond the borders of their country depart on what for many of them turns out to be a perilous journey. It is an ordeal difficult to survive, and of those that do, an unknown magnitude is detained somewhere along the route, sometimes traded as slaves to willing buyers. "Economic refugees" who somehow manage to climb the walls erected around the "safe havens," are often disallowed entry and sent back to where they "belong." The exclusion of alien intruders on the basis of their distinctive "otherness" is not restricted to the economically advanced quarters of the world but is not less ferociously practiced elsewhere. In our introductory chapter, we have commented on the wave of identity movements and parties sweeping through the political landscape that, though rightist in their appeal, are also joined by large segments of the working classes increasingly signaling their restiveness. The mainstream electorate wants to see citizenship restricted to those who are "our own," hitting out against all those who cannot claim Blut und Boden heritage. People of different religious or ethnic stock are disparaged and discriminated against, marginalized or even totally excluded from occupying economic and societal space. It is a racialized mindset that not only is manifest at the level of the nation-state but also, having become normalized in the age of imperialism, aims to set the civilizations of the Global North apart from those of the Global South. The sloping divide separates a forward and privileged segment of humanity from the disprivileged majority of the human species tainted with the stigma of backwardness.

The United Nations' Universal Declaration of Human Rights of 1948 asserts that social security is an inalienable human right. To implement this lofty declaration requires political will in combination with administrative aptitude, and today, both are missing at the global level. National states have lost much (though certainly not all) of their sovereignty, a loss of power that has not been compensated by supranational agencies. The ILO is the one organization vested with the mandate for a social compact; it has consistently failed to deliver what its conventions promise. The IMF agrees that fiscal policy can be a powerful instrument for redistribution but fails to act on it. As a major protagonist of neoliberalism, the World Bank should be held co-responsible for the obscene inequality in wealth and income that has materialized, but this taskmaster of corporate finance has been erroneously conferred by the United Nations with counseling on how to combat poverty. A supranational authority capable of halting and reversing the trend of ever more accumulation versus immiserization is clearly lacking. We live in a transitional period in which many challenges can no longer be dealt with by national authorities, and not yet (if ever) by supranational or world authorities. In the contemporary global world, there is no equivalent of the nation-state at the world level that could implement fiscal and welfare policies, anti-trust controls, and labor and environmental laws aimed at regulating markets and at correcting market failures. Nor is there a world independent judiciary that can control and sanction illegal behavior. Nor is there a democratic polity at the world level.

Unable to raise, let alone solve, the social question at the global level, the problem is referred back to where it started, within the perimeters of the nation-states. They can at least mitigate the severity of the global social problem by "good governance," which means limiting returns to shareholders; taxation to reduce extreme wealth; redistributing property and resources; restoring the public domain; and enhancing the bargaining power of people who lack representation, are prone to disenfranchisement, and are excluded from social provisioning. Critique of exclusionary policies seems to mainly address the state. In our opinion, rather than allow capital to remain shielded behind stare politics, it should be confronted head-on and held accountable for the well-being of both the laboring and the non-laboring poor in the world of today. The most likely consequence of what is in store may well be the collapse of what has become the hegemonic mode of production in today's world, as a result of its own internal contradictions. But the downfall of capitalism could be precipitated by the demise of political democracy. That eventuality is already signaled loud and clear, as can be illustrated also by the surrender of equality as a civilizational ideal. Our prognosis is inspired by the failure to reconcile the ever-widening gap in well-being with the dictum of social justice and universal franchise. A reversal of the steep inequality merely at state level is bound to remain a piecemeal endeavor, at best, with an enormous diversity in disparate parts of the world.

While there is a global trend toward growing precarity and insecurity, we should keep in mind that the differences between and within the North and the South are still enormous. According to the IMF, in 2016 the GDP per capita, in international dollars, was in the United States, 57,436; in Germany, 48,111; in Brazil, 15,242; in Nigeria, 5,942; and in Burundi, 814.[7] Naturally, international solidarity is extremely difficult under such conditions. The governments of the more privileged countries, with the support of majorities of their populations, try to defend their living standards and what is left of their systems of social protection by violently excluding migrants from poorer parts of the world. Labor movements are at a low ebb and trade-union density the world all over is probably less than 7 percent.[8] Collective bargaining for a better deal is considered counterproductive to higher dividends. The *World Employment Social Outlook 2017* reports that the ILO's social unrest index shows that with the current socioeconomic situation, discontent in recent years has heightened across almost all regions.[9] The misery and anger of the wretched of the earth cannot be wished away any longer. But will this looming threat persuade the powers that be to end the state of denial in which they want to keep the social question dormant?

NOTES

1. Diego Alejo Vázquez Pimentel, Iñigo Macías Aymar, and Max Lawson, *Reward Work, Not Wealth*, briefing paper (Oxford: Oxfam International, 2018), 8.

2. István Mészáros, *Beyond Capital: Towards a Theory of Transition* (New York: Monthly Review Press, 1995), 891.

3. Paul Bairoch, *Victoires et déboires: Histoire économique et sociale du monde du XVIe siècle à nos jours*, vol. 3 (Paris: Gallimard, 1997), 46–47.

4. International Labour Office, *World Employment Social Outlook—Trends 2017* (Geneva: International Labour Office, 2017).

5. Béla Hovy et al. *International Migration Report 2017* (New York: United Nations Department of Economic and Social Affairs/Population Division, 2017), 1–2. Note that economic motives seem to be

driving a majority of the migrants to the North, while the victims of forced displacement frequently stay in the South. According to the UN-DESA report quoted here, a majority of the world's international migrants live in high-income countries, while low- and middle-income countries host nearly twenty-two million, or 84 percent, of all refugees and asylum seekers.

6. Béla Hovy et al. *International Migration Report 2017*, 26.

7. All measured in Geary-Khamis international dollars.

8. International Trade Union Confederation, *Building Workers' Power: Congress Statement* (Berlin: ITUC, 2014), 8.

9. International Labour Office, *World Employment Social Outlook 2017*, 9.

INDEX

accumulation: dispossession and, 3, 20, 122; in Global North, 10; immiseration and, 248; in Latin America, 121; in Maoist China, 59, 61; neo-extractivism and, 135; subnational zones and, 80–81; in Western Europe, 32
Achcar, Gilbert, 194
Afghanistan, 200, 203
Africa: overview, 152–53, 164–65; church welfare institutions, 153; exclusion in, 1, 8, 153–56, 166n9; GDP in Nigeria and Burundi, 249; informal labor in, 160–63; labor movements in, 167n22, 167n31; migratory initiatives in, 166n15; mining sector, 161; SAPS and, 8–9; self-immolation, 66, 73; stabilization policy in, 156–60; tax havens in, 12; unemployed labor in, 167n16. *See also* South Africa
African Americans, 45, 49, 51–52, 52
African Labour Survey (ILO), 157, 158
African Survey (Hailey), 153–54
agrarian economy: ADB and, 12; agrarian/industrial transition, 2, 4–5, 10; agrarian radicalism, 44; Cambodia, 81; India, 99; Latin America, 117, 119; national sales tax and, 43; Turkey, 206n17
agricultural labor: in Cambodia, 81–82; in China, 59, 61, 76n46; manorial workers, 24
agriculture sector, 25, 42
Ali, Mehmed, 188, 190
alienation, 13, 240
All-China Federation of Trade Unions (ACFTU), 68
All India Congress Committee, 98
Ambedkar, B. R., 98, 111–12
Amendment 45 (Brazil), 138
American exceptionalism. *See* exceptionalism, American
American Federation of Labor and Congress of Industrial Organizations (AFL-CIO), 15
Americans for Prosperity, 53
Amin, Qasim, 188
ANC government, 180
Anderson, Perry, 135
Anti-Privatisation Forum, 180
antitrust policies, 45, 48
Antyodaya Anna scheme (India), 111
Apartheid, 174–76, 176tab10.1, 178, 181–82tab10.2, 183
apprenticeships, 24–25, 61
April Fifth Movement, 61
Arab Barometer Survey of 2011, 202
Arabian Peninsula, 13, 194, 197–98
Arab-Israeli wars, 200
Arab Spring, 201–4
ARAMCO, 198
Argentina, 117, 119, 123, 126, 127–28, 129
Argentinian Building Workers Union (Unión Obrera de la Construcción de la República Argentina) (UOCRA), 129
Arnold, Dennis, 12, 77–97
Article 331 of the Labor Tribunal, 139, 143, 144
ASEAN Economic Community, 90
Asia: agrarian resources in, 10; Asian Development Bank (ADB), 12, 89, 90, 92, 93, 94; Asian immigrant labor in South Africa, 173; East Asian production sites, 245; economies of, 37n31; exclusion in, 1;

South Asia, 115n14. *See also* China, People's Republic of; India; Mekong Asia special economic zones (SEZs); *specific countries*
al-Assad, Hafez, 194
asylum seekers, 249–50n5
austerity, 1, 135
Australia, 10, 32, 172
Austria, 31tab2.4, 31tab2.5, 32, 223
authoritarianism: overview, 69–70, 74; in China, 69–73; disempowerment, 71; dispossession, 70; indebtedness, 70–71; in India, 101; precariats' struggles for livelihood, 71–73; Trump's, 55
automotive sector, 137, 140, 143, 144, 147, 151n23

Bähre, Erik, 183
Bairoch, Paul, 28, 246
Bajap Political Party (BJP), 110, 114
Baltics, 216, 220
Banco Nacional de Desenvolvimento Econômico e Social (National Economic and Social Development Bank) (BNDES), 136
Bangladesh, 17, 18
Basic Income Grant (BIG), 14, 179–80, 183, 185
Batatu, Hanna, 194
Bavet, Cambodia, 83–84, 91–93
Bavet SEZ, 91–93
Bazler, Joseph, 127
Belgium, 31tab2.4, 31tab2.5, 32, 34
Benin, 165
Beveridge, William, 1
Bhatt, Ela, 114
BIMARU states, 112
Bismarck, Otto von, 58, 131, 193
BJP (Bajap Political Party), 110, 114
Block, Fred, 14, 40–57
Bolsa Familia poverty reduction program, 134, 209
Bonded Labour System (Abolition) Act of 1976, 101
Brazil: overview, 134–36, 149–50; courts in, 150n7; GDP, 249; informalization in, 147–49; job demographics in, 150n20; labor cost, 150n7; labor legislation, 137–38; land struggles in, 145–47; militant workers' movements in, 17; military coups, 123; My House My Life (Minha Casa Minha Vida) (MCMV) in, 151n38; neo-extractivism, 134–51; outsourcing, 138–44; Rio de Janeiro, 148, 149; subcontractor strikes, 136–37; tertiarization in, 144–45; tourism sector, 135; trade unionism, 16tab1.1, 127–29; Vaguismo in, 119; World Cup (Brazil), 135. *See also* CSB (Companhia Siderúrgica do Brasil) (Brazilian Steel Company)
Brazilian Center of Analysis and Planning, 121
Brazilian Steel Company (Companhia Siderúrgica do Brasil) (CSB). *See* CSB (Companhia Siderúrgica do Brasil) (Brazilian Steel Company)
Brazilian Workers Party (Partido Trabalhista Brasileir) (PTB), 137
Breman, Jan, 1–22, 14, 24, 98–115, 152, 208, 213, 244–50
Britain: Brexit, 1; collective bargaining, 32; Friendly Societies, 25; take-off of economy of, 37n31; TUC (Trade Union Confederation), 15, 21–22n21; union densities, 29; on wage fixing in Africa, 168n35
Buchowski, Michal, 213
Burawoy, Michael, 229
bureaucratization, 7, 8, 63
Burma, refugees from, 85–87, 93, 94

Cambodia case study: overview, 77–78, 81–82, 93–94; Bavet SEZ and, 91–93; GDP (gross domestic product), 78, 82; Mae Sot SEZ and, 91map5.2; migrants from, 87; minimum wage, 82fig5.1; selective hegemony in, 79–81; social security initiatives, 82–85, 95nn25–26
Cambodia National Rescue Party, 84
Cambodian People's Party (CPP), 81, 84
Campbell, S., 87
capital: decentralization of formation of, 25; ILO and, 18; informalization of, 11, 11–12; labor and, 109, 116, 122, 137–38, 245, 247; neo-extractivism, 134–51; outsourcing and, 138–40, 140–44; production and, 10; societal control and, 14; subcontractor strikes and, 136–37; tertiarization and, 144–45. *See also* Brazil
capitalism: overview, 244; casino capitalism, 14; commodity chains, 64; dissolution of alternatives to, 7, 245; divergent national varieties of, 209; downfall of, 249; in England, 35n6; globalized capitalism era, 244; ILO and, 18; in India, 110; market capitalism, 246; neoliberal capitalism, 245; occupy movements against, 1; rise of, 27–28; social capitalism, 246; socializing of, 245; social question and, 244; subsumption and, 120; uneven development of, 1, 247. *See also* dependent capitalism; global capitalism
Cardenismo, 119

Cardoso, F. H., 121, 138, 149
carteira de trabalho (working card), 147–48
Car Wash (Lava Jato) investigation, 134
Castel, Robert, 6, 21n7, 26, 121, 130
casual wage labor, 34, 35n4; in Brazil, 134, 138; commercialization and, 4; extraction of, 154–55; in precapitalist societies, 23–24
catch-up economies, 9, 14, 17–18, 19, 247
Central and Eastern Europe (CEE): overview, 208–9, 224; Bulgaria, 216, 220; class struggles without class in, 218–20; illiberal Visegrad Bloc in, 220–24; labor weakness in, 211–15; neoliberal consolidations in, 215–18; post-socialist liberalization, 9; re-industrialization of, 209; transitional recession in, 209–11
Central Unica dos Trabalhadores (Central Worker's Union) (CUT), 129
Central Worker's Union (Central Unica dos Trabalhadores) (CUT), 129
Chávez, Hugo, 119
chengguan (para-police force), 73
Chhouk Bandith, 84
child benefits, 6; in Africa, 159; in Brazil, 137; in Poland, 217; in South Africa, 181tab10.2
child labor, 26, 29, 30
Child Support Grant, 181tab10.2, 185
Chile, 117, 123, 127
China, People's Republic of: overview, 58–59, 73–74; *Communist Manifesto* (Marx) and, xiin2; construction workers, 65–66; economy of, 60–61, 63, 70–71, 72, 76n46, 137; Five-Year Plans (China), 69; guild traditions, 60; high-growth market reform, 62–69, 73; infrastructure investment, 65; iron rice bowl, 59; labor in, 7, 63, 66–67, 245; land use, 7, 76n46; multinational corporations, 74n17; precarity/precarious labor in, 59–62, 63–66, 74n17; propaganda, 61; revolutions in, 60, 61; service sector, 66; state regulation in, 7, 58; Tiananmen uprising of 1989, 63; union densities in, 16tab1.1
Chinese Communist Party, 60, 68
Chinese workers, 17, 59, 60, 61
Christian evangelicals, 45, 52
citizenship, 6, 37n37, 59, 245
class compromise, 5–6, 7–9, 11
la classe dangereuse, 2, 5, 25, 108, 109, 219
Clement, Carine, 9
Clément, Karine, 227–43
Clinton, Hillary, 51, 52–53
Clinton administration, 46
CLT (Labor Code), 137–38
Cock, Jacklyn, 183
Code de Travail for French Africa, 157, 158
coercion (violence), 80–81, 117
collective bargaining: bargaining power, 16, 245, 248; bias, 17; as counterproductive, 249; institutionalization of, 29, 30–32; in Latin America, 127; NGOs and, 72; in South Africa, 173, 177; in South Africa under Apartheid, 176tab10.1; systems of, 15; trade unionism and, 5; wage concessions, 46
collective consumption, 43, 43–44, 76n46
collective security claims, 58–59
colonialism, settler: overview, 170–72, 184–85; in Africa, 154; as civilizing mission, 7; cooperation and conflict: social protection beyond policy, 180–84, 181–82tab10.2; in Global South, 7; social question in the settler colony, 172–75; in South Africa, 170–75, 170–87
COMAU subcontractor, 143
Committee of Experts on the Application of Conventions and Recommendations, 164
commodification: commodity chains, 64; of land/labor, 3, 4, 5; social relations, 2; vocational education, 74n17
common labor, 14, 15
commons custom, 3, 6, 73
communist socialism, 18, 58. *See also* Russia; state socialism
Companhia Siderúrgica do Brasil (CSB) (Brazilian Steel Company), 135, 136, 139, 140–44, 148, 149
competition: in CEE, 217; effect of, 246; entrenchment and, 47–48; financial sector, 47; labor contracts and, 32; pharmaceutical sector, 47; restoration of, 43; social-security arrangements, 26–27
computerization, 10, 33
Congress of South African Trade Unions (COSATU), 178–79
Congress Party (India), 99–103, 106–7, 110–11
Constitutional Court, 223
construction sector: Brazil, 135, 136, 148; China, 65–66
consumption, 43; cheap imports, 17–18; individual consumption, 43; levels increase, 245
contingent labor, 41, 46, 246
contract manufacturing, 60, 63–64
Cook, Linda, 234
Cook, Maria, 127
Cooper, Fred, 156, 163

corporatism compact, in MENA region, 193–201
COSATU (Congress of South African Trade Unions), 178–78
cottage industries, 25
countermovements: in CEE, 221; global social compact architects, 18–20; in Latin America, 116, 126–29; militant wage protests, 78; mobility, 78; social protections and, 78; threats of, 81; trade unionism, 15–18, 16tab1.1
cradle to grave care, 6, 59
Crouch, Colin, 57n30
CSB (Companhia Siderúrgica do Brasil) (Brazilian Steel Company), 135, 136, 139, 140–44, 148, 149, 151n26
CUT (Central Worker's Union) (Central Unica dos Trabalhadores), 129
Czechoslovakia, 32
Czech Republic, 209, 210, 216, 221

Darwinism: neoliberal, 218, 219, 220; social, 108, 213, 218
Davies, D. I., 21–22n21
debt burden: Argentina, 128; Austria, 223; Brazil, 135; China, 70–71; Global South, 8; India, 101, 102; Latin America, 124; MENA region, 191; social debt, 128; South Africa, 183–84; student loans, 54; US, 47, 50–51, 54
De Castro Gomes, Angela, 137
decolonization, 8, 156–60, 192
de-democratization, 47, 48, 57n30
deindustrialization, 25, 145–47
Deng Xiaoping, 63
Denmark, 29, 31tab2.4, 31tab2.5
dependent capitalism: industrialization and, 138; labor under, 116–17, 129–31; marginality, 120–23; nationalism and, 117–20; neoliberalism and, 123–26; populism and, 123; post-liberalism and, 126–29
deregulation: EU and US, 137; in Latin America, 125, 135, 138; in Russia, 230
Desmond, Matthew, 51
De Soto, Hernando, 125
destitution, 2, 13, 111, 172
desubjectivation, 235–36, 238–39, 240
differential reductionism, 59
Disability Grant, 181tab10.2
disabled, 4, 181tab10.2, 245
disempowerment, 71, 221
disenfranchisement, 2, 115n14, 221, 249
displacements, 13, 249–50n5
dispossession: accumulation and, 20; in Asia, 10, 70, 76n46; in CEE, 221; in Europe, 3, 10; immiseration from, 2; in India, 112, 113; neo-extractivism and, 135; redistribution and, 3
Donzelot, Jacques, 26
Druck, Graça, 124
dualism (structural heterogeneity), 120
Ducpetiaux, Edouard, 25
Dzurinda, Mikuláš, 217

Eastern Europe. *See* Central and Eastern Europe (CEE)
Eckert, Andreas, 8–9, 152–69
ECLA (Economic Commission for Latin America), 119, 124, 128
Economic Commission for Latin America (ECLA), 119, 124, 128
economics: bottom-up push, 95n25; cash economy, 24; economic dualism, 19; economic dynamism, 48, 56n20; family economy in China, 76n46; financialization of economy, 45, 135; free-market economics, 12, 45; gig economy, 41, 70–71, 72; market economy, 43, 44; planned-economy period (China), 59; recessions, 163, 209–11; rentier economy, 145–46, 149; trickle-down economics, 2, 9, 19, 20; village-based economies, 7
Edin, Kathryn J., 51
education: education access, 1; higher education, 46; human development indicators, 196tab11.1; in India, 107, 110; racialized inequality, 176tab10.1; upward mobility and, 244; in US, 42, 44, 50–51; vocational schools in China, 74n17. *See also* students
Edwards, Sebastian, 123, 126
Egypt: administration of, 188; Arab uprisings in, 202–3; education in Nasser period, 195; food subsidies budget, 206n25; indirect British rule, 191–82; landless peasants, 194; *lumpen intelligentsia*, 202–3; Ottoman bureaucracy in, 190; Suez Canal, 191; U.S. military and development aid to, 199
elderly, 4, 181–82tab10.2, 245
emancipatory movement, 2, 137, 245
emigration, 13, 28–29, 28tab2.2, 37n28, 81
Employer Federation, 137
employment: in Brazil, 151n26; employment formalization, 19; full employment standard, 29, 33, 58, 245; in Global South, 246; hire-and-fire, 11, 34; liability for, 24; nonstandard, 246; permanent employment, 59–62; standard contracts, 6
empowerment, 110, 137, 163

enrichment, 47, 48
entitlement, 110
entrenchment, 47–48
entrepreneurship, 37n36, 70–71, 138, 163
environmental regulations, 14, 146, 147, 151n26
equality, 18, 205n5, 249
Esping-Andersen, Gosta, 152
Estado Novo, 137
EU (European Union). *See* European Union (EU)
Europe: dictatorships collapse in, 245; dispossession in, 3, 10; European migrants, 10; great transformation in, 3–4; implosion of state socialism in, 245; Red Cross, 153; Second World, 7
European Bank of Reconstruction and Development, 217
European Union (EU): Brexit, 1; integration of, 33; market access to, 92; poverty/social exclusion in, 35; steel industry, 137; Visegrad countries and, 216, 217, 219, 221, 224
Everything but Arms duty-/quota-free arrangement, 92
exceptionalism, American: overview, 40–42, 54–56, 56n2; consequences of conservative policies, 44, 47–49, 54; divergences after the New Deal, 43–44; divergent responses to, 51–54; internal factors ending, 41–42; polarization and, 49–51; reality of, 42–44; right-wing policies and, 44–47
exclusion: in China, 59, 71; critique of policies of, 249; in EU, 35, 121; in India, 14, 110–12, 115n14; non-deserving poor and, 247; in socialist welfare system, 7
executive compensation, 45, 47
Expanded Public Works Programme (EPWP), 182, 182tab.10.2
exploitation: in Brazil, 135; in Cambodia, 83–85; in catch-up economies, 17–18; commodification and, 5; different rates of, 246; in Global South, 122; lack of protections against, 13; in Latin America, 123; market-based, 36n15, 37n15; in Russia, 227–43

Fabian, Johannes, 153
Fakier, Khayaat, 183
family: dissolution of, 50; family allowances, 159, 168n35; family economy in Africa, 161; family economy in China, 76n46; marriage, 76n46; personal dependency relationships, 117; strains on, 12–13; in Western Europe, 25
Fan Lulu, 64
Federal Farm Loan Act of 1916, 43
Federation of Independent Trade Unions of Russia (FNPR), 231
feinha (little ugly), 140, 150n17
Ferguson, James, 88
Ferguson, Thomas, 56n20
Fidesz party, 223
financial sector: banking, 12, 45; credit availability, 43; expansion of, 46; government rescue, 47; mortgages, 43, 50, 135; small-cash transfers, 14
Finland, 28–29, 31tab2.4, 31tab2.5
flexibilization, of labor market, 18, 33–34, 66, 123–24, 136, 245
Forced Labor Convention of the International Labor Organization of 1930, 155
Fordism, 122
foreign direct investment (FDI), 90, 209
"For Fair Elections" movement, 232
"For honest elections" movement, 242n17
formal employment, 11, 116; in Africa, 155, 162–63; in Brazil, 138, 147–48; in Cambodia, 82; in Mekong Asia, 80
formal-informal divide, 8
France: collective bargaining, 32; French Revolution, 23; health insurance coverage, 31tab2.4; July Revolution in 1830 (France), 25; *mutualités*, 25; pension insurance coverage, 31tab2.5; take-off of economy of, 37n31; union densities in, 16tab1.1
franchising, 35
Franco, Tania, 124
Freeman, Richard, 17
French, John, 137
French West Africa, 155–59
Friedman, Eli, 68
Friedman, Milton, 45
Friendly Societies, 25
"From the Marginality of the 1960s to the 'New Poverty" of Today" symposium of 2004, 122
Fujita, K., 85

Gandhi, Indira, 101
Gandhi, Mahatma, 100, 112
Gandhian movement, 98–99, 102
Garibi Hatao (Get Rid of Poverty) slogan, 101
Garretón, Manuel Antonio, 118
GDP (gross domestic product), 65, 249; Brazil, 134; Cambodia, 77; in CEE, 209, 216; India, 101, 110; in MENA region, 200; Thailand, 77
Gehlen, Arnold, 164
Gelvin, James, 194

General Maintenance Unit (GMC), 143, 150n19
Germany: economy of, 3–4, 37n31; GDP, 249; *Hilfskassen auf Gegenseitigkeit*, 25; insurance coverage, 31tab2.4, 31tab2.5; labor in, 25, 34; social-security arrangements, 27–28; supply chains, 209; unions in, 16tab1.1, 32
ghost factories/workshops, 63–65, 140
Gimpelson, Vladimir, 234
Gini index, 189, 195, 205n5
global capitalism: overview, 9; in China, 58; divergent trajectories of, 10–11; effects of competition of, 246; informalization of, 11–12; land flight effects pm, 13–15; strains on family and reciprocity, 12–13; wealth/poverty divide and, 20
global economic crisis of 2007, 35, 41, 246, 247
globalization process, 18–20, 20, 116
Global North: class compromise, 5–6; colonial rule by, 7; development in, 1; differences within, 249; divergent from Global South, 9–15, 244, 249; divergent trajectories between Global South and, 10–11; economic informality, 246; insecurity in, 246; *la classe dangereuse*, 2, 5, 25, 108, 109, 219; neoliberal strategies in, 9; poverty in, 246; precarity debate, 122; sloping divide from Global South, 248
global public governance, lack of, 12, 248
Global South: class compromise, 7–9; debt crisis in, 8; decolonization of, 8; differences within, 249; divergent from Global North, 9–15, 10–11, 244, 249; economic informality, 246; economic refugees, 10, 249–50n5; inactivity in, 246; inequality crisis in, 245; informalized labor of, 18; labor movements and, 29; migration from, 247, 249–50n5; neoliberal strategies in, 9; sloping divide from Global North, 248; structural unemployment, 246; structural unemployment in, 247
Goods and Services Tax (India), 111
Government Work Report (China), 71
Gramsci, Antonio, 32, 117, 118
Great Depression, 20, 118, 155
Great Leap famine, 59
Great Leap Forward, 61
Greece, 23–24, 32, 188, 209–10, 216
Growth Acceleration Programs (Programa de Aceleração do Crescimento) (PACs), 136–37
Guinea, 164
Gyurcsáni, Ferenc, 222

Hacker, Jacob, 49
Hailey, William Malcolm, 1st Baron Hailey, 153–54
harmonization, 33, 71
Harris, Kevan, 1–22, 8, 188–207, 244–50
Hart, Gilian, 79
Harvey, David, 149
health care: access to, 87; in Brazil, 137, 143; family economy in China and, 76n46; in German East Africa, 154; health insurance coverage, 6, 31tab2.4, 31tab2.5, 43–44, 95n26; higher expenditures for, 33; in India, 110; poverty and costs of, 50; for self-employed, 30; social question and, 1; upward mobility and, 244
Heng Sour, 84, 92
Hezbollah, 203
Hilfskassen auf Gegenseitigkeit, 25
Hirschman, Albert, 29
Hitler, Adolf, 215
Hobsbawm, Eric, 190
Hochschild, Arlie, 53
Hodgson, Marshall, 189
Hoffman, Kelly, 123–24
Holy Ghost Fathers, 153
homo economicus, 19
housing: in Brazil, 136, 137, 151n38; cooperative housing societies, 7; family economy in China and, 76n46; in India, 110; mortgage debt, 50; social question and, 1; US costs of, 50
Huang Yan, 64
Hu Jingtao, 71
hukuo (household registration) system, 59, 62
human development indicators, 196fig11.1
Hundred Flowers Campaign, 60, 61
Hungarian National Bank, 223
Hungarian revolt, 61
Hungarian Right, 219
Hungary, 209, 214, 216, 217, 218, 220, 221, 222, 223
Hun Sen, 84

Ianni, Octavio, 119
Igoty (in-kind benefits), 230
Iliffe, John, 155, 158, 172
illiberalism, 221; overview, 208–9; class struggles and, 218–20; neoliberalism and, 215–18; polarizaition and, 211–15; transitional recession and, 209–11; Visegrad bloc and, 220–24
ILO (International Labour Organization). *See* International Labour Organization (ILO)
IMF (International Monetary Fund). *See* International Monetary Fund (IMF)
immigrants/immigration: Asian immigrant

labor, 173; modern slavery in Africa and, 164; at risk of poverty/social exclusion, 35; Tea Party activists and, 53; Trump administration and, 55
immiseration, 1, 248, 249; acceleration of, 2; behavioral economics and, 19; political effects of, 1
import substitution industrialization (ISI) model, 118, 119, 122, 128
inclusion, 14, 80, 106–8, 244
income inequality, 19, 44–45, 47, 54, 245, 248
indebtedness. *See* debt burden
India: Anglo-Persian treat of 1812, 205n10; climate of defiance in, 112–14; debt bondage in, 101, 102; development improvements, 100–104; exclusion in, 14, 110–12; Food Security Act (India), 111; GDP (gross domestic product), 101; Hinduist neoliberalism, 110, 115n14; inclusion in, 14, 106–8; informality remedy, 104–6; informal sector, 103–4; labor in, 17, 102–3, 245; landless class in, 98–102, 106; militant workers' movements in, 17; post-colonial development, 98–100; regional variation in, 112–13; social security spending, 101; state of denial in, 108–9; union densities in, 16tab1.1; Union Network International, 17
Indian Labour Conference, 111
indigence, 2–3, 11
Industrial and Commercial Workers Union (ICU) (South Africa), 174
Industrial Conciliation Act of 1924 (South Africa), 174
industrialization: in Brazil, 136, 138; in Global North, 10; import substitution industrialization (ISI) model, 118; in India, 112–13; in Latin America, 118, 120, 121; social struggles, 6; in South Africa, 177
industrial relations: in China, 59; in South Africa, 177; standard model of, 18
industrial reserve army, 121, 158
Industrial Revolution, 23, 25, 118
industrial serfdom, 25
industrial working class, 10, 42–43
inequality: in Brazil, 138; Gini index, 189, 195, 205n5; hierarchy of, 59; institutionalization of, 60; racialized inequality, 176tab10.1; responsibility for, 248; reversal at state level, 249; social inequality, 122, 205n5; sustainable development and, 19
infitah (openness) years, 198
Informal Economy Workers' Syndicate (Sindicato dos Trabalhadores na Economía Informal) (SINTEIN), 129
informal employment, 12, 116; in Africa, 162–63, 165; in Brazil, 135, 138, 147–48, 151n39; in Cambodia, 82; in Latin America, 122, 123–24
informality: in Africa, 152–69; independence and, 160–63; in India, 104–6; in Latin America, 123–25; poverty and, 78; return to in Global South, 246; in Russia, 236–39; SEZs (special economic zones), 77. *See also* economic informality
informalization of labor: features of, 11–12; in Mekong Asia, 80; in South Africa, 177; trade unionism and, 18; in US, 41, 49; in Western Europe, 35
informal workers, 8, 18, 35, 73
infrastructure, 42, 44, 46, 99, 110
insecurity, 59, 244, 246, 249
insurances, 29, 30, 31tab2.4-2.5, 37n36
internal orientalism, 213
International Alliance, 7–8
International Confederation of Free Trade Unions (ICFTU), 15, 16
International Federation of Trade Unions (IFTU), 15
International Finance Corporation, 82
internationalization: in China, 63, 71; in Latin America, 123
International Labour Organization (ILO), 82; criticisms by, 164; on decent work, 122; on informality, 123; labor rights and, 18–20, 157; male employment and, 125; purchasing power, 246; report on work arrangements, 35; as social compact architect, 18, 248; social unrest index, 249; tripartite formula of, 18; urban informal sector, 162–63; weak points of, 18; working classes and, 15
International Monetary Fund (IMF): economic informality, 245; on GDP, 249; IMF riots, 197; Kahn and, 223; redistribution and, 248; SAPS and, 8
International Monetary Fund (IMF) riots, 197
International Trade Union Confederation (ITUC), 16–17
intifadas, 203
Iran, 192, 193, 199, 201, 203, 219
Iraq, 194, 203
Ireland, 31tab2.4, 31tab2.5
Islam/Islamic law, 3, 188, 189, 199–200
Israel, 203
Italy, 16tab1.1, 31tab2.4, 31tab2.5, 37n31, 37n34, 193
Ivory Coast, 164

Japan, 16tab1.1, 37n31
Japanese lean model, 144
Jiang Zemin, 71
Jobbik party, 219, 223
Jordan, 199
Judah, Ben, 228
Justice and Development Party (AK Party), 201

Kaczynski government, 222
Kahn, Dominique Strass, 223
Kalb, Don, 9, 208–26
Kalecki, Michal, 33
Kapeliushnikov, Rostislav, 234
Kassalow, Everett, 31–32
Keiser, Thorsten, 25, 36n15
Kemalism, 190, 192, 193, 201
Khodorkosvky, Michail, 233
Khrushchev, Nikita, 215
Kirchner, Cristina Fernández de, 128, 129
Kirchner, Néstor, 128, 129
kolonos agoraios, 23–24
Kozina, Irina, 234
Kurdish Workers' Party, 203

labor: bonded laborers, 101; capital and, 116; commodification of, 4–5; control of, 117; cost comparisons, 150n7; demand limitations, 10; dependent capitalism and, 129–31; flexibilization of, 123; forced labor, 154–55, 164; free wage labor, 15, 24; independent contractors, 41; inequality of, 245; informalization of, 11–12; labor access, 154; labor contractors, 61; labor mediators, 34; labor supply shock, 17, 245; labor time regulation, 29, 30, 30tab2.3; in Latin America, 116–17; nationalism and, 117–20, 123; neoliberalism and, 123–26; post-liberalism and, 126–29; recognition of, 58; relative surplus labor, 121; reorganizational struggles, 134–51; sunset workers, 143; temporary-employment agencies, 34, 35; temporary labor, 41, 60–62, 246; unemployed labor, 3, 4, 5, 34, 167n16, 182tab10.2; unfree labor forms, 7, 24; unprotected labor origins, 23–25. *See also* migrant workers; outsourcing; subcontracting; wage labor
Labor Code (CLT), 137–38
Labor Contract Law (China), 66, 69
labor contracts, 7, 21n7, 87–88; flexibilization, 34; ILO report on, 35; individualization of, 17; standard labor contracts, 6, 11; unlimited duration, 29, 32
laboring poor: catch-up economies and, 247; low cost of production and, 17–18; in Mekong Asia, 80; purchasing power of, 246; underfunding of social safety net, 14
Labor Law (Brazil), 140
Labor Law (China), 64, 66–67
labor legislation: basic rights and, 6; in Brazil, 137–38; in Latin America, 118; in South Africa, 173; subcontracting and, 139
labor market: deregulation, 19; flexibilization, 18, 33–34, 66, 123–24, 136, 245; in India, 100; interventions, 94n7; polarization and, 49; racialized inequality, 176tab10.1
labor movements: in Argentina, 119; in Brazil, 136, 146–47; cross-sectional labor movement, 146–47; decrease in, 249; growth of, 27–28, 27tab2.1; labor activism in China, 60; in Latin America, 123; undermining of, 9; weakness of in US, 44
labor movements in Africa, 167n22
Labor Party, 154
labor power, 11, 58
labor question and dependent capitalism in Latin America: marginality question, 120–23; national development state and, 117–20
labor question in Latin America: marginality question, 120–23; national development state and, 117–20
labor relations, formal/informal divide, 116
labor rights: in Brazil, 137–38; globalization process and, 18–20; ILO and, 18, 157; inclusion and, 244; public support and, 244; strikes and, 71–72; trade unionism and, 244
labor struggles, in Brazil, 134–51
labor struggles in Brazil: overview, 134–36, 149–50; from factory struggles to land struggles, 145–47, 147–49; informalization of, 147–49; outsourcing and, 138–40; outsourcing in the CSB and, 140–44; states of labor, 137–38; subcontractors on strike, 136–37; tertiarization and, 144–45
Labour Relations Act (LRA) of 1995, 177
land issues: land dispossession, 76n46; land distribution, 99; land flight, 13–15; land laborers, 24; land-tenure patterns, 193; land use rights, 76n46; smallholders, 24. *See also* Brazil
landless class: in Africa, 160, 165; in Asia, 10; in China, 70; in Europe, 4, 5; in India, 98–102, 106, 107, 108, 112; Landless Peoples Movement, 180; in Middle East, 194; in South Africa, 171, 172, 180

The Land of Too Much (Prasad), 42
Laos, 77, 87
Latin America: overview, 116–17; Andean countries, 117; Bolivia, 129; decolonization of, 8; exclusion in, 1; labor under dependent capitalism in, 129–31; marginality and, 120–23; Mexico, 16tab1.1, 117, 119, 126; national-popular state period, 117–20, 123; neoliberal period, 123–26; post-liberal period, 126–29; Southern class compromise in, 8; urbanization in, 8; Uruguay, 117, 127; Venezuela, 119. *See also* Brazil; Mexico
Latvia, 217
Law 4330 (proposed), 139–40
Law and Justice for Poland, 224
League of Nations, 18, 155
Lebanon, 201, 203
Lee, Ching Kwan, 1–22, 7, 58–76, 150n7, 244–50
left-wing movements, in MENA region, 193
Lei 4330 (Brazil), 135
leprosy, 153
Levy, Joaquim, 135
Lewis, Oscar, 122
liberalization: in China, 63; in Latin America, 123, 125; in post-socialist Eastern Europe, 9
The Liberation of Women (Amin), 188
Libya, 194
Li Chun-yun, 72
life-cycle events, 12
life expectancy, 196tab11.1
Li Keqiang, 71
Lula administration, 135, 138
Lula da Silva, Ignazio, 134–35, 138
Lumpenproletariat (rabble working class), 5
Luxemburg, 32

Mae Sot, Thailand, 85–86, 89–91, 91fig5.2, 93
Magyar Garda, 223
Mahatma Gandhi National Rural Employment Guarantee Act (*narega*), 107
“Make America Great Again” slogan, 41
Malaysia, 16tab1.1
MAN-AG, 144
manufacturing sector: in Cambodia, 82–83, 82fig5.1, 90, 92; in CEE, 209; contract manufacturing, 63–64; in Thailand, 86, 90; US advantage in, 43; US jobs decrease in, 40, 53
marginalization, 13, 120, 120–23, 121, 244
marketization, 144, 229
market reform/regulation, 9, 62–69, 248
Marschalck, Peter, 28
Marx, Karl, 5, 117, 121
Marxism, xiin2, 121, 200, 241
Master and Servants Ordinance, 154
maternal capital program, 231
Maul, Daniel, 164
means test, 4
Mekong Asia special economic zones (SEZs): overview, 77–78, 93–94; Cambodia case, 81–85, 82fig5.1, 91–93; selective hegemony and, 79–81; SEZs and, 89–93, 91map5.2; Thailand-Myanmar border case, 79map5.1, 85–88, 89–91
Memoir on Pauperism (de Tocqueville), 3
memorandum of understanding (MOU) agreements, 87
MENA (Middle East and North Africa) region, 189; decolonization of, 192; European imperialism in, 191–92; interwar period, 192; social justice in, 190. *See also* Middle East; North Africa
Mészáros, István, 246
metalworker’s union (SMSF), 137, 144–45, 147, 149
Mexico, 16tab1.1, 117, 119, 126
micro-entrepreneurs, 64–65
middle class salariat, 135
Middle East: overview, 188–89; Arab uprisings, 205n10; colonial rule in, 190–93; demonstration in, 12; MENA empires, 189–90; nationalization in, 8; postwar corporatist compact, 193–201, 196fig11.1; state bureaucracy expansion, 8; Sunni militias, 203; tax havens in, 12; time of monsters, 201–5; urbanization in, 8
migrants: exclusion of, 249; from Global South, 247, 249–50n5; land dispossession in China and, 76n46; in Thailand, 96n39. *See also* migrants in Mekong Asia; migrant workers
migrants in Mekong Asia: overview, 77–78, 93–94; in Cambodia, 81–85, 82fig5.1, 91–93; selective hegemony and, 79–81; SEZs and, 89–93, 91map5.2; in Thailand-Myanmar border case, 79map5.1, 85–88, 89–91
migrant workers: in Africa, 162; in China, 61, 70; individualization of, 12–13; labor migration, 33; marginalization of, 13; recruitment of, 32; urban laboring class, 10; wage income of in China, 76n46
millenarian movements, 190
Millennium Development Goals (MDG) of World Bank, 2, 9, 19, 20
Mines and Works Act of 1911, 173
mise-en-valeur thesis, 7–8

missionaries, 153, 190
mobility: for labor migrants, 12; mass mobilizations in Argentina, 129; in Russia, 230–32; as workers' countermovement, 78
mobilizations in Mekong Asia: overview, 77–78, 93–94; in Cambodia, 81–85, 91–93; selective hegemony and, 79–81; SEZs and, 89–93; in Thailand-Myanmar border case, 85–88, 89–91
modernization, 117, 126
Modi, Narendra, 110, 111, 114
Mollona, Massimiliano, 8, 134–51
Morel, Regina, 146
Morris, J., 238
Mossadeq, Mohammad, 193
MOU process, 96n39
Munck, Ronaldo, 8, 116–33
Muslims: appeasement of in India, 110; exclusion of in India, 113, 115n14; forced sterilization of in India, 101; Muslim Brothers, 199; in Self-Employed Women's Association (India), 114
mutualités, 25
Myanmar, 77, 85, 87, 90
My House My Life (Minha Casa Minha Vida) (MCMV) in Brazil, 151n38

narega (Mahatma Gandhi National Rural Employment Guarantee Act), 108
Nasser, Gamal Abdel, 188, 193, 194, 195
National Commission on Enterprises in the Unorganized Sector (NCEUS), 109
National Commission on Rural Labour (India), 101
National Economic and Social Development Bank (Banco Nacional de Desenvolvimento Econômico e Social) (BNDES), 136
National Health Security Act (Thailand), 88
nationalization, 8, 87–88, 117–20, 123, 193
National Labor Law (China), 67
National League for Democracy (Thailand), 86
National New-type Urbanization Plan (China), 70
National Party, 154
National Socialism (Austria), 32
National Socialism (German), 32
national-socialist (*stricto sensu*) mobilizations, 218–19, 220, 221
National Social Protection Strategy, 95n25
National Social Security Fund (NSSF) of Cambodia, 95n26
National Verification (NV) system of Thailand, 96n39
Native Land Act of 1913, 172, 174–75
Navalny, Alexei, 233, 241
NCEUS (National Commission on Enterprises in the Unorganized Sector), 109
neo-extractivism: defined, 135. *See also* Brazil
neoliberal consolidations: uneven, combined, contradictory, in Central and Eastern Europe, 215–18
neoliberal democracy: overview, 170–72, 184–85; social protections, 180–84, 181–82tab10.2; social questions, 175–80; in South Africa, 170–87, 176tab10.1
neoliberalism, neoliberal democracy; entrepreneurship and, 163; in Global South, 9; ideology of, 1, 2; ILO and, 18; in India, 110; informal sector and, 163; in Latin America, 123–26; non-deserving poor label under, 247; social question and, 245; strained public budgets under, 14; World Bank (WB) and, 248
Netherlands, 31tab2.4, 31tab2.5, 32
New Deal, 43, 44, 55
The New Woman (Amin), 188
New Zealand, 10, 32
NGOs (non-governmental organizations), 68–69, 71, 72, 95n25, 163
Nigeria, 249
Nixon, Richard, 215
No Land! No Vote! slogan, 180
non-deserving poor label, 247
non-laboring poor: pauperism/pauperization, 14; relief for, 4; underfunding of social safety net, 14
North Africa, 188; Algeria, 194; demonstration in, 12; migrant worker recruitment from, 32; nationalization in, 8; state bureaucracy expansion, 8; urbanization in, 8
Northern class compromise, 5–6
Norway, 28–29, 31tab2.4, 31tab2.5
Nun, José, 121, 122

Obama coalition, 52–53, 54
obligatory insurance, 29, 30, 31tab2.4-2.5
oil industry, 197, 199; oil crisis of 1974, 33; OPEC price hike, 197, 200
old age pension, 14, 29; for farmers, 30; in South Africa, 154, 178, 181tab10.2, 183
Oliveira, F. de, 118, 121
Olympic Games (Brazil), 135
on-call enterprises, 64–65
on-demand drivers, 72–73
Ong, Aihwa, 80–81

oppression, 13, 113
Orange Free State, 172
Orban, Viktor, 218, 219, 222–23
Organisation for Economic Co-operation and Development (OECD), 33, 34, 67
Other Backward Casts, 113, 114
Ottomans, 189–90, 191
out-of-work benefits, 34
outsourcing: backsourcing, 143; in Brazil, 136–39; defined, 138; in Mekong Asia, 86; tertiarization as, 144–45
over-unemployment, 28, 29
Oxford Handbook of the Welfare State, 152

PACs (Programa de Aceleração do Crescimento) (Growth Acceleration Programs), 136–37
Pact Government of 29-1929, 154
Pahlavi monarchy, 193
paid leave, 6, 29
Pakistan, 17, 18
Palestine, 188, 203
Paraguay, 129
Partido dos Trabalhadores (PT) (Workers' Party), 134, 136, 145, 147, 149
Partido Trabalhista Brasileir (Brazilian Workers Party) (PTB), 137
passive revolution, 32, 33
paternalism, 7, 60, 166n15, 217
pauperism/pauperization, 5, 14, 20, 23
pensions: in Brazil, 137; in Cambodia, 95n26; in India, 111; pensioners, 22n24; pension insurance coverage, 6, 31tab2.5, 33; pension insurance coverage in Western Europe, 31tab2.5; pension levels, 176tab10.1, 217; pension privatization, 173; permanent primitive accumulation, 122
Peronism, 119
Persian Empire: Anglo-Persian treat of 1812, 205n10; anti-imperialist revolts, 190; centralization of, 190; Qajar dynasty, 190; territory loss, 191
Petrobras, 134
pharmaceutical sector, 47
Philippines, 16tab1.1, 17
Phnom Penh, Cambodia, 81, 83–85, 93
picket (*piquetero*) movement, 129
Pierson, Nicolaas G., 26
Piketty, Thomas, 9, 44–45
piquetero (picket) movement, 129
Plan D expansion, 140, 141
Poland, 4, 212, 214, 216, 217, 220, 221, 224
Polányi, Karl, 4, 14, 127, 128, 193, 218
polarization, 49–55, 211–15
Polish Right, 219, 222
Poor Laws, 3, 4
Poor White Problem, 172
population issues, 28tab2.2, 33, 158
populism: in Brazil, 149–50; Brexit, 1; developmentalist, 8; in Eastern Europe, 213, 216, 217, 221, 223, 230; in India, 112; in Latin America, 112, 119, 125–26, 129, 192; Putin's, 228, 233; in South Africa, 185; surge in, 1; in US, 1, 41, 53, 54; xenophobism and, 1
Portes, Alejandro, 123–24
Portuguese colonies, 155
Postan, Michael, 24
post-Apartheid period, 177–79, 180, 181tab10.2
post-liberalism, 126–29
post-socialism: overview, 208–9, 224; class struggles without class, 218–20; illiberal Visegrad Bloc, 220–24; labor weakness, 211–15; neoliberal consolidations, 215–18; transitional recession, 209–11
poverty: behavioral economics and, 19; Bolsa Familia poverty reduction program, 134; destitution and, 2; in EU, 35; in Global North, 246; global poverty line, 9; health care costs and, 50; in India, 101; informality and, 78; in Latin America, 122; in Mekong Asia, 80; multiracial poverty, 172; poverty alleviation, 2, 19; poverty industry, 122; poverty wages, 245; poverty/wealth divide, 19; precarity and, 20; pro-poor growth enclaves, 12; in Russia, 229; social question and, 2; urban poverty in Africa, 158; working poverty, 246. *See also* Africa
"Poverty and Sharing Prosperity" (World Bank), 19
Poverty Reduction Strategy Papers (PRSPs), 9
Prasad, Monica, 42–44
Prayut Chan-o-cha, 90
precarity issues: overview, 58–59, 73–74; behavior economics and, 19; in China, 63–66; construction workers and, 65–66; economic downturn and, 69–73; global factories, 63–65, 249; in Latin America, 116, 120–23; market reform and, 62–69; outsourcing as, 138; precarious labor, 63, 74n17, 80, 246; regulation and, 66–69; service sector workers, 66; in socialist welfare system, 7; state socialism and, 59–62; in Western Europe, 35
predatory capitalism, 12, 15, 20, 112, 146
Price, Richard, 29

price scissors, 59
private-sector unionization, 41
privatization: in banking, 12; in Brazil, 151n39; in CEE, 221; in China, 74n17; in Latin America, 122, 123, 125, 136, 140–42; in Russia, 230
Profintern, 15
profit rates, 33, 246
Program of Environmental Compensation (PAC), 146
proletarianization, 25, 60, 197
pro-poor growth enclaves, 12, 77
prosperity, 14, 19–20, 40
protectionism, 33–35, 34tab2.6, 43
protective labor legislation, 29, 30
protests: in Brazil, 135; in France, 25; militant wage protests, 78; occupy movements, 1; self-immolation, 12, 73
Provident Fund (Government Employees) Ordinance of 1942, 154
public benefits, 4–5, 245
public domain, 7, 248
public economy, 6, 6–7, 20
public relief: in India, 111; Poor Laws, 3, 4; Reform Act of 1832 (Great Britain), 4; social grant program, 178–79; social-insurance arrangements, 37n36, 94n7; unemployed labor and, 5
public space, 12, 232–34
public transport, 7, 135
public works, 7, 111
purchasing power parity (PPP) index, 9, 195, 246
Putin, Vladimir, 219, 231, 233, 238, 242n17
Putin administration, 230, 233

Qatar, 190, 197
quarterization, 139
Quijano, Aníbal, 121, 122
quinterization (*quinterização*), 140

racism: alien subordination and, 13; *mise-en-valeur* thesis as, 7–8; racial democracy, 192–93; racial harassment, 33; racialized inequality, 176tab10.1
Rand Revolt strike, 174
Reagan, Ronald, 45
Reagan administration, 45, 47
recentralization, 190
recessions, 163, 209–11
reciprocity, 12–13, 13
Red Cross, 153
Red International of Labor Unions (RILU), 15
redistribution of sources of existence, 3, 20, 137, 247, 248
Reform Act of 1832 (Great Britain), 4
reforms: in Brazil, 135; in China, 62–69; in US, 55, 56; in Western Europe, 29
refugees: from Burma, 85–87; detainment of, 13; economic refugees, 10, 249–50n5; rejection of, 1; from Visegrad countries, 220
regulatory policies: in Brazil, 146; in China, 59, 62, 66–69, 73; exemptions from, 14; top 1 percent and, 47; in US, 44, 45, 47
remittances, 183
rentier economy, 145–46, 149
repression, 17–18
resistance, 55, 138, 228–30
Revolution of 1848 (France), 25, 26
rights: basic, 6, 71, 245; Civil Rights Movement, 44; collective rights, 127; exclusion from, 115n14, 245; rights to the city campaign, 146–47, 148; Universal Declaration of Human Rights of 1948, 248; voting rights, 48. *See also* labor rights
Rogers, Joel, 56n20
Roma, 219–20, 222, 223
Romania, 210, 214, 216, 217, 220
Rosstat (Russian State Statistical Agency), 234
Rostow, Walter, 37n31
Rousseff, Dilma, 134, 135, 137, 139, 149
Rousseff administration, 138
rural issues: population, 24, 81; precariousness, 59; rural producers, 7; rural-urban divide, 59; rural-urban migration, 118; rural/urban transition, 2, 4
rush-order workshops, 64–65
Russia: overview, 227, 240–41; desubjectivation in, 235–36; economic revival, 230–32; exploitation in, 239–40; formal control, 238–39; grassroots social movements, 230–32; informality, 234–35, 236–39; *mir*, 3; power relations, 238–39; precariousness, 235; public sphere, 232–34; resistance in, 228–30; Russian economic crisis of 2014, 237, 238; Russian Federation, 16tab1.1; Russian workers, 4, 17; shock therapy, 9; tax havens in, 12; ultraliberal policies, 228–30; unemployment rate in, 242n6
Russian Longitudinal Monitoring Survey of the Higher School of Economics (RLMS-HSE), 234
Russian State Statistical Agency (Rosstat), 234

Safavids, 189
safety net programs, 14, 49–50, 127, 173

safety rules, 29, 137, 143
salafism, 200
Salvation Army, 153
Sanders, Bernie, 41, 49, 52–53, 54
Saudi Arabia, 198
Scandinavian countries, 34, 46
scarcity, 7
Scheduled Castes, 99, 100, 110, 114
Scheduled Tribes, 99, 100, 110, 114
Schengen agreements, 216
Scully, Ben, 8, 13, 170–87
selective hegemony: overview, 77–78, 93–94; in Cambodia, 81–85, 91–93; SEZs and, 89–93; social question and, 79–81; in Thailand-Myanmar border case, 85–88, 89–91
Self-Employed Women's Association (India), 114
self-employment, 2, 10, 11, 34, 247; in China, 66, 72–73; ILO report on, 35; in India, 114; in Latin America, 123
self-immolation, 12, 73
Senegal, 155, 159, 165
service sector: in Brazil, 135, 138; in China, 66, 67, 73
SEZs (special economic zones): overview, 89, 93–94; Bavet SEZ, 91–93; defined, 77; Mae Sot SEZ, 89–91, 91map5.2; proliferation of, 78
shadow workers, 63–65
Shaefer, H. Luke, 51
Shanghai, 60, 61
shoe manufacturing, 82, 82fig5.1
SIGMA managerial system, 141, 143
Simkins, Charles, 175
Sindicato dos Trabalhadores na Economía Informal (Informal Economy Workers' Syndicate) (SINTEIN), 129
Sisters of Cluny, 153
slavery: abolition of, 7; chattel slavery, 40; in Latin America, 117, 137, 145; modern slavery in Africa, 164; US economy and, 42
Slovakia, 209, 210, 216, 217, 221
Slovenia, 209, 210, 216, 217
Smith, Gavin, 81
Smith, Stephen, 169n56
SMSF (metalworker's union), 137, 144, 147, 149
social assistance: in Brazil, 137, 148; in Southeast Asia, 94n7; in Western Europe, 25, 26
social capitalism, defined, 246
social compact: global social compact architects, 18–20; Global South and, 7; ILO and, 248; in MENA region, 190, 192, 195
social Darwinism, 108, 213, 218
socialism, state: Arab socialism, 193; in CEE, 214; Eurocentric model of, 135; insecurity and unemployment, 244; precarious versus permanent proletariats under, 59–62; socialist caste system in China, 59; US prosperity and, 40; welfare system exclusions, 7
social justice, 44, 190, 230–32, 249
social protections: contributory access to, 247; countermovements and, 78; exclusion from, 249; migrant exclusion and, 249; secondary benefits, 34; in South Africa, 173, 176tab10.1, 180–84
social question: defined, 1; as European discovery, 23; initial meaning of, 244
social safety nets, 14, 49–50, 127
social security arrangements, 6, 26–27, 34, 37n37, 246
Social Security Fund (Thailand), 87
social security initiatives: in Cambodia, 82–85; global importance of, 157; mutual-aid societies, 5; in Southeast Asia, 94n7; standard contracts and, 6; in Thailand, 87–88
Social Security Law of 2002 (Cambodia), 84
solidarity: African solidarity, 153; in CEE, 214; social consciousness and, 2; in South Africa, 179
Solidarity Economy Board (Brazil), 129
Solidarnosc, 221
Sombart, Werner, 40
Somkiat Chawatsriwong, 87–88
South Africa: overview, 170–72, 184–85; access to state-provided transfers in, 14; Afrikaners, 172, 173; European migrants, 10; militant workers' movements in, 17; as neoliberal democracy, 175–80, 176tab10.1; as settler community, 8, 172–75; social protections, 180–84, 181–82tab10.2; union densities in, 16tab1.1; welfare state programs in, 154; women in, 13
South America: European migrants, 10; redistribution in, 3
South Asia: laboring poor in, 246; majoritarian politics, 115n14
Southeast Asia. *See* Mekong Asia special economic zones (SEZs)
Southern class compromise, 7–9
South Korea: militant workers' movements in, 17; take-off of economy of, 37n31; union densities in, 16tab1.1
Soviet Union: communist revolution, 18; ILO and, 18; industrialization plans, 193; invasion of Afghanistan, 200; Kitchen Debate, 215;

labor supply in, 245; Sino-U.S. détente, 198; Soviet-style neoliberalism, 228–35
special economic zones (SEZs). *See* SEZs (special economic zones)
stagnation: in Africa, 156; in Asia, 82; in Eastern Europe, 210, 212, 221; of Global South, 7; in Middle East, 200; of US economy, 40, 41, 48
Stalin, Josef, 215
standard employment relationship, 29, 32, 130, 246
Standing, Guy, 122
state protections, 25–29, 26tab2.1, 28tab2.2, 59
state regulation: in China, 58; under Ottomans, 190; union strength and, 38n41
state socialism: in China, 58, 61; collapse of, 1; dual labor system, 60; precarious versus permanent proletariats under, 59–62
steel industry: in Brazil, 137, 143; in EU, 137; in US, 137
Stenning, Alison, 210
Sternberg, Fritz, 37n28
Stigler, George, 25
Streeck, Wolfgang, 33
street vendors: in Africa, 163; in China, 66, 73; in India, 114
strikes: in Africa, 167n22; air traffic controller strike of 1981, 45–46; in Brazil, 136–37, 142; in Cambodia, 83–84; labor rights and, 71–72; Russian miners strikes, 230; in South Africa, 173–74; Trans-Siberian Railway blockade, 230
structural adjustment policies (SAPS), 8
structural heterogeneity (dualism), 119, 122
students: student interns, 64, 74n17; student loans, 50–51, 54; student movement, 45; teacher-student ratios, 176tab10.1
Stumm, Carl Friedrich, 26
subcontracting, 34; in Brazil, 135, 136–37, 138, 140–44, 149; in China, 64–65; defined, 138; ILO report on, 35; legal aspects of, 139; tertiarization as, 144
sub-Saharan Africa, 153, 161, 246
subsidiary responsibility, 143
subsidies, 14, 197
subsistence: in China, 58, 66, 73; family economy in China and, 76n46; in Myanmar, 85; smallholders and, 24, 25
subsumption, 120, 123
Sudan, 191
suffrage, 6, 42, 111–12
supranational authority, lack of, 12, 248
surplus population, 10, 13, 20
sustainable development: employment formalization and, 19; inequality and, 19
Sweden: emigration, 28–29; health insurance coverage, 31tab2.4; pension insurance coverage, 31tab2.5; take-off of economy of, 37n31; Urban Law, 24; welfare state in, 37n37
Switzerland, 31tab2.4, 31tab2.5
Syria, 188, 194, 203

al-Tahtawi, Rifa'a, 188
Taiwan, 37n31
Tanganyika, 154
Tatmadaw (Myanmar military), 85
taxation: in Brazil, 146, 148; increase in, 7; in India, 110, 111; opposition to increases in, 44, 45; reduction in, 14, 45, 47, 54; reform legislation, 48; revenues from, 43–44; supply-side tax cuts, 45; tax havens, 12; top 1 percent and, 47
Taylor Commission, 180
technological innovation, 44, 46–47, 63–64, 136, 138
Tequila Crisis, 126
tertiarization, 135, 139, 142, 144–45, 149, 150n7
Thailand-Myanmar border case study: overview, 77–78, 79map5.1, 93–94; Bavet SEZ and, 91–93; GDP (gross domestic product), 77; Mae Sot border district, 85–88; Mae Sot SEZ and, 89–91, 91map5.2; national and social security initiatives, 87–88; passport/work permit registration, 96n39; selective hegemony in, 79–81
Therborn, Göran, 135, 218
Tilly, Charles, 24
Tocqueville, Alexis de, 3, 42
top 1 percent, 45, 47, 112, 245
trade liberalization, 123, 125
Trade Union Confederation (TUC), 15, 21–22n21
trade unionism: in Africa, 167n31; in Brazil, 127, 137–38; collective bargaining and, 5, 15–16; confederations, 27–28, 27tab2.1; Davies on, 21–22n21; decrease in, 17, 33–34, 53, 249; at global level, 15–18; in India, 114; informalized labor and, 18; informal workers and, 18; labor rights and, 244; in Latin America, 117, 126, 126–29, 137; membership of, 15, 16, 22n24, 29; national trade unions, 26tab2.1, 27–28; policymaking process and, 18; in South Africa, 174; union densities, 16–17, 16tab1.1, 29, 34tab2.6, 44

transnational agencies, 8–9, 17. *See also* IMF (International Monetary Fund); WB (World Bank)
Transnationals Information Exchange (TIE), 17
travail précaire, 130
tribal communities, 155; conservation of, 154; decimation of, 10; in India, 113; mainstreaming of, 102; in MENA, 189
Tribunal Superior de Justica (High Court of Justice) (TSJ), 150n7
tripartism, 212
tripartite formula of ILO, 18
Trump, Donald, 1, 41, 49, 52–53, 54
Trump administration, 55
Tunisia, 73, 194, 202
Turkey, 192; agricultural holdings, 206n17; comparisons to, 207n40; Kemalism, 190, 192, 193; migrant worker recruitment from, 32; postwar elite rule in, 201; union densities in, 16tab1.1
Twenty Point Program, 101

Ukraine, 220
underemployment, 13, 245, 246
UN-DESA report, 247, 249–50n5
UN Development Goals (UNDG), 157
unemployment, 11; in Africa, 155, 158, 167n31; in Brazil, 135; in China, 66; conferences on struggle against, 37n34; cyclical unemployment, 246; defeat of under state socialism, 244; in Global South, 13, 246; public benefits and, 49–50, 245; in Russia, 242n6; in South Africa, 173, 179
unemployment insurance, 29, 37n36, 176tab10.1
Unemployment Insurance Fund (UIF), 182, 182tab10.2
unionization. *See* trade unionism
Union Network International, 17
Unique Cash Transfer scheme (India), 111
United Arab Emirates (UAE), 197
United Kingdom: health insurance coverage, 31tab2.4; labor movements in, 29; pension insurance coverage, 31tab2.5; union densities in, 16tab1.1
United States: agricultural labor, 42; day laborers, 41; death rates, 48–49; Federal Reserve System, 43; GDP, 249; global role of, 45; hegemony of, 193, 198; intergenerational mobility, 41; labor cost comparisons, 150n7; Latinos/Latinas in, 49, 51–52; military interventions, 203; political socialism, 49, 54; state building in, 42; steel industry, 137; stock market crash of 1929, 118; Supreme Court, 48; Tea Party activists, 53; technological innovation, 44, 46–47; union densities in, 16tab1.1; wage stagnation, 40, 41; Western European immigration, 29. *See also* exceptionalism, American
Universal Basic Income (UBI) scheme (India), 111
Unorganized Workers' Social Security Act of 2008, 109
UN Universal Declaration of Human Rights of 1948, 248
upward mobility: in Brazil, 138; US decrease in, 40, 48, 54
urbanization, 8; in Africa, 158; in Cambodia, 81; in China, 70; in India, 113; in Latin America, 118, 121; in South Africa, 177; Urban Law, 24; urban marketing, 161
urban laboring class: in China, 7, 10, 59, 63; in India, 10; in Latin America, 121; Southern class compromise and, 7–9; in Western Europe, 25

Vaguismo, 119
van der Linden, Marcel, 1–22, 2, 23–39, 152, 208, 244–50
Vargas, Getúlio, 136
Vargas administration, 137
Vietnam, 77, 90
Vietnam War, 45, 198
Vinogradova, Elena, 234
Visegrad countries: defined, 209. *See also* Central and Eastern Europe (CEE)
vocational education, 74n17
Volkswagen (VW), 144–45, 147
Volta Grande municipality, Brazil, 135, 136, 141, 145–47, 148, 149
von Holdt, Karl, 184
voting rights, 48, 180

wage labor, 116; in Africa, 159, 161; deferred wages, 247; dispatch workers, 66, 67; family allowances and, 159; flexibilization of, 18; high wages, 29, 246; ILO and, 18; in Latin America, 137; living wage, 245; minimum wage, 11, 137; overage paid laborers, 11; part-time jobs, 34, 41; in precapitalist Western Europe, 24; privatization in Brazil and reduction in, 151n39; pro-poor growth enclaves, 12; wage laborers, 35n4
Wallerstein, Immanuel, 9
Wall Street meltdown of 2008, 46, 47, 50–51, 223

Washington Consensus, 123, 126
wealth disparity, 20; in US, 44–45, 47, 54; WB and, 19, 248
We Are Poor but So Many (Bhatt), 114
Weber, Max, 3–4, 20n3
welfare state: in Brazil, 137; comparisons, 207n40; decolonization and, 8, 156–60; exclusion and, 8, 166n9; expansion resistance, 44; growth of, 6–7, 244; origins of, 58; public authority and, 6; in South Africa, 177–78; in Soviet Union, 229–30; in US, 43
welfarism, 7, 134, 138, 244. *See also* India
Western Europe, 23–39; overview, 23; Anglo-Persian treat of 1812, 205n10; average work hours annually, 30tab2.3; capital accumulation and, 32; capitalism in England, 35n6; contractual labor relations in Germany, 36n15; economies of, 37n31; emigration from, 28tab2.2; freedom of association, 26tab2.1; freedom of trade, 26tab2.1; Golden Age, toward the, 29–32, 30tab2.3, 31tab2.4, 31tab2.5; health insurance coverage, 31tab2.4; mass emigration, 37n28; migratory pressures from Africa, 169n56; national trade-union confederations, 26tab2.1; origins of unprotected labor, 23–25; pension insurance coverage, 31tab2.5; population of, 28tab2.2; protection decrease in, 33–35, 34tab2.6; social insurance arrangements, 37n36; social question in, 23–39; state protection beginnings, 25–29, 26tab2.1, 28tab2.2; unprotected labor origins, 23–25; welfare regimes of, 207n40
White, Lynn, 61
whites: with college degrees, 54; death rates, 48–49; non-college-educated whites, 52–53; welfare for whites only, 153–56; white privilege, 43, 49
Whyte, Martin, 59
Wickham, Carrie, 202
women: in African employment, 156–57, 159, 163; in China, 66; education of, 196tab11.1; exclusion of, 5, 35, 125–26; exploitation of, 82–85; gendered labor, 29, 30, 78, 156–57; in India, 114; in MENA empires, 190; second-wave feminism, 45; in South Africa, 178; strain on, 13; suffrage for, 6; urban marketing and, 161; US political protests of, 55; workforce participation, 125–26, 151n39
workers' coalitions, 27tab2.1, 29, 30
Workers' Party (Partido dos Trabalhadores) (PT), 127, 134, 136, 145
working class: in Africa, 161; bargaining power of, 6, 245; in Brazil, 137; changing composition of, 17; Chinese rural migrants, 63; debt burden, 135; emancipation of, 244; in Russia, 238; subcontractors, 135
working conditions/hours, 6, 11, 29, 30tab2.3, 35, 136
Workmen's Compensation Fund (Thailand), 87
world authority, lack of, 12, 248
World Bank (WB): CEE and, 217; on decreasing indigence, 9; economic informality, 245; Edwards, Sebastian, 123, 126; as global social compact architect, 18–20; influence of, 230; on MENA region, 200; on MENA social compact, 195; neoliberalism and, 248; on poverty, 122; SAPS and, 8. *See also* Millennium Development Goals of World Bank
World Confederation of Labor (WCL), 16
World Development Report of 2015, 19–20
World Employment Social Outlook 2017, 246, 249
World Trade Organization (WTO), 230

xenophobism, 1, 33, 184
Xi Jinping, 69, 71
Xi Jinping government, 72
Xue Hong, 64

Yeltsin, Boris, 228
Yugoslavia, 32, 214

Zhou Enlai, 62
Zucman, Gabriel, 12

CPSIA information can be obtained
at www.ICGtesting.com
Printed in the USA
LVHW021705260619
622440LV00004B/23/P

9 780520 302402